Human Rights and International Relations
in the Asia-Pacific Region

Human Rights and International Relations in the Asia-Pacific Region

Edited by
James T. H. Tang

PINTER
London and New York

Distributed exclusively in the USA by St. Martin's Press Inc.

PINTER

An imprint of Cassell Publishers Limited
Wellington House, 125 Strand, London WC2R 0BB, England

First published in 1995

Distributed exclusively in the USA by St. Martin's Press, Inc.
Room 400, 175 Fifth Avenue, New York, NY10010, USA

British Library Cataloguing in Publication Data

A CIP catalogue record for this book is available from The British Library
ISBN 1 85567 216 2

Library of Congress Cataloging-in-Publication Data
Human rights and international relations in the Asia-Pacific region /
    edited by James T. H. Tang.
        p.   cm.
    Includes bibliographical references and index.
    ISBN 1-85567-216-2
    1. Civil rights–Asia.   2. Human rights–Asia.   3. Asia–Politics
and government–1945–   I. Tang, James Tuck-Hong. 1957-
JC599.A78H83   1994   94-26946
323'.095–dc20   CIP

Typeset by GCS, Leighton Buzzard, Beds.
Printed and bound in Great Britain by SRP Ltd, Exeter

CONTENTS

PART III INSTITUTIONAL AND REGIONAL PERSPECTIVES

PART IV CONCLUSIONS

NOTES ON CONTRIBUTORS

Amitav Acharya is a Senior Fellow at the Centre for International and Strategic Studies, York University, and Director of the Southeast Asia and Security Project at the University of Toronto-York University Centre for Asia Pacific Studies. He studied in India and Australia, obtaining his Ph.D. from Murdoch University. Author of *U.S. Military Strategy in the Gulf: Origins and Evolution under the Carter and Reagan Administrations,* Dr Acharya has written extensively on regional security issues and ASEAN foreign policies. He co-edited *Cambodia: The 1989 Paris Peace Conference and After: Background and Documents,* and his work *A New Regional Order in Southeast Asia: ASEAN in the Post-Cold War Era* was published as Adelphi papers no. 279 by the Institute of International and Strategic Studies in London.

William J. Barnds is a foreign relations consultant and President of the Japan Economic Institute of America from 1985 to 1990. He was previously Director of the Subcommittee on Asian and Pacific Affairs of the House Foreign Affairs Committee, and served as a Professional Staff Member of the US Senate Committee on Foreign Relations. He is author and editor of five books on American foreign policy and Asian affairs, including *Japan and the United States: Challenges and Opportunities* and *China and America: The Search for a New Relationship.*

Mely Caballero-Anthony is a research officer at the Centre of Asian Studies, University of Hong Kong. A graduate of the University of the Philippines, she has worked and taught in several Southeast Asian countries, including the Philippines, Malaysia and Brunei. Her research interests are in international relations and foreign policies of Southeast Asian countries. She is co-editor (with Somak Tambunlertchai) of *The Future of Asia-Pacific Economies: Challenges to South Asia.* She is now completing a Ph.D. thesis on conflict resolution and regional organizations at the University of Hong Kong.

Joseph Chan is Lecturer in Political Theory, Department of Politics and Public Administration, University of Hong Kong. Currently completing a D.Phil. thesis on Aristotle's political theory for Oxford University, Joseph Chan studied in the Chinese University of Hong Kong and the London School of Economics. His principal research interests are in Aristotles political theory and contemporary political philosophy. His articles have appeared in academic journals including *Ethics* and *History of Political Thought.*

Michael Freeman is Deputy Director of the Human Rights Centre at Essex University. Dr Freeman obtained a LLB from Stanford University and his Ph.D. from the University of Essex. He is author of *Edmund Burke and the Critique of Political Radicalism* and co-edited (with David Robertson) *Frontiers* *of Political Theory*, and also published extensively on political theory and human rights question in academic journals. He is now completing a manuscript entitled *The Social and Political Theory of Genocide*.

Yash Ghai is Sir Y. K. Pao Professor of Public Law at the University of Hong Kong. He has taught at Warwick University, Yale Law School, University of East Africa, Upsala University and the National University of Singapore. Professor Ghai has published extensively in public law. His most recent publications include: *Heads of State in the Pacific: A Legal and Constitutional Analysis* (1990, with Jill Cottrell), *Public Administration and Management in Small States* (1991), *Law, Politics and Administration of Decentralisation in Papua New Guinea* (1992, with A J Regan), and *The Hong Kong Bill of Rights: A Comparative Approach* (1993, co-edited with Johannes Chan). Professor Ghai has advised various governments, the UNCTAD, and UNCTC on public law and other legal matters.

Francisco Nemenzo is Professor of Political Science at the University of the Philippines, where he was Dean af Arts and Sciences from 1982 to 1985 and Vice-Chancellor of the University's Visayas campus between 1989 and 1992. Professor Nemenzo was educated in the Philippines and the United Kingdom obtaining his Ph.D. from the University of Manchester. He has published widely. He co-authored (with Ed Garcia) *The Sovereign Quest: Freedom from Foreign Military Bases*, and co-edited (with R.J. May) *The Philippines After Marcos*.

Constantine Pleshakov is Director of the Pacific Studies Center, Institute of US and Canada Studies, Russian Academy of Sciences, Moscow. He studied at the College of Afro-Asian Studies, Moscow University where he obtained his Ph.D. Dr Pleshakov has published works on international relations in East Asia and post-communist Russia's problems.

James T. H. Tang is Lecturer in International Relations at the Department of Politics and Public Administration, University of Hong Kong. Dr Tang obtained his M.Phil. from Cambridge University and Ph.D. from the London School of Economics. He has also taught in the National University of Singapore. Dr Tang is author of *Britain's Encounter with Revolutionary China*. He has also written on East Asian politics and international relations. His research interests include Chinese foreign policy, political developments of Hong Kong, and politics of trade in the Asia-Pacific region.

Seiichiro Takagi is Professor of Political Science and International Relations, Graduate School of Policy Science, Saitama University, Japan. Professor Takagi, who received his Ph.D. from Stanford University, has published extensively on Chinese foreign relations especially with the United States and Japan. He held visiting appointments at the Brookings Institution and Stanford and was Director for the Japanese Side, the Contemporary Japanese Studies Programme, at Peking University between 1991 and 1992.

Paul Taylor is Reader in International Relations at the London School of Economics and Political Science. Dr Taylor, who obtained his Ph.D. from the

University of London, is author of several books on international institutions and international cooperation, and co-editor (with John Groom) of several books on international organizations. Dr Taylor's most recent book is *International Organization in the Modern World: The Regional and the Global Process*.

Lawrence T. Woods is Associate Professor of International Studies and Asia-Pacific politics at the University of Northern British Columbia, Canada. Dr Woods received his Ph.D. from the Australian National University. His principal research interests include: international organizations, the politics of Pacific economic cooperation, and international relations of the Asia-Pacific region. He is the author of *Asia-Pacific Diplomacy: Nongovernmental Organizations International Relations and Regional Economic Cooperation*. He has also published numerous articles on international relations in the Asia-Pacific and the role of nongovernmental organizations.

Zhou Wei is Associate Professor in the Department of Law, Shantou University, the People's Republic of China, and Director-designate of a proposed Human Rights Center in the University. Dr Zhou obtained a master's degree in law from Jilin University and completed his Ph.D. at the Faculty of Law, University of Hong Kong. His major research interests are Marxism and human rights.

PREFACE

This book is a collective attempt to examine post-Cold War human rights problems in the Asia-Pacific region. Contemporary human rights debates often evolve around themes such as universalism versus cultural relativism, and political and civil rights versus economic and social rights. This volume's focus – the East Asian-Western discord over human rights, involves complex and conflicting philosophical, political, social, economic, and moral issues. The human rights debates, often conducted within the context of the Western liberal tradition, have been further complicated by the recent emergence of an East Asian model of economic and political development.

Although liberal democracies claimed victory in the Cold War, they have been troubled by economic difficulties, political problems, and social ills at home. In contrast to the Western experience, many East Asian states have managed to achieve spectacular economic success with effective governance. While their success is in part attributable to their penetration of an increasingly interdependent global market economy, the region's experience has been seen as providing a distinctive approach for human development. This vision has presented a challenge to Western liberal political and economic thinking, provoking intense discussions on the implications of a possible clash between the two civilizations. As the 21st century approaches, it is clear that human rights are set to be a major source of conflict in world politics.

Contributors in this volume seek to clarify the issues surrounding the East Asian challenge to the universality of human rights in the context of the post-Cold War international environment, and evaluate the impact of recent domestic economic and political changes on the regional human rights agenda. The book also ponders on the prospects of developing a regional framework for the protection of human rights and for resolving differences over human rights in the Asia-Pacific region.

With diverse backgrounds, the contributors come from: Canada, China, Hong Kong, Japan, the Philippines, Russia, the United Kingdom, and the United States. There are two lawyers with expertise in human rights issues, and two political theorists. The majority, however, are international relations scholars. Human rights problems have often been discussed in moral and legal terms in the field of international relations, but there are relatively few works analyzing the political and economic dimensions. This is therefore not only an attempt to contribute to the contemporary debate of human rights, but also an effort to broaden the international relations perspective on the subject.

As a collective effort, the project is, first and foremost, the direct outcome of all the authors' own work. Several contributors also made useful suggestions and comments about the project as a whole. The contributors have been extremely patient with my requests for revisions and with my other queries. I am grateful to them for their excellent contributions and for making the book a reality.

The project has been facilitated by my participation in three meetings in different parts of the world during 1993. The idea of the project originated from an international colloquium on human rights and foreign policy organized by the Department of Political Science (which has been renamed as Department of Politics and Public Administration) at the University of Hong Kong on 11 March 1993. The meeting in Hong Kong, stimulating as it was, raised more questions than answers.

A more coherent set of questions which formed the basis of this project was formulated after the colloquium. Ideas for a book project were finalized a couple of weeks later during the concluding session of the North Pacific Cooperative Security Dialogue in Vancouver. Human rights as a form of unconventional international security threat was among the issues discussed in the meeting. Amitav Acharaya, Seiichiro Takagi, and Lawrence Woods agreed to contribute to the book after discussing the project with me in Vancouver. When I returned to Hong Kong I persuaded Mely Caballero-Anthony, Joseph Chan, and Yash Ghai to take part in this project.

The overall plan of the book was in place when I went to Vienna to attend the Non-Governmental Forum during the United Nations World Conference on Human Rights in June 1993. I was introduced to the world of human rights, and witnessed at first hand the multifaceted nature of the issues involved. I also collected useful documents and relevant materials for the project. As a newcomer to the field I was overwhelmed in Vienna, but the experience also helped me to crystallize the central themes of this volume and become more aware of the complexities of the task, and the limitations of the project.

I am indebted to the organizers and fellow participants of the three meetings. Ian Scott proposed the colloquium on human rights and foreign policy in the first place and went on to organize it as well as to secure financial support for bringing in overseas participants. As a co-organizer of the colloquium I am also grateful to Professor Wang Gungwu, Mr John Kamm, and Professor Byron Weng for their support. Our research students, in particular, Mely Caballero-Anthony, Mary Hogan, Winnie Lam, Kevin May, Winston Ng, Czeslaw Tubilewicz, Sangeeta-Matta Verma, and John Ward proved to be a wonderful support team.

The North Pacific Cooperative Security Dialogue was initiated and co-organized by Paul Evans, Director of the Joint Centre for Asia-Pacific Studies, Universities of York and Toronto, and David Dewitt, Director, Centre for International and Strategic Studies at York University. Brian Job, Director of the Institute of International Relations, University of British Columbia, was a hospitable local host during the Vancouver session. My trip to Vienna for the NGO forum was supported by the Department of Political Science at HKU. Manfred Nowak of the Ludwig Boltzmann Institute of Human Rights (BIM) directed my last minute request for participation to the Joint NGO Planning Committee with promptness.

I also wish to thank diplomatic missions in Hong Kong from several countries for supplying me with their governments' statements and speeches on human rights issues, particularly those made in the Bangkok preparatory meeting and the Vienna world conference. These countries are: Australia, the Republic of Korea, Indonesia, Japan, Singapore, and Thailand.

Several non-governmental organizations; their representatives, and other individuals have also been generous in sending me useful publications. Asia Watch, Amnesty International, International Alert, and HURIDOCS have all been helpful in entertaining my requests. I am particularly grateful to: Vicky Shu from Asia Watch and Cori Ng of Amnesty International. I also want to thank Phil Harris, Editor of *Terra Viva* for generously sending me a complete set of the newspaper which covers the Vienna World Conference on Human Rights and parallel events, and Pranay Gupte, Executive Editor of *Earth Times*, who sent me a special wrap-up issue on the Conference.

The late John Vincent's works on human rights and international relations have been a source of inspiration for this project. The positive response of Michael Leifer, my teacher and friend, to the preliminary proposal also gave me confidence in pursuing for its eventual publication. Paul Taylor, in addition to being a contributor, brought this project to the attention of Pinter Publishers. Other friends and colleagues, including, Brian Bridges, Andrew Byrnes, Johannes Chan, Judith Dueck, Rita Kwok, Tieu Tieu Le Phung, Christine Loh, Alex Schmid, Sing Ming, and Jo Jo Tam, assisted me in different ways. Morgan Acker's encouragement and enthusiasm about the project is also very much appreciated.

In editing this book I received important editorial support from Sangeeta-Matta Verma, who sorted out the contributors' notes, assisted me in compiling the bibliography, and helped organizing things in general. Her work made the editing task less arduous. Josy Chan provided typing support with great efficiency.

As always, I am grateful to my wife, Helen Siu-Hong, whose love and concrete support have been an important source of encouragement to my academic endeavours, this project is not an exception. My three year-old daughter Jean Wyng Ji's insistent demand for her father's attention also provided much needed impetus for not delaying the project for too long.

J. T. H. Tang
Hong Kong, 1994

LIST OF ABBREVIATIONS

AFP	Armed Forces of the Philippines
AMRSP	Association of Major Religious Superiors in the Philippines
ANZUS	Australia–New Zealand United States Security Treaty
APEC	Asia Pacific Economic Cooperation
ASEAN	Association of Southeast Asian Nations
ASEAN–ISIS	Association of Southeast Asian Nations–Institute of Strategic Studies
ASEAN–PMC	Association of Southeast Asian Nations–Post Ministerial Conference
BN	Barisan Nasional
CRS	Catholic Relief Services
DRP	Drought Recovery Programme
EC	European Community
FLAG	Free Legal Assistance Group
GATT	General Agreement on Tariffs and Trade
HURIDOCS	Human Rights Information and Documentation System International
IASC	Inter-Agency Standing Committee
ICCPR	International Covenant on Civil and Political Rights
ICESCR	International Covenant on Economic, Social and Cultural Rights
ICRC	International Commission for the Red Cross
IGO	International Governmental Organizations
INGO	International Non-Governmental Organizations
IPR	Institute of Pacific Relations
JCP	Japan Communist Party
LDP	Liberal Democratic Party
MFN	Most Favoured Nation
MITI	Ministry of International Trade and Industry
NATO	North Atlantic Treaty Organization
NGO	Non-Governmental Organizations
NIE	Newly Industrializing Economies
NORAD	North American Aerospace Defence Command
NPT	Nuclear Non-Proliferation Treaty
OAS	Organization of American States
ODA	Official Development Aid
OECD	Organization for Economic Cooperation and Development
PAFTAD	Pacific Trade and Development

PAHRA	Philippines Alliance of Human Rights Advocate
PBEC	Pacific Basin Economic Council
PCHR	Presidential Commission of Human Rights
PECC	Pacific Economic Cooperation Council
PIOOM	Interdisciplinair Onderzoeknnar Oorzaken van Mensenrechte schendingen (Interdisciplinary Programme of Research on Root Causes of Human Rights Violations)
PRC	People's Republic of China
SAARC	South Asian Association for Regional Cooperation
SEPHA	Special Emergency Programme for the Horn of Africa
SLORC	State Law and Order Restoration Council
SPF	South Pacific Forum
TFD	Task Force Detainees
TYLP	Third Year Loan Programme
UMNO	United Malays National Organization
UN	United Nations
UNDA	United Nations Development Agency
UNDP	United Nations Development Programme
UNDRO	United Nations Disaster Relief Organizations
UNHCR	United Nations High Commission for Refugees
UNICEF	United Nations Children's Fund
UNPROFOR2	United Nations Protection Force 2
US	United States
VOA	Voice of America

1
HUMAN RIGHTS IN THE ASIA-PACIFIC REGION: COMPETING PERSPECTIVES, INTERNATIONAL DISCORD, AND THE WAY AHEAD

JAMES T. H. TANG

Human rights concerns have come to the forefront of the international stage in the post-Cold War world. As the United States trumpeted ideological victory in the aftermath of the Cold War, East Asian states mounted a challenge to Western beliefs on human rights. In the Asia-Pacific region, the different human rights positions of East Asian states and the West have generated tensions with far-reaching regional and global implications. This book addresses the post-Cold War East Asian challenge to the contemporary 'Western' understanding of human rights and its implications for regional international relations. The volume also explores the prospects for a regional approach to resolving human rights differences and better human rights protection.

In December 1990 when the United Nations decided to convene a World Conference on Human Rights, the international environment seemed to offer a historical opportunity for the creation of a new world order in which human rights would occupy a central place.[1] The euphoria, however, was misplaced. Although the global confrontation between the Soviet bloc and the Western alliance was over, regional and ethnic conflicts emerged. Differences between the developing world and the industrialized West over political and economic problems have remained, and human rights issues became a source of international tension. In fact the preparatory work for the world conference soon ran into difficulties because of disagreements over procedural matters. The confrontations concerning the objectives of the conference between Western and Asian governments eventually led to questions about whether or not the whole affair would be nothing but an exercise on protocol.[2]

Instead of focusing on further developments of the global human rights protection system on the basis of the liberal tradition, UN member states became logged in debates about fundamental conceptual issues on human rights. Several Asian states sought to redefine the concepts of human rights by questioning the applicability of universal human rights in different cultural, economic and social settings. The Asian regional preparatory meeting which took place in Bangkok between 29 March and 2 April 1993 provided an opportunity for Asian governments to put forward their definition of human rights on the global agenda. The Bangkok Declaration, signed by over forty Asian governments, did not reject universal human rights. But the declaration suggested that universality should be considered 'in the context of a dynamic and evolving process of international norm-setting, bearing in mind the significance of national and regional particularities and various historical, cultural and religious backgrounds'.[3] The Asian states also sought to link development issues with human rights questions and emphasized the importance of non-interference.

In the event, the World Conference on Human Rights which took place in Vienna between 14 and 25 June 1993 did not turn into a battleground between Asian and Western governments as some participants had feared. None the less, their division was clear: Western governments criticized the human rights conditions in the Asian region and maintained that universal standards in human rights should be observed; East Asian states accused the West of using human rights to interfere with the domestic affairs of other countries, and ignoring the different economic, social and cultural conditions in the developing world.[4] This East Asian challenge, however, has also taken a new dimension beyond the question of cultural relativism which has been extensively discussed in existing works on human rights.[5] The post-Cold War confrontation between East Asia and the West over human rights also has to be understood in the context of the spectacular economic development in the Asia-Pacific region.

The emergence of the Pacific region as a focal point of global economic activities has led to intense discussions about whether a fundamental shift in world politics has taken place, marking the beginning of a new epoch.[6] The growing importance of the Asia-Pacific region has also prompted suggestions that international relations as conducted by East Asian states will provide a Pacific paradigm of the future.[7] As the debate about the meaning and theoretical implications of the Pacific phenomena among international relations scholars becomes fashionable, some East Asian states seem to have drawn the conclusion that the East Asian mode of development has proved to be more successful than the Western model. They assert that their political systems and economic policies are better than the Western political models, and they can offer 'an alternative vision of the values needed for a better world'.[8]

Western values appear to be set on a collision course with Asian traditions and economic priorities in the form of a 'clash of civilizations'.[9] To what extent can different interpretations of human rights exist in the contemporary world? Have human rights differences between the industrialized North and the developing South replaced the East–West ideological confrontation as the major source of international conflict? Can the differences over human rights between East Asian countries and the West be resolved?

Human rights and post-Cold War international relations in the Asia-Pacific region

Human rights questions have been on and off the agenda of world politics since the end of the Second World War. The holocaust in Europe and Japanese atrocities in Asia generated political momentum in the immediate post-war years for the establishment of an international human rights protection system. The adoption of the Universal Declaration of Human Rights in 1948 was a testimony to the international commitment to human rights protection. However, developments in international human rights protection have seen rather uneven progress in different parts of the world over the last half century.

Amnesty International, a leading international non-governmental organization, has been highly critical of the human rights effort of the UN. In a submission to the Vienna World Conference on Human Rights entitled *Facing up to the Failures*, the organization suggested: 'The United Nations is still critically failing to address some of the most fundamental violations of human rights which are still occurring on a horrifying scale in the world today.' Amnesty International concluded that the human rights mechanisms and procedures have not been able to eradicate human rights violations by governments.[10] While many other observers would share Amnesty International's disappointment, they probably would agree with Philip Alston that the development in the global framework within the UN system since the 1940s 'would have been considered inconceivable by the vast majority of observers in 1945'.[11]

Regional human rights protection systems have also evolved in different parts of the world. The European system which has been characterized as an enforcement regime is the most developed, with comprehensive coverage, a highly developed set of mechanisms and procedures, and a high degree of national compliance. Elsewhere regional arrangements for human rights have been established, with the exception of the Asian region where no region-wide human rights protection system exists.

Over the past four decades the international human rights debates have often been carried out in ideological terms because of Cold War politics. Western criticism of human rights violations have been targeted primarily at communist states, conveniently overlooking violations committed by anti-communist authoritarian regimes. Moreover, anti-colonialism, the struggle for national independence and nation-building have been the central focus of political attention in a region newly freed from Western colonial rule. Human rights have usually been accorded low priority by Asian states which have devoted their energy to developing their economies and creating national identities. Cold War confrontation and the struggle for independence have therefore shaped the agenda of human rights in Asia for more than forty years.

The end of the Cold War brought important changes to the pattern of international relations in the Asia-Pacific region, but the changes which are taking place differ significantly from those of Europe. Post-colonial nationalism, cultural differences and historical rivalry often complicated Cold War politics in the region. Soviet communism never had the same degree of dominance over the Asian region. The Sino-Soviet split and other conflicts among communist states have prevented the emergence of a pro-Soviet bloc in the region. The US policy of containment has been centred upon a network of bilateral security alliance rather than a central command defence pact like

NATO in Europe. The global bipolar rivalry at least offered predictability and also suppressed regional conflicts and differences over issues such as human rights.

As Western governments come under domestic political demand to press for improvements in human rights conditions in East Asia, there is a growing sense of uncertainty and concern about the role of the United States in the Asia-Pacific region. With the end of the super-power confrontation, regional international relations have ceased to be dominated by the global power structure. Issues such as the continuing confrontation between rival parties in divided nations like Korea and China, and conflicts over disputed territories have become key regional concerns. In the longer run, many Asian states are concerned that the reduction of a US military presence would lead to, borrowing from the title of the classic work by the historian A. J. P. Taylor,[12] a struggle for mastery of East Asia and other new forms of regional conflicts.

Human rights differences between East Asian states and the United States may influence American policy towards the East Asian region with far-reaching consequences. The collapse of Soviet communism came at a time when East Asian states have already become more confident of their political and economic capacities and more assertive internationally. Human rights issues have already complicated the bilateral relationship between the United States and East Asian countries such as China. The difficulties over the granting of the most-favoured-nation tariff status to China by the United States is just one example of how human rights problems have affected economic relations. Conflicts over human rights will also have implications for regional security and economic development.

Another dimension in the human rights issue is a changing domestic human rights agenda in many East Asian states. The renewed international attention to human rights has coincided with a more vocal domestic articulation of human rights concerns in the region brought about by social, economic and political changes which have come about in the post-decolonization era. Regional and local non-government groups have become far more aggressive in championing human rights protection.

In a region which has been dominated by authoritarian regimes, political structures in countries like South Korea, Taiwan and the Philippines have undergone significant changes in the past ten years. These 'newly liberalizing states' have sought to accommodate a more pluralistic polity and become more responsive to a widening domestic human rights agenda. In some other East Asian states, however, economic success has not led to political liberalization. Countries like China have undergone dramatic changes since the late 1970s, but the state's response to the changing economic and social conditions has been greater assertiveness—leading to a policy of economic liberalization, but the tightening of political control. International pressure on East Asian states over human rights issues has been interpreted by such states as attempts to undermine their political positions and therefore a threat to regime survival. The Beijing government's uncompromising stance towards political dissidents during the visit of the US Secretary of State Warren Christopher in early 1994 is probably also a response to the perceived threat to the leadership's authority.

Human rights differences between the Western World and East Asian countries can therefore be a major source of friction, creating problems for the Asia-Pacific region's search for a post-Cold War regional security structure and closer regional economic cooperations.

The East Asian challenge

The post-Cold War international debates on human rights have been referred to as a clash between the post-colonial approach and the neo-colonial approach. The post-colonial approach, developing from the liberal tradition, emphasizes the interdependence of states, and the triumph of the liberal democracies against authoritarianism. The neo-colonial approach sees a continuation from the colonial era to the present, rather than the creation of a new world order, with Western industrialized countries continuing their exploitations of the developing world with new allies in the form of the ruling classes in the developing world or major multinational corporations.[13]

The Western approach to human rights, which places more importance on civil and political rights and the universality of human rights on the basis of the liberal tradition, is usually associated with the post-colonial approach. The Asian position on human rights, which stresses the importance of economic and social rights, as well as cultural differences in Asia, has been identified with the neo-colonial approach. While these two approaches provide useful analytic frameworks in understanding the differences between the Western and Asian positions on human rights, it does not address the East Asian challenge which has been built on the economic success of the region.

The remarkable economic success of a number of East Asian countries since the mid-1960s has often been linked to state policies. The relationship between government policy and the spectacular record of high growth of nine economies in the region—Japan, Hong Kong, South Korea, Singapore, Taiwan, Indonesia, Malaysia, Thailand and China—has been the subject of a World Bank policy research report.[14]

These economies, characterized by the World Bank as high-performing Asian economies, have consistently outperformed practically any other group in the world since the 1960s. They grew more than twice as fast as the rest of East Asia, three times as fast as Latin America and South Asia, and five times faster than Sub-Saharan Africa. Even the oil-rich Middle Eastern economies and industrialized OECD group were easily outperformed. Their success is clearly not an accident. As the World Bank put it, 'If growth were randomly distributed, there is roughly one chance in ten thousand that success would have been so regionally-focused'.[15] While there are a number of fundamental economic factors behind the phenomenal East Asian success story, researchers from the World Bank also concluded that systematic government intervention in fostering development can be observed. Another feature of the East Asian 'miracle' is that the improvement in economic performance has been matched by declining inequality. Human welfare has improved dramatically as a result of the strategy of 'shared economic growth'.[16]

The critical role of the state in 'guiding' the economy to the right direction in most of the successful East Asian economies has challenged the liberal economic assumption that the state should be a neutral incentives regime. This has given rise to the the statist perspective that government policy is the key in understanding the success of East Asian economies. While the statist perspective has been challenged, and competing perspectives have been articulated,[17] the critical role of the state in the East Asian economies has been widely acknowledged. Indeed, interest in the 'state' among social scientists has been revived.[18]

The academic debate on the role of the state, however, may seem irrelevant to political élites in the region, who believe that the formula of success has been found. They suggest that a politically stable environment, brought about by a strong and dominating but competent government committed to a developmentalist strategy, is the best way to go ahead. East Asian states have become more assertive in defending their political power and in presenting a different approach to human rights problems.[19]

The East Asian challenge can be seen in cultural, economic and political terms. Culturally, they assert that the Western-centric approach ignores the specific cultural traditions and historical circumstances of Asian societies whose interpretations of human rights are different from the Western tradition. Economically, they maintain that the priority of developing Asian societies has to be the eradication of poverty, i.e. the right to survival must come first. Politically, they charge that Western political models are not appropriate for Asian societies, and argue that political stability under the capable leadership of a good government is far more important. They also question the motives of the West by accusing the Western countries of having double standards and using human rights merely as an instrument in advancing Western economic or security interests. In some ways the East Asian states' reaction to Western pressure on human rights questions can be characterized as a realist response: Western human rights policy has been seen as 'power politics in disguise' — an instrument for advancing Western political and economic interests.[20]

But if both the post-colonial and neo-colonial approaches cannot adequately describe the nature of the East Asian challenge to human rights problems in the Asia-Pacific region, the realist interpretation clearly has its limitations too. The growing pressure on the East Asian countries' stance on human rights comes not only from Western governments and citizens' groups (both international and regional). The rising importance of international institutions and increasing demands for better human rights protection within the East Asian region are relevant features in the evolution of the contemporary understanding of human rights protection. To describe the current international conflicts over human rights problems in the Asia-Pacific region as East Asia versus the democratic West oversimplifies the growing complexity of contemporary international relations.

An alternative regional approach?

The purpose of this introduction is to provide a background to the existing human rights debates in the Asia-Pacific region, and to raise questions on the nature of the East Asian challenge and its implications for international relations in the region. It does not seek to answer the substantive issues raised, which is the task of the contributors in this volume. Several chapters in this book will examine the roots of the human rights differences between East Asia and the West and the extent to which the universalist notion of human rights is relevant in the East Asian context. Contributors will also discuss the impact of economic and political changes on the human rights debate in the Asia-Pacific region. Finally, the book will explore the possibility of an alternative regional approach to human rights protection.

The book is divided into four parts. The four chapters in Part I, which focus on the critical questions related to the different perceptions and interpretations of human rights in Asian and Western societies, address the conceptual dimension of the East Asian challenge. Michael Freeman assesses the contrasting views about human rights in the West and Asia. Joseph Chan attempts a philosophical appraisal of the arguments put forward by the Asian states, and examines whether their positions could be justified in philosophical terms. Mely Caballero-Anthony focuses on the relationship between human rights, economic development and democracy by looking at developments in Southeast Asian countries. Yash Ghai concludes Part I with a critical review of the notion that there is a uniform Asian perspective and provides an analysis of the different views on human rights in Asia.

Part II concentrates on the positions of different Pacific rim countries, including the United States, the People's Republic of China, Japan, the Philippines and Russia. These chapters examine post-Cold War changes in these countries as well as the impact of the recent economic, social and political transformation on human rights debates in the region.

William Barnds begins this part with a survey of American human rights policy. He explores the American domestic agenda and legislative processes that have shaped US human rights foreign policy and the likely American influence on human rights development in Asia. Zhou Wei's chapter on the development of human rights study in China is an attempt to examine not only the nature of the academic debates on human rights but also the Chinese state's changing attitude towards human rights and the impact of international opinion on the Chinese leadership. Takagi's contribution examines the foreign policy dilemma facing the Japanese government over human rights problems in China. His chapter assesses the Japanese government's balancing act of maintaining a friendly relationship with post-Tiananmen China while upholding human rights principles.

Franciso Nemenzo and Constantine Pleshakov's contributions complete the discussion in this part by looking at the effects of political liberalization on human rights protection. Both contributors examine the dramatic changes which have occurred, but at the same time caution that human rights situations are still difficult even after the collapse of dictatorial regimes. International pressures, however, have worked in different directions in the Philippines and Russia. The Marcos dictatorship was a US ally in the Cold War whereas the Soviet Union was the target. The United States therefore supported Marcos despite his authoritarian policies. Nemenzo also highlights the importance of 'people's diplomacy' and the links between human rights advocates in the Philippines and the world human rights movement. Pleshakov is concerned with the complex consequences of the disintegration of the Soviet Union and the emergence of a new human rights agenda for Russia both domestically and internationally.

Part III discusses the institutional and regional dimensions of human rights problems in the region. The essays in this part consider the institutional dimension in a broad sense: the mechanisms for addressing international and regional human rights conflicts. Paul Taylor takes a global perspective by examining the UN approach to humanitarian assistance. His analysis concentrates on human rights violations as a result of war and natural calamities and the international community's mechanism in addressing such problems. He contributes to the debate by addressing not only the questions of whether international intervention is justified or not, and how the operation of humanitarian assistance could be carried out, but also the relatively unexplored issue of how the withdrawal of international intervention could be executed. Lawrence Woods assesses the important question of whether the existing framework of economic cooperation could be built upon as the basis for resolving human rights differences and improving human rights conditions in the Asia-Pacific region. Amitav Acharya examines ASEAN's attempt to develop an alternative approach to the management of human rights problems with reference to Myanmar.

Finally in the concluding chapter in Part IV, the editor reviews the evolving human rights agenda in the Asia-Pacific region. The chapter identifies existing efforts in the promotion of a human rights system in the region and examines the problems surrounding the establishment of regional arrangements for international human rights protection in the Asia-Pacific region. In concentrating on the information exchange and research dimension, the concluding chapter explores an alternative approach to improved human rights protection in the Asia-Pacific region.

Notes

1. General Assembly Resolution 45/155.
2. See *Human Rights Monitor*, no. 21, May 1993. In this special issue on the World Conference on Human Rights, there are detailed accounts of the background leading to the conference and the difficulties encountered during preparatory work.
3. Declaration adopted by the ministers and representatives of Asian states in Bangkok, 2 April 1993, in preparation for the World Conference on Human rights. Japan and Cyprus signed but expressed reservations on the statement.
4. A detailed day-to-day account of the World Conference on Human Rights in Vienna and the parallel non-governmental organization activities including the NGO Forum between 10 and 12 June 1993 can be found in *Terra Viva*, an independent daily published by the Inter-Press Service between 11 and 25 June 1993, covering the world conference and associated events.
5. See, for example, James C. Hsiung (ed.), *Human Rights in East Asia: A Cultural Perspective* (New York: Paragon House, 1985).

6. See, for example, Peter A. Gurevitch, 'The Pacific rim: current debates', *The Annals*, special issue on 'The Pacific region: challenges to policy and theory', vol. 505, September 1989.
7. James Kurth, 'The Pacific basin versus the Atlantic Alliance: two paradigms of international relations, *The Annals*, ibid.
8. Tommy Koh, 'The 10 values that undergird East Asian strength and success', *International Herald Tribune*, 11–12 December 1993, p. 6. See also Interview with Lee Kuan Yew, *Time*, 14 June 1993, pp. 20–1.
9. Samuel P. Huntington, 'The clash of civilizations?, *Foreign Affairs*, vol. 72, no. 3 (September 1993), pp. 22–49.
10. Amnesty International, 'Facing up to the failures: proposals for improving the protection of human rights by the United Nations ', Report to the World Conference on Human Rights, Vienna, June 1993, p. 2.
11. Philip Alston, 'Human rights in 1993: how far has the United Nations come and where should it go from here', Workshop discussion paper for the Non-Governmental Organization Forum, Vienna, June 1993, p. 3. A more comprehensive review of the United Nations work in the field of human rights is in Philip Alston (ed), *The United Nations: A Critical Appraisal* (Oxford: Clarendon Press, 1992).
12. A. J. P. Taylor, *The Struggle for Mastery in Europe, 1848–1878* (Oxford: Clarendon Press, 1954).
13. Christopher Tremewan, 'Human rights in Asia', *The Pacific Review*, vol. 6, no. 1 (1993), pp. 17–30. My summary is a very simplified version of Tremewan's arguments.
14. *The East Asian Miracle: Economic Growth and Public Policy*, (New York: Oxford University Press for the World Bank, 1993).
15. *ibid.*, p. 2.
16. *ibid.*, pp. 3–6 and 13.
17. See, for example, Steve Chan and Cal Clark, 'Changing perspectives on the evolving Pacific Basin: international structures and domestic processes', in Cal Clark and Steve Chan (eds), *The Evolving Pacific Basin in the Global Political Economy: Domestic and International Linkages* (Boulder: Lynne Rienner Publishers, 1992), pp. 1–26.
18. A general discussion of the role of the 'state' is in Peter B. Evans, Dietrich Rusechemeyer and Theda Skocpol (eds), *Bringing the State Back In* (Cambridge: Cambridge University Press, 1985). For discussions about the East Asian situation, see Frederick Deyo (ed.), *The Political Economy of the New Asian Industrialism* (Ithaca: Cornell University Press, 1987); Jeffrey Henderson and Richard P. Appelbaum, 'Situating the state in the East Asian development process', in Richard P. Appelbaum and Jeffrey Henderson (eds.), *State and Development in the Asian Pacific Rim* (Newbury Park: Sage, 1992), pp. 1–26.
19. See, for example, Lee Kuan Yew, 'Democracy and human rights for the world', speech delivered at the Create 21 Asahi Forum, Tokyo, 20 November 1992, as released by the Singapore government.
20. See Jack Donnelly's 'Twentieth–century realism', in Terry Nardin and David R. Mapel (eds.), *Traditions of International Ethics* (Cambridge: Cambridge University Press, 1992), pp. 85–111.

PART I
CONCEPTUAL PERSPECTIVES

2

HUMAN RIGHTS: ASIA AND THE WEST

MICHAEL FREEMAN

Introduction

It is useful to think of human life in the contemporary world as organized at four levels. First, there are individuals, who are born, have names, live lives, have good and bad experiences, and die. Second, there are cultural communities and practical associations, to which individuals belong, in which they pursue their goals, and which give meaning to their lives. Third, there are nation-states; which are the principal organizers of communities, associations and individuals. Fourth, there is the world system, to which nation-states and transnational communities and associations belong, in which they pursue their goals, and which provides a framework for their actions.

The world system is supposed to be regulated by the United Nations, which has a similar function in relation to its member states as they have to the communities, associations and individuals within their jurisdictions, although it lacks the power which states normally command. The UN claims to represent 'the international community' as states claim to represent their nations. As a sort of world government, it has a legislative code. This code includes the doctrine of human rights. This doctrine prescribes certain relations between states and the individuals within their jurisdictions. The UN constructed this doctrine in response to the barbarous actions of Nazi-German imperialism and to the economic and social misery of the Depression. In doing so, it drew on two Western political traditions: the opposition to despotic government that had its origins in England, America and France in the seventeenth and eighteenth centuries, and the struggle of the poor through trade unions and socialist organizations for decent conditions of work and standards of living. Although the UN human rights doctrine was formulated in terms of Western traditions, it addresses universal problems (despotism and poverty) and has been supported by non-Western governments, non-governmental organizations and individuals.

During the Cold War the human rights concept was distorted by the ideological battle between capitalist West and communist East. Western governments emphasized civil and political rights in their critique of communism. The communist states defended themselves by appealing to the doctrine of state sovereignty, and counter-attacked by criticizing Western capitalist societies for their failure to realize economic and social rights, for racial discrimination and imperialism. This conflict popularized the simplistic view that there were two types of human rights, one Western and bourgeois (civil and political), the other Eastern and socialist (economic and social). This distinction led to historical and political errors. It suppressed recognition of the traditional struggles for economic and social rights in the West and the place of civil and political rights in the socialist tradition. It blurred the conceptual and empirical relations between the political and the economic. Those who gave priority to freedom over bread assumed that starving people could be free, while those who gave priority to bread over freedom assumed that starving people did not need to be free. Both assumptions are questionable.

At the same time international relations were characterized by another division. This had several names: imperialism and anti-imperialism, colonialism and anti-colonialism, developed and developing countries, the West and the Third World, North and South. These names referred to a division between two sets of peoples, which had three significant features: it was not directly part of the Cold War; it was a direct product of European imperialism; and it was a division between rich and poor nations. Although some societies of the Third World were socialist, others capitalist, and many had mixed economies, and although the states of the Third World formed different political and military alliances with the Cold War powers, the historical experience of imperial domination by the West and the weak position of these societies in the international economy dominated by the West led them towards the Soviet view of human rights, emphasizing state sovereignty as a defence against 'neo-imperialism' and economic development as having priority over civil and political rights.

Western governments, having won their Cold War with communism, have taken their fight for human rights to the Third World. This has brought them into conflict with some Asian governments. Human rights violations in several Asian countries have been targets of Western criticism. However, the economic success of some East Asian societies has given their governments the confidence to resist this initiative on the basis of what they believe to be the proven worth of their cultures. What appears, from the Western perspective, to be a noble campaign for universal human rights, is interpreted, from an Asian perspective, as cultural imperialism.

In this confrontation two issues have been carried forward from the Cold War. The first is the conflict between the principle of universal human rights and that of non-interference in the internal affairs of sovereign nation-states. The second is the relative priority of civil and political rights, on the one hand, and economic and social rights, on the other. But there is a third, new element in the situation. The renewed assertion of non-Western cultural values has called into question the universalist interpretation of human rights. Some Asian governments accuse the West of trying to impose on them alien values derived from the Western liberal tradition.

Asia and human rights

There was no explicit concept of human rights in East Asian culture before the reception of Western political ideas at the end of the nineteenth century. Confucianism, for example, laid the foundations of ethics in certain social relations and the mutual obligations that were inherent in them.[1] The official ideologies of Tokugawa Japan and Yi dynasty Korea associated inequality with order and equality with chaos. There were no theoretical limits to the authority of the state. Yet protests occurred. In Korea, for example, the Tonghak movement emerged in the 1860s to challenge the neo-Confucian regime with an egalitarian, anti-Western ideology. We should therefore remember, when we consider Asian objections to the human rights doctrine on the ground that it entails the domination of Asia by the West, not only that violations of human rights in Asia entail the domination of some Asians by others, but also that this domination is often not culturally acceptable to those who are dominated. Political oppression in Asia can be and has been criticized by Asians on Asian cultural grounds that have some family resemblance to the human rights doctrine. Western ideas of rights were imported into Asia because there was indigenous dissatisfaction with the old order and because Western ideas of rights and democracy helped Asian protesters to articulate their goals and principles.[2]

Objections to the application of universal human rights standards to Asia on the ground that such standards are alien to Asian traditions rest on an oversimplified account of those traditions. Traditions are complex and change over time. The sources of change may be internal and/or external. External changes may be imposed by imperialist coercion or accepted voluntarily by peoples dissatisfied with their own traditions. The mere fact that a cultural influence is 'alien' does not mean that it is harmful nor is there anything shameful in learning from others. Asian élites have been keen to learn economic and technological skills from the West. They cannot consistently reject the human rights doctrine only because it is not part of the traditional culture. The question as to whether Asia should or should not adopt the human rights doctrine should not be settled either by looking backwards to tradition nor to the external origin of the doctrine. The test should be whether it is useful and morally acceptable now.[3]

Traditions can also be manipulated to serve contemporary political purposes. If the doctrine of human rights can be misused to disguise Western neo-imperialism, the doctrine of cultural relativism can be misused to conceal or to justify oppression by Asian élites. As Asians would be unimpressed by a justification of Western imperialism on the ground that imperialism was a Western tradition, so, for example, justification of discrimination against Asian women by Asian men on the ground that it is an Asian tradition is similarly unconvincing.[4]

The Asian response to Western criticisms of human rights violations in Asia sometimes takes the form of a moral critique of the West. Asians argue that the social achievements of Western societies are sufficiently questionable that the West has no right to give moral lectures to Asia.[5] This response is, however, inconsistent with that of cultural relativism. If the West should not criticize Asia for human rights violations on the ground that this is to impose alien cultural standards on Asia, then Asians should not criticize the West for its failure to conform to Asian moral standards. The Asian moral critique of the West may be justified, but it presupposes common moral ground between Asia and the West, and thereby undermines the relativist objection to Western critiques of Asia. This common ground exists because Asian élites have chosen to adopt important features of Western culture, especially those associated with the capitalist and socialist paths to economic development. In view of this, appeals to traditional culture are further weakened.

Another common Asian argument assigns priority to economic development. It assumes the validity of the human rights doctrine, but accords priority to economic, social, cultural and development rights over civil and political rights. The argument is that economic development, with its associated economic and social rights, requires stability, and the stabilization of society under conditions of economic development requires both authoritarian government and respect for traditional cultural values. The relation between human rights and economic development is, however, complex and not well understood, both because the concept of human rights is complex and because the empirical connections are complex. Although there are a few examples of successful economic development under authoritarian regimes, many such regimes have failed to achieve stability or economic development. Even where political repression and economic success have been combined, we should not assume that the former was necessary to the latter. If human rights violations are conceded to be wrong in themselves, but are justified on the ground that they are a necessary means to the good of economic development, the justification of the wrong is weakened by the failure to show that it is indeed a necessary means to the good end.

In March 1993 when Asian governments met in Bangkok to prepare for the UN World Conference on Human Rights in Vienna, they adopted a common position in the form of the Bangkok Declaration. The Bangkok Declaration recognized human rights as universal, but insisted that they be interpreted in the context of historical, cultural and regional particularities. Some universalists believe that this particularization of human rights betrays the universalist principle.[6] Yet universalists would be wrong to insist that particular public policies can be deduced directly from universal human rights principles. The Bangkok principle of cultural diversity may be a cover for human rights violations, but it is also inconsistent with the view that human rights are alien to Asian culture.

If universalists underestimate the importance of cultural differences between the West and Asia, those who speak of Asian culture underestimate its diversity. Japan expressed some dissent over the Bangkok Declaration. Human rights are viewed differently in China and the Philippines, and in the ruling and opposition parties in Taiwan. Throughout much of Asia, governments face criticism from Asian human rights organizations. Many of these Asian organizations reject the absolute priority of economic over political rights and believe the two to be mutually dependent. The human rights culture is no longer Western. It is no longer a matter of agreement among state élites. It is a global politico-cultural movement. The myth that the concept of human rights is alien to Asian culture is being challenged by Asian people.[7]

The universality of human rights

The claim that human rights are universal entails neither that all societies should have the same institutions nor that non-Western societies should abandon their cultural heritage in favour of the Western way of life. Those who believe that human rights are universal also believe that there can be diverse institutional means to implement these rights. Many cultural practices either lie outside the domain of human rights or are protected by the human rights doctrine. Article 27 of the Universal Declaration of Human Rights, for example, states that everyone has the right 'freely to participate in the cultural life of the community'.

However, the concession by universalists that the human rights doctrine is consistent with institutional and cultural diversity leaves open the question of whether the doctrine is Western and therefore not universal. Here it is useful to distinguish between the concept of human rights and conceptions of human rights.[8] Concepts are general ideas. Conceptions are specifications of those ideas. There is therefore a strong and a weak version of the thesis that the human rights doctrine cannot be universal because it is Western. The strong version says that the concept of human rights is Western and therefore inapplicable to Asia. The weak version allows that the concept is universal but claims that different conceptions are appropriate to different cultural areas. The strong version is advanced by some Asian intellectuals. The weak version is the position of the Bangkok Declaration.

Three uncontroversial points should clarify the issues. The first is that the concept of human rights refers to a set of international legal texts. The concept has, therefore, a basis in international law. The second point is that the concept of universal human rights is inherently non-Western in the sense that it assigns equal rights to every human being just because they are human and consequently accords no privileges to Westerners.[9] The third point is that the belief that the human rights doctrine is Western in its historical origin is itself not an exclusively non-Western idea but is the standard view of Western historians of Western political thought.[10] The concept of human rights, therefore, is legally international, philosophically universal and historically Western.

What is at issue is not any of these points but the question as to whether the claim that the human rights doctrine is universal is an example of Western cultural imperialism. The claim that it is arises from the combination of resistance to Western imperialism and the Western historical origins of the human rights doctrine. The claim is commonly made by contrasting the modern Western human rights doctrine with traditional Asian culture. However, the actual role of the concept of human rights in contemporary East–West relations is better understood if both East and West are examined from a historical point of view.

We have already seen that Asian history contains challenges to political authority, which were articulated in the Western discourse of human rights at the beginning of the twentieth century. Western history, too, contains traditions of political authoritarianism and social hierarchy. As Asians then and now have turned to the concept of human rights to articulate their opposition to oppression, so have Westerners since the seventeenth century and so they do today. As the introduction of the concept seems alien to Asian culture and unwelcome to Asian élites, so it was in the West. The Eastern and Western time-frames are different, but the political process of claiming human rights is rather similar. In the West the struggle for civil and political rights arose in response to the demands made by the modernizing state, while claims for economic and social rights arose in response to the demands of industrial capitalism. These rights claims were resisted by governing elites as politically subversive, obstructive of economic development and culturally repugnant. The Western and Asian stories are more similar than they are often made out to be.[11]

The classical statement of human rights theory is still that of John Locke.[12] This is often considered to be a paradigm of Western liberal theory and to incorporate many of its defects. The critique of Lockean liberalism and its theory of rights finds the source of its errors in its *individualism*, precisely the idea that is commonly said to distinguish Western from non-Western cultures. According to this critique, Locke and most liberals after him ground their moral and political theory in an 'abstract' individual, who is non-social and anti-social. The Lockean–liberal individual is said to have rights independently of and in opposition to society. It is supposed to follow that these rights-holders are self-centred beings indifferent to the good of society. This conception of individual rights is commonly contrasted with non-Western conceptions of the collective good to show not only that the Western conception of rights is culturally peculiar to the West but also that it is morally inferior in privileging individual self-interest over the common good.[13]

There is, however, a strong tradition in Western political theory that objects to the concept of individual rights precisely on the ground that it mistakenly regards the human individual as non-social and consequently grounds a political theory that is incompatible with an orderly and flourishing society.[14] Thus, the distinction between liberal individualism and its critics is not the same as the distinction between Western and non-Western thought. Opposition to liberal individualism and its theory of individual rights is just as Western as is support for these ideas.

The critique of Locke's individualism is also based on a misunderstanding of his theory. Locke's was a Christian doctrine. The ground of morality for him was the existence and nature of the Christian God. Locke presented God primarily as the creator of the world and, in particular, of human beings. Morality arose from the *relations* among human beings established by God. This morality consisted of the *obligations* each individual had to respect the fundamental interests of every other individual and the rights each individual had and might seek to preserve against unjust violation by others. Locke's theory of individual rights was a moral theory of the social relations among individuals, and was based upon a theory of fundamental religious obligation.

It was not a rights-based theory and Lockean rights were not non-social. Locke's theory of social relations is, therefore, not as different from the Confucian as contrasts between Western individualism and Chinese ethics usually suggest.

What is distinctive in Locke is his explicit emphasis on the rights which are correlative with duties in social relations. Locke's conception of rights provides the standard form of rights claims in modern Western liberal philosophy: to say that an individual A has a human-right to X is to say that there is a social relation between A and some other person(s) or organization(s) B such that there is a strong moral reason for holding that B has a duty towards A with regard to X. According to liberal theory, the doctrine of human rights is not only a doctrine of human duties among individuals but one of obligation to those social institutions that protect rights. The liberal theory of human rights, by requiring respect for the fundamental rights of each individual, requires support for the social system of mutually sustaining rights and duties. In the words of Alan Gewirth, 'the emphasis on individual rights is not only compatible with, but requires a conscientious concern for, the common good'.[15]

The social character of Locke's theory of rights can be further explained by one of his examples. He invites us to imagine a Swiss and an Indian making an agreement in the woods of America. Such an agreement, he says, is binding because the moral obligation to keep faith belongs to men as men.[16] Although this is a proposition about individual obligation, the individuals concerned are not non-social. They are Swiss and Indian, members of particular societies. Also, Locke's 'individualism', far from licensing the indulgence of unrestrained self-interest, places a *stricter* moral obligation on the parties than a more communitarian theory might do: neither the Swiss nor the Indian may appeal to the customs of his society to break faith with another human being. Finally, Locke's individualism, far from being 'imperialistic', entails a universal, egalitarian morality. In the woods of America the Swiss and the Indian meet as moral equals. Locke rules out the possibility that the Swiss may break faith with the Indian because he (the Swiss) is European or Christian or 'civilized'.

The Lockearn–liberal theory of rights is, however, a theory of the rights of *individuals*, and this individualism may seem alien to non-Western cultures. I return now to my proposal that we think of the contemporary world as organized at four levels: individual, community/association, nation-state and world system. The human rights doctrine is based on an agreement among nation-states at world-system level to impose upon all nation-states obligations to respect certain rights of individuals. The objection to this doctrine on the ground that it is an example of Western cultural imperialism claims that this analysis disguises the reality that one set of nation-states (the West) is imposing upon another set of nation-states (those of the Third World) and the communities and associations that they represent an alien culture that gives priority to the individual level over both that of community/association and that of the nation-state. However, we have already seen that the Locke–Gewirth conception of individual rights does not give the individual *priority over* community or nation-state but sets the defence of individual rights within a framework which requires support for the common good of associations, communities and nation-states.

Liberal individualism is more social than it is often thought to be, and non-Western collectivism more individualistic. In the Confucian ethic of social relations, for example, one crucial relation is that of husband and wife: a relation between individuals. A theory of social duties that eliminates individuals eliminates individual duties, which collectivist ethical doctrines do not normally intend. The justification for requiring an ethic for the individual level is, therefore, in part that the other levels cannot flourish if the individual level does not flourish.

What distinguishes the liberal theory of rights is not the denial that individuals have obligations to community and state, but the belief that human life is led by individuals. Individuals suffer or are happy, succeed or fail in their purposes, perform good or bad actions, do or do not fulfil their obligations to society. This form of individualism is compatible with the following 'communitarian' propositions: the identity of individuals is to a large extent constituted by their communities; individuals can normally flourish only in communities; the interests of communities should often be given priority over those of its individual members. Liberal individualism is, however, distinctive in denying that communities can be valuable independently of good individual lives.

The ground of this theory is the good human life. Good human lives are fundamental values in both 'individualist' and 'communitarian' moralities and in Western and non-Western cultures. I shall now use two ideas proposed by Joseph Raz. The first is a definition of rights discourse. To assert that an individual has a right is to claim that an aspect of his well-being is a ground for a duty on another person. The second is the logical proposition that assertions of rights are intermediate conclusions in arguments from ultimate values to duties.[17] Liberalism holds the good individual life to be an ultimate value which justifies the ascription of rights to, and duties on individuals. To assert that an individual has a right is to claim that he or she has some interest related to having a good life that imposes a duty on others.

The concept of the good human life must take account of two necessary features of the human condition: the vulnerability of individuals to harm and the capacity of individuals for action. Richard Rorty has suggested that the harms to which humans are vulnerable can be divided into two types: pain and humiliation.[18] Freedom from pain and humiliation are normally aspects of the good life that entail the right of every individual not to be subject to the arbitrary infliction of pain and humiliation by others and the duty of every individual not to inflict arbitrarily pain and humiliation on others. The condition of arbitrariness indicates that rights are not absolute because one right may conflict with another. It may be that the promotion of good lives requires the infliction of pain and humiliation on some individuals. This is not to endorse the utilitarian ultimate value of maximizing utility but to acknowledge that the ultimate value of good individual lives may require the infliction of harm, for example by way of reasonable punishment for wrongful acts. Such punishment is not arbitrary if it is justified by the ultimate value of promoting good lives.

The human capacity for action may be expressed in various ways: in morally worthy deeds, in intellectual creativity, in religious piety, in devotion to one's community, in the creation of wealth, etc. Good lives are those in which the capacities of individuals are developed and employed. Not all expressions of human capacities are good and should be permitted, for individuals have the capacity to harm others. But individuals have the right not to be subjected to arbitrary restriction of their capacities. Restrictions are not arbitrary if they are justified by the ultimate value of promoting good lives. Capacity rights are the other side of the coin of harm rights in that the restriction of capacities is harmful (i.e. causes pain and humiliation) to individuals. Individuals may, of course, choose to suffer pain and/or humiliation in pursuit of some good justified by an ultimate value. Such a choice does not in itself violate any right of the chooser, since the right is not to have harm arbitrarily inflicted by others.

The ultimate value of the good life and the derivative values of avoidance of arbitrary harm and the development and expression of capacities justify particular human rights. The right to a fair trial, for example, is justified in order to minimize the probability that the infliction of punishment will be arbitrary. The rights to freedom of expression, movement, association, religion and participation in the culture of one's community are justified as expressions of human capacity.

The liberal theory of human rights seeks to restrict the power of governments. Arguments that the theory is Western and alien to non-Western cultures often ignore the fact that the target of human rights concerns is much more commonly the actions of governments than the cultural practices of their peoples. Many non-Western governments proclaiming that the human rights doctrine is an example of Western imperialism and alien to the culture of their peoples are engaged in the destruction of the culture of their peoples in the name of economic development.[19] Liberals believe that governments, because they control exceptionally large concentrations of power, have an exceptionally large capacity to harm the individuals, communities and associations under their power. Individual rights are not secure unless they are protected from the use of power by governments to harm them. Insecurity is bad because it is painful and/or because it inhibits the development and exercise of human capacities. In order to provide adequate security for individuals, liberals emphasize the importance of embodying fundamental rights in law and requiring that governments be subject to the rule of law.

All human individuals have rights to secure. All are vulnerable to the violation of their rights by governments. The liberal theory of human rights does not seek to protect only the Western way of life. It seeks to protect diverse ways of life from violation by governments. Whatever one's chosen way of life, one has an interest in having it protected against arbitrary interference by government. Governments may restrict rights if this is necessary to promote good lives. Those governments which violate human rights justify their actions on precisely these grounds. The moral weakness of their position is that the violation of rights is clear, whereas the necessity of the violation is uncertain. On the liberal view, neither the sovereignty of the state nor economic development as such justified the violation of human rights, since neither necessarily minimizes arbitrary harm nor optimizes the development of individual capacities. This view is universal and not imperialistic because it subjects all governments to the same criterion of the promotion of good lives.

This theory treats rights neither as basic nor as the whole of morality. They are not morally fundamental because they are derived from ultimate values, but individuals have fundamental rights because those rights are necessary to realize ultimate values. They establish *minimum standards for decent governmental practice*. They are universal because every individual has a fundamental interest in having a good life. They are not, however, absolute, but may be limited only when they impose unreasonable burdens on others.[20]

We can now evaluate the moral status of three defences commonly presented against the claims of universal human rights. The first is the doctrine of state sovereignty. States are not good unless they promote good lives for communities, associations and individuals. Thus states are legitimate only if they respect human rights. There is no moral reason to respect the sovereignty of an illegitimate state. The second is the priority of economic development. However, economic development is good only if it promotes the good communities, associations and individuals. In so far as economic development is necessary to meet the minimum standards required by human rights, there is no conflict between the two. Where there appears to be such a conflict (e.g. between political and economic rights), the theory of human rights requires careful analysis of which rights of which individuals are being violated to promote which other rights of which other individuals, and critical examination of the claim that such violations are necessary to improve the promotion of good lives. The third defence is based on the right of political and cultural self-determination. There is here a self-contradiction, for objection is made to the concept of universal human rights on the basis of a supposed universal human right. The right of self-determination is a right of peoples and may not therefore be cited to defend the violation of human rights by governments. Also, the right of self-determination, like all rights, is derived from ultimate values and may be justly exercised only with due regard to other fundamental rights.

The concept of human rights is therefore universally applicable. What should we think of the Bangkok principle that, although the concept is universal, there may be different conceptions of human rights in different political, economic, social and cultural contexts? Western governments and human rights activists have opposed this idea because they believe that it disguises the desire to perpetrate gross human rights violations. The Bangkok principle may be right in theory but wrong in practice. The principle is justified by Dworkin's argument that general concepts have to be interpreted in particular circumstances. Both the meaning of human rights principles and the balancing of conflicting rights and values must be context-dependent. Yet there is reason to believe that this valid theoretical principle is being used by some Asian governments to conceal or to justify unjustifiable human rights violations. Naïve acceptance of the Bangkok principle may entail endorsement of oppression. Dogmatic denial may entail moral imperialism. Neither extreme is justified.

The human rights doctrine, because of its Western origins and its place in Western foreign policy, has suffered from guilt by association with imperialism. As a consequence, those who wish to protect the cultures in which they take pride have viewed with suspicion a doctrine that they mistakenly perceive to be hostile to those cultures but which in fact seeks to protect them from violation by their governments. The human rights doctrine is not imperialistic, because it seeks to protect the vulnerable from the powerful, whereas imperialism constitutes the domination of the weak by the powerful. There may be conflict between the doctrine and some elements of some cultures, but only when those cultures endorse oppression of some members of society by others.

What is to be done?

Politics is driven by power, more or less constrained by justice. Power works by pretending to be just. In thinking about human rights we should distinguish between what justice requires and what those with power demand. Yet in deciding what should be done we have to take account both of the principles of justice and the realities of power. There is no doubt that many serious violations of human rights take place around the world. That this is true and morally deplorable is not only a Western view. Asians are deploring human rights violations by Asians, as Westerners are deploring human rights violations by Westerners.

There is a global debate about human rights because there is a global world system in which global economic, political and cultural networks co-exist with national and local economies, political systems and cultures. The values of political self-determination and national economic development are values of the global culture. Both the political and the economic relations of this culture are highly dynamic. This has ambiguous implications for human rights. On the one hand, those with power wish to control these developments and this may lead to the suppression of human rights. On the other hand, the processes themselves can generate forms of people power which demand respect for human rights. This is more clearly true in capitalist systems in which market freedoms can easily spill over into demands for political freedoms. But it may also be true of socialist systems committed to economic development. Technology links economic development with political freedom. Development is impossible without participation in the world technological system, but modern technologies of communication and transportation make rigid forms of political authoritarianism more difficult to maintain.[21]

Kishore Mahbubani from Singapore has called for a dialogue of equals on human rights between Asians and Westerners on the basis of mutual respect. He complains that no level playing-field has been created for such a dialogue.[22] The doctrine of human rights itself endorses precisely such a dialogue of equals. It notes, however, that no level playing-field exists for dialogue between nation-states and their governments, on the one hand, and the communities, associations and individuals whom they govern, on the other. Dialogue presupposes certain rights of the participants. If the dialogue on human rights is not to protect interests only at the nation-state level, the voices of individuals, communities and associations must be heard. The human rights question is not properly an issue between East and West at all. It is a question of how governments can be truly responsive to the people they claim to serve. What is required, then, is dialogue among governments, the institutionalization of transnational, non-governmental dialogue and the institutionalization in all societies of those fundamental human rights which guarantee to individuals, communities and associations protection from arbitrary government and empower them to contribute creatively and constructively to the good life in common.

Notes

1. Chung-sho Lo, 'Human rights in the Chinese tradition', in UNESCO (ed.), *Human Rights : Comments and Interpretations* (Westport, Conn: Greenwood Press, 1973), p. 187.
2. Ian Neary, 'The Hyongpyongsa, the Suiheisha and the struggle of human rights in East Asia' (unpublished, 1993).
3. Boo Tion Kwa, 'Righteous talk', *Far Eastern Economic Review*, 17 June 1993, p. 28.
4. Neary, op. cit., pp. 5, 11, 19.
5. Kishore Mahbubani, 'Live and let live: allow Asians to choose their own course', *Far Eastern Economic Review*, 17 June 1993, p. 26.
6. Susumu Awanohara, Michael Vatikiotis and Shada Islam, 'Vienna showdown', *Far Eastern Economic Review*, 17 June 1993, p. 17.
7. Sidney Jones, 'The organic growth: Asian NGOs have come into their own', *Far Eastern Economic Review*, 17 June 1993, p. 23.
8. For the distinction between concepts and conceptions, see Ronald Dworkin, *Taking Rights Seriously* (London: Duckworth, 1978), pp. 134–6.
9. Alan Gewirth, *Human Rights: Essays on Justification and Applications* (Chicago: University of Chicago Press, 1982), p. 1.
10. Jack Donnelly, *Universal Human Rights in Theory and Practice* (Ithaca: Cornell University Press, 1989), part II.
11. Neary, op. cit., pp. 6, 16, and Donnelly, op. cit.
12. John Locke, *The Second Treatise of Government* (Cambridge: Cambridge University Press, 1970).
13. Julia Tao, 'The Chinese moral ethos and the concept of individual rights', *Journal of Applied Philosophy*, vol. 7 (1990).
14. Jeremy Waldron (ed.), *Nonsense upon Stilts: Bentham, Burke and Marx on the Right of Man* (London: Methuen, 1987).
15. Gewirth, op. cit., pp. 13–14, 18–19.
16. Locke, op. cit., paragraph 14.
17. Joseph Raz, *The Morality of Freedom* (Oxford: Clarendon Press, 1986), pp. 180–1.
18. Richard Rorty, *Contingency, Irony, and Solidarity* (Cambridge: Cambridge University Press, 1989).
19. Donnelly, op. cit.
20. James W. Nickel, *Making Sense of Human Rights* (Berkeley: University of California Press, 1987), pp. 4, 49–50, 96–8.
21. Ann Kent, *Between Freedom an Subsistence* (Hong Kong: Oxford University Press, 1993), pp. 236–7.
22. Mahbubani, op. cit., p. 26.

3

THE ASIAN CHALLENGE TO UNIVERSAL HUMAN RIGHTS: A PHILOSOPHICAL APPRAISAL*

JOSEPH CHAN

Introduction

The Bangkok Declaration, adopted by Asian governments in April 1993, as a representative proudly claims, 'stakes out a distinctively Asian point of view' on issues of human rights.[1] The Declaration and the high-sounding claims of some Asian states have triggered off a heated and on-going debate between Asia and the West on human rights issues. Asian states seem to have gained confidence in believing that their cultures and ways of life have merits and strengths which are wanting in Western industrial countries. This confidence finds concrete expression in their attitudes toward human rights. This essay is an attempt to evaluate, from a philosophical point of view, the Asia challenge to universal human rights.

Most Asian governments do not deny the concept of human rights and its importance. Nor do they deny that human rights are universal. However, they do stress the idea of diversity as much as universality about human rights. The Bangkok Declaration holds that Asian governments

recognize that while human rights are universal in nature, they must be considered in the context of a dynamic and evolving process of international norm-setting, bearing in mind the significance of national and regional particularities and various historical, cultural and religious background.[2]

Singapore, the most outspoken Asian state in the debate, warns that 'universal recognition of the ideal of human rights can be harmful if universalism is used to deny or mask the reality of diversity'.[3]

It is not clear whether this argument merely qualifies or in effect denies the very idea of universality. In any case, if more weight is attached to particularistic considerations, the more likely is the universality of human rights to be stripped of its substantive content. Moreover, once particularist arguments are taken on board in the debate about human rights, it seems difficult to bar these considerations from reaching the very foundation of human rights. Noting the danger of this slippery slope, the Vienna Declaration states categorically that 'the universal nature of [human] rights and freedoms is beyond question'. In addressing the issue of particularities, the

Declaration holds that

> While significance of national and regional particularities and various historical, cultural and religious backgrounds must be borne in mind, it is the duty of States, regardless of their political, economic and cultural systems, to promote and protect all human rights and fundamental freedoms.

Despite its rhetoric, this paragraph fails to explain how particularities can be properly taken into account in such a way that the universal nature of human rights can be preserved. It leaves room for Asian governments to argue that because of their particularities, they are entitled to adopt a unique approach in understanding and implementing human rights. However, universalists and human rights advocates obviously would not be happy with this vague rhetoric. They would insist that particularities should not affect the basic understanding and content of universal human rights. Here lies the crux of the debate. While the Asian governments acknowledge the universality of human rights and while the West concedes that particularities do matter, the two sides have very different views of how the two ideas should be related. How can universality and particularities be balanced? Would particularities affect human rights all the way down, from the substantive content of human rights to the problem of their ranking and implementation?

A philosophical perspective

In what follows I shall attempt to evaluate this debate from a philosophical perspective. I shall consider whether there is a case for the claim that particularities of societal contexts can generate a legitimate diversity of approaches in understanding, ranking and implementing human rights. To pursue this evaluation four questions are considered here: (1) What does the idea of universality amount to? (2) From the philosophical point of view, are there any universal human rights? (3) How should particularities be taken into account in considering universal human rights? (4) Can the particularities of societal contexts justify Asian governments adopting a different approach (es) to human rights, and if so, how?

Before we approach these questions, there are several important points to note. First, human rights issues are never purely academic or philosophical in nature. They are also political, reflecting power relations within and between states. The Bangkok Declaration is not so much a theoretical treatise as a political gesture directed against the ever-growing Western political pressure put on Asia to improve their human rights record. Some of the arguments put forward by some Asian governments may be self-serving excuses for their violations of human rights. Clearly particularities in the Asian context do not justify gross violations. No matter how much we might disagree with Singapore's defence of her own human rights record, the following statement by the Foreign Minister of Singapore should command universal agreement:

Diversity cannot justify gross violations of human rights. Murder is murder whether perpetrated in America, Asia or Africa. No one claims torture as part of their cultural heritage. Everyone has a right to be recognized as a person before the law. There are other such rights that must be enjoyed by all human beings everywhere in a civilized world.[4]

In trying to find out whether there is any theoretical space for Asian states to adopt a different approach to human rights, I do *not* intend to defend such violations.

Second, one may wonder why we need to approach the problem philosophically. Have not all Asian states agreed upon the Universal Declaration of Human Rights (hereafter the Universal Declaration)? Is this fact alone not a good reason to charge the Asian states with their violations? According to this view, what is at stake here are just plain violations. The debate does not involve any difficult theoretical or philosophical issues.

I do not think this view gives a correct picture. The 'success' of modern human rights talks conceal difficulties, and human rights agreements are sometimes more apparent than real. It is true that, ideologically, human rights are exalted to a very high status and carry powerful rhetorical force. Human rights are most fundamental rights applicable everywhere, and any violations of them are instances of serious injustice or great offences to human dignity. Furthermore, the Universal Declaration is signed by almost all states in the world and is thus an influential and useful instrument to promote human rights. However, the high political status of human rights is not accompanied with an equally high intellectual regard or respect. Neither is the agreement on the Universal Declaration married with a similar agreement in the interpretation and implementation of human rights.

Many philosophers have been reluctant to endorse the long list of rights in the Universal Declaration. Philosophers tend to prefer a shorter list with just a few rights such as the right not to be tortured, the right to a fair trial, and the right not to be subjected to exploitation.[5] Furthermore, some philosophers do not admit or deny the claim that economic rights are human rights.[6] Some do not even include the right to vote or the right to free speech in their lists.[7] One reason for such reluctance might be that philosophers take more seriously than politicians the universality of human rights.[8] Universal human rights should represent minimal moral standards required of states, and they should be ideologically neutral with respect to diverging political and economic systems in the world. The universal, minimal and neutral character of human rights is essential to the moral justification of international interventions into countries' internal human rights situation. But for many philosophers there is reason to doubt whether all the 'human rights' in the Universal Declaration are of this character.

The Universal Declaration is not a sacred text but the outcome of political debates and bargaining. In addition, agreement upon a list of human rights itself does not entail that there will be no serious controversies over the meaning and implementation of the rights. Consider the right to self-determination and the right to development. It is not clear what these rights mean, to say the least. Who are the people entitled to self-determination? Does

it imply the right of any ethnic community of a multinational state to secede?
Is the right to development an individual right or a collective one? Does it
impose a duty upon the state in which the right-holders reside or upon
foreign states? Some states may have expressed disapproval in discussing
whether these rights should be endorsed in international human rights
instruments, but their objections failed to convince the majority.

Indeed human rights issues are more messy than many people would like
to admit. A careful philosophical analysis is required to provide both a sound
basis for human rights and theoretical guidance for resolving disputes over
their interpretations. In this essay I hope to contribute, in a limited way, to this
task by offering a philosophical analysis of the issues of universality and
particularities and the relationship between them.

The universality of human rights

Are human rights universal? To answer this question, we need to know what
human rights are. Most rights are rights to something, for instance, the right
not to be tortured and the right to free expression. Human rights are of course
also the right to certain protection or service. But when the notion of 'human
rights' is used as a general term, it refers not to the specific content of the
rights but to the nature of a group of rights which share a certain common
characteristic. The common characteristic which the notion of human rights
highlights is its *condition of possession*. The notion of human rights specifies the
condition under which a would-be right-holder is entitled to possess a human
right. The notion tells us that a right is a human right if and only if a person
is entitled to it solely by virtue of being human, irrespective of sex, race,
religion, nationality or social position.[9] Now if a person is said to have a
human right (on the ground that he is a human being), then by implication
all other human beings also have that right. On this view, then, it is necessarily
true that human rights apply to all human beings. Human rights are necessarily universal.

The claim of universality stated in the Vienna Declaration and the Universal
Declaration is, therefore, clearly right. Indeed it is this feature which partly
explains the force of the language of human rights. M. Cranston, for example,
writes:

A human right by definition is a universal moral right, something which all men,
everywhere, at all times ought to have, something of which no one may be deprived
without a grave affront to justice, something which is owing to every human being
simply because he is human.[10]

Notice that Cranston's view of universality here is comprehensive. Human
rights apply to all human beings, *everywhere and at all times*. Thus this notion
of universal human rights implies that these rights are trans-historical or
ahistorical.

While this notion of universality gives force to human rights, it also sets a
very stringent requirement for their existence. At the justification level, uni-

versality serves as a *condition* of the existence of human rights. For a right to be a human right, it has to satisfy the universality requirement, i.e. the right in question has to be applicable to all human beings at all times and all places. Are there any human rights understood in this sense? No doubt there are, but perhaps only a few. The right not to be assaulted and tortured are examples. Apart from these specific rights, other rights that might pass the test of universality are likely to be highly general and are derived from minimal moral principles necessary to every human community. They are, for example, the right to life, the right to justice or fair treatment, and the right to freedom.

However, many rights listed in the Universal Declaration are specific rather than general, and they do not seem to be applicable at all times. Some rights in that list presuppose certain modern ideas or institutions or they require certain social conditions which were not available in pre-modern times. A clear example is the right to elect political representatives in the form of universal and equal suffrage. This is a modern idea, and its realization requires modern institutions (such as political parties) and relatively advanced social conditions (such as literacy and well-established mass media). Freedom of marriage was once also inconceivable in many countries, and the right to social security benefits requires a modern state bureaucracy with relatively advanced economic conditions.

To resolve this difficulty, it would be sensible to admit that not all rights in the Universal Declaration are trans-historical. The notion of universality should thus include an element of historicity: human rights are universal in the sense that they are applicable to all human beings in all places *in a particular era*. In fact, some human rights scholars propose to take the Universal Declaration as 'a minimal response to the convergence of cross-cultural human values and the special threats to human dignity posed by *modern* institutions' (emphasis added).[11] They claim that in the contemporary world, almost all societies, including Asian ones, have modern institutions such as the modern sovereign state, the bureaucracy, the market, and large-scale industrial organizations and enterprises. Traditional communities have either broken up or become too weak to protect powerless individuals from the invasion by these powerful institutions. Human rights are then instruments to ensure that individuals have something to fall back on to protect themselves in these situations.

While this qualified view of the notion of universality makes it easier to justify the existence of human rights, it also creates the possibility that human rights can vary if fundamental interests and threats vary. Scholars holding this view recognize that 'precisely what those [standard] threats are, and which it is feasible to counter, are of course largely empirical questions, and the answers to both questions will change as the situation changes'.[12] Jack Donnelly frankly admits the contingency of 'contemporary' human rights:

Our list of human rights has evolved and expanded, and will continue to do so, in response to such factors as changing ideas of human dignity, the rise of new political forces, technological changes, new techniques of repression, and even past human rights successes, which allow attention and resources to be shifted to threats that previously were inadequately recognized or insufficiently addressed. Such evolution is particularly clear in the emergency of economic and social human rights.[13]

Are there universal human rights in this qualified sense? Is it true that, despite the diversity of cultures and societal circumstances that exist among societies today, it is sensible to talk about uniformity in (a) fundamental human interests and (b) standard threats posed by modern institutions that would justify the human rights in the Universal Declaration?

Is there any uniformity in fundamental human interests? No doubt there are some rights in the Universal Declaration which are grounded in universal human interests such as survival and physical security. These rights are, for instance, the right to life, the right against torture and the right to protection of the family. But civil and political rights are grounded in personal autonomy, which would appear to be somewhat culturally relative. Freedoms of conscience, expression, association and movement and the right to political participation are to a significant extent justified by the value of personal autonomy (although they are also partly justified by the value of democracy). Now personal autonomy is a matter of degree. Our lives can be autonomous only to a certain degree. Almost all cultures today would regard that a certain degree of personal autonomy is desirable. It would be hard to imagine a culture or moral tradition today that would totally deny the value of personal autonomy.

That said, different cultures and political ideologies do ascribe different weights to that value. The liberal culture and ideology attach almost absolute weight to personal autonomy, and this explains their rejection of paternalism. Non-liberal cultures, however, do not give such a prominent place to autonomy. It is at this point that an Asian view could probably arise. While Asian cultures do not deny the value of personal autonomy, they put great emphasis on communitarian values such as family bondage, communal peace, social harmony, sacrifices for the community and patriotism. These Asian values need not lead to a denial of civil and political rights. But they may lead to a different understanding of the scope, weight and ranking of these rights. This point will be pursued in greater depth in the final section.

Let us first complete our present discussion by considering the factor of standard threats. Do individuals and societies in the contemporary world face similar threats? Without doubt there are certain threats common to all societies. Modern governments are very powerful and individuals certainly face the threats of the abuse or corruption of governmental power. However, Asian states claim that developing countries and their people face a unique set of threats and problems, posed not by modern institutions but by their specific social contexts. Ali Alatas, Minister of Foreign Affairs of Indonesia, declares:

Indonesia is also of the firm view that in evaluating the implementation of human rights in individual countries, the characteristic problems of developing countries in general, as well as the specific problems of individual societies should be taken fully into account.[14]

Unlike Western industrial states, many developing countries are post-colonial states facing poverty and political instability. According to China and other Asian states, the threats people face in these countries are colonialism, foreign domination and poverty. Thus China claims that these 'special circumstances' call for two kinds of 'human rights' which are important to developing countries: 'For the vast number of developing countries, to respect and protect human rights is first and foremost the full realization of the rights to subsistence and development.'[15] This statement also reflects a priority of human rights. Because of their special circumstances, the Asian states claim, they may adopt a different view as to the ranking and implementation of human rights. But is this claim true?

Is the Asian perspective defensible?

I shall distinguish the defensible and the indefensible in discussing an Asian perspective of human rights. Let us first deal with the indefensible. Arguments put forward by Asian states are often weak, not well supported by normative arguments and empirical evidence, and sometimes even mutually inconsistent. Two arguments which involve contradictions within their overall position will be considered.

While most Asian states agree that human rights are universal, they also emphasize the importance of particularities. But some of their formulations regarding the role of particularities are too sweeping and overstated. The Chinese representative to the Vienna Conference presented the case in the following way:

The concept of human rights is a product of historical development. It is closely associated with specific social, political and economic conditions and the specific history, culture and values of a particular country. Different historical development stages have different human rights requirements. Countries at different development stages or with different historical traditions and cultural backgrounds also have different understanding and practice of human rights. Thus one should not and cannot think the human rights standards and model of certain countries as the only proper ones and demand all other countries to comply with them.[16]

The logical conclusion of the argument in this passage amounts to a flat denial of universality. The particularities of a country are so deep that they would require a set of understanding and practice of 'human rights' radically different from that of another country. Human rights are thus no longer valid or applicable across cultures or countries. Thus, no human rights can be universal. This is obviously inconsistent with China's and other Asian states' commitment to universality.

There is another contradiction in the arguments by Asian states. Article 10 of the Bangkok Declaration holds that Asian states 'reaffirm the interdependence and indivisibility of economic, social, cultural, civil and political rights, and the need to give equal emphasis to all categories of human rights' (emphasis added). One message behind this Article is that it would be wrong to put civil and political rights above economic rights. Another implication clearly follows: one should not give higher priority to economic rights. But a strong preference for economic rights is clearly expressed by Asian states. In his speech to the Vienna Conference, Liu Huaqiu, Vice-Foreign Minister of China, echoed the Bangkok Declaration and said that 'the various aspects of human rights are interdependent, equally important, indivisible and indispensable'. But he immediately added a point which completely contradicts the previous one:

For the vast number of developing countries, to respect and protect human rights is first and foremost to ensure the full realization of the rights to subsistence and development. When poverty and lack of adequate food and clothing are commonplace ... priority should be given to economic development.[17]

How can it be consistent to hold on the one hand that economic and political rights are indivisible, indispensable and equally important but on the other that in some situation economic rights are more important than political rights? Such a strong preference for economic rights and the right to development can also be found in the Vienna Conference speeches by representatives of Singapore, Indonesia and Thailand.

What do these contradictions tell us about the view of Asian states on human rights? It does not seem groundless to think that their 'endorsement' of the universality of human rights and their 'insistence' of the equality of economic and political rights are nothing more than lip-service. The political motives behind the concerted actions of Asian states on human rights issues are therefore questionable. What they are most concerned with, in reality, might simply be economic development and political stability, not the protection of human rights. Thus said, it would be wrong to infer that, from a philosophical point of view, there is no legitimate room for an alternative perspective of human rights to be derived from the particularities of the Asian context. I shall argue that a certain degree of diversity in understanding the scope, limitation and ranking of human rights can be reasonable and legitimate.

Many Asian states have called for 'greater recognition of the immense complexity of the issue of human rights due to the wide diversity in history, culture, value system, geography and phases of development among the nations of the world'.[18] Singapore, for example, claims that although there is a small hard core of rights that are truly universal, most rights are, however, essentially contested concepts. Although there may be a general consensus over these rights, this is 'coupled with continuing and, at least for the present, no less important conflicts of interpretation'.[19]

The notion of 'essentially contested concepts' may be too strong if it means that the *core meaning* of a right can be interpreted in a number of different ways incompatible with one another. This would in effect destroy the principle of universality. A more moderate claim is plausible, however. It is not the meaning but the scope, weight and ranking of rights which may be contestable and allow systematic ideological differences. The scope, weight and ranking of rights are important and interrelated issues. Human rights in the Universal Declaration are often vague and general. Few if any of them are absolute. Many are subject to derogation in time of state emergency or to limitation in the name of the interest of society. Some rights may be limited if they conflict with the rights of others. Limitation of rights would restrict their scope of application. Whether a right should be limited has to depend on its weight and on how the interests of the right-holder are to be balanced with the interests of others.

Article 29 of the Universal Declaration specifically deals with possible limitations on human rights:

In the exercise of his rights and freedoms, everyone shall be subject only to such limitations as are determined by law for the purpose of securing due recognition and respect for the rights and freedoms of others and of meeting the just requirements of morality, public order and the general welfare in a democratic society. (Article 29(2))

The International Covenant on Civil and Political Rights also contains several limitation clauses. According to such clauses, certain civil and political rights may be limited on some of the following grounds: national security, public safety/order, public health, public morals, and protection of others' freedoms and rights. It is also specified that limitations on these grounds must be 'provided by law' and 'necessary in a democratic society'. These grounds and conditions of limitations stated in the above two documents are clearly necessary. But the generality and vagueness of those terms and concepts allow for various interpretations. It is at this point that culture or ideology-based interpretations are both inevitable and sometimes legitimate. Different cultural and ideological perspectives would strike the balance between the individual's interest and the public interest in different ways. Sometimes these differences can be significant.

Of course interpretations of the limitation clauses should not be arbitrary. There are some general principles to follow. First, like any treaty, a limitation clause should be interpreted in good faith in accordance with the ordinary meaning and purpose of the clause or article. Now since the purpose of the Universal Declaration or the Covenant on Civil and Political Rights is to protect human freedoms and rights, it follows that in any interpretations rights should be read broadly and limitations on rights narrowly.[20] The second is the principle of proportionality. Any limitations imposed must be proportionate to the legitimate aim pursued.[21]

However, even given these principles, controversial interpretations and judgements concerning the proper scope of rights and their limitations can still arise. It is now widely recognized in the international law of human rights that, when adjudicating matters involving the balancing between the individual's interest and the public interest or morals of a country, it is better to leave a 'margin of appreciation' to the contracting states. This principle of 'margin of appreciation' has been applied by the European Court of Human Rights. The Court admits that it is impossible to find 'a uniform European conception of morals' to guide interpretations.[22] Neither is it possible to find a standard of public interest common to all democratic societies. With regard to political, social and economic issues, opinions can reasonably differ within and between democratic societies. Thus contracting states should be given a degree of discretion in the concrete applications of the limitation clauses.

A case in point is the *Handyside* case. This case concerned a publication of a textbook for schoolchildren which contained a good deal of radical material, including a controversial chapter on sex. This book was banned in England but not in other European countries. The justification of such a limitation of freedom of expression was that this was necessary in a democratic society for the protection of morals. The European Court decided that since 'it is not possible to find in the domestic law of the various Contracting States a uniform of European conception of morals',[23] the authorities in England should be given a wide margin of appreciation to make judgements, in this case, on public morals and on the balance between this and freedom of expression.

There are many other human rights cases which involve controversies over a wide range of issues including military punishments, immigration, private property, homosexuality, freedom of expression and so forth.[24] In a detailed study of the development of international law by the European Court of Human Rights, J. G. Merrills observes that there are two competing schools of 'court's jurisprudence' in Europe, namely conservatism and liberalism, which have had much influence on the Court's decisions on human rights cases.[25]

These two ideologies imply two systematic, competing views on the relative importance of the values of individual freedom on the one hand and order, communities and traditions on the other. Conservatives strongly believe in the family, conventional morality, especially sexual morality, and property right. They also put a high priority on the maintenance of order and preservation of state institutions such as the monarchy, parliament, courts and the police. Liberals, in contrast, value highly individual rights and equality, and stress the role of the state in reforming institutions and practices which violate individual rights. Merrills' survey shows that these two ideologies have proved significant in the Court's cases on a variety of human rights issues, including detention, the police's technique of interrogation, the family, sexual morality and military discipline.[26]

It is thus clear that even if there is agreement on a list of human rights, substantial and significant controversies concerning their scope and limitation can still arise. The limitation articles or clauses in contemporary international human rights instruments are deceptively simple and they conceal intense disputes and controversies. Even within the relatively well-developed regional framework of human rights in Europe, where there is a 'common heritage of political traditions, ideals, freedom, and the rule of law', it is difficult to reach consensus on the parameters of the notions of 'democratic society' and 'public morals'. It would be no surprise to find that this problem is even greater at the international level.[27]

Furthermore, as Merrills rightly points out in his study, 'decisions about human rights are not a technical exercise in interpreting texts, but *judgments about political morality*' (emphasis added).[28] The reason for this is obvious. As the above discussion shows, the determination of the scope, limitation and ranking of human rights necessarily involves judgements about political morality. Different theories of political morality would give rise to different views of the proper scope of human rights. Arguably these issues are as important as the justification of the existence of human rights.

It is this link between human rights and political morality that opens up the room for Asian states to claim that they may have a different understanding of the scope of human rights. Of course, from a philosophical perspective, how different their understanding can be is a difficult question, which can only be answered by considering the concrete details of the specific political morality and social context of each of the Asian societies. This is a task beyond the scope of this essay. My main emphasis lies rather on the theoretical claim that there is room for variations in the determination of the scope of human rights. This essay can only illustrate this claim by making some generalized and sometimes impressionistic remarks about the political moralities and social contexts of Asian societies.

Asian societies in general seem to embrace a set of attitudes towards issues of values and morals which is different from that of the West. Many Asians do not value personal autonomy as highly as Western liberals do. In Asian political moralities, we can see a stronger emphasis on the stability, harmony and prosperity of society and a greater reverence for traditions, elders and leaders. Asians in general also have a more conservative attitude towards sexual morality. These conceptions of values and morals would inevitably influence the balancing between individual freedom and the interest of society. Thus it is no surprise that the scope and limitation of human rights drawn by Asians would be different from those of the West, let alone the fact that Westerners can sometimes differ quite widely among themselves.

Take as an example the limitation clauses which contain the phrase 'necessary in a democratic society'. The European Court understands the spirit of democracy to be 'pluralism, tolerance and broad-mindedness'. Democracy does not imply that the views of the majority always prevail. Individuals and the minority should be protected and given a fair and proper treatment.[29] It is doubtful whether many Asians would fully accept the spirit of pluralism and tolerance as understood by Western liberals.

While Western liberalism does have its followers in Asia, fewer Asians would defend the right to publish pornography or the right of homosexuals; nor do they find the legal enforcement of morals objectionable in principle. Some Asian societies seem to value the preservation of a common religion or common morals more than individual autonomy, and they might want to restrict individual freedom for this purpose. For example, Salman Rushdie's book, *The Satanic Verses*, was considered to be 'blasphemous' in some Islamic societies in Asia. People in these societies may judge that artistic expressions should be limited if they contain language insulting or hostile to their religion. It would be difficult to argue that this judgement must be wrong and that the banning of this book in these places violates the human right to freedom of expression.

Consider two other examples. China's birth control policy imposes financial penalty on families in the city with more than one child. Many people in China suggest that their country faces a long-term problem of overpopulation which, if left uncontrolled, would threaten the survival of the whole country. The Chinese government thus argues that such restriction of the individual freedom in family planning is necessary to protect the public interest.[30] There might be disputes on whether such a policy is really necessary. But since this judgement involves highly complicated social and economic problems in China, it would not be wrong to apply the principle of the 'margin of appreciation' in this case. Consider another example. In Singapore, there is a law which empowers the police and immigration officers to 'test the urine for drugs of any person who behaves in a suspicious manner. If the result is positive, rehabilitation treatment is compulsory'.[31] This act would be seen by Western liberals as an unjustifiable invasion of privacy. But for some Asians this amount of restriction may be seen as a legitimate trade-off for the value of public safety and health.

The claim for allowing a different scope in human rights interpretation that this essay defends is a moderate one. To prevent misunderstanding, a few words of caution are necessary. First, the above argument does not legitimize wholesale rejections of human rights or sweeping accusations that human rights are Western-biased, overly individualistic and so forth. Human rights are by their nature instruments to protect individuals from invasion by the government or society. They simply reflect that individual freedom and dignity are fundamental values. Of course, individual freedom is not absolute and often needs to compete with other values. A Western, individualistic approach can emerge when the scope and limitation of rights are to be drawn and conflicting values and rights ranked and traded off. An Asian approach or approaches can also emerge here. In fact, both the Universal Declaration and the International Covenant on Civil and Political Rights contain clauses of limitation and derogation which are wide enough to allow a diversity of approaches generated by different political moralities and societal contexts.

Second, the essay does not accept that all limitations on human rights in Asia can be justified in the name of a different political morality or a unique societal context. We need to observe some general guidelines in interpreting the limitation clauses in international human rights instruments. For instance, the principles of necessity and proportionality are essential. To justify restriction of a human right, it has to be shown, firstly, that the right to be restricted is in conflict with a legitimate aim, and, secondly, that the restriction is absolutely necessary and proportional to the protection of that legitimate aim. Many restrictions of human rights which occurred in Asia do not pass these tests. China's suppression of freedom of expression and political activities can hardly be defended by the claim that this is necessary to public safety or national security. There is simply no good empirical evidence to support this claim. Nor can Singapore's severe restrictions of the freedom of the press and detention of dissidents without trial be justified by similar reasons.[32]

Third, in interpreting the political morality of a country, the government of that country does not monopolize the right of interpretation. Some Asian countries, such as Indonesia and Singapore, stress the notion of consensus in matters of interpreting political morality. But 'consensus' in reality probably means the imposition of government's ideology on its citizens. The Singaporean government proudly claims the following: 'We do not think that our arrangements will suit everyone. But they suit ourselves. This is the ultimate test of any political system.'[33] While this claim may contain an element of truth, the crucial condition for such a test to be meaningful is that citizens have complete freedom to express their opinions. The fact is, however, that there are a number of authoritarian regimes in Asia where the courts are not fully independent in judging political cases and their citizens, very often, are unable to challenge critically the regime's legitimacy. It would be difficult to tell whether people in these regimes really find their arrangements suitable to themselves.

To conclude, human rights are general and vague. They allow plenty of room for reasonable disagreements over their scope and limitation. Thus a diversity of approaches can be legitimate as far as these disagreements are concerned. Because of their specific political moralities and societal contexts, Asian states can claim a wide (but surely not arbitrary) margin of appreciation in interpreting the proper scope and limitation of human rights. Asian states are entitled to claim no less than this. But also no more.

Notes

* I wish to thank James Tang for helpful comments and Johannes Chan for directing my attention to Merrills' book cited in this essay.

1. Bilahari Kausikan, 'Asia's different standard', *Foreign Policy*, no. 92 (Fall 1993), pp. 24-41.
2. The Bangkok Declaration, Article 8. The Declaration has been published in the *Law and Society Trust Fortnightly Review*, (vol. 3, no. 57 1 May 1993).
3. Won Kan Seng, 'The real world of human rights', speech by the Singapore Foreign Minister, Second World Conference on Human Rights, Vienna, 1993, p. 2.
4. Wong, ibid., p. 4.
5. H. A. Bedau, 'International human rights', in Regan and VanDeVeer (eds), *And Justice for All: New Introductory Essays in Ethics and Public Policy* (New Jersey: Rowman and Littlefield, 1973); J. Feinberg, *Social Philosophy* (New Jersey: Prentice Hall, 1973), p. 96.
6. M. Cranston, *What are Human Rights?* (New York: Basic Books, 1973); A. J. M. Milne, *Human Rights and Human Diversity: An Essay in the Philosophy of Human Rights* (London: Macmillan, 1986).
7. Milne, op. cit.
8. Bedau, op. cit., pp. 291-2.
9. Milne, op. cit., p. 1; J. Nickel, *Making Sense of Human Rights* (Berkeley: University Press, 1987), p. 3.
10. Cranston, op. cit., p. 36.
11. Jack Donnelly, *Universal Human Rights in Theory and Practice* (Ithaca: Cornell University Press, 1989), p. 122.
12. H. *Shue, Basic Rights: Subsistence, Affluence and U.S. Foreign policy* (New Jersey: Princeton University Press, 1980), p. 33.
13. Donnelly, op. cit., p. 26.
14. Ali Alatas, 'Indonesia against dictates on rights and wants better mechanism for rights', speech by the Minister of Foreign Affairs of the Republic of Indonesia

given at the Second World Conference on Human Rights, Vienna, 1993, p. 17.

15. Liu Huaqiu, 'Proposals for human rights protection and promotion', speech in Vienna, 1993, published in *Beijing Review*, 28 June–4 July 1993, p. 9.

16. ibid.

17. ibid., p. 9.

18. Alatas, op. cit., pp. 8–9.

19. Wong Kan Seng, 'The real world of human rights', speech by the Singapore Foreign Minister, Vienna, 1993, p. 4.

20. L. Henkin (ed.), *The International Bill of Rights: The Covenant on Civil and Political Rights* (New York: Columbia University Press, 1993), p. 24.

21. P. Sieghart, *The International Law of Human Rights* (Oxford: Clarendon Press, 1983), p. 94.

22. J. G. Merrils, *The Development of International Law by the European Court of Human Rights* (Manchester: Manchester University Press, 1988), p. 146.

23. ibid., p. 145.

24. ibid., pp. 136–59; Sieghart, op. cit., pp. 85–103; Yash Ghai, 'Derogations and limitations in the Hong Kong Bill of Rights', in Johannes Chan and Yash Ghai (eds), *The Hong Kong Bill of Rights: A Comparative Approach* (Hong Kong: Butterworths Asia, 1993), pp. 161–98.

25. Merrills, op. cit., pp. 207–29.

26. ibid., pp. 216–19, 220–9.

27. A. C. Kiss, 'Permissible limitations on rights', in Henkin (ed.), *The International Bill of Rights*, op. cit., pp. 306–7.

28. Merrills, op. cit., p. 149.

29. Sieghart, op. cit., p. 93, and Merrills, op. cit., p. 129.

30. *Human Rights in China* (Beijing: Foreign Language Press, 1991), Chapter VIII. The author, however, believes that forced abortion is unacceptable.

31. Wong, op. cit., p. 9.

32. Kausikan, op. cit., p. 38.

33. Wong, op. cit., p. 10.

4
HUMAN RIGHTS, ECONOMIC CHANGE AND POLITICAL DEVELOPMENT: A SOUTHEAST ASIAN PERSPECTIVE

MELY CABALLERO-ANTHONY

The issue of human rights, by definition, breeds confrontation. Raising the issue touches on the very foundations of a regime, on its sources and exercise of power, on its links to its citizens or subjects. It is a dangerous issue.[1]

Introduction

The issue of human rights has never been debated with as much vigour in Southeast Asia. The rhetoric and reality of human rights have become a major preoccupation among Southeast Asian states. While the debate on human rights is not new, it is the 'alternative' view to what constitutes human rights that has made this discourse take on a new dimension.

In the international arena, human rights problems have figured prominently amongst the many new issues that have emerged in the post-Cold War era in the Southeast Asian region. For example, member states of the Association of South East Asian Nations (ASEAN), comprising Brunei, Indonesia, Malaysia, Philippines, Singapore and Thailand, have found it necessary to address this issue within the new framework of international relations. Southeast Asian states could not possibly ignore the rhetoric and debate on human rights as they continually work towards becoming active actors in the international stage.

It was not that long ago when one hardly heard anything on human rights from the governments in this region. The tendency then was to dismiss rather than address this issue and the preferred response was to be non-committal. The reverse seems to be the case of late with Southeast Asian states like Myanmar and Vietnam joining the world discourse on human rights and espousing the same approach.[2] The eagerness of the Southeast Asian states to be heard can be read as part and parcel of the new global trends that have emerged as a result of the constantly changing international environment: the end of the Cold War, the collapse of communism in Eastern Europe and demise of the Soviet Union; the slackening growth of the economies in the developed West; the rapid growth and dynamism of newly industrializing economies (NIEs), ASEAN and China. At the same time, the decline and break-up of the Soviet Union and the United States' intervention in the Gulf

War suggest that the international system is becoming unipolar.

Thus at both ends an atmosphere of new found confidence prevails. While we see a confident West, in particular, the United States, espousing human rights in international affairs and promoting it globally, we also have an equally confident Southeast Asia, particularly among ASEAN states, facing up to criticisms of their human rights records, and challenging the United States on its application of human rights policies. These events reflect yet another significant development in the international arena where states in Southeast Asia are now more assertive in putting forward their position(s) in international forums. These also represent efforts by small states to resist what they perceive as attempts by more powerful states to dominate prominent issues in the global agenda.

In Southeast Asia the governments of Indonesia, Malaysia and Singapore have been the most vocal in openly challenging the Western view on human rights. They have frequently called on the West to stop 'lecturing' Asians and instead to listen to what they have to say. They have also called for a better understanding of the unique conditions of their respective states, taking into account the socio-economic realities and the political contexts within which they operate. What these states are actually saying is that collective economic needs must come first and that individual rights as enshrined in the West are to a certain extent 'irrelevant' to their culture or stage of development.[3]

The debate on human rights is often seen as a confrontation between the West and the East. It presupposes that there is in fact this wide gap between the Western concept of human rights and that of Asia. Is there a unique Southeast Asian concept of human rights that is at variance with that of the Western version? This chapter examines the Southeast Asian perspective on human rights with reference to the questions of development and democracy. It is an attempt to determine to what extent this perspective is really different from the West. In analysing the impact of human rights on inter-state relations, this chapter focuses primarily on governmental positions. This in no way suggests that the regional perspective is only confined to official positions. Regional non-governmental groups very often reject government views.

Human rights: a regional perspective

The Western media have sometimes projected the image that Asians in general regard human rights as something alien, a Western concept that is deemed incompatible with Asian traditions, values and cultures. This perception has to be carefully considered as it is not only facile but vacuous. Statements made by Southeast Asian governments and non-governmental organizations (NGOs) do not confirm that human rights are regarded only as a Western concept and thus irrelevant to the people. On the contrary, in spite of all the rhetoric, many Southeast Asian governments and NGOs have affirmed the universality of the rights as enshrined and codified in the Universal Declaration of Human Rights and reflected in the two international covenants: the International Covenant on Civil and Political Rights and the International Covenant on Economic, Social and Cultural Rights. How some

Southeast Asian countries may seem to differ, at least as far as the governments are concerned, is in the approach taken in the implementation of these rights. This position can best be summed up in two ways: situational uniqueness of human rights, and the sequential ordering of rights.

In March 1993 Thailand played host to the UN-sponsored Asia-Pacific Regional Conference on Human Rights in preparation for the United Nations World Conference on Human Rights. The Bangkok Declaration maintained that there can only be one set of fundamental human rights for whatever part of the world, but the *approaches* to its implementation may vary from country to country. This idea could not have been summed up more succinctly than by Thai Prime Minister Chuan Leekpai in his opening address when he said:

Perception of rights does not exist in pure air. It is a result of complex inter-action among several groups in the society . . . therefore, it is natural that approaches to the implementation of fundamental rights vary because of differences in socio-economic, historical, cultural backgrounds and conditions.[4]

The 'situational uniqueness' approach does not offer a different or alternative concept of human rights. The premise in fact maintains that rights as enshrined in the Universal Declaration of Human Rights are universal. These include, among others: the right to life; the rights against torture and slavery; the right to due process of law; the right to basic human needs, i.e. freedom from hunger and poverty; and the right to social dignity and respect. But while governments in the region reaffirm the universality of rights, their reservations on the full implementation of these rights which are contingent upon and predicated on the situational uniqueness of each state have now been taken to mean a difference in concept.

Thus the so-called human rights confrontation between the West and the East, in this case the Southeast Asian states, emerged from the Asian states' insistence that these rights should be implemented according to the stages of a country's development. The official Southeast Asian position is that the situational uniqueness of each state may, to a certain extent, necessitate the sequential ordering of rights. The international community should, therefore, take a more holistic approach in the discussion, implementation and evaluation of human rights practices of other states.

The link between different approaches to human rights and different economic, political and socio-cultural contexts within which societies operate has become the most controversial issue in the human rights debate. In Southeast Asia, the consensus among governments is that the *situational uniqueness* approach provides an alternative framework for discussing and promoting human rights. The ASEAN states have taken the lead in this direction. During the UN World Conference on Human Rights held in Vienna in June 1993 ASEAN states proposed that the world community should consider the question of *situational uniqueness*.[5] This approach has become the key plank of many Southeast Asian states on this controversial issue and has been recommended as one of the guiding principles in the code of conduct for ASEAN member states in international relations. Human rights issues therefore have been included on the foreign policy agenda and have made an important impact on inter-state relations.

One can summarize the position of the major Southeast Asian states on human rights via five principal elements. Firstly, these states argued that there should be comprehensiveness and non-selectivity of rights. Civil–political rights and socio-economic rights are not mutually exclusive as both are equally important, especially for developing states. The Southeast Asian states believed that Western states, like the United States, often confuse rights with Western liberal democracies.

Secondly, the Southeast Asian states considered that individual rights must be balanced with societal/communal rights. In ASEAN, for example, communal rights are seen to be equally important as the rights of the individual who are responsible to the society. ASEAN believe that there need not be a clear-cut contradiction of individual versus communal rights in promoting human rights. However, in achieving this balance within the context of the developing states in the region, it is sometimes inevitable that individual rights are limited for the sake of the community's interest, hence the expediency of sequential ordering of rights.

Thirdly, given the need to balance (a) civil and political rights with socio-economic rights and (b) individual rights with that of the community, within the context of the situational uniqueness of each state, the Southeast Asian states assert that there can be no superior model for human rights, as there can be no superior model for development and democracy.

Fourthly, as human rights call for the exercise of self-determination, human rights and their implementation should not be imposed upon and dictated by the outside but should instead evolve along their own course. It follows that the Southeast Asian states' right to development as another way of implementing human rights should be respected.

Finally, the Southeast Asian states argued that the four points should form the foundation for international relations if human rights were to be included on the foreign policy agenda. Human rights issues should therefore be depoliticized and not linked to development aid and commercial cooperation.

Such arguments, however, have been criticized and even rejected by the West, particularly the United States as nothing more than an excuse for the non-observance of human rights. But in their bid to promote an alternative perspective, many Southeast Asian governments have been aggressively campaigning for a 'pragmatic approach'. They continue to assert that in promoting human rights the situational uniqueness of each state has to be considered and that the sequential ordering of rights can at times become a necessity if human rights are to be meaningfully realized at all. In responding to criticisms about their own human rights records, these states have closed ranks in calling for a review of certain human rights provisions propounded by the West. They have also stressed the need for new forums where the 'playing field is levelled'.[6]

Behind the posturing, however, there is still no consensus even among Southeast states themselves on the issue of sequential ordering of rights. The lack of consensus, though not openly acknowledged clearly reflects the complexity of the human rights issue. More importantly, it brings into focus the problematic relationship between socio-economic rights and political rights on one hand, and the issue of democracy on the other.

Economic development, democracy and human rights

The glittering economic success of East Asian states has been somewhat tarnished by the way some governments have controlled domestic political activities. These governments justify their policies as necessary for a stable political environment and economic development. The political expediency for economic development rationale is one of the major bones of contention in the human rights debate. In Southeast Asia two problems can be identified: (1) Can there be an acceptable definition of what constitutes a stable political environment? (2) How does one decide whether or not political expediency is in fact legitimate?

'Poverty makes a mockery of all civil liberties,' said Singapore Foreign Minister Wong Kan Seng when he elaborated on the Singapore government's position on why political rights have to be considered in tandem with economic rights.[7] To Singapore and perhaps to most, if not all, ASEAN states political rights are deemed meaningless without a decent standard of living. And in many Southeast Asian societies, what is considered the greatest oppression is not necessarily political but economic, or social, or cultural. Many Southeast Asian states claim that economic development is the liberating force that can precipitate crucial changes in their societies.

Economic development is the only force that can liberate the Third World. Probably the most subversive force created in history, it shakes up old social arrangements and enables more people to take part in social and political development.[8]

Unchecked state power, however, may easily lead to totalitarianism, despotic rule and corruption. The economic development imperative very often merely provides justification for the perpetuation of power among a self-selected group and restricts citizens' participation in affairs of the state.

The performance of Southeast Asian governments and their claims have to be weighed against the general opinion of the citizens. But the Southeast Asian experience clearly also has to be seen in the context of problems and internal crises in their national-building process during the last four decades. In examining the record of political and economic developments in Southeast Asia the ASEAN experience is perhaps the most instructive.

Among the ASEAN states, Thailand and Indonesia have been characterized as military-dominated regimes. The evolution of these two regimes has been attributed to a number of factors.[9] Among these were the lack or absence of political institutions and declining economic conditions when mounting insurgency problems and separatist movements were threatening a breakdown of the political–economic system.[10] Since 1935 Thailand has had a number of *coups d'état* and at least sixteen changes to its constitution, but the country has managed to maintain a certain level of political stability. Two of Thailand's institutions—monarchy and a strong bureaucracy—have had a large part to play in maintaining the peace and political stability. Moreover, its military government, though authoritarian, was not repressive. Its judiciary maintained its independence and Thailand's press has been regarded as one of the freest in Asia. But an important element that lent legitimacy to what otherwise would have been an illegitimate political system was Thailand's steady pursuit of economic development.[11]

The continuing efforts of successive Thai governments to achieve economic development objectives have enabled Thailand recently to join the ranks of newly industrializing economies (NIEs). The significance of this economic success was that, after a long history of military authority, Thailand's economic growth resulted in a growing middle class which eventually played a crucial role in breaking the monopoly of military power, as displayed in the May 1992 demonstrations in Bangkok. Buoyed by its political development, Thailand is now working towards a more stable and sustainable democratic system. Compared with Thailand's relatively peaceful transitions, Indonesia has had a far more turbulent political history. After a bitter struggle for independence from the Dutch in 1949, Indonesia was still grappling with a battered economy and regional divisions when it was plunged into yet another mayhem after an abortive *coup* in 1965.[12] While *coup* after *coup* has plagued Thailand, Indonesia since the 1960s has experienced relative political stability. Indonesia has had a unitary basis of government with a 1000-member People's Consultative Assembly, elected every five years, which in turn elects the President of the republic. It is described as a constitutional democracy with a multi-party system dominated by the Golkar party which has a strong military background. President Suharto, who was a former military general, has been Indonesia's president since the failed *coup* in 1965, the longest-ruling president in Southeast Asia.

But considering the immense size and diversity of the nation, Indonesia has come a long way since her independence and the establishment of the New Order in 1965. Observers are amazed at the ability of the leadership to maintain a firm grip of the political system of Southeast Asia's biggest and most populous state. Indonesia has a multi-ethnic population of 179 million, even more than the combined total population of the rest of ASEAN. It is now one of the fastest-growing economies in the region with record GDP growth rates averaging 6–7 per cent in the last five years.[13] The government credits its present political system for providing and maintaining the stability essential for realizing its economic goals.

However, Indonesia has been one of the Southeast states singled out for human rights abuses. Its annexation of East Timor in 1976, the secessionist movements that followed and the unfortunate shooting of civilians by the military in the capital, Dili, in mid-November 1991 have marred the image of the government. Indonesia has also earned the reputation of being intolerant to foreign press. It has expelled Australian journalists for 'unfavourable' reporting and has banned coverage of politically sensitive issues. The Australian media's 'intrusion' in Indonesia's domestic affairs has been an irritant in relations between Jakarta and Canberra. At this juncture it is tempting to ask whether political rights have to be sacrificed for the sake of economic development. But the answer may not be readily available.

In contrast to Thailand and Indonesia, the military has had no major role in the political development of Malaysia and Singapore, except for a very brief period when the military in Malaysia was represented in the National Operations Council in 1969 after the race riots of that year.[14] The governments of

Malaysia and Singapore, however, have been characterized as being 'soft-authoritarians' — politics have been dominated by single parties.[15] These single parties have monopolized political power for the past thirty years.

In Malaysia, the Barisan Nasional (BN) or National Front party has been the ruling party since independence in 1957. The BN is an alliance party made up of three major parties drawn along the three major ethnic groups representing the ethnic composition of the state: the United Malays National Organization (UMNO), the Malaysian Chinese Association and the Malaysian Indian Congress. UMNO, however, holds the most number of seats in the government being the dominant party, and determines political leadership. Singapore, on the other hand, has the People's Action party, which was established in 1959. It has been Singapore's ruling party since its dismemberment from Malaysia in 1965, and to many observers it is the only party. The opposition parties have been almost negligible based on their performance at elections and number of seats held in Parliament.[16]

These two 'soft-authoritarian' states have displayed an intolerance for dissent. Singapore has been criticized for its restrictions on the freedom of expression. Like Indonesia, it has also banned circulation of magazines and periodicals which have published articles perceived by the government as being unfavourable. But what is deemed to be gross 'violations' of human rights is not so much the restrictions on freedom of expression but rather on the government's so-called social engineering policies such as its population policy of 'stop at two' in the early 1980s which was implemented by a number of tax and financial disincentives, only to be reversed in 1987 when the declining birth rate caused great concern; the introduction of incentives to marry within the same social rank, and, quite recently, the government's ban on chewing gum in the republic. The government has staunchly defended its policies, citing the need to develop a disciplined, resourceful and highly motivated population to make up for the country's size and lack of any other resources. Singapore is the smallest state in ASEAN but it also happens to be the most economically developed state in the region.[17]

The Malaysian government for its part has been criticized for using ethnic issues to control political activities. For instance, on 27 October 1987 the Malaysian government under its Internal Security Act arrested leaders of certain interest groups, political parties and church-based organizations, and at the same time suspended the publishing licences of three newspapers on the grounds that the government wanted to avert a possible ethnic tension. Another example which is regarded as a sign of the Malaysian government's intolerance for dissent was the sacking of the Lord President and two Supreme Court judges in 1988 following a High Court ruling in February that UMNO was an illegal party after the opposition party Semangat '46 challenged the results of the UMNO general election. When the case was going to be heard by the Supreme Court, the government removed the Lord President and the two Supreme Court judges because the government feared that the Supreme Court panel headed by the Lord President was not going to rule in its favour.[18]

Whenever political rights have been curtailed, both the Singapore and Malaysian governments have cited national security and stability as justification for their actions. The Internal Security Acts in both countries allow the government the legal power of arbitrary arrest and detention without trial. The Malaysian government has, on many occasions, emphasized the need to maintain racial harmony among its multi-ethnic population. Periodic 'checks' and certain political sacrifices are therefore considered by the government as the necessary evils for the sake of maintaining national unity and stability.

'Soft-authoritarian' states though they may be, Malaysia and Singapore have nevertheless set themselves up as good examples of fast-growing, modernizing regimes. Both states have maintained good public order and favourable business environments. Singapore prides itself on its high standard of living, a well-educated population and an efficient and incorruptible bureaucracy. Malaysia also shares the same successes as Singapore. It has relatively autonomous institutions, particularly the judiciary which has had a significant role in governance. The unfortunate event in 1988, however, has cast a doubt on its independence. With governments that are activist and states that are strong, both Malaysia and Singapore have established impressive social security policies. The quality of life in these two states is the envy of some Southeast Asian neighbours.

In contrast, the Philippine experience has often been used to illustrate further the ASEAN argument that political rights are meaningless in the absence of a healthy socio-economic environment. While one can argue that the Philippine case is also uniquely different given its chequered political history – particularly the martial law regime under Marcos – the political instability, confusion, incoherence and the lack of political control that were prevalent during the Aquino administration and the perceived indecisiveness of the present leadership are viewed by others as a case of a democracy that does not work. The inability of the government to solve the law and order problem in the country is seen as a serious weakness. The Philippines now lags behind her ASEAN neighbours in economic growth and has had to face tough developmental problems.

In analysing the situation in the Philippines after the 1986 People's Power revolution that toppled the dictatorial Marcos regime and finding out what went wrong, one has to be conscious of the other deeply rooted structural problems which have seriously impeded the realization of the country's developmental objectives. It is a very complex process, and the solutions to the problems clearly are not to be found in controlling and/or limiting political rights. After going through a painful and cathartic experience of severe political repression, consideration of a political system that is anything but democratic would be the ultimate tragedy to the Filipinos.

Just as it would be too dangerous to attribute the political, economic and social problems of the Philippines to its recently revived democratic system, it would also be simplistic to accord the success story of some ASEAN states to their political systems and to their approach to political rights. Among ASEAN states, four of them had a record of steady growth and development, with Singapore in the lead followed by Malaysia, Thailand and now Indonesia. The ASEAN experience, however, may not have convincingly demonstrated that the sequential ordering of rights is a necessary condition for development. After all, development is a multi-dimensional process with no hard and fast rule by which to proceed. But having gone along their own paths towards economic and political development, some ASEAN governments are convinced that their approach to rights is correct. Feeling confidently that their own models of political systems do work and, more importantly, that their systems can deliver despite being considered 'undemocratic', some Southeast Asian states are now challenging the Western model of liberal democracy.

If a democratic system is determined by four criteria—free and fair elections, freedom of political organization, freedom of expression, and availability of alternative sources of information[19]—then many Southeast Asian states are not full democracies. But some Southeast Asian governments can arguably claim that subject to certain limitations, their political systems can be said to have satisfied the basic criteria of democracy. And, if the litmus test to legitimacy is popular support determined through periodic elections, elections in Indonesia, Malaysia and Singapore which have returned the same governments to power would tell their own story.

The Western definition of democracy, particularly the American model of democracy, is not only unacceptable to many Southeast Asian governments but it is also regarded as a manifestation of the stronger West imposing its own values on the weaker nations. This is perhaps why nowadays one hears of an alternative model of democracy—Asian democracy—being propagated by states like Malaysia and Singapore. To them, the minimalist definition of democracy by the West, i.e. multi-party elections and freedom of expression, overlooks the very fundamental goal of democracy which is good governance.

In this same vein, the different approach to the implementation of human rights within the region is not considered as incorrect as is otherwise opined by the West. Some Southeast Asian governments are quick to correct details of certain reports of violations of human rights within their countries and to point out certain human rights violations in the West. They are challenging the West to accept the existence of diversity between their respective communities and the right of states to determine their own systems that are suitable to particular circumstances. Over time, suggested one Singapore official, 'a Darwinian process will establish itself . . . [and] the virtues of these systems speak for themselves'.[20]

National sovereignty and international intervention

Southeast Asian states have strongly resisted attempts at intervention by the West over the human rights issue. Intervention, the crux of the human rights debate between Southeast Asian states and the West, centres on the following questions: can and should the international community intervene? when to intervene? and how?

For many Southeast Asian states no state can dictate and make judgements on others about human rights. Accordingly, Southeast Asian governments have often asserted that foreign policies should not be linked to human rights. Southeast Asian states have criticized the West, particularly the United States, for its inconsistencies and double-standards in human rights policies. At the Vienna Conference on Human Rights, Indonesian Foreign Minister Ali Alatas declared:

Any approach to human rights which is not motivated by a desire to protect these rights, but by disguised political purposes or worse, to serve as a pretext to wage a political campaign against another country, cannot be justified . . . Indonesia, therefore, cannot accept linking questions of human rights to economic and development cooperation, by attaching human rights implementation as political conditions to such cooperation. Such a linkage will only detract from the value of both.[21]

Statements like this reflect the pervasive attitude in the region and are likely to drive a wedge in the relations between the West and Southeast Asia.

Governments in the region have argued that Western attitudes towards human rights problems are nothing more than functions of the self-interests of the states concerned and have little to do with the promotion and protection of human rights. Their position is that, instead of supporting the development of the region which will consequently lead to the realization of full democracy, the West has been 'sabotaging' the economic success of East Asia.[22] Specifically, they have attacked the US policy of linking development aid with human rights. This policy of aid conditionalities, imposing economic sanctions and using diplomatic *démarches* are perceived by the region as examples of power politics: the stronger West attempting to dominate and bully the weaker and less developed East.

The inaction of the United States and the European Union to the tragic events in the former Yugoslavia — the so-called 'ethnic cleansing' being carried out by the Serbs and Croats against the Muslims in Bosnia, and the US silence over events in Algeria, as contrasted to the American tirade against Iraq — are regarded by some Southeast Asian states as examples of Western double standards. Suspension of trading privileges and economic aid such as the US announcement to link the granting of most-favoured-nation trading preference to China's human rights records, the threat to suspend preferential tariff treatment under the US generalized system of preferences unless Malaysia and Indonesia stop violating workers' rights, the suspension of aid to Indonesia by the Netherlands after the November 1991 incident in East Timor have been seen as protectionism under the guise of human rights advocacy.

This line of reasoning again gives rise to a number of complex debates that only adds to the difficulty in reaching consensus on the question of international intervention. The most obvious questions are: What happens in cases of heinous crimes being committed by the state on its populations such as shooting down innocent demonstrators, arbitrary arrests and torture, abuse of women and children, slavery, and so on? Should the world community step back and merely watch while these are going on?

While shying away from criticisms of their own human rights records and stridently attacking the West, Southeast Asian states have not actually ruled out intervention. They had, for example, joined the earlier demand for sanctions against South Africa and, of late, urged the West to do more to stop the ethnic cleansing in former Yugoslavia. But these more vocal calls for direct intervention are more of an exception than the norm. There is an unwritten understanding within the states in the region not to interfere in each other's domestic affairs. ASEAN's efforts over the last thirty years towards building trust and confidence with each other is too good a capital to risk.

The history of intra-mural conflict and tension within the states in Southeast Asia which surfaced after the end of the Second World War suggested to them that the best guarantee to regional peace and stability was mutual understanding and respect. Thus in the mid-1970s, when ASEAN states were working towards the strengthening of the group as a regional organization, no attempts were made to isolate the communist states like Vietnam, Laos and Cambodia. In fact the ASEAN states' vision of reaching a *modus vivendi* with their communist neighbours was only altered when Vietnam occupied Cambodia in 1978. For more than a decade ASEAN worked towards the settlement of the Cambodian conflict, but cautious efforts have been made to exclude domestic issues, such as human rights, from their regional agendas.

When events in the Philippines during the Marcos regime turned for the worst after the assassination of Ninoy Aquino and when there was increasing momentum to topple the administration, ASEAN governments refrained from doing or saying anything. It was only in 1987, a year after Corazon Aquino took power, when the government's survival was seriously threatened by a series of *coup* attempts and when the ASEAN summit was scheduled to be held in Manila, that the ASEAN heads of state decided to go and attend the summit as an expression of support for the Aquino administration. But during the 1988 events in Myanmar when the military junta refused to recognize the results of the national election, shot and detained student demonstrators, and put Aung San Suu Kyi under house arrest, ASEAN governments did no more than express concern in carefully worded statements. The same response was true during the 1991 shooting of demonstrators in Dili, East Timor and at the height of the May 1992 demonstrations in Bangkok.

But this preference for non-intervention may be slowly changing. ASEAN states, for example, were for a time divided over the repressive regime in Myanmar. Singapore had earlier advocated for a 'pro-active' approach, otherwise known as constructive engagement, but Malaysia had insisted that Yangoon should change its political and economic system to ease the suffering of its people. Eventually the ASEAN states agreed to ask Thailand to take the lead in pressing the military junta in Yangoon to institute democratic reforms.

There are also indications of a *perestroika* in some states on human rights questions. Conscious of the criticisms about its human rights record and perhaps in an effort to boost its image, Indonesia has announced the setting up of a national human rights commission.[23] This announcement was made during the human rights workshop held in Jakarta in January 1992, two months after the Dili incident. This commission would be the second national commission to be set up in the region, the first being in the Philippines. In 1993 Malaysia also joined the United Nations Commission on Human Rights for the first time and announced its intention to play a pro-active role on major issues pertaining to human rights.[24] At the regional level, the association of ASEAN think-tank bodies known as the ASEAN Institute of Strategic Studies (ASEAN-ISIS) has also announced proposals to set up a regional human rights body to promote and protect human rights in the six member countries. While the proposal is still being worked out, it is thought that the regional body would act as a centre for information-sharing and dissemination and, if necessary, would serve as a fact-finding body to determine cases of human rights violations.[25]

This new thinking within ASEAN represents a shift to the usually defensive posture of the governments, indicating that they are willing to meet the West half-way on human rights. The first indication of this new thinking was reflected in the observations made by the former Prime Minister of Singapore, Lee Kuan Yew, during his recent visit to China when he was reported to have said:

while countries could legitimately differ on the right balance between freedom and order in their societies . . . people all over the world have the right to be treated in a humane way by their own governments—that cruelty and brutality are not acceptable.[26]

The practical consequence of human rights abuse was also acknowledged by another Singaporean official who put it this way: 'Any society that is at odds with its best and brightest and shoots them down when they demonstrate peacefully, as happened in Burma in 1988, is headed for trouble.'[27]

But while these positive developments are taking place, going by the statements of government officials and the initiatives undertaken by respective governments on human rights, one thing has remained consistent: Southeast Asian states continue to reject linking human rights to the promotion of liberal democracy, as well as trade and aid matters.

Conclusions

Southeast Asian states do not have an alternative concept of human rights. What they have is a different approach to the implementation of rights. These states, particularly ASEAN members, have henceforth called on the West to recognize that diversity does exist, and to be more understanding of Southeast Asia's values and socio-economic needs before attempting to prescribe a better way to observe human rights. In doing so, they placed greater emphasis on the necessity to balance political rights against economic rights, and the need for the international community to come up with a more balanced approach to human rights.

However, while different priorities and approaches in different societies at different stages of development exist, these should not be used as an excuse for ignoring political rights. There is always the danger of misrepresenting the priorities in a state and disregarding popular opinion. Thus, in addressing these issues, those advocating a different approach to human rights have to recognize the rightful role of the people. In keeping with the confidence brought about by progress in their respective economies, Southeast Asian states must be cognizant of the changing needs of their own people to allow for more meaningful participation and discussion by people at all levels. In the establishment of national mechanisms for the promotion and protection of human rights, Southeast Asian states should provide guarantees of independence and accessibility. Furthermore, the development of non-governmental organizations (NGOs) in their own states must be allowed. The governments must themselves recognize that the NGOs' role in the respective states is equally germane to the development of human rights.

If the Southeast Asian states affirm the universal importance of human rights, they must also open themselves up to the scrutiny of the international community. At the same time while Western initiatives to include human rights in the international agenda have raised international concern over human rights questions, a better appreciation of the diversities which exist in Southeast Asia is also important. Neat generalities about human rights sometimes can cause problems. The use of sanctions in cases of gross human rights violations, for example, may not necessarily produce the desired effects, and should therefore be examined more closely and considered more carefully. As a measure of last-resort sanction, conditions should be made clear and the application of the criteria must be uniformly applied and not arbitrarily determined.

In conclusion, what may seem as a divisive issue in relations between states, the so-called confrontation between the Southeast Asian states and the West on the subject of human rights should, in fact, be seen as a positive development in international relations when such important issues as human rights are increasingly discussed in a multilateral international forum. The fast-changing global environment no longer makes it possible for states to exist in isolation. With the advances in information technology the world is shrinking and economies are becoming borderless with international trade. Human rights concerns can no longer be suppressed in the name of economic development. All states, regardless of their stages of development, must improve their human rights records. They need to be reminded that what may seem to be momentarily tolerable will not be excused for ever.

Notes

1. Stanley Hoffman, 'The hell of good intentions', *Foreign Policy*, no. 29 (1977–78), p. 8.
2. At the Asia-Pacific Regional Conference on Human Rights held in Bangkok in March 1993, the Burmese representative bluntly told the West not to dictate its own norms and standards of human rights to Asian countries, while the Vietnamese representative denounced the linking of economic aid with human rights. See *Far Eastern Economic Review*, 15 April 1993, and the *Straits Times*, 2 April 1993.
3. Indonesia has earlier argued that states have the right to set their priorities. See the *Straits Times*, 15 June 1993.
4. *Straits Times*, 30 March 1993.
5. *Far Eastern Economic Review*, 17 June 1993. See also *Jakarta Post*, 16 and 17 June 1993, and the *Straits Times*, 17 June 1993.

6. During the First ASEAN Congress in Kuala Lumpur in October 1992, a Singaporean official expressed what he perceived as an imbalance in the relationship between the West and ASEAN: that the West is vastly more powerful so ASEAN must address this global imbalance by speaking more strongly (so as to make the playing-field levelled). *Far Eastern Economic Review*, 20 October 1992.
7. Speech by Singapore Foreign Minister Wong Kan Seng at the UN World Conference on Human Rights, Vienna. See the *Straits Times*, 17 June 1993.
8. In Kishore Mahbubani's speech at the Asian and American Perspective on Capitalism and Democracy, excerpts printed in the *Star* (Malaysia), 5 April 1993. He is Singapore's Deputy Secretary in the Foreign Ministry.
9. See, for example, Harold Crouch, ' The military and politics in Southeast Asia', and Ulf Sundhaussen, 'The durability of military regimes in South-east Asia', in Zakaria Hj. Ahmad and Harold Crouch (eds), *Military–Civilian Relations in South-East Asia* (Singapore: Oxford University Press, 1985).
10. Chai-anan Samudavanija, 'Thailand: A stable democracy', in Larry Diamond, Juan Linz, Seymour Martin-Lipset (eds), *Democracy in Developing Countries: Asia*, Vol. 3 (Boulder, Colo.: Lynne Rienner Publishers, 1989), pp. 304–46.
11. ibid..
12. There are several works that give comprehensive accounts of Indonesia's New Order. See for example, Harold Crouch, *The Army and Politics in Indonesia* (New York: Cornell University Press, 1978); Leo Suryadinata, *Military Ascendancy and Political Culture: A Study of Indonesia's Golkar* (Ohio: Ohio University Press, 1989).
13. See *Regional Outlook: Southeast Asia, 1993–1994* (Singapore: Institute of Southeast Asian Studies, 1993).
14. Chandra Muzaffar, 'Ethnicity and Ethnic Conflict in Malaysia', in Claude E. Welch, Jr. and Virginia A. Leary (eds), *Asian Perspective on Human Rights* (Boulder, Colo.: Westview Press, 1990), pp. 107–41.
15. Robert Scalapino calls some governments in Asia as 'authoritarian-pluralist' and categorizes them as 'hard-authoritarian' and 'soft-authoritarian'. See Chan Heng Ghee's article on 'Democracy, human rights and social justice', printed in the Sunday edition of the *Straits Times*, 22 November 1992.
16. For general reference on the political systems of Malaysia and Singapore, see Zakaria Hj. Ahmad (ed.), *Government and Politics of Malaysia* (Singapore: Oxford University Press, 1987) and Jon S. T. Quah, (ed.), *Government and Politics of Singapore* (Singapore: Oxford University Press, 1987). See also Chan Heng Chee, *The Dynamics of One Party Dominance: The PAP at the Grass-roots* (Singapore: Singapore University Press, 1976).
17. See *Regional Outlook: Southeast Asia 1993–1994*, op. cit.
18. Chandra Muzaffar, op. cit., p. 117. For a more detailed account, see *Aliran Monthly* (Malaysia), vol. 8, no. 4 and vol 8, no. 6 (1988) as cited in Muzaffar, op. cit.
19. Robert A. Dahl, 'Democracy and human rights under different conditions of development', in Asbjorn Eide and Bernt Hagtvet (eds), *Human Rights in Perspective: A Global Assessment* (Oxford: Basil Blackwell Ltd., 1992), pp. 23–51.
20. In Kishore Mahbubani's speech, see note 8.
21. See full text of Ali Alatas' speech at the UN World Conference on Human Rights, *Jakarta Post*, 18 June 1993.
22. Malaysia's Prime Minister Datuk Seri Dr Mahathir Mohamed was reported to have made this point on several occasions. He cited the economic chaos in the former communist states in Eastern Europe wherein these states have been forced to beg for aid as a case in which the 'West' uses human-rights policy as a tool of dependency. See *Far Eastern Economic Review*, 17 June 1993.

23. *Straits Times*, 13 December 1992.
24. *Star* (Malaysia), 29 January 1993.
25. *Straits Times*, 13 May 1993.
26. See Mike Yeong's 'ASEAN meets West half-way on human rights', in the *Straits Times*, 26 October 1992, p. 24.
27. In Kishore Mahbubani's speech, see note 8.

5
ASIAN PERSPECTIVES ON HUMAN RIGHTS

YASH GHAI

Introduction

In the contemporary debates on human rights, it is generally assumed that there is one Asian view of human rights, and that it is opposed to the traditions of individual human rights that first developed in the West. It is easy to believe that there is a distinct Asian approach to human rights, because some government leaders speak as if they represent the whole continent when they make their pronouncements on human rights. This view is reinforced because they claim that their views are based on perspectives which emerge from the Asian culture or Asian realities. The gist of their position is that human rights as propounded in the West are founded on individualism and therefore have no relevance to Asia which is based on the primacy of the community. It is also sometimes argued that economic underdevelopment renders most of the political and civil rights (emphasized in the West) irrelevant in Asia. Indeed, it is sometimes alleged that such rights are dangerous in view of fragmented nationalism and fragile statehood.

It would be surprising if there were indeed one Asian perspective, since neither Asian culture nor Asian realities are homogeneous throughout the continent. All the world's major religions are represented in Asia, and are in one place or another state religions (or enjoy a comparable status: Christianity in the Philippines, Islam in Malaysia, Hinduism in Nepal, and Buddhism in Sri Lanka and Thailand). To this list we may add political ideologies like socialism, democracy or feudalism which animate peoples and governments of the region. Even apart from religious differences, there are other factors which have produced a rich diversity of cultures. A culture, moreover, is not static and many accounts given of Asian culture are probably true of an age long ago. Nor are the economic circumstances of all the Asian countries similar. Japan, Singapore and Hong Kong are among the world's most prosperous countries, while there is grinding poverty in Bangladesh, India and the Philippines.

The economic and political systems in Asia show a remarkable diversity, ranging from semi-feudal kingdoms in Kuwait and Saudi Arabia, through military dictatorships in Burma and Cambodia, effectively one-party regimes in Singapore and Indonesia, communist regimes in China and Vietnam, ambiguous democracies in Malaysia and Sri Lanka, to well-established democracies like India. There are similarly differences in their economic systems, ranging from tribal subsistence economies in parts af Indonesia through highly developed market economies of Singapore, Hong Kong and Taiwan and the mixed economy model of India, to the planned economies of China and Vietnam. Perceptions of human rights are undoubtedly reflective of these conditions, and suggest that they would vary from country to country.

Perceptions of human rights are also reflective of social and class positions in society. What conveys an apparent picture of a uniform Asian perspective on human rights is that it is the perspective of a particular group, that of the ruling élites, which gets international attention. What unites these élites is their notion of governance and the expediency of their rule. For the most part the political systems they represent are not open or democratic, and their publicly expressed views on human rights are an emanation of these systems, of the need to justify authoritarianism and repression. It is their views which are given wide publicity domestically and internationally.

There are other Asian voices as well. There are, admittedly somewhat muted or censored, the voices of the oppressed and the marginalized. There are the passionate voices of indigenous peoples whose cultures are destroyed by governments which claim to be the custodians of Asian cultures; they speak in a language which finds few resonances even in the West (because their language is threatening to the system of the market). There is the voice, rising in density, of the middle classes, with a stake in affluence whose new-found prosperity and economic enterprise show to them the virtues of the legal protection of property and the rule of law. There are the strident voices of ethnic minorities who seek collective autonomies which challenge governments' claims of political monopoly and state sovereignty. There are the well-modulated voices of the non-governmental organizations, which provide the most consistent and coherent alternative view of human rights to that of governments.

The unity of governments is more apparent than real. Although the Bangkok Declaration[1] was endorsed by all the Asian governments at the April 1993 Asian regional preparatory meeting for the Vienna World Conference on Human Rights, some of them have a firm commitment to human rights and their record is better than one might expect from their endorsement of the Declaration. India is one example. Along with some other states, it is committed to human rights by its constitutional instruments, has a strong and independent judiciary, and despite problems and setbacks tries hard to maintain human rights. Nor is their adherence to traditional values and rules absolute; the Indian Constitution prohibits many traditional and religious practices like the discriminatory and degrading treatment of lower castes and provides for an equal treatment of women with men.[2]

The reason for presenting a united front is not unconnected with a perceived North–South confrontation (as is evident from the Bangkok Governmental Declaration, which stressed the need to avoid the application of 'double standards' in the implementation of human rights and its 'politicization').[3] Asian governments feel that since the end of the Cold War, the West has focused its attention on what it perceives to be the 'undemocratic' nature of Third World polities. In Africa and Latin America the concern with human rights is seen to be an instrument for the establishment or strengthening of the market, in an attempt to restrict the interventions of the state in economic relations. In Asia, however, the key economies are heavily market-oriented, and for the most part are successful. Even China is now turning to the market, which is widely credited for its economic success. So the emphasis on human rights is not necessary as a spur to the market (and indeed, as I explore later, the relationship between the market and human rights is problematic).

Some Asian governments consider that Western pressure on them for an improvement in human rights is connected with the project of Western global hegemony. This is to be achieved partly through the universalization of Western values and aspirations, and partly through the disorientation of Asian state and political systems (and the consequent negative effect on their burgeoning economies). They have fashioned their response accordingly. There is some danger in this internationalization of the Asian debate on human rights. It shifts the focus away from the practices of Asian governments and the restrictions on human rights. It enables the governments to attack as Western stooges indigenous supporters of human rights. It leads to spurious stereotypes, of 'orientalism' and 'occidentalism', with either defensive Eastern counterparts of Western universalism or aggressive retreat into an imagined past or culture. It politicizes the question of human rights in an unproductive way.

The 'official' Asian view of human rights

The 'official' stance on human rights of a number of influential Asian countries (Singapore, China, Malaysia, Indonesia) has developed primarily in response to two contingencies: the imperatives of control and confrontation with Western pretensions. They are therefore formulated somewhat defensively. It also means, because they are an engagement and a debate with the West, that they are formulated in universalistic terms, in the usual discourse of human rights. Several ingredients constitute such official views. One which flows directly from both the contingencies is the assertion of 'domestic jurisdiction' over human rights. Human rights are encapsulated within state sovereignty; the national treatment of human rights is no concern of other states or the international community. Self-determination, a concept which has been used to advance claims of human rights, is regarded as irrelevant to independent states. This position runs contrary to the contemporary view that human rights are a matter of international concern and that their gross violations entitle the international community to intervene in domestic situations to redress violations.

In its white paper *Human Rights in China* (1991), the Chinese government stated that 'Despite its international aspect, the issue of human rights falls by and large within the sovereignty of each state'.[4] The Chinese delegation to the UN Commission on Human Rights at its meeting in February 1993 urged that the World Conference in Vienna should 'reiterate the principle of state sovereignty contained in the UN Charter and international law which is basis for the realisation of human rights. Only when the state sovereignty is fully respected can the implementation of human rights be really ensured'.[5] This is also pre-eminently the position of the other countries mentioned above.

Another element in the official view is the relativity of rights, determined by the economic and political circumstances of each country. The Bangkok Governmental Declaration

recognises that while human rights are universal in nature, they must be considered in the context of a dynamic and evolving process of international norm-setting, bearing in mind the significance of national and regional peculiarities and various historical, cultural and religious backgrounds.[6]

This stance reflects the position in the Chinese white paper which states:

the evolution of the situation in regard to human rights is circumscribed by the historical, social, economic and cultural conditions of various nations, and involves a process of historical development. Owing to tremendous differences in historical background, social system, cultural tradition and economic development, countries differ in their understanding and practice of human rights.[7]

The Chinese use this framework to establish the priority of social and economic rights in their country, and much of the white paper is taken with an account of the ending of pre-communist regime practices of feudalism and other forms of human exploitation and the steady progress since in nutrition, education, health, the position of women and the disabled. Other countries too have used the state of national economic development as explanations for the failure fully to guarantee the complete range of human rights ('to eat their fill and dress warmly were the fundamental demands of the Chinese people who had long suffered cold and hunger').[8]

There are two major implications of this relativist position on human rights. The first relates to conditionalities of political stability, and the other to the primacy of economic development. The implications of the first represent restrictions on civil and political rights. A forthright statement of this position is to be found in pronouncements of the Singapore government following the detention of various social workers and activists in May 1987. The Minister for Home Affairs, for example, in reply to US Congressmen who had written to complain about the detentions, compared the 'resilience and cohesiveness' and shared values of the nation of the United States (which presumably makes possible the tolerance of human rights) to the fragility and heterogeneity of Singapore. He suggests:

We are vulnerable to powerful centrifugal forces and volatile emotional tides. Like many other developing countries, Singapore's major problem of nationhood is simply to stay united as one viable nation . . . In our short history, Singapore has repeatedly encountered subversive threats from within and without . . . To combat these threats to the nation, the usual procedures of court trials, which apply in Singapore to most criminal cases, have proved totally inadequate. The very secrecy of covert operations precludes garnering evidence to meet the standards of the criminal law for conviction. In many cases of racial agitation, the process of trial itself will provide further opportunity for inflammatory rabble rousing . . . Singapore cannot be ruled in any other way . . . Preventive detention is not a blemish marring our record; it is a necessary power underpinning our freedom.[9]

Another aspect of Singapore bypassing the formal legal system, with its guarantees of openness and fairness, not discussed in the minister's reply, is the tapped and doctored 'confessions' extracted from the detainees under some coercion, and then shown on national television as proof of guilt and calculated to destroy their credibility and dignity.

These remarks were directed at a justification of administrative powers of detention without any kind of trial, but similar arguments have been used to justify other curtailments of civil rights, like the right to associate and assemble, to peaceful marches, to speech and expression. The Chinese white paper says that the people's right to subsistence will be threatened in the event of social turmoil or other disasters, and that it is the fundamental wish and demand of the Chinese people and a long-term, urgent task of the Chinese government to maintain national stability and concentrate their efforts on developing productive forces.[10]

The economic backwardness of Asia has been used to establish the primacy of economic development over human rights. The argument is, in part, that civil and political rights are neither meaningful nor feasible in conditions of want or poverty. Therefore the first priority of state policy must be to promote economic development. It is implied that economic development may well require restrictions on human rights, both to provide a secure political framework in which it can be pursued and to remove obstacles in its way (e.g. through forced movement of people from lands required for 'development'). The opposition of human rights and development is assumed rather than proved by argument and illustration. It is also used to establish the priority as between different kinds of rights, in which civil and political rights occupy a lowly position (in part a response to an argument that human rights are indivisible, and all of them enjoy an equal status).

The emphasis these governments purportedly place on economic development has led them to support the right to development. This right is a matter of considerable contention internationally, with developing countries arraigned on the side supporting it, and most developed countries united in their opposition to it. It certainly does not have the quality of other kinds of rights which are intrinsic to individuals or groups and for the most part are entitlements against the state. Nevertheless the General Assembly of the United Nations adopted, in the face of abstentions by most Western states, a Declaration on the Right to Development on 4 December 1986.[11]

The Declaration ties the realization of human rights in the developing countries to international economic aid for them and gives to 'peoples' (presumably meaning 'states') the right to 'participate in, contribute to, and enjoy economic, social, cultural and political development, in which all human rights and fundamental freedoms can be fully realised'. In return for these, several concessions are made in emphasizing the indivisibility of rights and the claims of individuals to full participation in development and in the fair distribution of the benefits resulting from it.

The Declaration is a blurry document, trying to be all things to all persons. So while there are sections of it which can be used to advance the (more traditional) cause of human rights, the gist of it seeks to establish reason for the failure of the realization of human rights in the international economic and political systems (including encroachments on the principle and practice of self-determination), while affirming that the primary responsibility for human rights are vested in states as part of their sovereignty. In other words, the rich countries must provide economic assistance to the poor countries, but must not question their human rights situation. (The Western riposte to the Declaration has been a massive imposition of political conditionalities on economic assistance and indeed, in the case of China, on economic relations and cooperation). The Declaration is also an attempt to provide an alternative framework for the international discourse on human rights. It shifts the focus from domestic arenas (where most violations of human rights take place) to the international, and takes attention away from specific rights, for example speech, assembly, social welfare, to an ambiguous portmanteau right of development, for which, in the nature of Third World affairs, the state must take the responsibility in defining and implementing it. Through the Declaration, Asian governments seek to promote the ideology of developmentalism, which justifies repression at home and the evasion of responsibility abroad.

Another Asian initiative in changing the framework for the discourse on human rights is even more fundamental. The approaches discussed so far have taken the Western discourse as the main framework and have advanced qualifications to it or provided justifications for derogation from its values. Some governments have put forward the argument that the cultural matrix within which relations between individuals and the state are embedded are fundamentally different in Asia from that in the West. This matrix governs the nature and salience of human rights. This approach has been taken up aggressively in Singapore and Malaysia (less so in China, where the government's residual loyalty to Marxist thought is inconsistent with the adoption of this cultural approach, especially since so much of it is based on semi-feudal thought in Asia). I take as the basis of my discussion of this point an official statement of the government of Singapore, *Shared Values* (1991).[12]

The context of the white paper on *Shared Values* is a concern of the government that the cultural values of its people are under attack from foreign ideas and values. It poses the rhetorical question, 'Can we build a nation of Singaporeans, in Southeast Asia, on the basis of values and concepts native to other peoples, living in other environments?' It goes on: 'If we are not to lose our bearings, we should preserve the cultural heritage of each of our communities, and uphold certain common values which capture the essence of being a Singaporean.'[13] It then finds certain perceptions and values which are common to the different ethnic communities of Singapore and which also distinguish them from societies in the West.

The key section of the white paper is devoted to a discussion of the relationship between the individual and society. Disputing the proposition that values are universal and common to all mankind, it states that there is a major difference between Asian and Western values in the balance each strikes between the individual and the community; Asian societies emphasize the interests of the community, while Western societies stress the rights of the individual. The Singapore society has always weighted group interests more heavily than individual ones. 'This balance has strengthened social cohesion, and enabled Singaporeans to pull together to surmount difficult challenges collectively, more successfully than other societies. An emphasis on the community has been a key survival value for Singapore.'[14]

The core values of the Asian society are identified as placing society above self, upholding the family as the building block of society, and resolving major issues through consensus instead of contention. There is a strong element of Confucianism in this elaboration, although the government denies that the values it propagates are purely Confucian. It does, however, pick up an element of Confucian teaching as particularly relevant to Singapore.

The concept of government by honourable men (junzi), who have a duty to do right for the people, and who have the trust and respect of the population, fits us better than the Western idea that a government should be given as limited powers as possible, and should always be treated with suspicion unless proven otherwise.[15]

The supremacy of political authorities is emphasized by the first of the Shared Values, 'Nation before Community'.

Another aspect of Asian values, implicit though not explicit in the white paper, is the importance of duty as a counterpoint to right. The cohesion of society as well as the fulfilment of the individual is secured through a chain and hierarchy of duties. (The primacy of the notion of duty is emphasized elaborately both in the Chinese and Indian constitutions).[16] The individual does not disappear altogether as a bearer of rights in the Singapore white paper. However, characteristically the concern with the individual is expressed more in terms of the obligations of the community to look after its less advantaged members. (In Singapore there is a twist to this, in that the 'community' in question is the ethnic community of the individual, not the state, 'to avoid the dependent mentality and severe social problems of a welfare state as experienced in many developed states',[17] laying the foundations of a kind of community corporatism in the wake of declining popularity of the ruling party, showing how much these questions are viewed in that country from the perspectives of governance and management.)

Cultural 'embeddedness' is not the only justification for this view of the relationship between the individual and the community and the interposition of the family. It is also said to be rooted in more pragmatic considerations. The white paper hints at this, but it has been developed elsewhere. In Southeast Asia at least, there is a strongly held view that an authoritarian political system is the secret of its economic success, and the frequent Singaporean mocking of the democratic efforts of the Philippines (with a rather inefficient economy) is advanced as proof of it. But there is also the belief that it is not the individual but the family (tied in to a network of clan associations and relationships) which has been at the forefront of the phenomenal economic success of the region. It appears to be the view of a significant number of people (primarily but not only among the business community as is certainly evident in the debates in Hong Kong) that this combination of authoritarian rule and family and kinship networks lies at the root of economic success.[18] This model (which reverses the normal understanding of the relationship between the market, individualism and the rule of law) is seen to be threatened by democracy and human rights. Hence democracy and human rights are not high on many people's agenda.

A critique of the official perspectives

In this section I offer a brief critique of some aspects of the official perspectives outlined above (although these views are not entirely devoid of merit). The 'communitarian' argument suffers from at least two weaknesses. First, it overstates the 'individualism' of Western societies and traditions of thought. Even within Western liberalism there are strands of analysis which assert claims of the community (e.g. Rousseau); and most Western human rights instruments allow limitations on and derogations from human rights in the public interest, or for reasons of state. Western courts regularly engage in the task of balancing the respective interests of the individual and the community.[19] Furthermore, liberalism does not exhaust Western political thought or practice. There is social democracy, which emphasizes collective and economic rights, and Marxism, which elevates the community to a high moral order and is also reflective of an important school of Western thought. Even within liberal societies there are nuances in the approach to and the primacy of human rights, as becomes evident when one examines the differences among the United States, Canada, France and the United Kingdom. There is much celebration in Western political thought of 'civil society'.[20]

Secondly, Asian governments (notwithstanding the attempt in the Singapore white paper to distinguish the 'nation' and the community) fall into the easy but wrong assumption that they or the state are the 'community'. (A similar conflation occurs in the African Charter of Human and Peoples' Rights.)[21] Nothing can be more destructive to the community than this conflation. The community and state are different institutions, and to some extent in a contrary juxtaposition. The community, for the most part, depends on popular norms developed through forms of consensus and which are enforced through mediation and persuasion. The state is an imposition on society, and unless humanized and democratized (as it has not been in most of Asia), it relies on edicts, the military, coercion and sanctions. It is the tension between them which has underpinned human rights.

In the name of the community, most Asian governments have stifled social and political initiatives of private groups. Most of them have draconian legislation, like the British colonially inspired Societies Act[22] which gives the government pervasive control over civil society. Similarly rights to assemble and march peacefully have been mortgaged to the government. Governments have destroyed many communities in the name of development or state stability, and the consistent refusal of most of them to recognize that there are indigenous peoples among their population (who have a right to preserve their traditional culture, economy and beliefs) is but a demonstration of their lack of commitment to the real community. The vitality of the community comes from the exercise of the rights to organize, meet, debate and protest, dismissed as 'liberal' rights by these governments.

It is ironic that the 'community' is much more lively and significant in the supposedly individualistically orientated Western states than in Asian states which are in the custody of governments which pay lip-service to the primacy of the community (even to the extent, as in Singapore, of defining values for the community!). Nor is the tight regulation of society as in Singapore and Malaysia particularly Confucian. Confucius argued against reliance on law or coercion, and advocated a government of limited powers and functions.

Another attack on the community comes from the economic policies of the governments, and for the most part these are market policies. Although Asian capitalism appears to rely on the family and clan associations, there is little doubt that it weakens the community and its cohesion. The organizing matrix of the market is not the same as that of the community. Nor are its values or methods particularly 'communitarian'. The moving frontier of the market, seeking new resources, has been particularly disruptive of communities which have managed to preserve intact a great deal of their culture and organization during the colonial and post-colonial periods. The emphasis on the market together with individual rights of property is also at odds with communal organization and enjoyment of property (and a further irony is that Asian leaders who allege their allegiance to communal supremacy and values are among the most ardent opponents of a Marxism that espouses the moral worth and authority of the community).

Market policies have relied greatly on multinational capital and corporations, which have brought new values and tastes, and are increasingly integrating their economies and élites into a global economy and culture. Indeed it is these very considerations which prompted the Singapore white paper, but the contradictions of official policies largely escaped its authors. It totally ignored the impact, indeed the onslaught, of modern technologies on traditional communities.

A final point is the contradiction between claims of a consensus and harmonious society and the extensive arming of the status apparatus. The pervasive use of draconian legislation like administrative detentions, disestablishment of societies, press censorship, sedition, etc. belies claims to respect alternative views, promote a dialogue, and seek consensus. The contemporary state intolerance of opposition is inconsistent with traditional communal values and processes. I fear that the contemporary state processes in Asia are worse than the much-derided adversarial processes of the West, which at least ensure that all parties get a fair hearing.

Non-official voices

Non-official voices are many. For reasons of space, this section concentrates on the views of the non-government organizations (NGOs). But there are other voices that must be taken into account. The views on human rights of the most oppressed are not articulated, or, when articulated, are not heard. They are the worst victims of the denial of human rights, and in desperation they turn to violence or other dramatic challenges to authority. An important and articulate group are intellectuals who are alienated from the state, and for the most part are not apologists for the regime. Intellectuals respond to and engage in international debates, and like the NGOs they form networks with their counterparts in other parts of the world. Like the NGOs they have a commitment to human rights and democracy (even in China there is a growing and vibrant academic community with a keen interest in human rights and constitutionalism). They are less ready to accept Western conceptions in totality, and attempt to relate questions of human rights to specific national conditions.

An authoritative statement of the position of Asian NGOs was issued on 27 March 1993 on the occasion of the Asian intergovernmental conference on human rights preceding the Vienna World Conference.[23] It endorsed its commitment to the view that human rights are universal, and are equally rooted in different cultures. While it supported cultural pluralism, it condemned those cultural practices which derogate from universally accepted human rights. Since in its view human rights are of universal concern and universal value, it does not regard the advocacy of human rights as an encroachment upon national sovereignty. Indeed it recommends international cooperation and solidarity for the promotion of human rights as a refutation of claims of national sovereignty over human rights issues. The NGOs' signatories of the statement support the principle of the indivisibility and interdependence of human rights.

If in these perspectives the views of the NGOs are at variance with those of governments, there is some common ground on other points. The NGOs attribute the poor state of human rights to the international economic order, whose reform, through structural changes as well as the adoption of a Convention on the Right to Development, they urge. Unlike the governments, they see a much closer connection with domestic oppression and international exploitation, in the collaboration of local economic and political élites with multinational corporations and aid agencies. Unlike the governments, they are critical of the consequences of the market system. They share with governments the desire to establish a broad framework for the analysis of human rights, but their framework (unlike that of governments which is informed by a statist view of development) is suffused with notions of social justice, eradication of poverty through equitable distribution of resources and the empowerment of people, especially women and other disadvantaged communities.

The NGOs also part company from governments in their assessment of the state of human rights, which they find marked by massive and terrible violations of these rights and pervasive lawlessness on the part of state authorities. They deplore the militarization of their governments and societies which is a primary cause of these violations. Their prescription for the ills of their countries is thorough-going democracy and an unambiguous recognition and enforcement of human rights.

Conclusions

It is clear that it is no longer possible for Asian governments, NGOs or scholars to ignore the international discourse of human rights. Nor have they chosen to do so. Even China has engaged vigorously in this discourse, refusing to accept a purely defensive position even in the face of criticisms about the massacre in Tiananmen Square, arbitrary detentions, extensive use of capital punishment, and prison labour. It has instead opted to establish the legitimacy of a distinctive approach to human rights. Other countries have also tried to establish a distinctive Asian approach. This is surely a correct position for the context of human rights is delineated by the social and economic conditions of the place and the time. So-called universal human rights of the West have evolved over a long period of European history, responding to the changing configurations of power and the tasks of each epoch of history. Claims of universality and indivisibility of rights are hard to sustain in the face of the West's history of the oppression of its own people and of others, with slavery which once enjoyed religious approbation, abuse of child labour, the exploitation of colonies and the other depravations of imperialism and racism. Nor is the process complete. Social welfare rights were acknowledged only in this century, and the appalling degradation of the environment has now set the stage for a new conception of rights and responsibilities, in which the community will have to be accorded a key position as a bearer of rights as well as duties. There is no reason why contemporary concerns and fads in the West should define the parameters of international discourse in and aspirations of human rights.

If human rights have to be located in their social and economic contexts, what are the appropriate features that constitute the context for them in Asia? We should first perhaps abandon the search for a set of features that explain the whole Asian context, since there is such a marked diversity among Asian countries. There appears to be no common context between the small, urbanized, economically prosperous Singapore and the vast, impoverished, largely rural India. I have already indicated that the attempt to establish a common context through the invocation of a common and distinctive culture is spurious. I do not argue that culture is irrelevant, but that the implications drawn from it by governments are disingenuous.

If one may generalize (despite my preceding remarks), the following specifics of the Asian situation stand out. The first point is that the function of human rights (and discourse on them) in Asia is quite different from that in the West. Human rights in the West have responded to the configurations of power and economic relationships as they have evolved over a long period. They are consequently consistent with the patterns and structures of authority, and people's aspirations as well as expectations. There are no serious competing paradigms of political organization. The role of human rights is to fine-tune the administrative and judicial system and fortify rights and freedoms that are largely uncontroversial. In Asia, on the other hand, human rights have a transformative potential. They are a constant challenge to vested interests and authority in societies riven by enormous disparities of wealth and power, with traditions of authoritarianism and the helplessness of disadvantaged communities, of militarization and the conjunction of corrupt politicians and predatory domestic and international capital. Human rights are therefore a terrain for struggle for power and the conceptions of good society. It is for this precise reason that Asian governments have engaged in the debate with the West which I outlined above; the real audience is their own people.

The second point is that there are massive violations of human rights in Asia; of women and children, of lower castes and otherwise disadvantaged communities, of ethnic minorities, of workers. Violations range over the whole conspectus of human rights; civil and political rights, as well as cultural, social and economic; there are mass killings and widespread disappearances; torture; wide displacements of communities from their traditional abode; arbitrary detentions and extensive censorship of thought and expression. The state is a major culprit, brutalizing whole populations, but massive violations also take place in and through civil society, sometimes with the connivance of the state, and frequently reflecting feudalistic and patriarchal dimensions of culture. Social conflicts, particularly those stemming from ethnic or caste differences, have politicized and militarized civil society in many states. These developments should caution us against over-romanticization of civil society (which in India, for example, is a major source of the oppression of millions of people, through murder and rape, bonded labour, and a web of discriminatory and punitive customs and practices).[24]

The third point is that despite these violations, human rights consciousness is low. Explanations for this paradox may lie in the weight of oppression over centuries, a fatalistic acceptance of one's miseries, obstacles placed in the way of those who would seek to make explicit to the downtrodden the causes of their oppression. It certainly lies in the ethnic divisions of societies; ethnic consciousness can dull human rights consciousness, for the oppression of others is frequently viewed as their just rewards. A major challenge to human rights workers is undoubtedly this ethnic consciousness which compels a perception of outsiders as less than human. Another cause of low human rights consciousness may be widespread poverty. Poverty is a great cause of the denial of human rights. The international system refuses to accept this reality—for largely political reasons. It refuses to acknowledge that poverty destroys human dignity, and without human dignity there can be no human rights or indeed the capacity to challenge the system of oppression.

Thus, economic development is undoubtedly important. But not just any kind of economic development. Economic growth must be accompanied by a wide measure of egalitarianism, the protection of the rights of workers, particularly migrant workers, and democratic practices at work-places. Nor must economic growth be undertaken at the expense of land, customs and autonomy of long-settled communities. Unless these and other community concerns are safeguarded in the process of economic growth, development is perverse and adds to the violations of human rights and dignity.

A further point about human rights in Asia is that challenges to their violations are not individual-based but group- or class-based. This is particularly the case in multi-ethnic states. The protection of human rights is therefore pursued through the group. This fact, and that the state is a major violator of human rights, suggests strategies that are different from the traditional Western approaches, which are legalistic and court-centred. Asian strategies cannot realistically be court-centred, however favourably the judiciaries may be disposed towards human rights (and for the most part they are not). Human rights awareness and mobilization based on connections between them and their oppression are a fundamental starting point (connections for which neither local governments nor the West is anxious should be made).

Nor must the terrain of struggle be purely domestic. Despite the resistance of governments, the realization of human rights in each country is intimately tied to wider global forces (particularly in the contemporary world-wide pursuit of marketization). Even today many governments in the Third World are surrogates for external economic and political interests, and it is necessary to take the battle to the homelands of these interests, just as it is necessary to recruit foreign interests to put pressure on domestic governments which deny their people the right to participate in decisions affecting their own destiny. Fruitful Asian perspectives on human rights must therefore transcend obfuscation of culturalism, locate human rights in the contingencies of their political economy, and urge struggle domestically as well as globally.

Notes

1. The Declaration was published in the *Law and Society Trust Fortnightly Review*, vol. 3, no. 57 1 May 1993, pp. 1–3.
2. Indian Constitution, see Articles 14 and 17, and the Directive Principles of State Policy (particularly Articles 42 and 46) which sets a wide agenda of social reform consisting largely of attack on traditional values and practices.
3. These differences dominated the World Conference on Human Rights in Vienna in June 1993. These differences could not be reconciled, although in the end they were papered over by genuflections to a series of contradictory positions. Perhaps the basic achievement of the World Conference was that it kept open the possibility of further dialogue rather than achieving any meaningful consensus on substance or procedure. For details see The Declaration, *Law and Society Trust Fortnightly Review*, op. cit., paragraph 7.
4. *Human Rights in China* (Beijing: Foreign Languages Press, Vol. 1, 1991). The white paper was published by the State Council to refute the charges of human rights violations in China. The quotation occurs on p. 2.
5. Statement by Zhang Yishan, Alternate Representative of the Chinese Delegation at the 49th Session of the Commission on Human Rights (February 1993), p. 2.
6. The Declaration, *Law and Society Trust Fortnightly*, op. cit., paragraph 8.
7. *Human Rights in China*, op. cit., p. 2., footnote 2
8. *Human Rights in China*, op. cit., pp. 4–5, footnote 2.
9. Letter written by the Singapore Minister for Home Affairs, Mr Jayakumar, dated 24 June 1987, addressed to US Congressmen who had written to complain about the detentions.
10. *Human Rights in China*, op. cit., p. 8.
11. The Declaration is reprinted in the *Compilation of International Human Rights Instruments* (Geneva: The Human Rights Centre, 1991). I have criticized the Declaration in *Whose Human Right to Development?* (London: Commonwealth Secretariat, 1989).

12. *Shared Values*, Cmd. 1 (Singapore: Singapore National Printers Ltd. Government Printers, 1991).
13. Quoted in presidential address to Parliament in January 1989, p. 1.
14. Presidential address, paragraph 26, p. 5.
15. Presidential address, paragraph 41, p. 8.
16. Chapter 2 of the Chinese Constitution is entitled 'The Fundamental Rights and Duties of Citizens'. Article 42 states that Chinese citizens have the right as well as the duty to work and Article 46 says that they have the duty as well as the right to receive education. Other duties include safeguarding the 'unification of the country and the unity of all its nationalities' (Article 52); abiding by the Constitution and the law, keeping of state secrets, protection of public property, observing labour discipline and public order, and respecting social ethics (Article 53); safeguarding the security, honour and interests of the motherland and a prohibition against acts detrimental to the security, honour and interests of the motherland (Article 54); and to pay taxes (Article 56). Article 55 states 'the sacred duty of every citizen of the People's Republic of China to defend the motherland and to resist aggression' as well as 'to perform military service and join the militia in accordance with the law'.

    The Indian Constitution requires citizens, *inter alia*, to abide by the Constitution, protect the sovereignty, unity and integrity of India, to promote harmony and the spirit of common brotherhood amongst all the people of India, and to renounce practices derogatory to the dignity of women, and to safeguard public property and abjure violence (Article 51-A).
17. Presidential address, paragraph 38, p. 7.
18. I have reviewed this literature (and examined its implications for the centrality or otherwise of the rule of law) in 'Capitalism and the rule of law: reflections on the Basic Law', in Raymond Wacks (ed.), *Legal Theory: China, Hong Kong and 1997* (Hong Kong: Hong Kong University Press, 1993).
19. See, for example, Will Kymlicka, *Liberalism, Community, and Culture* (Oxford: Clarendon Press, 1989).
20. See John Keane (ed.), *Civil Society and the State: New European Perspectives* (London: Verso, 1988).
21. The African Charter was adopted in Nairobi in June 1981. Its preamble refers to the 'values of their historical tradition and the values of African civilisation which should inspire and characterise their reflection on the concept of human rights and peoples' rights'.
22. The Societies Ordinance of Hong Kong (before its recent amendment following the Hong Kong Bill of Rights Ordinance) is fairly typical of this kind of legislation.
23. The Bangkok NGO Declaration reprinted in *Law and Society Fortnightly Review*, vol. 3, no. 57 (1 May 1993), pp. 5–21.
24. The framers of the Indian Constitution were well aware of these problems of civil society. Article 15 declared illegal discriminations on grounds, *inter alia*, of caste, in, for example, access to wells, tanks, bathing ghats, roads and other places of public resort. Article 17 abolished untouchability and its practice in any form. Article 23 prohibited traffic in human beings and forced labour, particularly the traditional form of bonded labour known as 'begar'. There are various laws at the central and state levels to implement these provisions, particularly the Civil Rights Act of 1955 (expanded and renamed as the Scheduled Castes and Scheduled Tribes (Prevention of Atrocities) Act in 1989). Despite these attempts, the social and economic position of these disadvantaged communities shows little improvement.

PART II
COUNTRY PERSPECTIVES

6

HUMAN RIGHTS AND US POLICY TOWARDS ASIA

WILLIAM J. BARNDS

Introduction

Human rights issues have had an international as well as a national dimension since the late eighteenth century. The movement of political ideas and ideals back and forth across the Atlantic as men attempted to find a way to combine liberty and order was one of the earliest examples of a concept that has recently become commonplace, namely the interdependence of nations. There are, of course, great differences between the domestic and international environments and between constraints affecting a government's ability to promote human rights at home and abroad, for sovereignty stops near the water's edge, although even absolute sovereignty is now being questioned.

The United States is by no means the only nation in the world that is concerned with the international dimension of human rights. I believe that it is fair to say, however, that the United States has shown greater concern for human rights than any other major power, and that it has had a greater impact on developments relating to human rights than any other nation. These conclusions do not rest upon a view that Americans are better or more moral than the citizens of other countries, but only that certain elements in the American experience have influenced US policies and the attitudes of the American people since the beginning of our history as a nation.

The United States is unique among the major nations of the world in that it was created by an act of will by a group of individuals – the Founding Fathers – who won independence and established the nation on the basis of ideas concerning the relationship of men, government and society. (The fact that the Founding Fathers also had particular interests they sought to protect only demonstrates that they were not saints; it does not weaken the argument that the country was created on the basis of certain ideas.) This is quite different from the history of almost all other nations, which gradually emerged as a result of the experiences of a particular group of people living in a specific geographical area. Moreover, as the United States took on an increasingly multi-ethnic character because of the diverse origins of its immigrants, the importance of the American idea of limited self-government, of a written constitution, and of specific rights for its people became ever more important as a source of legitimacy for its political institutions.

Since the American revolution against the English crown was based upon the assertion that all men had certain inalienable rights, a certain universalist and missionary attitude on the part of the successful revolutionaries and citizens was virtually inevitable. The fact that America was a society in which some men, because of their race, and American women, because of their gender, were not accorded equal rights did not prevent many Americans from arguing that the United States had a universal message for the world. Americans have disagreed throughout their history, however, about whether that message should be spread by action or by example.

Having engaged in some ethnocentric prose, let me qualify this by two points. First, progress in other nations is almost always due primarily to the efforts of the people of such countries, not to outside influence. Second, Americans have often had — and many today still have — an exaggerated view of America's actual or potential influence. One example — really a caricature — is the mid-1940s statement of Senator Kenneth Wherry that 'We will lift Shanghai up, up, up until it is just like Kansas City'. Yet such views were a part of the traditional American view of this country's distinct role in China. Louis Halle has pointed out an example of this attitude well over a century ago:

As early as the 1850s, when the Taiping rebellion threatened anarchy in China, Mr. Humphrey Marshall, our American commissioner on the scene, reported that 'the highest interests of the United States are involved in sustaining China — maintaining order here and engrafting on this worn out stock the healthy principles which give life and health to governments, rather than to see China become the theater of widespread anarchy, and ultimately the prey of European ambitions.'

Here, at the outset of the contest among the great powers for influence in China . . . when we were still struggling to dominate our own continent, we were to undertake the establishment of order among hundreds of millions of alien people on the other side of the globe and to re-educate them.[1]

In this century, both World Wars and the Cold War had elements of human rights concerns involved in American participation, although concern for US security was the primary motivating factor. 'Making the world safe for democracy' in the First World War, and opposing Germany and Japan in the Second World War and the communist nations in the Cold War was due in part to the nature of these regimes. It must be acknowledged that large elements of expediency were involved — aiding Stalin against Hitler, for example, or supporting right-wing dictatorships (and Tito and later Mao) against the Soviet Union.

Yet during the Cold War the core of the anti-communist coalitions were democratic societies in Western Europe and Japan. Moreover, the United States favoured freedom for colonial nations (self-determination or collective human rights), although compromises were made in deference to our Western allies. Yet in broad terms, we were pursuing our values as well as protecting our security.

The present era of US human rights policy began in the mid-1970s. This occurred partly as a reaction to the US experience in Vietnam, which many Americans (and many young Democrats elected to Congress in 1974) believed represented an immoral policy. Henceforth higher moral standards should govern US foreign policy, in the view of these critics. Moreover, for a time in the mid-1970s communism appeared less of a threat to many Americans, especially when the communist take-over of South Vietnam did not lead to the feared domino effect. Another factor was the negative reaction of many Americans to the Nixon–Kissinger *realpolitik* approach to foreign policy. US foreign policy actions had previously been based primarily upon US security interests, but the rhetoric had normally been that of idealism. Nixon and Kissinger not only acted in *realpolitik* terms, but talked in terms of the balance of power. Their critics—including presidential candidate and then President Jimmy Carter—found it necessary to articulate a more 'moral' approach, and gave a higher priority to human rights.

Congress began passing new laws—and amending old ones—conditioning US economic aid, access to the US market and the right to purchase certain US products, and US arms sales and military aid according to the behaviour of foreign countries. The behaviour involved not only adherence to certain standards (usually loosely defined) of human rights, but to other country's policies on matters including nuclear proliferation, missile and other arms sales, and failure to curb the growth of crops that could be used to produce illegal drugs. The Congressional Research Service, in a 653-page study of economic sanctions imposed (or continued) for political purposes between 1979 and 1992, found that such sanctions were in force against forty-five countries ranging from Afghanistan to Zaïre during these years.[2] (Economic sanctions to protect US economic interests are also in force against many additional countries.)

Beyond the sanctions imposed by law (which often give the president power to waive the restrictions if he finds they would harm US interests), there have been numerous cases of the executive branch imposing sanctions for reasons of its own—or to head off tougher Congressional actions. In the early 1980s the Reagan administration, in reaction against President Carter's emphasis on human rights, downgraded this aspect of US policy. In time, however, it saw that stressing the value not only of market-oriented economies but also of human rights and democracy was a useful tool in the struggle against communism as well as a way to expand and deepen the moral content of US foreign policy.

Following a brief summary of the growth of US laws involving (non-economic) sanctions, this chapter considers how America's relative economic decline will influence its ability to influence Asian nations, looks at trends toward freedom in Asia, and concludes with some observations of the human rights policies of the Clinton administration towards Asia—especially the People's Republic of China (PRC). Limitations of space make it impossible to discuss the extremely complex matter of US views regarding the collective human right of self-determination, an issue that will confound many countries in the future.[3]

The scope of US laws

No comprehensive listing or examination of US laws designed to influence the behaviour of other countries is necessary to portray their scope—a few examples are adequate to do that. The following is a brief review of some such legislations, including: the Foreign Assistance Act of 1961, the Export Administration Act of 1979, the Trade Act of 1977, the Arms Export Control Act, Export Import Bank Act of 1945, the International Development Association Act, and the Trading with the Enemy Act.

The Foreign Assistance Act of 1961, as amended, prohibits foreign aid to any communist country, to any country that supports international terrorism, or that transfers nuclear enrichment equipment to a third country, or explodes a nuclear device (if it is a non-nuclear power).[4] The Export Administration Act of 1979, as amended, gives the president extremely broad authority to prohibit or curtail the export of any goods, technology, or other information subject to the jurisdiction of the United States to the extent necessary to further significantly the foreign policy of the United States.[5]

The Trade Act of 1977, as amended, authorizes the president to provide duty-free entry of articles produced by developing countries provided (among other conditions) that such countries adhere to 'internationally recognized worker rights' including the right to organize and bargain collectively, prohibit forced labour, and enforce acceptable working and safety conditions.[6]

The Arms Export Control Act prohibits the sale or lease of defence articles to any country which refuses to give the United States veto power over the transfer of such arms to third parties (excepting members of NATO and a few other countries), or to any country that transfers US weapons to a country that supports international terrorism.[7] Other important laws involved are the Export Import Bank Act of 1945, the International Development Association Act, and the Trading with the Enemy Act. Restrictions on economic relations with specific countries often are imposed as amendments to acts not specifically relating to foreign commerce or arms exports.

The International Financial Institutions Act also directs the president to press other members of such organizations to advance the cause of human rights by restricting aid to countries that engage in a 'consistent pattern of gross violations of internationally recognized human rights'.[8] Such policies may violate the charters of these international financial institutions, which provide that loans shall be influenced only by economic considerations. Administrations often try to justify such policies to other countries by arguing that unsettled conditions in potential recipient countries make loans economically unsound, while telling Congress it is opposing aid on human rights grounds.

Moreover, many restrictions are imposed by an executive order of the president under broad presidential powers to conduct foreign policy. The president can also direct the US member of the board of directors of the World Bank, the International Monetary Fund, or regional international economic organizations to vote against providing resources to nations whose policies are offensive to the United States. The United States has with varying success pressed its friends and allies to impose restrictions on their economic dealings with third countries in order to influence the latter's behaviour.

The point of this brief description of the US laws as well as US policies resorting to economic sanctions is not to argue that such laws or policies are mistaken, although few would agree with every measure. What is striking is the breadth of the sanctions, which apply restrictions on many actions of other countries that involve their domestic as well as international activities. Does the United States have the power to influence such a range of issues across the globe, and will it have such power in the future? In trying to answer these questions, it is important to remember that the United States has many non-economic ways of influencing foreign countries: the tradition of international political leadership, enhanced as a result of the collapse of communism in many countries; the attractiveness of US political values; and the influence of US culture and the example of the United States as a society (both of which have positive and negative impacts abroad). But US power and influence throughout the post-war era have rested to a major extent on its military strength and underlying economic power.

Two additional points should be borne in mind. First, administrations tend to apply the laws somewhat selectively, a practice Congress encourages by downplaying human rights violations in countries that have important groups of American supporters. Second, the requirement that the administration submit an annual report on human rights in all countries forces it to pay regular attention to this issue. Such reports also influence other countries, which often pay close attention to what is said about their performance.

With the US-led victory in the Cold War, with the demise of communism and the moves towards democracy in many former communist countries — as well as Latin America and parts of Africa — American leaders and people saw the remaining communist and authoritarian nations — especially in Asia — as anachronistic and on the defensive. Yet both in attitude and law the United States has generally made a distinction between advancing human rights and promoting democracy, while recognizing that human rights fare much better in democratic nations. In the Gallup poll taken for the Chicago Council on Foreign Relations in 1990-1, about one-half of the public and the foreign policy leaders listed defending human rights as a very important foreign policy goal, but only one-quarter of each group assigned a similar priority to promoting democracy.[9]

Yet many Americans — especially human rights activists and members of Congress — have, in my judgement, an exaggerated notion of the extent of US influence over other nations — especially Asian countries. They also downplay the need to make hard choices in foreign policy. For example, is it more important to improve human rights conditions in China (and if so, which human rights) than to reduce Chinese missile sales in unstable regions, secure Chinese help on non-proliferation issues, and prevent Chinese vetoes in the UN Security Council on peacekeeping issues? The answer may sometimes be yes, but it is hardly a self-evident answer.

Economic troubles and influence abroad

It is important to analyse the likely significance of US economic difficulties during the past decade regarding America's ability to press its views on human rights and democracy in the coming decade. In particular, does the shift in economic power from the United States to Japan matter in this context? Japan is an American ally that has usually followed the US lead in foreign policy, and cooperation between the two countries has been close in most aspects of Asian affairs, especially in the past fifteen years.

One reason for emphasizing the importance of Japan is that, despite close cooperation on most political security affairs, Japan and the United States have very different attitudes towards exporting their political values and culture. Japan has no missionary impulse, as do the Americans, British and French. It values harmony and tries to avoid confrontation in foreign as well as domestic affairs. Tokyo joined the Western nations in halting aid to China after Beijing's suppression of the democracy movement in 1989, but more to preserve harmony with its major partners than because of a conviction that this was the proper course to follow. At the Houston summit in 1990 Japan made clear that it intended to resume aid to China, arguing that stability and economic development would in time contribute to renewed progress towards political liberalization. In April 1991 Tokyo announced that henceforth a country's human rights record and its democratic orientation would be among the factors considered in granting it aid, but it remains unclear how strongly these guidelines will be followed.

Japan did temporarily suspend aid to Myanmar (Burma) after its brutal military regime suppressed a popular uprising in 1988 but argued, at least publicly, that it did so because conditions made economic development under such conditions unlikely. And when a military *coup* in Thailand early in 1991 led to a cut-off of US aid, Japan's aid resumed after a brief cut-off. The Japanese government not only refused to condemn the Thai coup regime's bloody crackdown on civilian protestors, but accused the demonstrators of provoking the regime's harsh reaction. Since about 70 per cent of Thailand's bilateral aid comes from Japan, the US aid cut-off had limited impact. The Thai populace, with the help of the king, managed to reverse the *coup*, but much more as a result of their own determination than of external pressure.

Without succumbing to economic determinism, it does not take profound insight to reach the conclusion that as countries become more dependent on Japan for economic aid, technology and private investment (in which Japan has overtaken the US lead in Asia) the US leverage over developments in these countries will decline.[10] Yet the United States has increasingly emphasized the promotion of human rights and democracy abroad as its relative economic power has declined, although these values continue to compete for priority against other US foreign policy goals.

America still retains many ways to influence events abroad, even in Asia where growing economic strength in other countries and Japan's increasing role reduce US leverage. Most Asian countries want a continued US military presence as a non-threatening 'regional balancer', even though the former Soviet Union is viewed with less apprehension than in the past. Most countries in the East Asian region — as well as most Japanese — do not want to see US military power replaced by that of Japan. And most Asian countries are still more dependent upon access to the US than the Japanese market for their exports, although that too is gradually changing as Japan opens its economy more to foreign goods. (Yet the rules of the General Agreement of Tariffs and

Trade (GATT) make no provision for restricting access to one's market to countries because of their internal political developments.) The United States can still influence Japan's foreign aid policy in many situations, but the amount of pressure required and the costs entailed are rising over the long term as US relative economic strength declines.

Japan's current economic troubles may somewhat slow its gains in relative economic power, but its large trade surpluses will continue to enable it to provide more capital and foreign aid to Asian countries than America. Moreover, as Asian countries increasingly trade with and invest in each other, their susceptibility to external pressure is likely to decline. The effect of the US relative economic decline probably will be felt in other areas of the world and in our relations with countries other than Japan.

If the US relative economic position continues to slide—especially if it continues to depend on foreign capital—its ability successfully to press other wealthy nations to follow its lead on human rights and democracy probably will gradually diminish. The energies and resources of Western European nations may increasingly be focused on Eastern Europe—and perhaps the former Soviet Union—limiting, though not eliminating, their concerns about such issues in the less developed countries.[11] Indeed, if the United States finds itself in another Gulf-type war and is again dependent upon foreign financing, our ability to influence our wealthy friends and allies on other issues could decline despite their dependence on American military power.

Asian trends

People do not live by bread—or rice—alone, and recently Asia has experienced growing pressures for greater popular participation in civic affairs. Several elements are behind these trends. Authoritarian regimes are hard pressed to accommodate the growing diversity of interests characteristic of increasingly complex societies, which creates pressures for political pluralism and greater respect for human rights.

Economic progress and rising levels of education and urbanization have created middle classes determined to influence civic affairs. While deference to authority has not been destroyed, it has declined. The communications revolution has enhanced the flow of aspirations as well as facts. Countries that have outward-oriented economies and that send thousands of citizens abroad each year cannot wall off their people from new ideas. Finally, the triumph of Western (and Japanese) economic and political systems in the Cold War has provided psychological and political encouragement to advocates of human rights and democracy and has placed authoritarianism on the defensive.

Yet nearly all of Asia's democracies are beset by greater or lesser strains that rule out complacency and make periodic setbacks likely. Pervasive corruption creates public cynicism in some countries. Ethnic and religious conflicts are rife in parts of Asia. Disaffected minorities are sometimes willing to resort to arms to seek self-determination, a tendency probably strengthened by events in the former Soviet Union. Political institutions and processes are developing, but they remain weak in much of Asia. Political parties often are little more than vehicles for fulfilling the ambitions of individual leaders, and independent judiciaries and the rule of law are only gradually taking root.

The collapse of communism and the advance of democratic forces on several continents have led to greater acceptance of the idea of universal political values, even ones that first arose in the West. Yet cultural pride and belief in certain core values from their own traditions will continue to lead many Asians to reject any mechanical transplant of Western political values and systems. Many Asians believe popular participation must be structured in a manner that does not undermine national unity and stability, which are both essential for economic progress. Awareness of their countries' vulnerabilities together with sensitivities over intrusions on their sovereignty, will make nearly all Asian countries cautious about pressing their neighbours over human rights abuses and authoritarian rule, and differences in approach to such issues are likely to characterize—and divide—Western and Asian nations.

Yet despite such differences, increasing numbers of Asians—and Asian non-governmental organizations—are pressing their governments not simply to reject Western concepts of human rights, and to recognize that there are certain universal norms despite cultural differences between nations. The Bangkok Declaration of April 1993 emphasized the importance of such cultural differences, but at the United Nations Human Rights conference in Vienna a few months later the universality of human rights was upheld, as well as the principle that the promotion of human rights is a legitimate concern of the international community.[12] US willingness to accept the concept of certain economic and social rights as fundamental was regarded by Asian countries as an important step forward, and probably was an important step towards making agreement possible at Vienna.

The Clinton administration and Asia

Before attempting to describe and appraise the human rights policies of the Clinton administration towards Asia, it is necessary to discuss briefly the policies of the Bush administration and their impact, for these had considerable influence on Clinton's approach to the issue. The Bush administration was almost by necessity focused largely on the Soviet Union, Eastern Europe and the Middle East in view of the dramatic events in these areas, but it could not ignore the situation in China after the 1989 upheavals there.

It is interesting to note that it was only in the mid-1980s that human rights in China became an important issue in Sino-American relations—although there had been some friction over these matters briefly in the late 1970s. The decline in Soviet-US hostility, and reforms in the Soviet Union, together with looser political controls in China, gave added prominence to human rights conditions within China, as did the riots and repression in Tibet in 1987. Voices within China calling for a more open political system, progress in South Korea and Taiwan, and a growing American awareness of both past Chinese abuses and present conditions led to greater American attention to human rights in China. It was, however, only with the repression that occurred during and after the demonstrations centred at Tiananmen Square in

1989 that the trickle of American concern became a flood.

The Bush administration imposed significant sanctions on its own initiative, while attempting to keep Congress from imposing even tougher sanctions — particularly the cut-off or conditioning of most-favoured-nation (MFN) treatment for Chinese exports. This is not the place to present a detailed discussion of the moves and counter-moves between the Bush administration, Congress and Beijing after 1989.[13] In effect, President Bush was successful in preventing China from losing its MFN tariff status. However, his lack of strong language concerning the repression, and the failure of the Chinese leaders adequately to respond to his restraint — and to some unilateral gestures towards China — forced him to undertake or acquiesce in stronger measures.

Three points need to be made about these measures in terms of their long-term impact. First, such measures as agreeing to support Taiwan's membership in GATT before that of the PRC, the late-1992 visit of the first cabinet-level US official to Taiwan since US–PRC normalization, and the sale of F-16s all enhanced Taiwan's position and increased its ability to pursue its more flexible diplomatic and economic diplomacy towards the PRC. Second, Beijing did recognize that it had to make some concessions to the United States if President Bush was to preserve the Sino-American relationship, which was becoming steadily more valuable to China. Some of these concessions were economic and diplomatic, but others involved human rights — at least at the margins.

Third, another measure that concerned Beijing was the US–Hong Kong Policy Act of 1992. While most of the provisions of the Hong Kong Act are 'sense of Congress resolutions' rather than US laws which must be enforced, some parts are law, although the president is granted broad waiver provisions. Yet the Act is a strong indication that if China does not live up to the provisions of the 1984 Joint Declaration regarding the rights specified for the people in Hong Kong it will do so at what may be a substantial cost to its relations with the United States. Beijing's failure to do so would look to Americans like the act of the village bully abusing someone much smaller, which — depending on just what Beijing did — could spark a powerful American reaction.

Thus after Tiananmen two decades of US bipartisanship in US policy towards China were disrupted, and with the election of President Clinton the PRC faced the possibility of an administration as well as a Congress committed to a tougher stance towards China.

The Clinton administration's policies towards democracy and human rights are still being formulated in mid-1993, but it is clear that they will not be made in a vacuum. Domestic priorities and pressures, US world-wide policies on human rights, other foreign policy issues and priorities, and the views of other countries will all influence American human rights policies toward Asia. To cite only two examples, the basic aim of the administration's foreign policy will be to keep out of trouble abroad as it focuses on domestic revival. It will not be looking for new foreign policy responsibilities, as its retreat from the president's campaign rhetoric on Bosnia and Haiti has already demonstrated. Human rights policies that carry substantial economic costs will be looked at with a jaundiced eye.

At the same time, human rights activists and interest groups are more of a Democratic than a Republican constituency, and their influence will be felt.[14] This factor—and President Clinton's and Secretary of State Christopher's own beliefs—means that human rights probably will receive somewhat greater emphasis under Clinton than they did under President Bush.

The administration's first Asian test involved the issue of China's MFN status, which under US law must be renewed by mid-year annually. Democrats in Congress and the human rights activists, who in earlier years had pressed for terminating China's MFN status or making it subject to tough and wide-ranging legislative conditions, found themselves in a dilemma as well as a fierce political struggle. It was politically easy and safe to urge toughness when a Bush veto was certain to protect the anti-MFN forces from the consequences of success. With Clinton having attacked the Bush administration for having coddled 'tyrants from Baghdad to Beijing', no such easy choice was possible. Business and farm groups with an economic stake in continued trade with China lobbied hard for a flexible approach. Moreover, friends of Taiwan and Hong Kong made a strong case that these areas would be badly hurt by an end to China's MFN status.

President Clinton was able to take advantage of these conflicting views and concerns by securing the agreement—or at least the acquiescence—of all the groups involved in handling the issue through an executive order rather than through the more formal process of legislation. China's MFN status was extended for a year, but with the provision that future renewals would depend upon an improved Chinese performance on human rights. Moreover, the administration stated that China's actions on nuclear non-proliferation issues, and arms and missile exports, would henceforth not be linked to the MFN issue. While there was some Republican grumbling about the Clinton policies, that party's support of the Bush approach made it difficult to criticize Clinton.

Beijing reacted with a few strong statements critical of any linkage between human rights and trade, but probably was privately relieved. In any case, it is unlikely to reduce its economic links with the United States substantially in order to decrease its future vulnerability to US pressure.

While the Clinton administration's handling of China's MFN status is a clear indication that it will deal with human rights issues in a flexible rather than a rigid manner, the MFN issue for China will remain on the agenda and be subject to events beyond American control. New political upheavals and repression in China could change the thrust of US policy. Similarly, Chinese actions seen as contributing to nuclear proliferation of missile build-ups could create intensified pressures to restrict China's MFN status—just as strong Chinese pressure on North Korea to curtail its nuclear programme could improve China's prospects for enjoying continued MFN status. Such linkage may not exist on a *de jure* basis but it does exist *de facto* in US public policy.

Another issue that reflects the Clinton administration's penchant for compromise and flexibility—which some would label abandoning principles and campaign promises—involves the proposed Radio Free Asia. Although no final determination had been made by mid-1993, the administration and Congress appear likely to reject both the establishment of an independent new radio system financed by the US government or simply the expansion of Voice of America broadcasts on internal affairs in Asian communist countries. The outcome probably will be the establishment of some form of a Radio Free Asia operating alongside the Voice of America but separate from it. Such a distinction may seem meaningless to Asian communist countries, but it does demonstrate US government resolve to exercise a measure of control rather than to establish an independent operation such as Radio Free Europe has been.

US success in furthering respect for human rights and democracy in Asia will, over the years, depend heavily upon two factors. The first is whether it can gain multilateral (and especially Japanese) cooperation. This will depend partly on US willingness to engage Asian nations in serious dialogues involving Asian as well as Western approaches to human rights and democracy, and to institutionalize multilateral approaches as well as to act—or threaten to act—unilaterally. Since America has accepted Asian proposals to supplement bilateralism with multilateralism in security affairs, such a move should be possible in the area of human rights as well—provided Asian countries are also willing to see human rights issues internationalized.

The Clinton administration's 14 June 1993 announcement that it would actively seek Senate ratification for four international treaties signed by the US government in earlier decades but never ratified—including the controversial International Convention on Economic, Social and Cultural Rights—will enhance US stature in Asian eyes if the ratification process is successful.[15]

Second, US influence on human rights and democracy will depend heavily upon how successful the United States is in dealing with the problems of American society—which are not solely economic—and upon its willingness to stay engaged in Asian political and security affairs as well as in the region's economic and cultural life.

Yet it is appropriate to conclude by reiterating an earlier point, which is that the key factor in the political evolution of Asian countries will be the efforts of the people in the countries themselves rather than the actions or non-actions of the United States and other external powers.

Notes

1. Louis J. Halle, *Dream and Reality* (New York: Harper and Brothers, 1958), pp. 219–20.
2. Erin Day, *Economic Sanctions Imposed by the United States Against Specific Countries: 1979 through 1992* (Washington, DC: Congressional Research Service, 1993).
3. For a valiant if not wholly successful effort to grapple with this issue, see Morton J. Halperin and David J. Scheffer with Patricia Small, *Self-Determination in the New World Order* (Washington, DC: Carnegie Endowment for International Peace, 1992).
4. US Senate Committee on Foreign Relations and US House of Representatives Committee on Foreign Affairs, *Legislation on Foreign Relations through 1992* (Washington, DC: US Government Printing Office, 1993), Vol. I, pp. 250–1 and 296–9.
5. ibid., Vol. III, p. 835.

6. ibid., Vol. III, p. 464.
7. ibid., Vol. I, p. 318.
8. ibid., Vol. III, p. 55.
9. John E. Rielly (ed.), *American Public Opinion and US Foreign Policy 1991* (Chicago: The Chicago Council on Foreign Relations, 1991).
10. For a useful description of the limitations of economic sanctions based on a conference at Freedom House in New York, see John Train, 'When can sanctions succeed?' *Wall Street Journal*, 14 June 1989.
11. In 1991 the EC began to move towards linking its foreign aid to Asian countries to their human rights records, as some EC member countries had done earlier. See 'Under Western eyes', *Far Eastern Economic Review*, 14 March 1991, pp. 20–1.
12. See Frank Ching, 'Asia , West reach compromise on human rights in Vienna', *Far Eastern Economic Review*, 15 July 1993, p. 26, for a succinct description of these matters. For a broader appraisal of the Clinton Administration's policy on human rights, see Susumu Awanohara, 'Do unto others . . .', *Far Eastern Economic Review*, 1 July 1993, p. 18.
13. For a description and appraisal of these moves and counter-moves, see Harry Harding, *A Fragile Relationship: The United States and China Since 1972* (Washington, DC: Brookings, 1992).
14. Many of Clinton's appointees are strong activists who are urging a strong US stance on human rights and democracy, such as Assistant Secretary of Defense designate Morton H. Halperin. See his article 'Guaranteeing Democracy', *Foreign Policy*, Summer (1993), pp. 105–22, for an assertion that an international guarantee for constitutional democracy should be supported under rather broad circumstances by the use of US military force.
15. For an argument that the International Covenant on Economic, Social and Cultural Rights is based upon democratic concepts rather than the arguments of authoritarian states (as many Americans charge), see Andrew Redding, 'Clinton is right on international human rights', *Wall Street Journal*, 15 July 1993, p. A13.

7
THE STUDY OF HUMAN RIGHTS IN
THE PEOPLE'S REPUBLIC OF CHINA*

ZHOU WEI

Introduction

The question of human rights has long been politically sensitive in the People's Republic of China (PRC). Prior to 1989 very few scholars dared to study and discuss it. Authorities in charge of ideological work maintained a negative attitude towards scholarly works on human rights. The turning point came after the events of 4 June 1989, when human rights in China attracted wide international concern and criticism.[1] Articles criticizing the bourgeois theory of human rights and 'human rights foreign policy' of Western imperialists appeared in major newspapers, magazines and academic journals in China. This marked the beginning of the large-scale study of human rights in the People's Republic.

In September 1990, the first conference specifically on human rights was convened by the Research Centre for Social Science Development of the State Education Commission, symbolizing the official blessing to research on this subject.[2] The publication of a white paper on *Human Rights in China* by the State Council in October 1991 not only presented the official views and interest in human rights, but also reflected a development in the study of human rights.

The change in the official attitude towards human rights problems has promoted studies in the subject, marking a historical turning point in human rights as a field of investigation. There were very few published works on the subject before 1989 but a large number have appeared since then, and the scope has broadened considerably. In China this phenomenon has been referred to as 'a hot wave of interest in studying human rights'.[3]

The study of human rights in the PRC therefore can be divided into two periods. The first is the period before 1989, during which the field of human rights study was almost non-existent. The second period starts after 1989 and can be divided into two stages: the first between 1989 and 1990 and dominated by traditional (Chinese) Marxist views on human rights and criticisms of bourgeois human rights theory; and the second, marked by the first officially sponsored conference on human rights, which began in September 1990. During the second stage, as a result of official support a number of conferences and seminars were organized and important theoretical issues on human rights were discussed from different perspectives.

The study of human rights before 1989

'Fighting for freedom and human rights' had once been one of the political slogans of the Chinese Communist Party before it came to power, and there had been some legislation concerning human rights protection in 'the red area' under Communist control in Northwest China.[4] However, human rights problems were largely ignored after 1949 because of ultra-leftist ideological influences. The study of human rights was regarded as unnecessary because when workers, peasants and other working people became masters of the country they had gained real democratic rights and freedom. The term 'human rights' was also criticized as a bourgeois concept, because 'it was the bourgeoisie who first raised the call for human rights'.[5] Against this background, there were few published works on human rights except the occasional criticism of bourgeois human rights theories.

During the late 1970s and early 1980s with the end of 'the Great Proletariat Cultural Revolution' and the ousting of 'the Gang of Four', a heated debate on questions about 'alienation in socialism' and 'humanism and human rights' emerged. The question was: Can there be a Marxist approach to humanism and human rights? During this period the impact of ultra-leftist ideas of the 'Great Cultural Revolution' was still very much alive and the debate on human rights rather political. The voices for human rights were weak — most people believed that human rights were a bourgeois concept. On the question of humanism, however, strong support was found in Mao Zedong's remark, 'Heal the wounded, rescue the dying, practise revolutionary humanitarianism'.[6] The focus of the debate shifted from human rights to humanism and alienation in socialism, but inevitably occasionally or implicitly it also raised issues concerning human rights.

Three different views can be identified in the debate. The first maintained that the notions of humanism and human rights had no place in Marxism; both were ruthlessly criticized by Marx and Engels as a bourgeois sham. Marxist human rights ideas were dismissed as old revisionism promulgated by the Second International. Human rights were, therefore meaningless for socialist China. Those who supported this view maintained that human rights might have been mentioned by Marx and Engels occasionally, but it was just a tactical slogan for class struggle.[7] The second view asserted that as the supreme form of social science Marxism encompassed the concepts of humanism and human rights. Those who articulated this position, however, argued that socialist rights were based on public ownership and therefore had transcended bourgeois human rights. According to this second school, humanism and human rights had been abandoned by Marxism as ideological weapons because these ideas would weaken the fighting will of the people.[8] A third view insisted that the principles of humanism and human rights should be included in, and considered as an integral part of, Marxism. Those adhered to this position argued that principles of Marxist humanism and human rights remained important even during the course of socialist revolution and construction.[9]

The first view had long been the official position, displaying an absolutely negative attitude towards human rights. The second one appeared to be more moderate but in substance it still did not take human rights seriously: while it recognized the notions of humanism and human rights, it regarded them as irrelevant. The third view abandoned the ultra-leftist stance by arguing that humanism and human rights were important even for socialist countries, but this position was criticized by the authorities as a bourgeois liberal view.

Although the debate was merely a preliminary one and the discussions were far from vigorous, it ended too early with the launching of 'the movement to clear spiritual pollution'. In October 1983, at the second plenary session of the Twelfth Party Congress of the Chinese Communist Party, the decision to 'clear spiritual pollution' was made. On 3 January 1984, Hu Qiaomu, an authoritative theorist, made a speech on 'some theoretical problems about humanism and alienation' in the Central Communist Party School, criticizing the writings on alienation and socialism. Such works were considered to be focusing too much on ideas opposing the leadership of the government and the party. 'Humanism,' he said, 'as a bourgeois outlook . . . is opposite to Marxist historical materialism.'[10] Subsequently the number of articles on the topic were reduced greatly. Public opinion quickly came in line with Hu's stance, and several prominent scholars also made public self-criticisms.[11] The debate ended. The study of human rights came to a stop.

With the deepening of economic reforms and growing interests in political liberalization, the traditional Marxist social sciences in China faced the challenge of shifting social reality towards the end of the 1980s. These were politically the most liberal years since 1949. The study of Western philosophy, economics and jurisprudence returned to China and studying Western theories became fashionable among academics. A huge number of books and articles on these topics were published, but only a few openly advocated the promotion of human rights in China. Xu Bing and Si Pingping's articles were two exceptional examples.

Xu Bing declared that human rights had already become a banner of the whole mankind. 'It, in the course of history, led mankind from barbarianism into civilization, from low-level civilization into high-level civilization, from autocracy to democracy and from the Rule of Man to the Rule of Law.' He also wrote: 'Marx did not negate human rights thoroughly, so human rights must be the starting point and the end of all the human activities.' While agreeing that human rights were class-related, he also argued that human rights were supra-class in nature. 'Rejecting the supra-class nature of human rights and one-sidedly emphasizing class nature of human rights will lead to neglect and violation of human rights.' He took the Cultural Revolution as an example and proposed to 'understand human rights afresh'.[12]

In Si Pingping's article judicial independence was identified as the key element in protecting human rights. Without judicial independence, there would be no protection of human rights in China.[13] Si maintained that since the Chinese Constitution stipulated that the People's Courts should administer justice independently in accordance with the law, and not subject to interference by administrative organs, public organizations or individuals, judicial independence is constitutionally guaranteed.[14] However, he pointed out that judicial independence had been interfered with by party organizations at various levels.[15] He also suggested that China should participate in the International Conventions on Human Rights.

The study of human rights between 1989 and 1990

Tens of articles on human rights had been published in major academic journals and newspapers by the end of 1990. This is indeed a relatively large number, for there had never been so many articles on this topic within so short a period since the foundation of the PRC. This might be due to the unexpected fierce criticism of the Chinese government by the international community: China could not remain silent when it was severely criticized for human rights violations.

The common features in these articles were their criticism of bourgeois human rights theory (which refers to domestic bourgeois liberal ideas) and repudiation of Western criticism on China's human rights record. This can be seen, sometimes, simply from their titles, such as 'Do not talk abstract human rights',[16] 'A critical analysis of bourgeois human rights',[17] and 'Two opposing approaches to human rights'.[18] These articles were written for political purposes rather than academic analysis and merely reflected the official stand. They focused on the following issues: first, criticizing the class nature of bourgeois human rights; second, advocating the protection of human rights in socialist China; third, emphasizing that human rights protection was purely an internal affair.

In criticizing bourgeois human rights, many of these articles maintained that, in accordance with Marxist views, human rights reflected class interests. Using a Marxist approach, these works regarded human rights as part of the superstructure, determined by the economic base on which they existed. Rights were therefore the products of economic relations. Private ownership determined the class nature of bourgeois human rights: they were the rights of capitalists, not of the working class. 'The core of bourgeois human rights,' argued one author, was 'bourgeois private ownership or property freedom.' Referring to Engels, Zhang suggested that bourgeois property was one of the essential rights of man.[19]

Reflecting the official stance on human rights, this group of writers asserted that the capitalist legal system only guaranteed individual rights to private property. But with the bourgeoisie declaring that human rights were universal and equally enjoyed by every person, the class nature of human rights was being overlooked. 'Human rights are always concrete, [they] belong to a certain class or a certain state,' announced Gu Chunde. He argued that 'the abstract man' in bourgeois human rights theory did not exist because a person must belong to a certain class; thus, the rights of an indvidual reflected class nature.[20]

These writers rejected the notion that human rights could be absolute and frowned upon what they regarded as unlimited rights in bourgeois theories. 'The Marxist view holds that human rights are restricted by law, and also by economic and cultural conditions.'[21] These writers accused those who advocated 'absolute human rights' of confusing the relationship between law and human rights. In their view, laws could not only protect and implement human rights, but also could restrict rights; absolute and unlimited human rights did not exist.[22]

On the question of socialist human rights, works reflecting the official position declared that China had always paid great attention to protecting its citizens' rights. They pointed out that rights of the Chinese people as stipulated by the Constitution and other laws, both substantive and procedural, have been protected and these rights are real and exercisable.[23] 'Our socialist rights,' wrote Professor Zhang Guangbo, 'which are based on public ownership and the principle of distribution to each according to his work, are really equal rights.'[24] Some of these works emphasized the historical achievement made by the Chinese people and government in seeking the right to subsistence.

Most of these articles insisted that the government's position towards the pro-democracy movement and the trial of the criminals participating in the activities were purely the internal affairs of China.[25] To support this stance, they pointed out that an individual is not a subject of international law and could only be protected by domestic law. Therefore human rights could only be an internal matter.[26] Moreover, under the principle of national sovereignty, one of the main principles of international law, international intervention could not take place under the guise of human rights protection. The principle of respecting state sovereignty should be the prerequisite to the protection of human rights. The argument that human rights are beyond national boundaries was, in their view, totally wrong and unacceptable to any sovereign state.[27]

Some of these writers, however, conceded that the international protection of human rights could be applicable in the case of collective rights.[28] They believed that human rights could be divided into domestic and international human rights. The former were the rights of citizens stipulated by constitutions; the latter were mainly collective rights proclaimed by international law. For them, the state should be entitled to implement human rights within its sovereignty, and should figure as the key element in human rights protection. Even international human rights protection would have to be implemented under the jurisdiction of the state.[29]

The study of human rights since 1990

The conference on human rights convened by the Research Centre for Social Science Development of the State Education Commission, which took place in Beijing in September 1990, is of historical significance: it marks the beginning of the officially organized study of human rights in the PRC. The original intentions of the authorities were 'not only to counter-attack both internal and external reactionaries, but also to meet the needs of socialist modernization and to set up and develop a Marxist theory of human rights'.[30]

The study of human rights since 1990 can be divided into two kinds: the first focuses on providing the authorities with arguments for political purpose; the second concentrates on the theoretical research in order to set up a Marxist system of human rights theory. Some works attempt to defend China's human rights record and explain the legal protection of human rights as provided by the Chinese constitution and laws. Most of these works have attempted to criticize and expose imperialistic 'human rights foreign policy'.[31]

The fruits of the first kind of study have been fully reflected in the white paper on *Human Rights in China*. The white paper was published for the purpose of helping 'the international community understand the human rights situation as it is in China', and 'educating the Chinese people to see clearly western human rights advocators' lies'. The Chinese version of the white paper was published in October 1991 and the English version in early November. Soon afterwards a reference booklet edited by the Hongqi (Red Flag) Press was also published as a study guide for the public on the white paper. The nationally organized studying of the white paper was similar to 'political study' of the Cultural Revolution period, and demonstrated that the authorities were determined to clarify 'confused ideas of human rights'.[32]

Not all recent scholarly works on human rights have been produced to defend the official position. Freer debates and discussions among academics, however, have also benefited theoretical analysis about human rights concepts. As a result some traditional (Chinese) Marxist views on rights and law have been criticized and even revised. Recent debates in the field have centred around four themes: the question of class and human rights; the relationship between individual and collective rights; the importance of social and economic rights versus political rights; and the question of international protection of human rights and state sovereignty.

Class and human rights

The relation between capital and freedom has become a major issue in the conceptual debates about class and human rights. One of the substantive issues being disputed was the leftist belief that human rights are simply the basic rights of citizens in the capitalist states.[33] Professor Zhang Guangbo of Jilin University has suggested that human rights reflect the fundamental interests of the bourgeoisie—the freedom of capital to survive, the freedom on the part of capitalists to invest, employ and exploit. These rights, for Zhang, are products of the capitalist commodity economy. In his view, under the capitalist system each person is free in form but the owners of capital enjoy the freedom to employ and exploit, and the labourers have to sell their labour and be exploited. The core of such human rights as promulgated in bourgeois constitutions as the basic rights of citizens is therefore the right to private property. Thus, Zhang suggests that the term 'the basic rights and duties of citizens' or 'citizen rights' should be used instead of 'human rights' in order to make a clear distinction from bourgeois private ownership, and to render the concept of rights more scientific.[34]

Zhang's criticism of bourgeois human rights has been to a large extent accepted by some Chinese scholars. But others disagree with his observation. Lin Rendong, a professor of Nanjing University maintains that human rights and citizens' rights were distinguished by Marx in his *On the Jewish Question*. For Marx, 'the rights of Man are in part, political rights', Lin suggests. He therefore argues that citizens' rights should be a form of human rights. But he also accepts that human rights are internal affairs of a country because 'legalization, certification and protection of human rights depend on legislation of the sovereign state'.[35] Lin's views are supported by Li Buyun, editor of *Studies in Law*. Li believes that human rights are not merely limited to 'citizens', and 'basic rights'. If 'human rights are citizens' rights', other human rights problems besides citizens such as refugees and stateless persons, and other 'non-basic rights', would be ignored.[36]

The question whether human rights are rights of the bourgeoisie class has continued to be a subject of concern among Chinese scholars. Zuo Yu and Shu Sheng, for example, classified bourgeois human rights as human rights and citizen rights in accordance with Marx's division of 'civil society' and 'the political state'.[37] They regard bourgeois human rights as exercised by members of the civil society as 'rights of Man', and rights which can only be exercised by citizens of a political state as 'citizens' rights'. Citizens' rights are political rights, and the rights of man are the rights of individual private life. They prefer terms like 'rights to property', 'rights of ownership' rather than human rights and conclude that the bourgeois rights of citizens simply protect private material interests.[38]

While some scholars obviously still consider human rights to be a class-related concept, open discussions on the subject have challenged the notion that human rights is an entirely bourgeois idea. The debate has marked the first step towards a better understanding of human rights. Many Chinese scholars have come to recognize the universality of human rights. Hence the remark, 'human rights are both class-related and universal'.[39]

Collective and individual rights

An equally controversial question is: Which is more fundamental—collective or individual rights? It has long been a moral norm in the PRC that individuals are subject to the collective. Thus, individual rights are subject to collective rights. Individual rights have long been criticized as abstract, while collective human rights have been considered as concrete and more important.

The relationship between individual rights and collective rights is clearly a critical question. Huang Nansheng, professor of philosophy at Beijing University, has suggested that Marxism never rejected individual human rights. Therefore, Huang argues, individual human rights should be respected.[40] Another writer, Zhang Wenxian, has gone as far as arguing that human rights are largely about individuals. In Zhang's eyes, collective rights are derived from individual rights, and human rights are but one of the many kinds of rights. His position is that while human rights should not be confused with collective rights, social rights and rights of the state,[41] collective rights are not more important than individual rights. He suggests that since the law confers rights on both the individual and collective, the two kinds of rights should be equally protected.

Zhang was not without his critics. Lu Deshan, for example, accuses him of 'negating collective human rights'. Lu suggested that the individual and collective are two different aspects of human rights: 'Collective human rights are not derived from individual rights.'[42] Zhang rebukes Lu's criticism by declaring that he did not negate collective human rights. In a spirited defence, however, Zhang maintained that 'collective rights should be a matter for international human rights'.[43]

The question of international human rights has been taken up by Xu Xianming who agreed that collective human rights were problems in international human rights law. But he suggests that the scope of internal human rights should be enlarged. Women, children and teenagers, elderly people, disabled people should be the subject of internal human rights law because these groups would have difficulties in exercising their human rights.[44]

While the debate on individual and collective rights continues, it has led to a better recognition by some scholars that individual rights should also be considered as human rights. There has also been wider acceptance that collective rights and individual rights are interrelated and should be equally protected.[45]

Political rights versus social and economic rights

A different but equally intriguing question posed by Chinese scholars since 1990 has been: Are some rights more important than others? The answer is clearly not straightforward. Li Buyun divides human rights into basic and non-basic rights. But he also points out: 'We have to stress the protection of basic human rights in both domestic and international societies.'[46] While supportng Li's argument that a distinction between basic and non-basic human rights can be made, Zhang Wenxian rejects the claim that economic, social and cultural rights are more important than political rights. Zhang believes that certain rights of the individual, as well as political rights and freedom together with economic and social rights, are all basic human rights.[47]

The inclusion of political and individual rights into basic human rights contradicts the official view that economic rights or rights to subsistence are more basic. But the question posed by writers such as Zhang as to what constitutes basic human rights has remained unresolved.[48]

International protection of human rights and state sovereignty

In discussing the relations between the international protection of human rights and state sovereignty, Chinese scholars are unanimous in believing that the former is subject to the latter.[49] Wei Ming, for example, holds the view that while the principle of human rights protection had been generally accepted, it has not yet been regarded as a fundamental principle of international law. International protection of human rights concerns merely collective human rights and individual human rights have remained essentially matters within the domestic jurisdiction of a state. 'Though international protection of human rights is of importance and, to some extent internationalized, the principle of state sovereignty is still the cornerstone of modern international law.'[50]

But many Chinese scholars also feel that the principle of state sovereignty is not unlimited. Xu Goujin, for example, has pointed out that while individual human rights should be regarded as domestic affairs within the jurisdiction of a sovereign state, a state bears direct and indirect international duties for the protection of international human rights. A state should therefore prevent crimes against international human rights as declared in international treaties, such as international terrorism, genocide and apartheid.[51]

. Other scholars feel that the international protection of human rights consists of two forms of protection: direct and indirect. Direct protection refers to direct interference by the international community, when a state commits crimes such as genocide or apartheid. Indirect intervention refers to the fact that, as sovereign, states are entitled to protect domestic human rights within their own jurisdiction. Indirect protection is regarded as the main form of international protection of human rights.[52] In spite of their different perspectives, most Chinese scholars agree that state sovereignty cannot be obstructed under the guise of the protection of human rights. This view can be seen as 'sovereignty is superior to human rights'.

Another group of scholars believe in the 'equal importance theory', namely, that the international protection of human rights and state sovereignty are of equal importance. Li Ming, for example, believes that the principle of non-interference is difficult to adhere to because the international community has increasingly paid much attention to and shown great concern for the protection of human rights, specifically the violation of human rights on a large scale, such as genocide, apartheid and slavery. While he has not gone so far as saying that the principle of non-interference is not applicable to human rights protection, his conclusion is: 'respecting human rights is a demand of modern times.'[53]

Another writer, Li Ling, offers a compromise solution to solve the conundrum concerning international intervention and sovereign rights. He suggests that the protection of human rights and state sovereignty are necessarily in contradiction. Putting the two concepts in opposing terms is absurd and distorts their value. He believes that there has been a tendency towards the 'internationalization of human rights' and 'relativization of state sovereignty'. The internationalization of human rights is observed as: the internationalization of the values of human rights, of human rights legislation and of the protection of human rights. The internationalization of human rights has restricted state sovereignty. But Li Ling concludes that 'neither violating human rights on the pretext of state sovereignty nor intervening sovereignty under the excuse of protecting human rights is good for world peace and world order'.[54]

Conclusion

The entire spectrum in the field of human rights study in China is beyond the scope of this brief review. Many other problems such as how to safeguard human rights, how to enforce human rights, and how to define the minimum standards of human rights have all generated considerable interest among Chinese scholars in recent years. If this chapter has not provided the full details concerning human rights studies in China, it has demonstrated that since 1990 these studies have come a long way, both in terms of quality and quantity.

The change of the official attitude towards the study of human rights after 1989 is of theoretical and practical significance. First of all, it represents the official acceptance of the term 'human rights'; therefore, the study of human rights may not be politically dangerous. Secondly, protecting and improving human rights as a long-term historical task for socialist states has been implicitly acknowledged. Thirdly, it represents a declaration that, instead of the very negative attitude towards human rights, Marxism is not generally against human rights.

This explains, largely, the 'hot wave of interest in studying human rights' among academic circles in China. Against this background, the study of human rights in China has achieved a lot. The more dogmatic traditional theory of human rights has, to some extent, been replaced. Some basic concepts are understood afresh; for instance, the term 'human rights' is no longer considered a bourgeois concept, the scope of human rights studies has been greatly enlarged, and individual rights have been recognized, to some extent, as human rights.

The influence of Western human rights theory has also become visible. Western terms and concepts, such as dignity, an individual's worth and personal freedom, have appeared in legal writings. Some other Western views have even been accepted; for instance, 'human rights are the rights of an individual because he is a human being'.[55] Citations of Western writers are commonplace among papers on human rights. Some Western works have also been translated into Chinese. Existing human rights studies have, to some extent, influenced the present official standpoint on human rights. Take the white paper *On Human Rights in China*, for example, which has adopted ideas from the articles published. Almost all the issues addressed by the white paper have been discussed in published human rights works.

China's human rights are, to a larger extent, determined by internal and international situations. Although the study of human rights in China is, to a certain extent, the product of international pressure, the impact of scholarly analysis and discussions on human rights questions on China's foreign policy should not be exaggerated. While the government has accepted human rights problems as an issue open to discussion, it will almost certainly try to keep human rights questions off its foreign policy agenda.[56] The government's position on international human rights has been clearly spelt out in the white paper:

. China advocates mutual respect for state sovereignty and maintains that priority should be given to the safeguarding of the right of people of the developing countries to subsistence and development, thus creating the necessary conditions for people all over the world to enjoy various human rights. China is opposed to interfering in other countries' internal affairs on the pretext of human rights and has made unremitting efforts to eliminate various abnormal phenomena and strengthen international cooperation in the field of human rights.[57]

Similarly, the speech made by Liu Huaqing, Vice Foreign Minister of the Foreign Ministry and Head of the Chinese Delegation to the United Nations World Conference on Human Rights in Vienna, reiterated the principle of non-interference, the rights of subsistence and development, and China's different cultural tradition.[58]

Confronting Western criticism of China's human rights record, however, China is and will remain defensive. During the Vienna Human Rights World Conference in June 1993, China shared the views of many other Asian neighbours against the position of Western nations. However, their common position has not provided an opportunity for the conclusion of a regional Asian treaty.

There is little sign that regional cooperation on human rights will become an important issue on the agenda of human rights study in China. But human rights study is definitely now shifting from abstract theory to specific issues with practical significance, for instance questions concerning the right to work, the right to a clean environment, and protecting human rights through due process of law. More recently some authors have also discussed the abolition of capital punishment and the restriction of administrative powers.[59]

As long as the government still aspires to the establishment of 'a system of Chinese (socialist) human rights theory', the study of human rights, building on the basis of the expanding efforts since 1990, will continue to develop in China. While the study of human rights in recent years has been obviously a response to increasing concern over human rights protection in the international community, the continuation of academic enquiry in the field will certainly, and most importantly, accelerate the change of human rights consciousness of the Chinese people.

Notes

*I would like to acknowledge the encouragement from Professor Ian Scott and Mr Albert Chen for the writing of this paper and the presentation at the international colloquium on human rights and foreign policy in March 1993 at the University of Hong Kong. I am also grateful to Professor Raymond Wacks, my supervisor at the University of Hong Kong, for his support to my research on human rights, and to Dr James Tang who helped me to improve the language and style of this paper.

1. The 4 June occurrence has not only been criticized by foreign governments, international public opinions and non-government organizations on human rights, but also by a United Nations Human Rights Committee (Sub-Commission on Prevention of Discrimination and Protection of Discrimination and Protection of Minorities) in its forty-first session in August 1989 in Geneva. It was 'the first time China or any other permanent member of the Security Council has been criticized by a United Nations Human Rights committee'. For details see *South China Morning Post*, 2 September 1989.

2. The Conference on Human Rights Theory was the first such function devoted to the scholary discussion of human rights issues. On 3 December 1988 the Chinese Society of International Law and the Chinese Association of United Nations had organized a symposium on the 40th Anniversary of Universal Declaration of Human Rights in Beijing. Although the development of international human rights law and China's human rights practice were discussed, it was a memorial rather than an academic occasion. For more information see *Chinese Yearbook of International Law*, 1989, p. 518. Human rights were also on the agenda of the

fourth national conference of the young scholars of international law which took place in Xian in late May 1990. A summary of the conference discussions concerning human rights problems can be found in 'The development, jurisdiction and other problems about human right' in *Legal System Daily*, 2 July 1990.

3. Wang Mingfu 'Value explanation and legal realization of human rights', *Nanjing Social Sciences*, vol. 2 (1992), p. 74.
4. Zhang Jinfan (ed.), *Legal History of China* (Beijing: Masses Press, 1987), pp. 489–90.
5. Xu Bing, 'The rise and historic development of human rights theory', *Studies in Law*, vol. 3 (1989), p. 1.
6. In Chinese, 'humanitarianism' and 'humanism' are both called 'rendaozhuyi' and no clear distinction is made between the two.
7. Xing Fengsi, *Humanism in European Philosophical History* (Beijing: People's Press, 1978). See also Zhi Qun, 'Which classes do human rights belong to?' *Xinhua*, 19 April 1979, and Ma Zheming, 'A critical analysis of philosophy of man', *Study and Research*, vol. 1 (1982), pp. 12–15.
8. Huang Nansheng, 'Some theoretical problems about humanism', *Peoples Daily*, 4 June 1981; Ling Jingyao, 'My views of humanity and humanism', *Wenhui Daily*, 8 February 1983; Wang Yilian and Zheng Zhongchao, 'On Marxism and humanism', *Journal of Central China Normal College*, vol. 2 (1983), p. 36.
9. Zhou Yu, 'Inquiring into some theortical questions of Marxism', *People's Daily*, 16 March 1983. See also Lan Ying, 'Are human rights a bourgeois slogan? Discussion with Comrade Xiao Weiyun', *Social Science*, vol. 3 (1979); Wu Daying, 'Analysing human rights historically and concretely', *Studies in Law*, no. 4, 1979; Wang Ruosui, 'A defense for humanism', *Wenhui Daily*, 17 January 1983; Ding Xueliang, 'Marxism is coherent with humanism', *Wenhui Daily*, 12 April 1982; Zhang Xiuping, 'Marxism including humanism', *Qilu Academic Journal*, no. 3 (1983).
10. Hu Qiaomu, 'Some theoretical problems about humanism and alienation', *Peoples Daily*, 4 June 1981, p. 3.
11. Among those scholars who made self-criticisms publicly: Zhou Yang, former Culture Minister, admitted his misunderstanding of humanism and alienation, *People's Daily*, 6 November 1983; Nu Xin, a scholar at the Central Communist Party School, confessed that he confused the differences between Marxism and humanism, and the use of Marxist Humanism was not acceptable, *People's Daily*, 9, 10 and 11 January 1984.
12. Xu Bing, op. cit., p. 8.
13. Si Pingping, 'Judicial independence and protection of human rights', *Science of Law*, vol. 5 (1989), pp. 14, 16.
14. The Constitution of the People's Republic of China (1982), Article 126.
15. Si, op. cit., p. 15.
16. Jie Hua, 'Do not talk abstract human rights,' *Study and Research*, vol. 10 (1989).
17. Yi Jia, 'A critical analysis of bourgeois human rights', *Modern Jurisprudence*, vol. 1 (1990).
18. Gu Chunde, 'Two opposing approaches to human rights', *Legal System Daily*, 11 November 1989, p. 1.
19. Friedrich Engels, 'Anti-Dühring', in *Collected Works of Marx and Engels*, vol. 27, p. 19.
20. Gu Chunde, op. cit., p. 1.
21. ibid., p. 3.
22. Jie Hua, op. cit., p. 38.
23. This is also one of the views expressed by the Chinese government shortly after

4 June. On 18 August, Yu Zhizhong, observer from China at the 41st Session of the Sub-Commission on the Prevention of Discrimination and Protection of Minorities, stated: 'The Chinese constitution and law effectively guarantee the citizens their political, economic, cultural and educational rights, right to religious belief and all the other basic rights.'

24. Zhang Guangbo, 'Adherence to Marxist views on human rights', *Chinese Legal Science*, vol. 4 (1990), p. 16.

25. This is also the view expressed by several Chinese leaders. See Fu Xuezhe, 'On problems about human rights', *Universities Social Sciences*, vol. 1 (1990), p. 14, and Gu Chunde, 'Two opposing approaches,' *Liberation Army's Daily*, 8 May 1991.

26. See Fu Xnezhe, op. cit., p. 16, and Li Huaping, 'Reflections on legal philosophy concerning certain problems of human rights', *Journal of China University of Political Science and Law*, vol. 3 (1990), p. 69.

27. Cheng Jirong, 'Adhere to Marxist human rights approach: critical analysis of France's Declaration of the Rights of Man and the Citizen', *Politics and Law*, vol. 2 (1990), pp. 1-5, and Lai Weifang, 'Rights and wrongs of the problems of human rights', *Study and Research*, vol. 10 (1989), p. 40.

28. Tian Jin, member of the Sub-Commission on the Prevention of Discrimination and Protection of Minorities and former Chinese ambassador to Sweden, spoke out at the 1990 World Law Conference in Beijing on the same issues. A heated debate among the participants followed. See also Zheng Yong, 'The origins and development of the human rights issue in the international arena', *Chinese Legal Science*, vol. 4 (1990), pp. 18-23.

29. Cheng Jirong, op. cit., p. 5 and Li Huaping, op. cit., p. 70.

30. Meng Chunjin, 'Insisting on the Marxist human rights view, rejecting the bourgeois human rights view: brief summary of the Universities Theoretical Conference on Human Rights', *Peoples Daily*, 17 September 1990, p. 5.

31. Some examples of the works which have attempted to defend the government's views include: Gu Chunde, 'Protection and Guarantee of human rights in China'; Wang Dexiang, 'The constitutional guarantee of human rights in China', *Studies in Law*, vol. 4 (1992); Dong Yunhu, 'Special importance of the right to subsistence to the Chinese People'; Lin Xiangquan and Li Qunxing, 'Protection of human rights by the Chinese Labour Law', *Wuhan University Law Journal*, vol. 2 (1992); Jie Tongwen, 'On some theoretical problems of the Marxist view on human rights', *Journal of China University of Political Science and Law*, vol. 1 (1992); Yang Xinghua, 'A critical analysis of human rights foreign policy of the USA', *Zhengming*, vol. 1 (1992); Xu Goujin, 'Limit of fulfilling duties of international human rights by state', *Chinese Legal Science*, vol. 2 (1992); Liu Wenzong, 'On human rights and human rights foreign policy of the USA: an international law perspective', *Peoples Daily*, 10 May 1992; Dong Yunhu and Liu Wuping, *World Documents of Human Rights* (Sichuan: People's Press, 1990).

32. Xu Jianyi (ed.), *Answers to the Questions from the White Paper on Human Rights in China* (Beijing: Chinese Youth Press, 1991), p. 4.

33. Zhang Guangbo, op. cit., p. 10, and Qiao Wei, 'Commenting on the rights of man', *Journal of Literature, History and Philosophy*, vol. 6 (1989), p. 3.

34. Zhang, op. cit., pp. 12, 17.

35. Lin Rendong, 'On human rights and Citizens' rights', *Nanjing Social Sciences*, vol. 1 (1992), pp. 45-7.

36. Li Buyun, 'On the three forms of human rights', *Studies in Law*, vol. 4 (1992a), pp. 12-3.

37. The terms 'civil society' and 'political state' are used by young Marx in his early works, such as *On the Jewish Question: Contribution to the Critique of Hegel's*

Philosophy of Rights.

38. See Zuo Yu and Shu Sheng, 'The basic content of human rights: human rights and citizens' rights', *Chinese Legal Science*, vol. 6 (1991), p. 15.
39. Guo Daohui, 'On the class nature and universality of human rights', *Peking University Law Journal*, vol. 5 (1991), p. 20.
40. Huang Nanshang, 'Marxist philosophy and human rights', *Peking University Law Journal*, vol. 3 (1991), pp. 38–9.
41. Zhang Wenxian, 'On the subject of human rights and subjects' human rights', *Chinese Legal Science* (1991), pp. 26, 27, 29.
42. Lu Deshan, 'Also talking about the subject of human rights', *Chinese Legal Science*, vol. 2 (1992), p. 22.
43. Zhang Wenxian, 'On the subject of human rights and the subject's human rights', *Chinese Legal Science*, vol. 5 (1992), p. 117.
44. Xu Xianming, 'Several theoretical problems on the subject of human rights', *Chinese Legal Science*, vol. 2 (1992), pp. 35, 38.
45. Luo Mingde and He Hangzhou, 'On the individual character of human rights', *Journal of China University of Political Science and Law*, vol. 1 (1993), pp. 58–9.
46. Li Buyun, op. cit., p. 13.
47. Zhang Wenxian, op. cit., p. 33.
48. This is a question that has bothered China's Marxist theorists for years. It emerged again in the debates on alienation, humanism and human rights in late 1970s and early 1980s.
49. Li Lin, 'A summary of symposium: under the guidance of Marxism, progressing to the study of the human rights theory', *Studies in Law*, vol. 5 (1992), p. 21.
50. Wei Ming, 'International human rights and non-interference in internal affairs', *Peking University Law Journal*, vol. 3 (1991), pp. 46, 49.
51. Xu Goujin, 'Limits of fulfilling duties of international human rights', pp. 16–17.
52. Li Linmei, 'The principle of sovereignty and international protection of human rights', *Journal of Foreign Affairs College*, vol. 1 (1992), p. 51.
53. Li Ming, 'Human rights in the Charter of the UN and problems of non-intervention in internal affairs', *Chinese Legal Science*, vol. 3 (1993), p. 43.
54. Li Ling, 'International human rights and state sovereignty', *Chinese Legal Science*, vol. 1 (1993), pp. 40, 41, 44.
55. Dong and Liu, *World Documents of Human Rights*, op. cit., p. 75, and Ye Lixuan and Li Shizhen, *Human Rights Theory* (Fuzhou: Fujian Peoples Press, 1991), p. 1.
56. Chinese political leaders Jiang Zhemin and Li Peng, for example, said so several times to some foreign visitors and they discussed human rights with some of their foreign guests. Some human rights delegations have also visited China since 1991.
57. State Council, *White Paper on Human Rights in China* (Beijing: Information Office of the State Council of China, 1991), p. 79.
58. Liu Huaqing, 'Speech at the UN World Human Rights Conference in Vienna', *Ming Pao* (Hong Kong), 21 June 1993, p. 32.
59. Yang Dunxian and Chen Xingliang, 'The existence and repudiation of capital punishment and the protection of human rights', *Peking University Law Journal*, vol. 6 (1992), pp. 57–63; Wang Tiancheng, 'Those who govern are governed by law: administrative laws and human rights', *Beijing University Law Journal*, vol. 5 (1992), pp. 29–36.

8
HUMAN RIGHTS IN JAPANESE FOREIGN POLICY: JAPAN'S POLICY TOWARDS CHINA AFTER TIANANMEN*

SEIICHIRO TAKAGI

Introduction

The management of Japan's relationship with the rest of Asia is beset with dilemmas inherent in the nation's self-image and history. Identifying itself as a major 'Western' power, but located in a region where non-Western institutions and values remain powerful and where memories of its aggression are still very much alive, Japan is often faced with ambivalent requirements and conflicting demands. However, merely balancing such demands has become increasingly inappropriate as Japan's political role has gradually expanded with its rising international economic standing. No country renders Japan's Asia dilemma more intractable than China. It is an enormous neighbour with which Japan must maintain a friendly relationship. The pre-1945 history of the Japanese invasion of China makes the effort to do so even a moral imperative in the minds of many Japanese. Yet China remains one of the countries with institutions and an ideology of which the Western world is most critical. Deng Xiaoping's reforms since late 1978 have made China's economy increasingly marketable and open to the outside world. At the same time, however, its political institutions and ideology have remained basically intact, thus becoming a focus of concern in the West.

In terms of issues, the protection of human rights and democratization are the ones that make Japan's dilemma most salient. On the one hand, most Asian countries have some form of authoritarian political system with questionable human rights conditions, especially on civil and political issues. Therefore, their leadership tends to perceive Western criticisms and demands over these issues as a threat to their regimes and to reject them as interference with their domestic affairs. On the other hand, Japan's commitment to democratic political institutions and the protection of human rights has become increasingly established in the post-war era, even though its impact on Japanese diplomatic behaviour has been rather limited.

The military suppression of the mass protest and the accompanying bloodshed around Tiananmen Square in Beijing at just before dawn on 4 June 1989 posed a tremendous challenge to Japanese diplomacy. With the Tiananmen incident, Japan's commitment to Western institutions and values was tested *vis-à-vis* its most important neighbour, a country extremely resistant to imposition of 'external values'. What made the challenge even more exacting was the fact that Japan's principal ally, the United States, was the leading force imposing sanctions on China as a result of the bloody suppression.

Human rights in Japanese diplomacy

Japan began post-Second World War reconstruction under the occupation of
the allied powers and in 1946 accepted a totally new constitution drafted by
the occupation authority, which spelled out a democratic political system for
Japan and guaranteed basic human rights to the people. The steady institutionalization of democratic practices and human rights protection since then
shows that these principles increasingly took root in the society. But it was not
until Japan was admitted to the United Nations in December 1956 that it
started to profess such commitment internationally.

Embracing the UN Charter and the Universal Declaration of Human
Rights, Japan participated actively in the UN deliberations on the Draft International Covenant on Economic, Social and Cultural Rights at the first opportunity in the eleventh General Assembly. The Japanese delegation focused its
discussions on the issue of improvement of living standards and emphasized
the importance of international cooperation.[1] Since then the UN has been the
primary setting for Japan's 'human rights diplomacy'. Japan's approach to
human rights issues in the UN has reflected the need to consider both the
Western political identity and the Asian geo-cultural identity from the very
early stages. Japan approached this problem by taking a moderate position
and opposing radical measures proposed by either side.

In the 1960s the UN deliberations on racial discrimination in South Africa,
which had begun in 1952, entered a new phase with the admission to the UN
of more than ten sub-Sahara nations. African nations, now more numerous,
proposed economic sanctions against South Africa and the issue became the
focal point of the UN debate on human rights. Japan took sides with
Asian–African nations by agreeing to place the issue on the General Assembly
agenda and professing opposition to racial discrimination. But it set itself
apart from them by arguing against hasty imposition of economic sanctions.[2]
When the UN deliberations on the draft Covenant on Political and Civil
Rights reached the final stage in 1966 and discussed the implementation
clauses, Japan again took sides with the Asian–African group. Japan opposed
the obligatory mediation of the violation charges against any country. It was
also critical of the proposal to allow violation appeals to the Human Rights
Commission by individuals and private groups on the grounds that it was
neither accepted by a sufficient number of countries nor was it practical.[3]

The 1970s saw the growing politicization of the human rights issue in the
UN. The traditional Western approach emphasizing the rights of individuals
clashed with the approach taken by Asian–African and socialist countries
which focused on the rights of groups.[4] Japan could do very little in this
situation. The introduction of the Human Rights Covenants (A and B) in 1976
created the means to deal with the issue but Japan had not ratified the
Covenants. Outside the UN, Japan came under attack from foreign countries
for certain human rights practices such as fingerprinting foreigners, including
those Koreans and Chinese who had been forced to move to Japan during the

war and had stayed. The Japanese government could only take a defensive position.

With the ratification of the Human Rights Covenants in 1980, so Japan's involvement in the issue gradually expanded during that decade. In 1982 Japan became a member of the Human Rights Commission under the Economic and Social Council of the UN. In 1984 two law professors from Japan took part, as individuals, in the Sub-Commission on the Prevention of Discrimination and Protection of Minorities (the Human Rights Sub-Commission), and Japan became involved in all the human rights fora in the UN. In the same year the Japanese Foreign Ministry created the Human Rights and Refugee Division within the UN Department to strengthen the handling of the issue.

The politicization of the human rights issue in the UN continued throughout the 1980s. But with increased involvement and international standing, Japan's attempt to defuse the issue was sometimes effective. In 1987 the deliberation on the US draft resolution on human rights conditions in Cuba was approaching its final stage and both the United States and Cuba tried hard to block each other. Japan conducted several consultations with each country in order to effect substantive improvement in Cuba. This effort was instrumental in the adoption of the Latin American proposal to send an investigation team to Cuba.[5]

Thus, even though human rights had not become a central element of Japan's foreign policy, by the end of the 1980s Japan's involvement in the issue had grown substantially and its role in international human rights protection had become increasingly significant.

Japan–China relations before Tiananmen

Since the normalization of Sino-Japanese relations in 1972, the bilateral relationship has experienced cycles of conflict mostly related to the emotionally charged issue of Japan's military ventures in China before 1945. Yet with each conflict the situation has become more containable and a deeper and more extended relationship has resulted. Thus just before the Tiananmen incident the relationship was in fairly good shape, with significant progress on all major aspects. Overall Sino-Japanese trade in 1988 had reached a record high of $19.3 billion. Japan had been China's leading trading partner for a number of years and China's share in Japan's total trade had risen steadily. China's balance of trade, which became a serious concern in 1985 when it imported from Japan twice as much as it exported, steadily improved and became a Chinese surplus of $400 million in 1988. These trends continued in 1989.

In terms of investment in China, Japan remained third after Hong Kong-Macau and the United States. This, together with insufficient technology transfer, was still the major cause of China's complaints. However, the amount of investment had been increasing and the content had begun to shift from service to manufacturing. With the signing of the Investment Protection Agreement in August 1988, a large-scale investment with significant technology transfer began (e.g. Matsushita's TV tube production). Since China de-

cided to accept economic assistance from the West in late 1978, Japan had
been by far the most willing provider. The total net disbursement by the end
of 1988 was over \$3.25 billion. In 1988 Japan provided 55.5 per cent of total
bilateral Official Development Aid (ODA) to China. Even including multilateral aid, Japan's share exceeds 35 per cent. In August 1988, Japan announced
the plan of the Third Yen Loan Programme (TYLP) for fiscal years 1990–5.
Within a year before the Tiananmen incident heads of both governments had
visited each other. During Japanese Prime Minister Noboru Takeshita's trip
to Beijing in August 1988 the Investment Protection Agreement was signed
and the TYLP was announced. In April 1989, just before the beginning of the
student demonstration, Premier Li Peng went to Tokyo.

Needless to say, problems remained. The legal complications of the
Guanghua dormitory issue, which led to a barrage of Chinese attacks in 1987,
were still unresolved. The occasional comments on the Second World War by
conservative politicians continued to irritate the Chinese every now and then,
the latest case being Takeshita's statement in February 1989 when he suggested in the Diet that any judgement on whether the Second World War was
a war of aggression on the part of Japan should be left to a later era. However,
these problems were effectively contained and did not become serious enough
to disrupt the basically good relationship. The international situation was also
favourable. The steadily improving relationship between the United States
and China since mid-1983 and the Sino-Soviet *rapprochement*, which culminated in Gorbachev's visit to Beijing in May 1989, made the friendly relationship between Japan and China compatible with the interests of both
superpowers.

Japan's Tiananmen shock

The bloodshed around Tiananmen Square caused a tremendous shock wave
in Japan just as in many Western countries. A Japanese public opinion poll
showed a sharp decline of respondents who mentioned China as one of the
three countries they liked, from 17.3 per cent in May to 4.9 per cent in June.
Correspondingly, those who mentioned China as one of the three countries
they disliked shot from 5.4 per cent to 27.1 per cent.[6]

Japan's official reaction, however, was somewhat different from Western
governments. The Japanese government was not uncritical but its verbal reaction was rather non-accusatory and circumspect. The earliest official statement made on 4 June by a Foreign Ministry spokesman merely said: 'We are
gravely concerned with the development of the situation where the military's
use of force led to bloodshed. The Japanese government strongly hopes that
the situation does not deteriorate any further.' The statement even showed
some understanding of the Chinese government's position by characterizing
the movement of the students and citizens as 'anti-government'.[7] Foreign
Minister Hiroshi Mitsuzuka was equally mild, saying on the same day: 'It is
regrettable that the bloodshed took place when China was making steady
progress along the line of liberalization. I hope the Chinese situation will
resume calm as soon as possible.'[8] Prime Minister Sosuke Uno's comment was

not made until the next day. In response to reporters' questioning he only said: 'We are seriously concerned. I pray for a return to calm.'[9] In response to the report that the US government had imposed sanctions including a ban on military sales and exchanges, the Japanese position vacillated. At first both Foreign Minister Mitsuzuka and Minister of International Trade and Industry Seiroku Kajiyama expressed reluctance to follow suit.[10] Soon after categorically denying that Japan would impose sanctions on China, however, Prime Minister Uno suggested that it was not yet time for making the decision.[11]

Generally speaking, while the public were not sufficiently outraged to demand sanctions, they were frustrated by their political leaders' rather muted public stance, especially in comparison with other Western leaders. When Takashi Ishiwara, Chairman of *Keizai Doyukai* (Japan Association of Corporate Executives), one of the four major business organizations, openly expressed this frustration and urged the government to make a more forceful statement, the organization received many encouraging calls from the public.[12] However, even when the government eventually took a critical stand, it remained reluctant to take sides. On 7 June, Uno finally said in the Diet: 'It is a grave matter [for the army] to point guns at the people. It should not have happened.' But he also said, 'we should avoid passing judgement of right or wrong', and ruled out sanctions.[13]

A corollary to this attitude is Japan's willingness to accept the principle of non-interference in domestic affairs, much more so than other Western nations. When Deputy Foreign Minister Ryohei Murata protested to the Chinese Ambassador Yang Zhenya by saying that the Japanese government 'cannot condone on humanitarian grounds' the actions of the Chinese government, he also confirmed that Japan had 'no intention of intervening in the domestic affairs' of China.[14] When the Chinese executed the participants in the demonstrations and the US government in protest imposed additional sanctions on 20 June,[15] the Japanese position was that it was a domestic problem of China and the Japanese government only expressed hope that the Chinese government would refrain from actions which would invite accusations from the international community.[16]

Another related characteristic was the relative lack of reference to human rights and democratic values. The first official reference to democracy was not made until 16 June, when Foreign Minister Mitsuzuka said that the continued crackdown on students and intellectuals by the Chinese government was 'not compatible with the basic values of Japan which is a democratic state'.[17] The first reference to human rights was even later. On 23 June Mitsuzuka finally said: 'Japan shared with the US and European nations concern over human rights and humanitarianism.'[18] Most of the official criticisms of the Chinese government were based on humanitarian grounds, not on appeals to human rights or democratic values. This tendency was not limited to the government. Even Ishiwara's criticism of the government's muted response characterized the incident as a 'humanitarian issue'.[19]

Unlike the relatively mild verbal response, actions taken by the Japanese government were not necessarily less severe than those of Western governments. But such measures were taken somewhat later and were presented in either a distinctly apolitical manner or with no clear political explanations. The

Ministry of Foreign Affairs officially advised Japanese citizens not to visit
Beijing even for business trips. This advice was issued immediately on 4 June
and was extended to the whole of China three days later.[20] On 20 June the
Foreign Ministry decided to freeze new economic assistance projects, including all the preparatory procedures for the TYLP for the fiscal years 1990-5. The
decision was related to the press immediately without an official statement.
The policy of avoiding minister-level contacts with China was revealed to the
press on 29 June. But a top Foreign Ministry official explained it as not
constituting a 'clearly defined measure'.[21]

Determinants of Japan's official reaction

One of the factors which restrained the government's reactions was the recognition that worse atrocities had been committed by the Japanese army
during the war and the political reality that it is still an issue, very much alive
if not always salient, in the relationship with China. Prime Minister Uno made
this point as early as 6 June when he denied the possibility of sanctions. This
consideration, along with geographical proximity, he maintained, made the
Japan–China relationship different from that between the United States and
China.[22] Similar feelings were widely held within and outside the government.
The government, especially the Foreign Ministry, was afraid that careless
criticisms could immediately invite counter-attacks from the Chinese leadership which might use it as a scapegoat to which to redirect students' frustration; then Japan's bilateral relations with China would deteriorate.[23] And, as
Prime Minister Uno stated on 7 June, a more immediate additional consideration was the concern for the safe evacuation of the 8,300 Japanese nationals
in China.[24]

   Another factor which restrained Japanese reaction, especially in the sphere
of economic sanctions, was the perceived danger of isolating and destabilizing
China. Prime Minister Uno expressed concern over the isolation of China as
early as 6 June.[25] From the Japanese point of view, the biggest step in this
direction would be cancellations of Official Development Aid (ODA). But the
Japanese government, especially the Foreign Ministry, believed that since
Japan was the biggest provider of ODA to China its suspension would be far
more destructive than economic sanctions imposed by any other Western
countries.[26] It is undeniable that part of the concern over economic disruption
was a consideration of business interests, which certainly were not negligible.
The business community was one of the most vocal groups pointing to the
danger of isolating China.[27] But that is not the whole story. The Japanese
government also feared that economic disruption might lead to political instability, which in turn could create instability in Asia and eventually the
world.[28]

   The fear of possible economic disruption and political instability in China
was linked to the concern that Japan might be inundated by Chinese boat
people. This fear was not based on fanciful imagination caused by the enor-
mity of the Chinese population; in fact, it had existed in the minds of some

since the 1970s, and assumed an added sense of urgency and came to be shared by more people in the year of the Tiananmen incident. From May 1989 there was a new wave of arrivals in western Japan of 'Vietnamese refugees' by boat. Many of those who arrived were suspected of being Chinese from southern China.[29]

Interestingly, especially in light of the US situation, the government's response to the Tiananmen incident did not become an issue in Japanese domestic politics. It is true that some of the stronger governmental statements were made in response to questions in Diet sessions. But most of the opposition parties issued statements only minimally more accusatory than the government. They were equally uncertain as to what measures should be taken and were equally reluctant to impose sanctions on China.[30] The only exception was the Japan Communist Party (JCP), which was anxious not to be associated with the Chinese Communist Party. In a Central Committee statement the party 'denounce[d] with anger the unspeakable act of violence committed by the leadership of the Party and the government'.[31] Their concern was not without foundation. The JCP turned out to be the only opposition party to lose in the Upper House election of July 1989 which resulted in the historic defeat of the ruling Liberal Democratic Party (LDP). The activities of private groups critical of the Chinese government were limited to helping Chinese students and issuing their own statements of condemnation. They had little impact on the policies of the Japanese government. In fact some critics expressed scepticism on 'human rights diplomacy' as a policy instrument of rich countries against countries that were weaker or hostile. One critic warned that if China's economy stagnated, it would cause misery inside China and also threaten China's neighbours. He asked: 'Which is the more serious human rights problem? [the armed suppression of demonstration or severe sanctions in the name of "human rights diplomacy"?]'[32]

If there were ample considerations which restrained the Japanese government from reacting forcefully to the Tiananmen incident, the possibility of Japan's own isolation among the Western nations exerted pressure in the opposite direction. Japan's relationship with China, important as it was, could not be promoted without blessing from other Western nations, especially the United States. Thus the Japanese government was quite sensitive to Western criticism of Japan's involvement in China.

In mid-June the *Financial Times* published an article which sarcastically described how hastily Japanese businessmen, who had just been evacuated on special planes, were returning to China. The newspaper commented that they put economic considerations ahead of moral concerns. This was exactly the kind of criticism the government was worried about. Instead of pointing out that businessmen from Western countries were behaving in similar ways, when Foreign Minister Mitsuzuka referred to the article a few days later, he evoked the image of thieves at the site of a fire and criticized Japanese businessmen.[33] Moreover, in spite of the business community's counter-criticisms, the Foreign Ministry formally requested three major business organizations on 22 June to 'be prudent' in sending their member companies' staff back to China.[34] What the Western country Japan was most concerned with was obviously the United States. Just weeks before the Tiananmen incident, US-Japan bilateral trade friction had reached another height when the US government had evoked the 'Super 301' provision of the 1988 Omnibus Trade and Competitiveness Act to name Japan as one of the countries with unfair trade practices. The 'revisionist' arguments, that Japan did not share Western values and institutions, had been gaining influence in the United States. There was fear in Japan that its moderate treatment of China might become the flashpoint of another round of 'Japan-bashing', especially in the Congress. The development in US-China relations and Congressional deliberation on China sanctions were closely followed in Japan.

The Japanese government decided to send Foreign Minister Mitsuzuka to the United States on 25 June to confirm that the differences between the two governments were not that great and took measures to bring Japan's words and deeds closer to the US position. The decision to freeze ODA programmes was made with this visit in mind.[35] In Washington, Mitsuzuka revealed Japan's decision to postpone the sixth Japan–China Ministerial Conference, which had been expected to be held in Tokyo later that year. At a meeting with the American Secretary of State James Baker, he also said that Japan 'could not condone as a human-rights problem' the armed suppression by the Beijing authority and emphasized 'the need for considerations not to push China back into isolation'. He argued that Japan and the United States might differ in their manner of expression and nuance but the basic thinking was the same. To his relief, Secretary Baker concurred.[36]

Japan's post-Tiananmen international manoeuvre

The occasion which threatened to challenge Japan's Western identity was the G-7 Paris Summit of the seven leading industrialized countries in mid-July 1989. The government started to think about the problem immediately after the Tiananmen incident.[37] By late June it concluded that it should conform with the position of the Western nations.[38] But Japan still found it difficult to join other G-7 members in supporting a resolution which would accuse China by explicitly naming it.[39]

Confronted with this challenge the Japanese government did not limit its effect to accommodation but actually tried to convince other members of the danger of isolating China. Mitsuzuka's trip to Washington in late June was the first step. Then at the ASEAN post-ministerial conference in early July, he tried to muster ASEAN support for Japan's position by pointing to the danger of pushing China back towards a closer relationship with the Soviet Union.[40] At preparatory sessions in Paris, the Japanese delegates reaffirmed its willingness to support, with economic aid, the US effort in assisting reform in Eastern Europe in order to secure American backing. They also expressed concern for Hong Kong in an attempt to gain British support.[41]

In the end the Summit did adopt the Declaration on China which reiterated their condemnation of 'violent repression in defiance of human rights'. But the sanctions mentioned were only those which were already in place and included no new measures. The Declaration included a passage which referred to avoiding the isolation of China, reflecting the Japanese concern. Japan's objective, however, was not simply to soften the Western accusation against China's human rights violations. The Declaration on Human Rights at the Summit clearly committed Japan to the Western position on human rights. The Declaration stated that human rights is a legitimate international concern, in clear opposition to the Chinese position that it should be under the exclusive control of state sovereignty. It also unequivocally gave priority to the rights to freedom of thought, conscience, religion, opinion and expression as the basis of other rights. The right to development, which China and many developing countries emphasize, was not even mentioned in the Declaration.

At about the same time as the Paris Summit, Japan was involved in another international forum on the Tiananmen incident, though not at the intergovernmental level, when it was brought up at the UN Human Rights Sub-Commission. A non-governmental Japanese member of the Sub-Commission, Professor Riboh Hatanos, took part in the deliberations with Japan–China relations in mind. In anticipation of a harsh draft resolution, Professor Hatanos was intending to argue for a more moderate version, and was prepared to abstain if a harsh version were to be introduced. However, since the Sub-Commission decided to use a secret ballot for this case, making it impossible for him to express his position through voting, he joined in the drafting of the resolution. In order to assure the widest possible support, the draft finally submitted was a very mild one. The resolution adopted on 31 August expressed concern only about 'the events which took place recently in China' and 'their consequences in the field of human rights', and made an appeal for 'clemency in favour of persons deprived of their liberty as a result of the above-mentioned events'. It neither made any accusation against the Chinese government nor mentioned Tiananmen, not even the date of the incident. Nevertheless, it is still the first case in which a human rights resolution on a permanent member of the UN Security Council was passed at the Sub-Commission.[42]

The re-normalization of the Japan–China relationship

After the relative success of the Summit and with the situation in China stabilizing, the major concern of the Japanese government was how to restore normal relations. The task involved encouraging non-governmental visits, ending the freeze in new economic aid, and rebuilding official contacts. Throughout this process the Japanese government continued to be sensitive to the positions of other Western nations, especially the United States without compromising its own initiative.

The first sign of relaxation came from the government. On 19 August it lifted the travel warning pertaining to China outside Beijing and resumed the economic assistance projects which had been temporarily suspended. The first major non-governmental visit to China was made in mid-September by the Diet Member's League for Japan–China Friendship, a non-partisan organization. The delegation was led by former Foreign Minister Masayoshi Ito and carried a message from Prime Minister Toshiki Kaifu. They were met by all key members of the post-Tiananmen Chinese leadership, including Premier Li

Peng, Party General Secretary Jiang Zemin and 'Paramount Leader' Deng Xiaoping. Ito told them frankly how China's international reputation had suffered because of the incident. Li Peng admitted that he understood the embarrassment of the Japanese engaged in business with China. He also said that they regretted the incident and that they would try to be more responsive to popular grievances.[43]

On 25 September the official travel warning was lifted for Beijing. A few days later a 150-member youth delegation led by a major LDP Diet member visited Beijing and Foreign Ministers of both countries met at the UN. In mid-November the Japan–China Economic Association, which consists of Japanese companies with business interests in China, sent a delegation of business leaders to Beijing. In observance of the suspension of official contacts, the Ministry of International Trade and Industry (MITI) and the Export Import Bank, which normally send their personnel as members of such delegations, avoided involvement on this occasion.

The sudden visit to Beijing by US National Security Advisor Brent Scowcroft and Under Secretary of State Lawrence Eagleburger in early December led to calls in Japan for the acceleration of the normalization process. The Japanese government decided to resume preparations for the TYLP within the Foreign Ministry and to invite Zou Jiahua, Chairman of China's State Planning Commission, to Tokyo in January 1990.

After Zou's visit to Tokyo the normalization process was bogged down for a while as the criticism within the United States of the Bush administration's secrecy in sending the Scowcroft-Eagleburger team stalled the US–China normalization process. But with the Bush administration's decision in late May to extend China's most-favoured-nation status for another year, the Japanese government judged that the worst was over with regard to US–China relations, and decided to work for the initiation of the TYLP after the G-7 Summit in Houston.[44] China's agreement in mid-June to allow Fang Lizhi, a prominent pro-democracy leader who had taken refuge in the US embassy after the Tiananmen incident, to leave the country removed another obstacle to Japan's effort.

Prime Minister Kaifu met President Bush on 7 July, just before the Houston Summit, and obtained his agreement concerning Japan's stance towards the TYLP. Because of this and other efforts of persuasion, when the plan was presented to the full Summit no country was irreconcilably opposed to it. However, the Political Declaration adopted at the Summit still included a section which, while acknowledging the recent progress, urged China to pursue further political and economic reform, especially in the field of human rights. It also reconfirmed the need of sanctions mentioned in the 1989 summit Declaration on China, though at the same time accepting the modifications which had been made during the year. Sensitive to Western reservations, the Japanese government offered to limit its loans to China in the fiscal year 1990 to humanitarian items and to lift suspension of the TYLP only in stages.[45]

In September former Prime Minister Takeshita went to Beijing to convey the Japanese government's decision. In the same month Education Minister Kosuke Hori attended the opening ceremony of the Asian Games in Beijing — the first minister-level visit to China since the Tiananmen incident. The negotiations for implementation of the first year stage of the TYLP began in October. However, as promised at the Houston Summit, the Japanese government limited the loan to humanitarian items and provided it in three instalments.

In early 1991, high-level official contacts were fully resumed. Key Japanese Cabinet members visited China in rapid succession: Finance Minister Ryutaro Hashimoto in January, MITI Minister Ichiro Nakao in March, Foreign Minister Taro Nakayama in April. From the Chinese side, Minister of Foreign Economic and Trade Relations Li Lanqing and Vice-Chairman of State Gu Mu visited Tokyo in April, followed by Foreign Minister Qian Qichen in June. In August Prime Minister Kaifu became the first G-7 leader to visit Beijing after the Tiananmen incident. He announced that in the fiscal year 1991 the TYLP would be provided in a lump sum and would not be limited to humanitarian items, thus completing the process of restoring normal relations.

Japan's post-Cold War human rights diplomacy

Reversing the tendency immediately after the Tiananmen incident, the process of normalization accompanied increasingly demanding Japanese official statements on China which, though still considerably milder than those of other Western leaders, made more explicit references to the 'Western' values of human rights and democracy. This reflected an increasing articulation of 'Western' values in overall Japanese foreign policy. In January 1990, Foreign Minister Nakayama had already told Zou Jiahua, then visiting Japan, that greater effort for the improvement of relations between China and Western countries should come from the Chinese side. When Prime Minister Kaifu declared to the Diet in March that Japan should make a contribution to the establishment of the post-Cold war 'new international order', he clearly stated that this order should embody respect for freedom and democracy.[46] In the same month, Japan joined other G-7 countries in presenting a draft resolution on China to the 46th session of the UN Human Rights Commission. The draft resolution endorsed the August 1989 appeal of the Human Rights Sub-Commission for clemency towards the detainees of the Tiananmen incident, welcomed the Chinese government decision in January 1990 to release 573 detainees, and urged it to continue to take measures along the same lines.[47]

The end of the Gulf War in February 1991 accelerated the search for Japan's role in the post-Cold War world through a disappointing realization that Japan's contribution of $11 billion, for which people had to bear additional taxes, did not earn any international appreciation. The discussion quickly focused on the Official Development Assistance (ODA), through which Japan was becoming the world's number one donor, as the principal tool. The consensus that emerged was that Japan should have a clearly stated principle for its ODA. This provided another opportunity for articulating Japan's commitment to democracy and human rights in its management of foreign relations. In April 1991, the government announced 'Four Guidelines' on ODA: the recipient countries were to be examined on (1) the trend in military expenditure, (2) the trend in development and production of weapons of mass destruction, (3) the trend in the arms trade, and (4) efforts being made for the promotion of democracy and a market economy and basic human rights and freedom conditions.[48]

During his visit to Beijing in August, Prime Minister Kaifu explained these Guidelines to the Chinese leaders. He urged them to join the Nuclear Non-Proliferation Treaty (NPT) and to support the Japanese effort to establish a registration system for the sale of international arms at the UN. He also pointed out that China's positive measures on democracy and human rights would enhance its international status. These guidelines were not directed to punish 'violators', but were clearly formulated to persuade recipient countries towards more acceptable behaviour. China's response indicated that this approach can work. Premier Li Peng told Prime Minister Kaifu that China had decided in principle to join NPT and appreciated Japan's effort to control the sale of arms internationally. He also indicated willingness to discuss human rights issues with the international community. When the ODA Charter, with four principles, was adopted by the Cabinet in June 1992, the first three items of the Guidelines were amalgamated into one principle but the fourth guideline (on the issues of democratization, marketization, and human rights and freedom) remained intact, constituting the fourth principle.[49]

In 1993 Japan's identification with the Western position on the issue of human rights and democracy went one step further, within the context of the World Conference on Human Rights. At the preparatory regional meeting for Asia held in Bangkok in March, the Japanese representative did not shy away from making the following arguments: (1) human rights are a universal factor common to all mankind and a matter for legitimate concern among the international community; (2) human rights should not be sacrificed for development; (3) when development assistance is to be provided full attention should be paid to the situation regarding human rights and freedom in the recipient countries.[50] Predictably, Asian countries attacked the Japanese position for being too Western, China being the chief accuser.[51] But that did not affect the basic position of the Japanese government. While Japan supported the consensus in the form of the Bangkok Declaration, which articulated the 'Asian position', out of 'a spirit of cooperation and compromise', at the same time it issued an 'explanation of the vote' which expressed reservations on some key points of the Declaration. In addition the Japanese delegation argued for the need of regional machinery for the promotion and protection of human rights.[52] At the UN World Conference in Vienna in June, the Japanese envoy, Nobuo Matsunaga, elaborated Japan's arguments in Bangkok.

Conclusions

The Tiananmen incident posed a tremendous challenge to Japan's management of foreign relations. The Asian dilemma it confronted was made more complicated by the highly critical issues of human rights and democracy in a major neighbouring country which had suffered Japanese invasion in the Second World War. Initially Japan emphasized the need to prevent the isolation of China while silently taking the same measures as the West. However, when Japanese leaders felt assured that China would not be isolated, their concern for Japan's own isolation among the Western powers became more important. Japan took the unequivocal step of identifying itself with Western values of democracy and human rights at the G-7 Paris Summit in July 1989. After the Summit, it expressed its commitment to Western human rights values with increasing clarity, while at the same time removing the post-Tiananmen sanctions. The end of the Gulf War in February 1991 provided further impetus to Japan's articulation of its human rights commitment. With a greater sense of its responsibility for the emerging post-Cold War world order, Japan's commitment to human rights and democracy was now embedded in the principle for its provision of ODA, the single most important resource Japan has in its international relations. This was confirmed at the World Conference on Human Rights in Vienna in June 1993 despite harsh criticisms by some other Asian nations, including China.

This, however, is not and should not be the end of the story. Japan's 'Western' identity in the field of human rights does not change its geo-cultural identity. Nor does such a commitment absolve Japan from the responsibility of finding ways to work with other Asian nations to effect substantial progress in human rights protection. Effective fulfilment of this responsibility requires further efforts within Japan as well as deeper understanding of other Asian nations. The critical issue would be a more straightforward acceptance of its responsibility for the damages it caused to Asian people during the Second World War. The recent political change in Japan which ended the decades-long LDP domination might turn out to be critical in liberating the Japanese from the mental and psychological restraints of the past, as the new prime minister's bold acceptance of the aggressive nature of the war suggests. This, along with the potential for the emergence of a more effective policy formulation process, represents an encouraging development but success is far from assured.

Notes

*I would like to thank Professor Akio Watanabe for his comments on the earlier draft, and Ms Keiko Okaido, Professor Koshi Yamazaki, Ms. Anne Emig and Ms. Keiko Okaido for the materials they made available to me.

1. Gaimusho (Ministry of Foreign Affairs), *Waga Gaiko no Kinkyo* (Recent Developments in Japanese Diplomacy) (1957), pp. 123–4.
2. *Waga Gaiko no Kinkyo* (1967), pp. 38–9.
3. *Waga Gaiko no Kinkyo* (1967), pp. 86–9.
4. *Waga Gaiko no Kinkyo* (1973), pp. 333–4.
5. Gaimusho, *Gaiko Seisho: Waga Gaiko no Kinkyo* (Diplomatic Blue Book: Recent Developments in Japanese Diplomacy) (1988), p. 82.
6. The poll is conducted by the Jiji News Agency every month and is published in their weekly *Shukan Jiji*.
7. Gaimusho (n.d.), *Chugoku no Jinkenmondai nitaisuru Wagakuni no Taioh* (Japan's Response to Human Rights Problems in China), p. 2.
8. *Nihon Keizai Shimbum* (Japan Economic Newspaper) hereafter *Nikkei*, 5 June 1989.

9. *Asahi Shimbum* (Asahi Newspaper), hereafter *Asahi*, 5 June 1989 (evening edition).
10. *Nikkei*, 6 June 1989.
11. *Asahi*, 6 June 1989.
12. *Nikkei*, 7 and 8 June 1989.
13. *Nikkei*, 8 June 1989.
14. *Asahi*, 8 June 1989.
15. The principal component of the sanctions was a ban on high-level official contacts and opposition to China loan programmes in international financial institutions.
16. *Asahi*, 24 June 1989.
17. *Asahi*, 16 June 1989 (evening edition).
18. *Nikkei*, 24 June 1989.
19. Ishiwara referred to the Tiananmen incident as a clearly humanitarian problem. See *Kekkei*, 7 June 1989.
20. The Ministry of Foreign Affairs' travel advice is divided into three categories according to the seriousness of the situation. The first category is called *Toko Jishiku* (travel advice to defer non-essential trips), the second is called *Kanko Ryoko Jishuku Kankoku* (travel advice to defer sightseeing tours), and the third is *Chu Kanki* (travel caution). The Ministry issued the category one travel advice during the Tiananmen crisis. None of the three categories is legally binding.
21. *Nikkei*, 30 June 1989.
22. *Asahi*, 6 June 1989.
23. *Asahi*, 7 June 1989.
24. *Asahi*, 8 June 1989.
25. *Asahi*, 6 June 1989 (evening edition).
26. *Nikkei*, 6 June 1989.
27. *Asahi*, 22 June 1989.
28. *Asahi*, 7 June 1989.
29. *Nikkei*, 30 August 1989.
30. *Asahi*, 5 June 1989.
31. *Nikkei*, 5 June 1989.
32. T. Okabe, 'Tenanmon-Jiken to Kongo no Chugoku' (The Tiananmen incident and China's future', *Kokusai Mondai* [International Affairs], no. 359 (2–16 January 1990).
33. *Nikkei*, 17 June 1989.
34. *Asahi*, 23 June 1989.
35. *Asahi*, 20 June 1989 (evening edition).
36. *Asahi*, 27 June 1989 (evening edition).
37. *Nikkei*, 6 June 1989.
38. *Nikkei*, 20 June 1989.
39. *Asahi*, 24 June 1989.
40. *Nikkei*, 7 July 1989.
41. *Asahi*, 16 July 1989.
42. R. Hatano, 'Jinken Shohiinkai no Kino: Sono "dokuritusei" to "seijisei" (The function of the Human Rights Sub-Commission: its 'independence' and 'political nature'), *Kokusai Jinken* (Human Rights International), no. 1 (1990), pp. 44–7.
43. *Asahi*, 18 September 1989.
44. *Nikkei*, 3 June 1990.
45. *Nikkei*, 10 July 1990 (evening edition).
46. Gaimusho, *Gaikou Seisho* (1990), p. 290.
47. Pakistan's motion of no action overruled this draft resolution.

48. Gaimusho Keizai Kyoryoku Kyoku [Department of Economic Co-operation, Ministry of Foreign Affairs], *Wagakuni no Seifu Kaihatsu Enjo* [Japans Official Development Assistance], (1991), p. 58.
49. Gaimusho Keizai-Kyoryoku Kyoku, (1992), p. 360. The other two principles are: Japan should pursue development compatible with environmental protection, and Japan should avoid the military use of aid and the aggravation of international conflict.
50. Seiichero Otsuka, 'Statement by Seiichero Otsuka, Minister, Embassy of Japan in Thailand and Representative of Japan to the Regional Meeting for Asia of the World Conference on Human Rights', *Jiyuto Seig*, vol. 44, no. 11 (1993), pp. 106–5.
51. G. Fairclough, 'Standing firm: Asia sticks to its view of human rights', *Far Eastern Economic Review*, 15 April 1993, p. 22.
52. Otsuka, 'Statement by Minister', pp. 105–6.

9

PEOPLE'S DIPLOMACY AND HUMAN RIGHTS: THE PHILIPPINE EXPERIENCE

FRANCISCO NEMENZO

Introduction

When the government is seen as a guardian of human rights, citizens turn to it for protection; but when perceived as a violator, people fight it with any weapon accessible. Forms of popular resistance may range from cracking political jokes to armed rebellion. People's diplomacy is a benign weapon the Filipinos learnt to use in the struggle against the Marcos dictatorship. The term 'people's diplomacy' is a term used by the Philippine mass movement and non-governmental organizations (NGOs) which simply means the efforts of private groups to counter the diplomatic initiatives of a repressive state.

Mass movements and NGOs resort to people's diplomacy when supposedly democratic governments—as a *raison d'etat*—subsidize, train and equip the armies of repressive states. At the height of the Cold War, for example, the self-designated leader of the 'free world' paid court to savage rightist dictators. US support for Ferdinand Marcos provoked opposition groups in the Philippines to protest along with the American people and America's allies. They lobbied the parliaments of democratic states as well as specialized UN agencies. They set up 'hotlines' with the foreign media and linked up with sympathetic organizations abroad, hoping they could bring pressure to bear on their respective governments to change their policies towards the Marcos dictatorship.

People's diplomacy has come to be recognized as a vital activity requiring specialized knowledge and skills. The Philippine Rural Reconstruction Movement has set up a People's Diplomacy Training Program to teach selected members of other NGOs and mass organizations the complex and delicate art of people's diplomacy.

The US-Philippines special relations

Their efforts were primarily directed at the United States because of the so-called 'special relations' between the Philippines and its former colonial master. It may be recalled that Spain ceded the Philippines to the United States under the Treaty of Paris of 1898. During the period of American rule, the United States cloned its own political institutions in the islands, and, in the guise of teaching Filipinos the art of democratic governance, nurtured a subservient native élite.

When the United States finally granted formal independence to the Philippines on 4 July 1946, this native élite was already well entrenched in the Philippine power structure. It was therefore relatively easy for the United States to extract economic and military concessions from the Philippines to ensure continuing dependency. Threatening to withhold funds for post-war rehabilitation, the United States coerced the Philippines into amending its constitution to allow American citizens and corporations 'parity rights' in the exploitation of natural resources and the operation of public utilities.[1] In 1947 the Philippine government also agreed to reserve huge tracts of land for US military bases.[2] This agreement was followed by the Philippine–US Military Assistance Pact and the Philippine–US Mutual Defense Treaty. Together they formed the legal infrastructure for 'special relations', a euphemism for neo-colonial servitude.[3]

Despite the semblance of sovereignty, the Philippines remained heavily dependent on US economic and military aid. Taking advantage of this, the US government and the local American business community brazenly meddled in Philippine internal affairs. While it would be simplistic to say that the United States dictated the course of events in the Philippines, it was presumed that no major political changes would occur without the acquiescence or instigation of Washington.

On this assumption, the ill-informed credit Ronald Reagan with the 'people's power' insurrection that sent Marcos tottering and shivering to Honolulu. Little known abroad is the complicity of Washington and the local American business community in propping up the Marcos dictatorship. On the eve of the 'people's power' insurrection, Reagan sent a special envoy— Philip Habib—to persuade Corazón Aquino and Salvador Laurel to accept a power-sharing scheme that would keep Marcos in the presidency. It was not until 25 February 1986, when victory was assured to 'people's power' by the defection of the 15th helicopter Wing and the 5th Strike Wing of the Philippine Air Force, that Reagan called for Marcos's resignation.[4]

A review of events in 1970–2 would show the political genius of Marcos and explain the popular revulsion at the 'special relations' which culminated in the eviction of the US military bases when the original agreement expired in 1991. At that time Marcos was beginning to appear as a 'lame duck' president. His second term was due to end the following year and, under the Philippine constitution of 1935, he would not qualify for re-election. He tried to circumvent the ban by calling a Constitutional Convention and inducing the delegates to favour a parliamentary system that would let him stay as prime minister. This collapsed when one delegate (whom Marcos trusted because he came from the home province of his wife) revealed in a privileged speech that Marcos had entrusted to him an enormous amount of money to bribe his fellow delegates into voting for a parliamentary system. This triggered a public uproar that wrecked his initial game plan.

Seeing him as a spent force, members of his own Nacionalista party began deserting like the proverbial rats from a sinking ship. They underestimated his wile. On 21 September 1972, literally at the stroke of a pen, Marcos reversed the wheel of fortune. Through a combination of terror, propaganda and diplomacy, he was able to prolong his presidency twelve years beyond the constitutional limit.

In the next section I shall discuss how he neutralized democratic pressures from abroad, thereby gaining a free hand to suppress the human rights of his people. In later sections I shall relate how the opposition employed people's diplomacy to mobilize international public opinion against the dictatorship around the human rights issue.

Courting a dictator

The 1935 constitution, under which Marcos was elected twice, provided that:

The President shall be Commander-in-Chief of all armed forces of the Philippines, and, whenever it becomes necessary, may call out such armed forces to prevent or suppress lawless violence, invasion, insurrection, or rebellion. In case of invasion, insurrection, or rebellion or imminent danger thereof, when the public safety requires, he may suspend the privilege of the writ of habeas corpus, or place the Philippines or any art thereof under martial law.[5]

Marcos invoked this provision, alleging that martial law was needed to quell the communist rebellion and the Moro secessionist rebellion in Mindanao.[6] There was no question that he had the authority to impose martial law. The legitimacy issue arose because many Filipinos believed that he broke the constitution by disbanding Congress, stripping the judiciary of independence, and investing himself with legislative power. In other words, the constitution was used to undermine constitutional government. Marcos himself popularized the self-contradictory term 'constitutional authoritarianism' to describe his regime.

In a manoeuvre that would have delighted Machiavelli, Marcos calculated all possible sources of opposition and took decisive steps to cripple or win them over. He realized, of course, that the United States constituted the most formidable obstacle. The Americans took pride in their former colony as a 'showcase of democracy in Asia'. It was for this reason that the colonial-minded opposition politicians and journalists expected the United States to intervene should Marcos attempt to shatter the 'showcase'. Although sceptical of America's commitment to democracy, the nationalist faction of the élite could think of no other means to avert the establishment of a dictatorship but to go to the Supreme Court. Only the left and the secessionists prepared for armed struggle.

In a sense, however, the opposition unwittingly paved the way. In the first three months of 1970, the left unleashed a wave of massive anti-Marcos and anti-American demonstrations. Remembered as the 'First Quarter Storm', this marked the beginning of a period of turbulence that lasted up to September

1972. Demonstrations spread to places outside Manila. Labour was restive and strikes became commonplace. Violent clashes marred the 1971 senatorial and local government elections. The worst incident was the bombing of a campaign rally that nearly wiped out the entire opposition senatorial slate. Meanwhile, in the rural areas the communist New People's Army went on the offensive; and in Mindanao, the Moro people launched a 'holy war' for a separate Islamic republic.

Riding on the crest of nationalist resurgence, the legislators clogged the dockets of Congress with bills nationalizing one industry after another.[7] In the emerging atmosphere it seemed a foregone conclusion that 'parity rights' would not be extended once the Laurel–Langley Agreement expired in 1974. American businesses were naturally worried. As early as February 1971, the Philippine–American Chamber of Commerce in New York drew up a dire scenario for American investments after the Laurel–Langley Agreement.[8] Their anxiety worsened when in August 1972 the Supreme Court (traditionally a bastion of conservatism) rendered a radical decision to the effect that all American investments which entered the country under 'parity rights' would automatically be nationalized upon the termination of the Laurel–Langley Agreement.[9] This was followed by another decision that American corporations in the Philippines could only employ Filipino managers.[10]

In an uncharacteristic show of forbearance, Marcos desisted from bold counter-measures, blaming the legal system for restraining the hand of authority. He thus allowed the radical movement to swell until it appeared sufficiently menacing to American interests. He moved only after the Supreme Court decisions by dispatching his key Cabinet members to Washington to convince the White House, the State Department, the Pentagon and key figures in the US Senate and House of Representatives of the grave danger confronting US economic and military interests in the Philippines.[11] He also conveyed the dire warning that, even with his best effort, he could not assure a two-thirds majority in the Philippine Senate to ratify a new set of treaties. The only way to secure American interests was to go beyond the limits of constitutional government. He had to be freed from a petulant Congress so that he could, by presidential decrees, unilaterally extend the crucial provisions of the Laurel–Langley Agreement and the Military Bases Agreement.

This diplomatic stratagem worked. The American business community in Manila welcomed martial law. A week after its declaration, Marcos received this telegram which the presidential drum-beaters played up in the controlled media:

The American Chamber of Commerce wishes you every success in your endeavours to restore peace and order, business confidence, economic growth and the well-being of the Filipino people. We assure you of our confidence and co-operation in achieving these objectives. We are communicating these feelings to our associates and affiliates in the US.[12]

The US government not only acquiesced to the dismantling of the 'showcase of democracy in Asia' but also lavished the new-born dictatorship with loans and military aid. Between 1970 and 1972 the Armed Forces of the Philippines (AFP) was receiving only $60.2 million per annum under the Philippine–US Military Assistance Pact. In the first two years of martial law, however, the figure leapt to $118.8 million.[13] There could be no nearer blessing for a dictatorship than to aid the expansion, training and arming of its chief instrument of repression. With this bounty, the AFP ballooned from any army of 60,000 in 1972 to 200,000 men in 1979.[14]

American economic interests were saved at the expense of America's political legacy. Marcos did away with constitutional government as understood in American jurisprudence. He replaced the 1935 constitution[15] with one that concentrated powers in his hands, as concurrent president and prime minister. The 1973 constitution, ratified by a rigged plebiscite, negated with the American principles of separation of powers and checks and balances. It authorized Marcos to legislate by presidential decrees.

While this new constitution guaranteed freedom of the press, Marcos allowed only those newspapers, radio stations and television channels that belonged to his relatives and cronies. The detention centres in Camp Crame and Fort Bonifacio were packed to the rafters. In the first three years of martial law over 50,000 persons were arrested and detained without trial. Of the 107 political prisoners interviewed by the Amnesty International fact-finding mission in 1975, seventy-one claimed to have been tortured.[16]

The radical activists who eluded arrest were forced to go underground. Those captured while hiding risked what Amnesty International calls 'extrajudicial executions'. Some of those tortured became physically or mentally maimed for life. Women were raped, men sexually humiliated. In the rural areas, villages were strafed and burnt, their residents herded to strategic hamlets. In Manila and other urban centres, shanty towns were demolished to create space for new hotels, shopping malls, luxury condominiums and the magnificent edifices built according to the caprices of Imelda Marcos.

The trade unions lost their right to strike. Civil servants lost security of tenure. Universities lost academic freedom. Business establishments had to give 'voluntary contributions' to Imelda's ostentatious projects. With no Congress or free press to restrain him, Marcos revoked the nationalization laws and projected the Philippines as an idyllic place for foreign investments.

The beginnings of people's diplomacy

After a brief visit to Manila in 1973, US Senator Mike Mansfield described the Philippines unkindly as 'a nation of 60 million cowards and one son-of-a-bitch'. He failed to foresee that the Filipinos would fight back and his government would lend a deaf ear to their cries for help.

The anti-Marcos traditional politicians who were spared arrest kept their peace. Some raised puny legal protests which the reconstituted Supreme Court readily dismissed.[17] Those who escaped to the United States (Marcos contemptuously branded them 'the steak commandos') lobbied in Washington, bewailing the death of democracy and pleading for the US government to cut military and economic aid to the dictatorship. But Richard Nixon and, after Watergate, Gerald Ford showed total indifference.

The election of Jimmy Carter rekindled the liberal opposition's faith in America as liberator since he adopted human rights as the centrepiece of his foreign policy. To their utmost dismay, however, Carter proved as uncaring about the human rights of Filipinos beyond showing concern for eminent individuals, for example when Benigno Aquino staged a hunger strike while in detention.

Seen from Manila, Carter's human rights policy appeared to apply only to the communist states, South Africa and Southern Rhodesia, and the anti-American dictatorships in the Third World. He refrained from badgering Marcos on human rights, lest he would make trouble for the bases. Of course, hopes for changing US policy vanished when Carter lost to Reagan. Washington's insensitivity loomed in abundant clarity when George Bush, as Vice-President, represented Reagan at the oath-taking of Marcos (after Marcos 'won' a phoney election over a hand-picked opponent) and expressed appreciation for the dictator's 'devotion to democracy'.

The left opposition[18] took a different path. Since Carter's presidency, left-wing groups also appropriated the human rights issue, but diversified their international contacts. Unlike the liberal opposition, they did not confine themselves to Washington. They carried their campaign to countries allied with the United States and found greater sympathy in Western Europe. Moreover, they addressed not primarily the governments but more the media, churches, trade unions, professional bodies and, of course, Amnesty International.

As international organizations, the Catholic and Protestant churches were most effective in 'people's diplomacy'. His Filipino congregation persuaded the Pope to defer a projected state visit as a gesture of protest for the persecution of church people.[19] When the Pope eventually decided to come, the jubilent Marcos reciprocated by 'lifting martial law' on 17 January 1981 with Presidential Proclamation No. 2045. But the trick was too transparent to allow John Paul II to pose as a saviour. The proclamation provided that the writ of habeas corpus would remain suspended for those in detention, and for all those who would be charged of insurrection, rebellion and sedition. The military tribunals would continue hearing all pending cases. Underscoring that the dictatorship would remain intact, it added that 'all proclamations, orders, decrees, instructions and acts promulgated, issued or done by the incumbent President constitute part of the law of the land and shall remain valid, legal, binding and effective even after the lifting of martial law'.

As soon as the Pope left, Marcos informed the bewildered nation that before 'lifting martial law' he had signed, on 12 September 1980, Presidential Decree No. 1737 ('Publc Order Act') containing all the obnoxious elements of martial law. Under this draconian decree, one could be arrested not necessarily for what one had done but even for what one was likely to do.

Human rights monitoring

People's diplomacy will have no impact unless there exists in the home country an extensive and efficient mechanism for monitoring and reporting atrocities. This is essential because most human rights violations occur in remote vllages or poor urban communities that do not normally attract media attention.

The Catholic, Protestant and Aglipayan[20] churches have networks reaching out to the far-flung areas. They also have international connections and enjoy a high level of credibility. The Association of Major Religious Superiors in the Philippines (AMRSP), representing sixty Catholic religious orders for men and ninety for women, established the Task Force Detainees (TFD). This is doubtless the most effective human rights monitoring organization. TFD has documented thousands of human rights cases from 1973 to the present. It has conducted fact-finding missions to scenes of massacre, strafing and burning of villages, hamleting, food blockades, etc. Working closely with the Protestants and Aglipayans in the Ecumenical Movement for Justice and Peace, TFD gets up-to-date reports from missionaries, parish priests and pastors all over the country.

Some religious orders and dioceses also have their own groups to assist the victims of atrocities. In addition, the Protestants have their Program Unit on Human Rights under the National Council of Churches of the Philippines and the Justice, Peace and Human Rights Desk under the United Church of Christ. There is a secular but church-related Protestant Lawyers League that takes up cases of victims who cannot afford the standard legal fees.

Besides these church-based groups, some lawyers have formed their own human rights organizations with fancy acronyms like FLAG and MABINI. Like the Protestant Lawyers League, they take up human rights cases in court and train 'paralegals' among law students and community leaders. Under Marcos, their members were subjected to constant harassment, some were assassinated by right-wing death squads.[21] Under Marcos, MABINI stood with TFD at the forefront of the human rights campaign, but under Mrs Aquino many of its members joined the Cabinet. FLAG (the Free Legal Assistance Group) and the Protestant Lawyers League have retained their credibility by keeping a distance from the government. Success killed MABINI!

Other human rights groups are directly affiliated to various left-wing organizations. Like TFD, they are active in people's diplomacy but they work mainly with Philippine solidarity groups abroad, about which more will be said.

People's diplomacy is only a secondary concern for many human rights groups. More urgent is saving the lives of prospective victims. When somebody disappears or is picked up by suspected military personnel who refuse to identify themselves or present a search warrant, that person is a candidate for torture and extrajudicial execution. Without wasting time, relatives and friends must contact a 'paralegal' or the nearest church. The latter in turn get in touch with a human rights lawyer. Torture is always performed in the first few days of captivity, while the victim undergoes what the military calls 'tactical interrogation'. This dreadful process is often done in 'safe houses', not in the regular detention centres.[22]

A 'safe house' is rented by a military intelligence unit, without the owner and neighbours knowing its diabolic function. Persons arrested illegally, i.e. without search warrants issued by the courts, are brought to safe houses, each well furnished with instruments of torture. If the intelligence unit is confident that nobody knows the identity of the arresting party, and especially if the abduction is done cleanly without anybody having seen the act, a victim can be tortured with impunity. If his body is irreparably mutilated, the soldiers may 'salvage'[23] him and dump his body into an unmarked grave.

This makes swift action imperative. The human rights lawyer immediately accompanies the closest kin to the military camps. The military officers initially deny responsibility, but when they know a search is on and the incident could blow up in the international press, that is sometimes sufficient to save the victim. Under martial law, soldiers were not scared of the courts; but they have always been scared of the foreign media since reports on gruesome incidents would tarnish the image the government was trying to build abroad. It is therefore important for the human rights groups to be known as having good contacts with the foreign media, who are pivotal in the human rights campaign.

The killings continue

The widow of Benigno Aquino (the most eminent victim of the dictatorship), Corazón Aquino placed human rights at the top of her campaign platform in the February 1986 snap election. Her first acts as President of the Philippines raised hopes for a decent, humane and democratic society. She released some 550 political prisoners in the TFD list, among them José Ma. Sison (founder of the Communist Party of the Philippines) and Bernabe Buscayno (better known as Commander Dante, the first commander-in-chief of the New People's Army). She restored the writ of habeas corpus. She also created the Presidential Commission on Human Rights (PCHR) with the most respected human rights advocate (Senator José W. Diokno) as chairman.[24]

But President Aquino did not go all the way. Painfully aware that the military faction that helped put her in office remained a potential threat, she allowed its leaders (Juan Ponce Enrile and Fidel Ramos) to hold back her hand. While Enrile and Ramos denounced General Fabian Ver's faction for atrocities and corruption, they opposed an all-out purge in the service. Diokno, on the other hand, was bent on probing the human rights records even of those who had belatedly turned against Marcos. In the ensuing conflict between the PCHR and the Enrile–Ramos group, Aquino deferred to the latter. Her executive order formally establishing PCHR did not grant it prosecutory powers. PCHR has remained a helpless consultative and advisory body. It investigates abuses of the military and police, but it is left to the Department of Justice to decide whether to charge the human rights violators in court.

What made the PCHR ineffective was Aquino's refusal to repeal Presidential Decrees Nos. 1822 and 1850 which provided that military personnel charged with crimes against civilians could only be tried by the military courts. She even refused to reassign military officers unless ordered by General Ramos. In effect, those who faced charges of human rights violations remained in their posts. As expected, the witnesses were too scared to testify.

When Diokno died a year later, Aquino packed PCHR with persons whose commitment to human rights is open to doubt. They were more concerned in helping the military denounce alleged abuses on the rebel side. Aquino's image as champion of human rights dwindled.

It declined further when, after a series of attempted *coups*, General Fidel Ramos emerged as the *éminence grise* in her government. Upon his insistence, the human rights lawyers were ousted from her Cabinet, including the first Executive Secretary, a prominent figure in MABINI. She also adopted the strategy of 'total war' that involved civilian agencies in counter-insurgency operations. Worst, she authorized the arming of right-wing vigilantes, village thugs who lost no time flaunting their power and perpetrating unspeakable brutalities. Some vigilantes belong to quasi-religious cults who believe that eating human brains while performing esoteric rituals will make their bodies invulnerable to bullets.[25] In a notorious case, an Italian priest in Mindanao, suspected of sympathy for the guerrillas, had his skull neatly sliced and emptied of the brain.

It would be dishonest to deny that the restoration of the writ of habeas corpus significantly reduced the number of political detainees. Unless charged of other crimes, such as the illegal possession of firearms, those arrested for rebellion can be released on bail. But this has also increased the number of extrajudicial executions.[26] Since it is now difficult to keep anyone in detention, rather than turn over the suspects to a detention centre only to be released, they are summarily executed.

Besides salvaging, there has also been a marked increase in assassinations. The most prominent victims were Rolando Olalia (president of the militant labour federation, Kilusang Mayo Uno) and Lean Alejandro (the best-loved student leader). Commander Dante barely survived a bold assassination attempt after appearing in a television talk-show. The Lawyers Committee for Human Rights and Asia Watch (both international fact-finding groups) bewailed the fact in October 1988 that 'since the overthrow of Ferdinand Marcos, human rights abuses in the Philippines had risen to high levels'.[27]

In view of continuing human rights violations, TFD and other human right monitoring groups have not closed shop. A broader organization—the Philippine Alliance of Human Rights Advocates (PAHRA)—has been established to heighten public awareness of the current human rights situation in the country and to pursue people's diplomacy. Their efforts in the international arena provoked Mrs Aquino to sound like Marcos, invoking national sovereignty to parry foreign criticisms of her human rights record.

There have been more tangible improvements in the human rights situation under President Fidel Ramos. This is paradoxical because Ramos was the Chief of the Philippine Constabulary whose strike forces spearheaded the rounding up of people when Marcos imposed martial law. Having turned against Marcos (his own cousin) in February 1986 and, together with the then Defence Minister Juan Ponce Enrile, led the mutiny that sparked off the 'people's power' uprising, he became Aquino's AFP Chief-of-Staff (and later Secretary of National Defence). In that capacity Ramos blocked Diokno's effort to cleanse the military of human rights violators. He was also the inventor of the 'total war' strategy and the patron of vigilante groups.

Since he assumed the presidency, however, Ramos has taken a surprisingly conciliatory stance. He had Republic Act No. 1800 ('Anti-Subversion Law') repealed. That law, enacted in 1957, classified membership in the Communist Party, or whatever the government brands as a 'communist front', a capital offence, and therefore ineligible for bail and subject to the death penalty. Under that law thousands (including Mrs Aquino's husband) were detained without trial during the martial law period.

In 1986 Ramos opposed the release of Sison and Dante, but after becoming president himself, he too unlocked the detention cells, releasing all communist and secessionist rebels as well as the military men involved in the *coup* attempts he had crushed. Furthermore, he reopened peace talks with all rebel groups. The democratic space has lasted longer under this hardened warrior than under 'the angel of peace', as Mrs Aquina used to be called.

Mrs Aquino, as noted earlier, ruled under the constant shadow of a military revolt. This accounted for her indecisiveness and vacillation. Being a military man himself (he graduated from West Point and fought in Korea and Vietnam), Ramos feels more confident in dealing with soldiers. He has done what Aquino dared not attempt, for example forcing the retirement of 'Scallywags in uniform' and arresting high-ranking officers suspected of kidnapping and protecting crime syndicates. No less than the Chief of the Philippine Constabulary and later Director-General of the Philippine National Police was forced out of the service, together with many generals and colonels.

While human rights violations still occur, the instances have been considerably reduced. More civilian witnesses are now willing to testify against erring soldiers. Ramos has also taken steps to disband the private armies and dissolve vigilante groups notorious for harassing the civilian population. None the less, human rights violations still occur and the possibility of renewed repression cannot be excluded. Ramos's unexpected leniency is inspired not by conviction but by a pragmatic desire to create the impression of stability, thus attracting foreign investments. This has made him more sensitive to world public opinion, but there is reason to doubt if he would sustain this position in the likely possibility that his Medium Term Philippine Development Plan proved to be a colossal failure.

The international network

Hundreds of thousands of Filipinos have emigrated, some residing abroad legally, others illegally. Not all of them are domestics and entertainers. In the United States, Western Europe and Australia, they include professionals, some former activists and a few who had a taste of torture and detention. In addition, there are citizens of these countries who have special affection for the Philippines, having spent time there as missionaries, businessmen, scholars or journalists. From their ranks are drawn the members of solidarity groups abroad.

Solidarity groups play a crucial role in people's diplomacy. The local monitoring groups channel through them news about human rights cases for dissemination to the media in their countries of residence. They engage in lobbying work in official circles and among political parties, trade unions, churches, professional organizations, and similar institutions that are influential with their governments. Of course, they also help raise funds for the movement back home.

Better organized and richer in experience, the Philippine human rights organizations no longer rely solely on Amnesty International. There are institutions abroad dealing especially with Philippine affairs. In Brussels, the Philippine International Centre for Human Rights lobby in the European Parliament while coordinating campaigns in various European countries. Similar structures exist in the United States, Australia and Japan—countries with concern for human rights and to whose governments and investors the Philippine government is beholden.

More than any single event, the assassination of Senator Benigno Aquino in August 1983 stirred the American conscience. The American media and the American senators and congressmen who were hitherto indifferent to the plight of the Filipinos started clamouring for official gestures of protest. Fact-finding missions descended upon the Philippines, only to confirm human rights violations. By 1985 the ailing dictator was beleaguered by adverse publicity and congressional denunciations, at a moment when he desperately needed economic relief for his bankrupt government. Thus, in November that year, he yielded to the demand for an internationally supervised election.

The February 1986 snap election marked the beginning of the end of the dictatorship. Marcos campaigned against the ghost of Benigno Aquino. As he was losing heavily to Aquino's widow, his henchmen cheated with impunity, in the presence of foreign journalists and photographers. They went to the extent of fabricating fictitious polling booths at the last minute. Worst of all, they tampered with the Commission on Elections computers that projected the provincial election results on the official bulletin board. When the computer operators walked out in protest, the credibility of the whole exercise fell apart.

This formed the backdrop to the 'people's power' uprising. Even before the military mutiny led by Ramos and Enrile, the brazen cheating in the election had already given rise to an insurrectionary situation.

Conclusions

The effectiveness of people's diplomacy depends to a large extent on the degree of a government's dependence on foreign aid and loans. Marcos had made himself vulnerable to international pressures after tearing down the protectionist barriers in a fruitless quest for export-oriented development. He borrowed recklessly from the multinational banks, looted a good part of the loans, and squandered the rest on the whimsical projects of his wife. He enlarged the military and equipped them with foreign donations. These, too, made him more vulnerable.

This paradox confronted the human rights groups with a painful dilemma. They form part of the national liberation movement whose cadres and activists are the usual victims of human rights abuses. They are fighting for independence from foreign, especially US, control; yet the logic of the struggle has forced them to appeal to world public opinion with the aim of inducing foreign governments, especially the United States, to put pressure on the Philippine government to respect human rights.

They have since resolved the paradox in their own conscience. They realize that no state, democratic or authoritarian, can invoke sovereignty to deny human rights to its citizens. When the Philippines signed the Universal Declaration of Human Rights, the Convention against Torture, and the International Covenant on Civil and Political Rights, it accepted a limitation to sovereignty and acknowledged that violations of human rights in any nation must also be a concern of others.

The benign image of the Aquino and Ramos governments overseas renders people's diplomacy more difficult to pursue. The foreign media have lost interest in the Philippines. News about atrocities in the Philippines no longer draw excitement because there are far more gruesome stories since the beginning of the 1990s from Bosnia and Somalia, and Rwanda. With no more military bases in its former colony, Washington ranks the Philippines low in its order of priorities.

None the less, the extensive local and international human rights networks have to be maintained while the struggle for social justice must continue despite the end of the Cold War. A shaky democratic space prevails as Ramos pursues his nebulous dream of turning the Philippines into a newly industrializing country by the year 2000. Having learnt a hard lesson in 1972, the Filipinos maintain constant vigilance.

Notes

1. 'Parity rights' refers to a special privilege granted to American citizens and corporations to invest in agriculture, mining and public utilities which the 1935 constitution had reserved exclusively for Filipino citizens and corporations. This is embodied in the Laurel–Langley Agreement that was due to expire on 3 July 1974, unless extended with the consent of two-thirds of the Philippine senate.
2. The original Philippine Independence Act was rejected by the Philippine National Assembly in 1933 because a nationalist majority led by Manuel L. Quezon objected to the military bases provision. Hence, the Philippine–US Military Bases Agreement of 1947 reversed the 1933 Filipino position.
3. Stephen Rosskamm Shalom, *The US and the Philippines: A Study of Neo-colonialism* (Philadelphia: Institute for the Study of Human Issues, 1981; and Quezon City: New Day Publishers, 1986).
4. Gemma N. Almendral, 'The fall of the regime', in Aurora Javate de Dios *et al.* (eds), *Dictatorship and Revolution: Roots of People's Power* (Metro-Manila: Conspectus, 1988), pp. 206–20.
5. Constitution of Republic of the Philippines (1935), Article VII, Section 10 (2).
6. Presidential Proclamation No. 1081, 'A state of martial law in the Philippines', 21 September 1972.
7. Philippine–American Chamber of Commerce, 'List of Filipinization bills filed in Congress', reprinted in Aurora Javate-De Dios *et al.*, op. cit., pp. 347–8.
8. Philippine–American Chamber of Commerce, 'Post-1974 prospect: statement on Philippine–American relations' (unpublished papers, February 1971), repro-

duced in Javate-De Dios *et al.*, op. cit., pp. 344–7.

9. 'Republic of the Philippines versus William H. Quash', *Supreme Court Reports: Annotated*, vol. 46 (17 August 1972).

10. 'Anti-Dummy Board versus Luzan Stevedoring Company', *Supreme Court Reports: Annotated*, vol. 46 (21 August 1972).

11. Interview with a former Cabinet member who requested anonymity.

12. James B. Goodno, *The Philippines: Land of Broken Promises* (London: Zed Books, 1991), p. 67.

13. ibid., p. 67.

14. Amnesty International, *Human Rights Violations in the Philippines: An Account of Torture, 'Disappearances', Extrajudicial Executions and Illegal Detention* (New York: Amnesty International USA Publications, 1982), p. 1.

15. Until 1973 the Philippines had a constitution that was ratified under the supervision of American colonial authorities. It installed a government closely patterned after the American model, with separation of powers, bicameral legislature, etc.

16. Amnesty International, *Human Rights Violations in the Philippines*, op. cit., p. 1.

17. 'Benigno Aquino versus Juan Ponce Enrile', *Supreme Court Reports Annotated*, vol. 59 (17 September 1974); and 'Javellana versus the Executive Secretary', *Supreme Court Reports Annotated*, vol. 50 (31 March 1973).

18. The term 'Left opposition' (as distinguished from the 'liberal opposition') is used here as a generic term to refer not only to the communist-led National Democratic Front but also to the social democrats (e.g., Pandayan), the independent socialists (e.g., BISIG) and the miscellaneous adherents of liberation theology.

19. Amnesty International, *Arrest, Detention and Political Killing of Priests and Church Workers in the Philippines* (London: Amnesty International Publications, December 1988.)

20. The Aglipayan church, officially named Philippine Independent church, broke away from Rome at the turn of the century. Fiercely nationalistic, it takes progressive positions on a range of social and political issues. It also has international connections through the Episcopalian church.

21. Amnesty International, *The Killing and Intimidation of Human Rights Lawyers* (London: Amnesty International Publications, 1988).

22. Amnesty International, *Human Rights Violations in the Philippines*, op. cit., pp. 3–8.

23. Having little respect for English grammar, the Filipino military uses the verb 'salvage' as a euphemism for murder or what Amnesty International calls 'extrajudicial execution'.

24. Leonora Angeles *et al.*, 'The quest for justice: obstacles to the redress of human rights violations in the Philippines' (unpublished research paper submitted to the University of the Philippines Centre for Integrative and Development Studies, July 1989), pp. 17–19. See also Alberto T. Muyot, *Human Rights in the Philippines, 1986–91* (Quezon City: University of the Philippines Law Centre, 1992), pp. 3–5.

25. Instances of these gory incidents are detailed in TFD case files. Some of the worst cases are described in Amnesty International, *Philippines: The Killing Goes On* (London: Amnesty International Publications, 1992) pp. 25–60; Angeles *et al.*, 'The quest for justice', op. cit., pp. 45–81; and Amnesty International, *Unlawful Killings by Military and Paramilitary Forces* (London: Amnesty International Publications, 1988). The last-mentioned is the report of an international fact-finding mission.

26. Angeles *et al.*, 'The quest for justice', op. cit., pp. 19–20.

27. Jeannie Green, 'The Philippines: human rights issues in US foreign policy,' *Harvard Human Rights Yearbook*, Vol. II, Spring 1989 (Cambridge, MA: Harvard Law School). This publication has since been renamed as the *Human Rights Journal of the Harvard Law School*.

10
HUMAN RIGHTS IN RUSSIA: THE DRAGON IS NOT DEFEATED

CONSTANTINE V. PLESHAKOV

Introduction

It is very tempting to present a general survey of human rights over the entire former Soviet Union, but this task is simply too enormous: the new independent states that replaced the former Soviet empire constitute a wide range of political and social environments—from relative political stability to fierce civil war—and they represent diverse cultural backgrounds—from North European (Baltic) to continental Moslem. Russia alone is a subject diverse and contradictory and a perfect example of a society in transition between totalitarianism and democracy.[1]

The essence and the history of the Soviet communist regime can be characterized in one sentence: shameless and boundless violation of human rights. It makes no sense to itemize abuses of human rights in the Soviet Union, for practically no human right was observed or respected. The dragon of totalitarianism simply destroyed individual rights. After the death of Stalin a limited degree of individual rights was gradually accepted. Khrushchev gave the peasants the right to move to the cities (having abolished the new serfdom). Since the 1950s people were put into prison only for opposing the regime while under Stalin even some of the most loyal subjects of communism may have had to face the firing squad. The priests were no longer sent to concentration camps; instead, they were required to report to the KGB, the government's intelligence agency, and could only be ordained with its approval. By 1985 life had become easier than in 1953, but the principal approach to human rights had remained practically unchanged. Only the penalty for demanding one's rights was changed: under totalitarianism it was death; now it was social ostracism.

International pressure upon the regime was a paramount factor introducing this change. The Soviet leaders after Stalin did not want to isolate themselves from the world behind the Iron Curtain: first, it was dangerous, for it increased the risk of military conflict due to misperceptions, and second, the West was now regarded as a supplier of artefacts for the élite and for the Soviet economy. If the Soviet leaders wanted to open up a bit, they could not avoid allowing their subjects a glimpse of the West. The West was definitely one of the main factors which had caused the softening of the system. For example, the Catholic church in the west of the country enjoyed much more freedom than the Orthodox church of its Slavic core: the Catholics were reluctantly regarded by Moscow as the community having special relations abroad, while the Orthodox Slavs lacked that protective shield.

The traditions of liberalism and the very notion of human rights were ruthlessly destroyed in the Soviet Union. It would have taken a long time for them to re-emerge were it not for one outside force: the West. The West through different channels (radio broadcasting was one of the most effective) had connected Soviet citizens with the world community where human rights were regarded as the basic criterion of the social progress.

Human rights: Russian tradition and the concept of universality

In the conflict between the state and the individual, the Russian Orthodoxy tradition yielded to the pressure of the state. The Orthodox church preferred not to fight for the protection of human dignity and human importance of Russian Christians. The clergies accepted their status as silent slaves of the throne. Humility and collectivism became the guiding principles of Russian life, and those who had promised to 'change everything' — Russian revolutionaries — gladly used the tradition prepared for them by the tsars and the hierarchy of the church. Soviet totalitarianism came into being without much difficulty; Russian liberalism with its concept of human dignity evident in the last decades of the nineteenth century was easily crushed and then erased from collective memory. Russian tradition supported the notion of state supremacy.

In this sense, it can be argued that the concept of human rights which had absolutely no cultural roots in Russian tradition is alien to Russia. The emergence of a mainstream Western civilization somewhere in the mid-nineteenth century, however, had a major impact on Russian mentality towards the conflict between the state and the individual. Western enterprise had reached and then united all cultures. The world had become much smaller and more compact. As inevitably as the adherence to modern guns and cruisers, the concept of human rights appeared in most Western societies. Earlier, during the reign of Peter the Great, imitating Western warfare techniques and trade policies of Western European countries such as the Netherlands, Britain and Germany was relatively easy because human rights problems had not yet become an issue of major concern. At that point the Westernization of Russia (or rather an incorporation of it into the mainstream Western civilization) could do without the rights of an individual. Later it was to become impossible to be a full member of the world community and not at least pretend to protect human rights. The concept of human rights came together with technology.

Under the Soviet communist system, the power of the state was almost unlimited, but the state was not able to isolate its citizens completely from the rest of the world. In spite of the xenophobic tendency of the communist regime, international interaction with the inevitability of a falling apple had included the Soviets into the mainstream Western civilization. In the aftermath of the collapse of communism, however, it would be premature to argue that Russia has come to share all the values of the Western world including the concept of human rights. It will take a long time to overcome the legacy of the past. Even the 'liberals' in today's Russia still have difficulties embracing wholeheartedly the concept of human rights because their consciousness is still rooted in a different tradition. But the process is already under way.

Myths and realities

The collapse of communism in the Soviet Union was not absolute. It has remained practically intact in most of the Central Asian states. However, when a new Russia emerged in 1991 after the catalysis of 19–21 August (the *putsch*), respect for human rights was proclaimed the pivot of the newly born state. Earlier, human rights were to be guarded as the treasures obtained in the struggle with the dragon of communism.

There was also the same factor again: the West was willing to see in the new Russia what it wished to see—a democracy adhering to the human rights principles. Naturally, Russia regarded itself at least as a moral ally of the Western capitals and had to play according to the rules of the game. But declarations were rather far from everyday practice. Russian leaders were more optimistic about their human rights image than the actual state of matters permitted. Russian foreign policy was tightly connected to Western support which could be available only to a democratic country. That is why Russian leaders tried to save as much face as possible, while doing as little as possible in practical terms inside the country. Their power-base allegedly relied upon absolute political freedom—but probably the only thing they could really boast about was absolute freedom of speech. Several major factors contribute to the present human rights situation in Russia and the outside world's perception of it. The latter is influenced by two great myths created by the international mass media and the wishful thinking of the politicians.

First, there is the myth about democracy in Russia. The image of Russia from the international arena is that democracy has triumphed with the collapse of communism and the major problem the country faces is the economic crisis. In reality, Russia is just at the starting point of the political process leading to democracy. Probably two things have misled foreign observers: the obvious presence of democratic institutions and the freedom of speech enjoyed by Russians and by the Russian media.

Second is the myth that the Russians are free at last. This derives from the first myth concerning the triumph of democracy and is again explained by superficial reading of the situation in which outward formal characteristics of democracy have been taken for democracy itself. Compared with the years of communist or, for that matter, tsarist rule the human rights situation in Russia has improved enormously. But human rights are being violated in Russia all the time and practically nobody is immune to unscrupulous violations. Several factors have contributed to this:

1. The traditional Russian system of values insists upon the insignificance of a private

individual relative to nation and state (and other minor communities). It is not a question for most Russians whether to violate human rights or not; the question is how to violate them in the way most productive for the state.

2. In objective terms, the Russian nation and state are now in crisis; the ghost of civil war is at the door; the country's disintegration is also a possibility. This economic crisis stems not only from the dismantling of communism, but also from structural problems in the economy. Russia now needs a strong state to cope with all these problems. Such strengthening of the state automatically means a certain offensive against individual rights; even when the rights of communist extremists are considered, such an offensive could create a dangerous precedent. The process that is going on in Russia could hardly be called reformist; it is chaos, and it is a general law that in chaos the first things to disappear are not bread and butter, but human rights.

3. The communist system has not actually been dismantled. While notorious totalitarian principles have been eliminated, the system has remained the same. Vital institutions and laws, principles and approaches have remained intact, surviving the democratic tide. The democratic tide, as it were, has removed only the coating from the Russian pyramid of power, with the foundations still intact.

4. It is worth asking the question: Who rules Russia today? If we take the vast majority of institutions and administrative bodies, the sad conclusion is that the bureaucratic lords have not been replaced, and that Russia is still ruled by the old communist nomenclature (or apparatchiks) which has only modified its verbal entourage but not the moral approach to the principles, methods and goals of governance.

No revolution took place in Russia in 1991. Communism was deprived of the right to call itself such, but not deprived of its authority as a social system violating human rights. Such influential social insitutions like the army and the secret police have remained intact, and practically all administrative units and all minor institutions are still run by the people who are supposed to have been ousted by liberals in 1991. The major issue of the new Russian revolution — the issue of power — has remained unresolved.

The combination of these four factors — cultural archetypes, antediluvian laws and approaches, the preservation of the same people at most of the important administrative positions, and total chaos — has led to a situation in which human rights are still not properly protected in contemporary Russia.

The forbidden zones

Several vast areas of social space are still completely closed to public control; glasnost and the presence of the democratic president in the Kremlin have changed nothing here. These are traditional Russia's legacy; the only innovation is that now it is possible to discuss them freely in the press. But when freedom of speech leads to nothing, it is actually not freedom of speech. An individual's rights can be protected as long as he or she stays outside the 'forbidden zones'. I am referring not to the gloomy cavity of the secret services, but to the triad of arbitrariness — military service, the penitentiary system and medical institutions.

When an individual joins the army or becomes a prisoner or a patient in a hospital, the person immediately leaves the 'normal' environment where at least some protection of law can be expected, and enters the domain of tyranny. The absolute vacuum of law in the triad of arbitrariness is a reality.

Military service has become not only a burden, but a terrifying prospect for young Russian males. The Russian army is still as bad as its Soviet predecessor was. The routine life of a private makes him subject to cruel punishments both from the officers and from his older comrades. The privates are beaten up, humiliated in all possible ways; they are deprived of free will; the situation with food and housing resembles that of the Dark Ages; the Russian soldiers dealing with state-of-the-art technology are themselves regarded as hostages in a medieval war. When an officer restrains himself fearing possible consequences, he will delegate the punishment functions to non-commissioned officers. It is a tradition in the army that all privates of the first year are considered literally as slaves of their older comrades, and cruelty is supposed to be the only way to bring up a 'real man'. It is not the problem of harassment, but that of depriving a person of all rights and turning him literally into a slave. If he becomes a 'real man', he will be cruel to his younger comrades in his second year—this can be unending.

Most of the cruelties and human rights violations in the army are not punished. The number of murders and suicides is enormous (of course, the real statistics are not known). The after-effects of the military service reveal themselves in mental and physical diseases, in broken wills and ugly behaviour patterns. Numerous lives are lost every year during military exercises; more coffins and no protection through law. The army is still often used as a survival kit for the economy: not only soldiers but even officers are sent to farms where they are regarded as cheap labour with the employer having no commitments towards them.

So far society has been unable to interfere. The only group really concerned —the parents of the privates—has formed a Committee of Soldiers' Mothers. The Committee has been granted access to the military establishments only after several ugly incidents in which the military police were involved, and the Minister of Defence himself has from time to time promised cooperation. So far the army remains an institution which threatens not only the souls but also the lives of Russian citizens. President Boris Yeltsin has signed a decree on alternative service in the army; it remains to be seen whether it will be properly observed: the experience of other former Soviet republics with alternative military service shows that frequently the conscripts are sent not to hospitals (to work as nurses) but to special construction units (to work as serfs).

The disintegration of the former Soviet Union brought other difficulties for the Russian army. Conscripts have been caught in the middle of inter-ethnic conflicts (Tadjikistan, the Caucasus). In the days when their country is not waging war with any nation, the conscripts find themselves in the crossfire of rival factions from the southern part of the former empire. The law does not guarantee them a free choice of whether to take part in the ethnic conflicts (and the government does nothing to protect or at least to define their status on the territory of the ex-Soviet republics). Those casualties cannot be justified by Russia's 'national interests'; the obligatory participation of Russian conscripts in combat outside Russia definitely violates their basic rights. Such participation is a serious international problem, but it is also a problem of human rights.

Similar to the military establishment, the penitentiary system has been described by its victims or independent observers as medieval in structure. Sometimes several dozens of prisoners (including teenagers) are put in a small cell where they have to take shifts in sleeping. The penitentiary system resembles the army in many ways. Prisoners' rights are not protected by law, but depend upon the whims of the warrant officers. Inner jail life is organized not according to the prison regulations, but to the laws of the criminal world. It is practically impossible to become immune to the cruel laws of this environment. Again, humiliation is a general rule, and the criminal world builds a strict hierarchy inside each cell and inside each jail. The laws offering protection to those awaiting trial are not clear. As soon as a person enters the prison doors, he or she is automatically deprived of all rights not only as a citizen, but also as a human being. The prisoners in the camps are used as an extremely cheap source of labour in the most dangerous and primitive spheres of economy. Their material environment is depressing in its quality.

Not surprisingly, the penitentiary system does not provide any form of rehabilitation; an enormous proportion of them are so spoiled by the organization of the inner criminal world and so embittered by the attitude of the authorities that they return to the path of crime when they are released. This tendency is especially frightening where young people are concerned, where one offence committed during one's youth can lead to entry into the criminal world with the obvious consequences for the future.

Medical care in Russia is another sphere of arbitrariness. It shares the same features with the army and penitentiary system and strikingly resembles a jail. As soon as an individual enters a hospital, the person or relatives have practically no chances to appeal to law, to say nothing of human compassion. The personnel of all clinics are free to engage in extortion of different levels and it is practically impossible to take legal action against the clinic or doctors. Patients are often deprived of such basic things as visits from their relatives and friends. Often such visits determine whether a person survives or not, especially when he/she requires continuous care that the clinic is unable or unwilling to provide.

The situation in mental asylums is especially difficult, for mental institutions are still completely closed to the influence of law and public opinion. It should be mentioned that a law guaranteeing the rights of the mentally disabled has been passed, but implementation is a major problem because the clinics are unwilling to open up and it is not in the state's interest to interfere. If an 'ordinary' clinic could be called a jail in a metaphorical sense, a mental asylum is literally a jail. The fact that political opponents are no longer put there ironically has made the situation worse, for Russian psychiatry has ceased to attract the attention of the international community.

The phantom of freedom

Since the collapse of communism, human rights are still subject to violation in many respects. There are several notorious cases. The institution of *propiska* (official registration) has remained intact. Introduced at the dawn of communism, *propiska* means that freedom of migration throughout the territory of Russia is very much restricted.

Under the registration system every Russian citizen is supposed to be registered in a particular police office at a strictly fixed address. No one can move to another city or even to another apartment without a complicated bureaucratic procedure. Russian citizens who move to another city officially have no right to employment and will face legal difficulties. Anyone visiting another city for a long business trip or for long vacations has to register in a local police office. *Propiska* therefore limits the right of the individual choice of a place to live, and also the place to work. Moreover, an individual without proper registration will not be able to obtain medical care except in an emergency—and even then with a lot of bureaucratic delays (thus opening ways for extortion). Registration at the address of relatives, including parents, usually involves complex court procedures.

Obviously, Moscow offers far more jobs and opportunities than any other city in Russia. For many years the right to be registered in Moscow was the most important ambition of thousands of people, giving rise to corruption and crimes and the ugly phenomenon of marriages of convenience (for one gains the privilege of *propiska* by the merit of marriage). The situation becomes even more complicated for one important reason: the system of official registration gives an individual a right to occupy an apartment for life and if the whole family is registered there, the right to live in the apartment will be passed on to the spouse and children. Privatization of apartments cannot really solve the problem, because even if an individual acquires an apartment registration to live in that city is necessary for the right to use the property. Of course, these regulations and restrictions are not so efficient as the political and economic system undergoes significant changes—a case when general inefficiency of laws can be considered a good thing.

This observation is also true for some other cases. For instance, discrimination on the basis of sexual orientation is still prevalent in Russia, and its official form until very recently was really terrifying. Russian law (Article 121 of the Law Code) until May 1993 bluntly stated that homosexual practice is an offence liable to imprisonment. Ironically enough, the law mentioned only male homosexuality (presumably, in Stalin's days they did not have any idea about female homosexuality).

Not surprisingly, Russian homosexuals were doomed to semi-clandestine existence. While they had access to the mass media and the state had so far tolerated them, according to the law they were automatically regarded as criminals, and they could not be sure when the law would be used against them. Attempts to attract the attention of parliament and government to change this absurd situation only succeeded in May 1993. Even if homosexuals are not regarded as criminals, discrimination against them in employment and a biased social attitude are common. Many are still in prison. The issue now is more a matter of discrimination than of legal punishment for sexual orientation. While there is some progress, learning to become tolerant towards the Russian homosexual community will still take a long time.

The rights of another group of minorities — the religious groups — are officially protected by law, but they still have to rely upon their individual survival skills. This is true, for example, of the Catholics in Russia who, while being equal to the Russian Orthodox church, are still discriminated against even in Moscow. To be a minority still implies facing a lot of trouble in Russia. It is still obligatory to declare your nationality when filling in all kinds of forms; every passport also bears this ethnic label. Some national minorities (like Russian Germans) are still deprived of the right to have territorial autonomy.

The case of discrimination against Jews used to be a big issue in the Soviet Union; in Russia, the situation has changed. Although the Soviet law regarded Jews as equal citizens, and Russian practice has really made them equal citizens in respect of their careers, anti-Semitism at a social level still exists. Extremist organizations enjoy the freedom of demanding Jewish blood. Only one or two cases have been brought to court. Which brings us to the problem of Russian fascism. Does freedom of speech allow a person to terrorize certain ethnic or social groups — Jews, liberals, Asians, anti-communists, etc.? The Russian Code of Laws prohibits propaganda of racist beliefs or violence. But it is usually not applied. Sometimes when ethnic and minority social groups are threatened by fascists, the law does not seem to offer them much protection.

Human rights and Russian foreign policy

The question of human rights is of paramount importance for Russian foreign policy. While this is a very intricate issue, the Russian government's approach to human rights violations is a case of double standards. While Russia's human rights standards ceased to be a critical issue in its relations with Western nations, ironically in the aftermath of the disintegration of the Soviet Union, the rights of the Russians outside Russia (not only ethnic Russians, but also those identifying themselves with Russia, including many Ukrainians, Jews, and Byelorussians) have become a major problem in Russian foreign policy. Outside Russia the rights of such 'Russian-speaking' people are violated in most of the new states. This violation takes different forms.

Apartheid is evident in the policy of Latvia and Estonia. During the general election in Estonia some 42 per cent of the population was deprived of the right to vote. The desire to make Russians second-class citizens, to force them eventually to leave the Baltic states, even takes on legal forms, with state violence not yet leading to bloodshed. In other parts of the former Soviet Union such as Caucasus, Central Asia, and Moldova the lives of Russians are threatened, and they have already become the object of severe new programmes. Even in areas of relative stability, 'mild' forms of discrimination can be observed, whereby Russian-speaking groups begin to lose their jobs and cannot enter the universities. Probably only in two Slavic republics — Ukraine and Byelorus — can Russians still feel free, but not entirely safe with the rise of local nationalism.

So far the Russian government has been unsuccessful in bargaining for the security of the Russian communities even with countries such as Estonia and Latvia which are more concerned about their international images. Russia has moral obligations towards more than 30 million of the people who have suddenly become outcasts. They have nobody else to appeal to, and Russia's moral and political retreat is quite understandably regarded as treachery. But there is another dimension to this problem. If the present regime under the control of the 'liberals' is unable to protect the human rights of its ethnic kin, Russian fascists are more than willing to exploit the issue in their attempt to seize power.

When Russia is unwilling to interfere, the isolated Russian communities must choose between submission to discrimination and revolt. The case of Pridnestrovye (in the territory of the republic of Moldova), when the Russians preferred military conflict to surrender, could be just the beginning of a new trend—a frightening prospect of ethnic conflict similar to what happened in the former Yugoslavia. So far, the Russians outside Russia have displayed patience—probably due to the psychological shock of abrupt change. Yugoslavia was troubled by violent ethnic disputes for a long time and was a united country for a relatively much shorter time. If the Russian enclaves explode in the former Soviet republics, Russian foreign policy may probably be swallowed up by the maelstrom of conflicts. Russian military interference has curbed the bloodshed in Pridnestrovye, but this is an exception rather than the rule. Russia's military participation on the side of Russians might be counterproductive and eventually lead to grave consequences.

Safeguarding the human rights of Russians in the territories of the former Soviet Unions has become a matter of national survival for Russia. The logical choice would be cooperation with other governments in protecting the rights of these Russians. The goal is: to help the Russians integrate into new entities as citizens possessing both equal political/economic rights and ensure their right to survive as different cultural/religious communities. This requires Russia to negotiate with the governments of the new sovereign states and at the same time to find the right third country as mediators (the Scandinavian countries, for example, seem a natural choice for regulating the human rights situation in Estonia and Latvia) in the negotiations.

Russian concern about human rights problems outside Russia, however, seems to be confined to Russians in the former Soviet republics. Russia's double standards are evident in its attitude towards other neighbouring countries with poor human rights records. Russia demands the guarantees of human rights for Russians outside Russia and does not care about the human rights of the others. The Russian government agrees to the non-democratic status of Russians in Uzbekistan, provided they possess equal rights with the locals. Moscow's position can be described in the following way: let the Russians abroad be equal with their new compatriots, be it in democracy or in autocracy. It is as true for China as for the Muslim Central Asian states.

Russia seems to have accepted that a stable political environment in its neighbouring area is preferable to political turmoil even if stability has to be achieved at the expense of human rights violations. For national security reasons Russia prefers to have a politically stable but morally imperfect Uzbekistan, China or Tadjikistan, rather than supporting the struggles for better human rights if it means unpredictable internal conflict among its neighbouring countries. Moreover, the Russian government fears that any attempt to impose democratic values upon its neighbours at the official level will be immediately seen as interference in their domestic affairs. If the United States can afford to take a moral position as the world's only remaining superpower, Russia hardly has the resources for doing the same. Russia is simply not prepared to endanger its geopolitical environment by officially supporting the cause of human rights in China or in Uzbekistan, demonstrating the sentiments that freedom of speech in a neighbouring country is not worth the national security of one's homeland.

Indeed, the efforts of Russian human rights activists from non-governmental organizations like Memorial in Moslem Central Asian republics have already created problems for the Moscow government. The role of Moscow's liberal press is also regarded by some Central Asian states as subversive, and many publications have been banned from those areas. But the Russian government has found itself embroiled in international disagreement over other human rights problems, too. In May 1993 five former Russian army soldiers were sentenced to death in Azerbaijan for participating in combats on the side of Armenia as mercenaries. Moscow has again found itself unable to solve this problem. Russian mercenaries are sought all over the south of the former empire by many rival factions.

One of the major tasks of Russian foreign policy is therefore to help the Russian people who have practically become hostages of the newly independent nationalist regimes in the former Soviet Union. Russia clearly cannot take in all 30 million or even any substantial portion of them. The only realistic step is to make the life of Russians outside Russia bearable. This involves active diplomatic interaction and sometimes possible sanctions against newly independent former republics which violate the basic human rights of Russian-speaking groups.

Russia clearly cannot claim to be an ideal state as far as human rights are concerned, given all the terrible violations and ugly distortions which occur there. Nevertheless, Russia, Ukraine and Byelarus are in the forefront of the democratic movement in the territory of the former Soviet Union, reflecting the sorry state of the general human rights situation in the former Soviet empire. Human rights problems will remain a difficult issue in Russian foreign policy for years to come.

Non-governmental groups and international intervention

Non-governmental human rights groups have been marginalized in contemporary Russia. This could probably be explained by the traditional attitude towards the rights of an individual. Russians have inherited not only the communist past, but also the tsarist Russian legacy which regards an individual as a non-entity in comparison to the state, church and other institutions. This neglect of an individual has a dual effect: people are not interested in general issues of human rights even in their own country; nor do they believe that the efforts of individuals can change the situation.

The most notable among Russian human rights groups is Memorial. This group is perhaps the best example of an internationalized human rights organization in Russia. It maintains links with the West, where it seeks support. Established at the dawn of perestroika to commemorate the victims of Stalin's terror, the organization soon discovered that it could not embrace only the remote past. Homage to the victims of Stalin has been paid even by the orthodox communists in Russia. The organization therefore shifted its attention to more current human rights issues. It is also committed to combating human rights abuses outside Russia in the territory of the former Soviet Union. It has become involved in some of the more notorious cases—for instance, in Uzbekistan, where the opposition leaders were arrested and harassed. In this sense Memorial is already an international organization with a network of support in other former Soviet republics.

Unfortunately Memorial is internally divided and so far has failed to provide leadership to the human rights movement. One major problem is the absence of a leader. Only one person—the late academician Andrei D. Sakharov—had the stature for this exceptional role.[2] Other leaders of the former dissident movement are either busy recriminating or suspecting each other of being KGB agents in the past. Some of them have emigrated and the rest have to struggle in the intricate art of political survival in contemporary Russia.

The role of non-governmental organizations in securing the rights of Russians outside Russia remains unclear. The main problem is that all the new regimes in the territory of the former Soviet Union are still not taking non-governmental organizations seriously. That probably can be explained by the legacy of totalitarianism: even the 'liberals' are unwilling to accept an idea that a group of private citizens can be influential. Many of them believe that the world could be run only in the corridors of power and not by the efforts of the concerned citizens. So far, non-governmental organizations do not look very viable in Russia. The only non-governmental institution which can be regarded with a certain amount of respect is probably the church. Human rights activists representing a church with an international reputation probably may have a better chance of influencing the politicians.

International pressure probably will have a greater impact on the human rights situation in Russia. So far there have been no international efforts in combating human rights abuse in Russia. From time to time visits by Western human rights activists to a prison or a mental clinic may create a scandal among the mass media and for middle-level bureaucrats, but the impact has been limited. In contrast to the human rights movement, the international green movement that has swept through Russia at least can be identified as part of a broader network. The international human rights movement has ignored Russia, under the misperception that democracy had after all triumphed in this part of the world.

It is only natural that the land with no experience in democracy could not become a paradise immediately after the collapse of the old regime. However, this does not mean that Russian society today should care only about bread; as we know, bread does not come without human rights. Much could be achieved in other areas: capital punishment; the rights of people violated by economic mismanagement; corruption of the judicial system and inability of the police and courts to attend to the basic problems of citizens' safety; the rights of women and children and probably many others.

At a time when new values are emerging in Russia, the influence of the world community upon it in the sphere of human rights is extremely important. It should be stressed that the sooner the West parts with the myth about the triumph of democracy in Russia, the better. A country in which human rights are violated is not only bad for its citzens, it could also become dangerous to the world. The dragon of totalitarianism is still not completely defeated in Russia. The country awaits St. George.

Notes

1. The following list of English-language works provides more information on the changes which have taken place in the former Soviet Union and recent developments in Russia: David W. Benn, *From Glasnost to Freedom of Speech* (London: The Royal Institute of International Affairs, 1992); Michael Binyon, *Life in Russia* (New York: Pantheon Books, 1983); Elena Bonner, *Alone Together* (New York: Alfred A. Knopf, 1986); David Cane, *Soviet Society Under Perestroika* (Boston: Unwin Hyman, 1990); Walter Lacquear, *The Long Road to Freedom* (London: Unwin Hyman, 1990); Tony Parker, *Russian Voices* (London: Jonathan Cape, 1991); Alexander Yanov, *The Russian Challenge and the Year 2001* (New York: Basil Blackwell, 1987).
2. See George Bailey, *The Making of Andrei Sakharov* (London: The Penguin Press, 1989).

PART III
INSTITUTIONAL AND REGIONAL PERSPECTIVES

11
THE ROLE OF THE UNITED NATIONS IN THE PROVISION OF HUMANITARIAN ASSISTANCE: NEW PROBLEMS AND NEW RESPONSES

PAUL TAYLOR

Introduction

This chapter is concerned with the infringement of human rights as an aspect of complex emergencies, which include threats to individuals from natural or man-made disasters, and even war.[1] In such circumstances it is likely that the rights of individuals will also be transgressed, often deliberately by warring groups and governments, and sometimes accidentally when government has broken down. Examples include Cambodia, Angola, Liberia, Mozambique, Somalia and former Yugoslavia, but there are others, and an increasing number in the early 1990s.

The United Nations organizations and the non-governmental organizations have been under increasing pressure to attempt to intervene in such emergencies, to provide humanitarian relief, to protect the peace through the use of peacekeeping forces and to help with the reconstruction of failing states. In a broad and in a narrow sense they have been concerned with human rights: broad in the sense of attempting to provide a minimum acceptable standard of physical welfare, narrow in the sense of attempting to correct the worse infringements of the standards of a civilized society.

In this chapter the problems which have arisen in the provision of such assistance will be discussed. The discussion is divided into three sections. First, the problems which arise at the point of involvement by international organizations in an emergency are examined. Second, the problems of providing assistance are evaluated. Third, the problems of recovery and rehabilitation, which could lead to the withdrawal of the international organizations, are considered. If the discussion occasionally appears to be overly optimistic it is because stress is upon trends or new arrangements which seem to be a move in the right direction, and not because they have led to successful outcomes. Who could think otherwise at a time of crisis in so many parts of the world?

Sovereignty and international humanitarian assistance

What considerations are relevant to the involvement of the international community within a country? A first response, and one which derives from a rather fundamentalist interpretation of Article 2(7) of the UN Charter, is that there can be no intervention within a state without the express consent of the government of that state. The implication appears to be that no form of behaviour of a sovereign government within its own frontiers is a matter of concern to outsiders. This position is probably most frequently illustrated in the arguments favoured by the government of mainland China.[2] This position might be compared with the other traditional view, namely that intervention within a country to promote human rights is only capable of justification on the basis of a threat to international peace and security. Evidence of this could be the appearance of significant numbers of refugees, or the judgement that in the circumstances of the emergency other states might intervene militarily. In the hands of liberal lawyers this condition appeared flexible enough to justify intervention to defend human rights whenever it seemed prudent. In the hardline view, however, it was a more difficult condition: though the Chinese did not dispute the general principle, and could not if they were to remain members of the UN, they saw it more as a way of defeating any proposal to intervene. The liberal perspective saw it as a bridge to action, the hardline as a way of creating barriers by denying there was a threat to international peace and security wherever possible.

In the last few years, however, other justifications for intervention, in the face of the government opposition have emerged, though they have remained controversial. It was pointed out that the UN Charter had not merely asserted the rights of states but also the rights of peoples, and that statehood could be interpreted as being conditional upon respecting the rights of peoples. For instance, the Preamble held that the organization was 'to reaffirm faith in fundamental human rights', and Article 1(3) asserted the obligation to 'achieve international cooperation . . . in promoting and encouraging respect for human rights and fundamental freedoms for all'. There was ample evidence in the Charter to justify the view that the sovereignty of states was not unconditional and that the extreme transgression of human rights could itself be a justification for intervention by the international community.

There were a few examples of this view in the early 1990s: the most clear was probably Security Council Resolution 688 which sanctioned the creation of the Safe Havens in Iraq at the end of the Gulf War, which were intended to protect the Kurds and marsh Shias against Saddam Hussein. The allies committed themselves to defend the Kurds and to provide humanitarian assistance. In the major UN pronouncements, e.g. A/43/131 and A/46/182,[3] there was consistent reference to the primary responsibility of the target states for dealing with complex crises within their frontiers, although A/46/182 implied some relaxation of this in its precise wording: it held that

the sovereignty, territorial integrity and national unity of States must be fully respected in accordance with the Charter of the UN. In this context, humanitarian assistance *should* be provided with the consent of the affected country and *in principle* on the basis of an appeal by the affected country.

The use of 'in principle' and 'should', implied that there could be occasions when government approval was not possible, but where intervention was nevertheless necessary.

There was discussion as to whether the existing procedures of the UN, relying in particular on the approval of the Security Council, could be regarded as an adequate authorization of such intervention, or whether further safeguards were necessary, such as as a two-thirds majority in the General Assembly and the supervision of the International Court of Justice.[4]

There were in practice ways of dealing with the problem by less direct means. A small number of international organizations, such as the UN Children's Fund (UNICEF) and the International Committee of the Red Cross (ICRC), were not required by their founding agreements, or the rules which governed their operation, to obtain the formal consent of governments for intervention. They naturally preferred this, but assumed that they could work on a territory unless expressly forbidden from doing so. In Cambodia UNICEF and ICRC had established a presence during the Vietnamese occupation and were allowed to operate throughout the area in a low-key way. The publicity generated by reports of massive starvation there by the journalist John Pilger, who had the support of OXFAM, not only led to serious quarrels between OXFAM and the other participating organizations, but invited the Vietnamese government to restrict aid to the area it occupied. Eventually aid had to be delivered to the Khmer Rouge area in the north west of the country from Thailand.[5] NGOs were also sometimes able to intervene without positive approval both because of their greater flexibility than the UN and their lesser sensitivity to political constraints.

So far the discussion has concerned the nature of the right to intervene in a state. But there is, of course, a prior question, that of obtaining information about whether human rights in any sense are being contravened. In the late 1980s and early 1990s there were a number of developments in this connection. In A/46/182 it had been argued that information on disasters, such as incipient famine or other forms of catastrophic failure, could be gathered by the existing development machinery, in particular the Resident Coordinator of the UN Development Programme (UNDP). A new organization could play a part in this collection, which will be discussed later in this essay, namely the Department of Humanitarian Assistence (DHA). It was also possible to use higher forms of technology. For instance, satellite observation could indicate the areas where it looked as if crops might fail because of inadequate rainfall and soil conditions.

But this kind of information was only part of the problem. In complex emergencies it was not just a question of the scarcity of physical resources but also of forms of man-made crisis. It looked as if the UN was entering a new phase in its history, one in which stress was placed on the gathering and analysis of a wide range of information on an increasing range of questions. It was, of course, only on the basis of adequate information that timely action could be taken. But the knowledge that such information was indeed being collected might also act as a deterrent to actions that could precipitate man-made disasters and abuse of human rights. It was as important to convince potential malefactors that they would be seen as it was actually to collect relevant information and intelligence materials.

But other forms of visibility were also now demanded. After the Gulf War it was proposed that there should be a register of arms sales and movements, and the UN was in the process of setting this up at the time of writing in late 1993. The point was made that collecting this information was not at all difficult since most of it was already in the public realm; bringing it together and making it available in what was called a Global Watch was, however, new.

Alongside this could be placed the proposal for an International Court of War Crimes, which was proposed during the war in Yugoslavia and which was also now to be established. This was not merely to bring the errant Serb leaders to book, but, at British insistence, was to obtain a general mandate to deal with those who committed crimes against humanity in times of war. It was striking that this went beyond the Nuremberg system in two ways. First, it was to be a permanent mechanism, and could therefore be seen as a system of justice detached from the issues in particular situations and the grievances or prejudices of victors: it was part of the process of strengthening the community of states. Secondly, it could deal with war in general and not just between states: the offences to be judged in Yugoslavia were committed in the course of civil war, and this was another sense in which the frontiers of states were being permeated more thoroughly. On two occasions in recent years the UN had required that data on war crimes should be collected — the Gulf War and Yugoslavia in Security Council Resolutions 674 (October 1990) and 771 (August 1992) respectively. International accountability was to be strengthened: human rights transgressions, even related to the conduct of war, were now more likely to be exposed to the attention of the international community.

A great change occurred in the 1980s with regard to the role of non-governmental organizations in this connection. There were still major complaints about the inadequate links between NGOs and IGOs and the latter still paid insufficient attention to the former and seemed to grant them, in Geneva and New York, what could only be called a 'grace and favour' relationship: they were called in at the discretion of the IGO. But there was considerable evidence to indicate that the gap was being closed, and that they were being brought more into the picture as their size and professionalism increased. They certainly played a vital role in a number of areas such as Somalia and Cambodia, both in the central mechanisms and in the field. NGOs also played a crucial role in identifying and advertising abuses of human rights: Amnesty International was perhaps the best-known organization in this area, but many other organizations were involved, such as Save the Children Fund, OXFAM, Catholic Relief Services, and many others.

The institutional dimension of humanitarian intervention

In the operations themselves, after a crisis had been identified, a number of further issues arose. General Assembly Resolution 46/182 had indicated that the international machinery then existing was unsatisfactory. It was proposed that a new institution should be set up to replace the main body previously entrusted with response to disasters, namely the UN Disaster Relief Organization (UNDRO). This new institution appeared in 1992, though at the time of writing it was still in the process of construction in the light of new reports and experience; its first head, Jan Eliason, was appointed in April 1992. By late 1993 this new institution was to fit into an emerging pattern of UN and NGO involvement in disasters. This section discusses the main features of the pattern which has emerged.

It was recognized that the funding of disaster relief had to be managed in such a fashion that donor states would have confidence that their money would be spent according to a well-constructed overall plan. It was necessary for requests for funding to be consolidated. The DHA took over major responsibility for this and, unlike previous efforts at rationalization in the UN system, it looked as if the DHA had succeeded in this enterprise. Appeals with regard to the Horn of Africa, including Somalia, were favourably received by the states in mid-1993, although inevitably some problems remained. Some of these were probably inherent in the process: NGOs complained that their efforts were not adequately reflected in the funds which they received through the appeals, and that they had too little input into the assessment.

Some specialized agencies suspected that their constitutional independence might be challenged by the new institution. Organizations like the UN High Commission for Refugees (UNHCR) were quick to react against any apparent attempt to extend the operational role of the DHA, and this was interpreted as including the assumption of responsibility for the initial response to a crisis. The most that could be expected was that the DHA would augment the existing arrangements by acting as a facilitator.

This was not, however, a trivial function. There was much to be done by way of promoting improved contacts between the various organizations involved in the routine of international governance and in the special circumstances of particular disasters. The DHA could make a major contribution by promoting plans for dealing with crises, with a role for the major contributors agreed in advance. It could also play a major role in collecting and analysing information, and in triggering a response. In performing these tasks it could work with the major inter-organizational committee involved in the area of disaster relief, the Inter-Agency Standing Committee (IASC), also established as a result of A/46/182, and it needed to develop its service function with regard to this committee. Of great importance was the promotion of the exchange of staff, in particular the placing of people with field experience in the central management mechanisms. In mid-1993 the DHA itself still had insufficient staff with field experience, and the agencies lacked sufficient contact with the NGOs. The role for the DHA was therefore that of a facilitator, a promoter of coordination and contacts, rather than of a manager.

There was a need for an agreed process for approaching problems. The demand for a new international resource in the shape of the DHA was well founded. But despite this imperative, it was also necessary to vary the in-country response so that it could be tailored more precisely to local circumstances. There could be no general ideal type of involvement. For example, it might be appropriate, as was the case with humanitarian assistance in Kenya in 1991–2, to have a sensitive response to the problems of consolidating the authority of national governments (see the further discussion of this in the next section). In other cases a chain of command that passed more clearly through UN mechanisms and that bypassed governments that were corrupt or tyrannical might be advisable. But the nature of the UN system meant that even when a tighter international effort was indicated it was a question of managing a pluralistic international system of organizations, be they agencies or states.

By mid-1993 a standard procedure for managing complex emergencies had emerged. The main elements were a chain of responsibility via a special representative of the Secretary General. Earlier operations had been led by specialized agencies, such as UNHCR in Yugoslavia, but the majority of involvements in Africa had been led by Secretary General Representatives and, as indicated below, for a number of reasons this appeared to be the way of the future.

Beneath the Representative the emerging pattern in 1993 was a troika of offices. Two of these had a DHA involvement: a political mechanism linked with DHA in New York (the political sections of the Secretariat under Marrack Goulding and James Jonah), and a humanitarian mechanism linked with DHA in Geneva. Both of these could be augmented according to the needs of the particular crisis. The third was the peacekeeping element, if required, which would be managed in 1993 by the peacekeeping section in the Secretariat in New York, acting under a mandate agreed in resolutions of the Security Council.

There were a number of reasons for the increasing tendency for disasters to involve a Special Representative of the Secretary General. One of these was to do with the initial stages of an intervention. The arguments were that if a complex emergency arose, normally this would mean that the existing mechanisms had in some sense been discredited. The process of development, which is the normal concern of the UNDP mechanism, would have failed, and it was likely that there would have been a failure in relationships between the Resident Coordinator and the government of the failing state, if that survived. There was a good case for a new start, and for injecting a new measure of authority in the form of the Special Representative.

There was, however, also the need for a trigger. The DHA could act in this capacity more readily than UNDP: it might be expected to have a more objective viewpoint concerning the various economic and social trends which it was observing. It could blow the whistle when the UNDP Coordinator hesitated to do this. In other words, the development process might be expected to form one loop of links between the international community and the failing state, but it would be necessary to embark upon a second loop if crisis turned into disaster.

In any crisis situation there may well be problems of security which produce problems of their own. The Secretary General Boutros Boutros Ghali in *An Agenda for Peace* [6] confirmed what seemed in mid-1992 to be an expanding range of UN security/peacekeeping operations. In addition to traditional forms of peacekeeping, he argued that two other forms of security activity by the UN were required. One was a flexible force capable of being moved into areas at short notice where a threat had been observed. The argument was that if such a force had been available for stationing on Kuwaiti territory before the Gulf War, Saddam Hussein would have held back. A second type of force was for use after a ceasefire, or settlement, and would be much more proactive than forces hitherto in defending the terms of such agreements.

New forms of intervention linking military and humanitarian activities had also been observed in the practice of the UN. In ex-Yugoslavia, UN Protection Force 2 (UNPROFOR 2) had been given in Security Council Resolution 770 of 13 August 1992 the mandate of ensuring that humanitarian assistance got through to areas facing deprivation.[7] They were also given a mandate to use force to ensure that such assistance was delivered. This was the first time that the military had been used in such a way, although the actual use of force to ensure delivery was avoided, largely because of fear of the consequences if more aggressive forms of delivery were embarked upon. In Somalia the United States volunteered to send 30,000 troops to protect the delivery of aid, an offer which was accepted by the Security Council in Resolution 794 of December 1992, though there was doubt about whether they were expected to protect the organizations and their representatives involved in aid provision. Although the force had been drastically reduced by mid-1993 and replaced by a UN force of equal, if not greater, size, the activity still had the special character that it engaged the military in the active pursuit of humanitarian assistance.

By late 1993, however, a number of problems had been observed by the UN in the use of military forces in these new ways. From a period of some optimism about such arrangements in the early 1990s—the time of the writing of *An Agenda for Peace*—a new pessimism had set in, such that the Secretary General himself was reported by October 1993 as having come to the conclusion that the UN should not go beyond traditional forms of peacekeeping.[8] It was not clear, however, whether this public doubt was part of an exercise to engage the attention of governments, or whether it was a genuine exercise in damage limitation.

There was a problem to do with the strategy of using peacekeeping forces. In traditional forms of peacekeeping, the UN force was at its strongest when adopting an interpositional role between two armies after a ceasefire had been agreed. The UN had also been involved in two instances of enforcement, which was closer to the pattern of involvement foreseen in the Charter in Chapter 7. The UN would commit itself to a principle reflected in a preferred outcome and would use force to realize this outcome. In practice, of course, the UN was never able to do this strictly according to the Charter, and only went to war on two occasions—Korea in the early 1950s and the Gulf in 1991—when the United States, as it were, acted as a hired gun.

The problem in the strategy of peacekeeping was that once the traditional peacekeeping role had been abandoned, for instance in the more proactive delivery of humanitarian assistance, it was very difficult to avoid being pushed towards the other extreme of the spectrum—enforcement. UN troops—especially the more effective and committed ones—were identified as enemies by parties to the dispute. They were more likely to be attacked and pushed into an escalation of the use of violence. This had clearly happened by late 1992 in Yugoslavia with the British forces, and in Somalia with the

Americans. In other words, the spectrum of conceivable UN use of the military had a hollow centre: once traditional peacekeeping had been abandoned there was pressure to move to the other end of the spectrum and engage in enforcement.

This led immediately to the second problem, or rather a set of interrelated problems. Governments were not prepared to accept the cost of financing the enlargement of operations, especially at a time when the economies of the developed states—the major contributors—were under pressure. Governments were also faced with another kind of humanitarian dilemma—how could they persuade their people to accept casualties among their forces when national interests were not directly threatened? Indeed, how could the killing of their people, in the cause of the very humanitarian principles that were being disregarded by those in the target state, be justified? The only response to this was to identify more closely the political purposes of intervention, which would lead to the conclusion that any separation of humanitarian, political and security concerns was difficult. It was often quite hard to make a convincing presentation of what principles needed to be defended. The risks seemed out of proportion with the gains.

There was also the problem of who would command such forces if involvement was accepted. UN command was acceptable for traditional low-key peacekeeping, but could governments allow UN commanders, or the Secretary-General, to take hands-on control of more deadly activities? The Americans in particular were clear that they would not hand over command of US forces to the UN, but other states had their reservations.

Such doubts were accentuated by the observation that forces originally committed for humanitarian purposes were being dragged into enforcement and targeted as enemies. In both Yugoslavia and Somalia, as more active peacekeeping was used, there were reports of national officers referring to their own governments for instructions about whether to comply with UN orders. Hence by late 1993 Boutros Boutros Ghali was thinking again about how far the extension of UN power could go.

The withdrawal of humanitarian intervention

In this discussion of the experience of humanitarian assistance one theme has as yet only been addressed obliquely. This concerns the guidelines which should be followed to facilitate withdrawal from crisis situations. Clearly questions about rehabilitation and recovery should form a part of thinking during involvement in, and the conduct of, such operations. The NGOs, IGOs and governments concerned should be posing three questions simultaneously: how to get in, how to be effective, and how to get out. The reader can identify two continua of concern; the humanitarian assistance process is at their point of intersection. First is the continuum of involvement, operation and withdrawal; withdrawal is itself obviously a fairly large category which will be further broken down below. Second is the continuum of emergency aid, political context and initiative, and security.

The reader will not be surprised to discover that this is a fairly brief section, in view of the slight experience of international organizations in successfully concluding a programme of humanitarian intervention. The best that can be done is to set out the various issues that arise in this situation and that need to be noted during the conduct and establishment of such operations.

The withdrawal phase can be broken down into at least four subphases. The first is the direct provision of relief to the human suffering and repair of the damage caused by the disaster. Second is the process of rehabilitation, the reinstatement of the integrity of individuals and their relationships, so that a potential for self-reliance is generated. Third is the process of reconstruction, during which economic, social, administrative and governmental arrangements are built up and made effective: the civil structure of the state is regenerated. And fourth is the process of development, which might be regarded as the norm for large parts of the globe.

One of the parts of this spectrum which has received relatively little attention is that concerned with rehabilitation and reconstruction. It should be focused at three levels at each of which there has been some evidence for new concern. At the local level it is necessary to work with and to enhance the capacity of existing local authority structures. It is also necessary to work with existing economic structures, in other words to provide food for work except in the worst of situations. Local merchants need to be enlisted in support of distribution programmes by allowing them to purchase food and sell it in the markets. Ingenuity has to be used in finding ways to provide currency for such purchases which does not appear simply to be given. Catholic Relief Services reported its experience with regard to moving from food aid to food self-sufficiency. This problem has indeed been much discussed in its technical aspects. But it was evident that the need for the effective micro-management of the process was still understressed. Too often this delicate evolution depended on the relatively uncoordinated interaction of a large number of groups, ranging from NGOs like CARE, OXFAM and Save the Children Fund, to UNICEF, World Food Programme, and the Food and Agricultural Organization. There was a need for sensitive micro-management and hence for specific coordinating mechanisms at the local level which, despite the good intentions of individual organizations, was not always available.

This suggested a need not only for linkage between the organizations dealing with the disaster, but also between them and the development agencies, as well as the closer involvement of the Bretton Woods organizations, in order to promote rehabilitation and development out of disaster relief.

Second there was a need to deal at country level. There was evidence in Somalia in the summer of 1993 of the beginnings of a major effort to regenerate the country's governmental and administrative structures. The DHA had embarked upon a major programme involving the setting up of regional administrations, and in 1993 was looking to recruit up to 1000 advisers to man these operations. The intention was not to subdivide the country, but to shape local government in consultation with established local clan authorities. Similarly there was an attempt to link the relatively stable, and semi-detached, northern part of Somalia now called Somaliland, through this process — not to force unity, but to generate reconciliation. The Catholic Relief Services (CRS) were, unlike ICRC, very proactive on this as they were anxious to bring about

reconciliation between conflicting groups wherever possible. In countries —
though there were few of them — where there seemed to have been a renewal
of civil authority as in Ethiopia, it was important to be flexible in the assistance arrangements, so that the international organizations worked with,
rather than against, the governments in question (see above). It was also
appropriate to work with existing stable governments, as in Kenya.

Thirdly, there was a need to do something at the international level. There
was some evidence of greater concern with this process on the part of the
leading states. The US Congress, for instance, had for the first time allocated
money specifically to reconstruction, as opposed to development or relief, in
autumn 1992. A total of $100 million had been allocated for relief, rehabilita-
tion *and* reconstruction in the Sub-Sahara region. Moreover, $15 million was
allocated for reconstruction through OFDA in three countries — Angola, Mozambique and Ethiopia — though because of the Somalia crisis in the event
only the money for Mozambique was allocated. There was also a more widespread realization among the leading developed countries that the relief of
debt repayment obligations was a necessary part of the reconstruction process.   To summarize: wherever possible food aid should not be allowed to
interfere with the process of growing local produce. In other words, there
should be help with seeds and the survival of livestock whenever this is
feasible as an alternative to food aid. There should be serious study of the
process of reconstruction after an emergency. The UN system and indeed the
NGOs have not yet acquired special expertise in this area, and it is arguable
that a new agency concerned with reconstruction should be established.

Emergency provision should not be at the expense of longer-term relief and
development operations. It is dangerous if 'hot' crises attract such a level of
funding that more routine programmes suffer. The UNICEF evidence is striking in this context: 50,000 children died in 1992 in 'hot' crises, but 13 million
died as a result of ailments like diarrhoea and dysentery in longer-term 'cold'
crises.

In promoting recovery and reconstruction more effort needs to be given to
support for internal migrants; no organization had a mandate to deal with this
problem in 1993, though UNDP and UNHCR had both acted in this context.
There are two aspects to this problem: one is that the provision of assistance
should not involve large movements of population. The setting up of the
special feeding centres by OXFAM and other agencies in the Ethiopian crisis
in the mid-1980s was generally regarded as a mistake, since accumulating
large numbers of people increased the prevalence of diseases and led to many
more deaths. Conversely, where there has been migration people should be
helped to return home to rebuild their lives.

The UN should build on local authority structures and set up an apparatus
for the recovery of the state. This involves the role of conferring legitimacy
to a new regime, and of helping it with the training and supply of adminis-
trators. To say this implies a position which would have been regarded as
being at least 'politically incorrect' just a few years ago. It implies a frontal
challenge to the terms of the General Assembly Resolution of December 1960
under which claims for independence by colonies were to be allowed uncon-
ditionally i.e. not dependent on meeting any kind of educational, social or

economic standards. The result of this policy, which was first resisted by the countries of the developed world and then welcomed as a way of abandoning their responsibilities, led to the setting up of a number of utterly incompetent and sometimes corrupt regimes which completely failed to provide for the welfare of their citizens.

In reconstructing states which have experienced major humanitarian crises and the collapse of administrative and political structures, the UN could take on a kind of modified trusteeship role. It could help create well-founded states. It could also issue certificates of legitimacy to new regimes, which is in fact what it purported to do when it helped set up and supervise elections in Namibia, Cambodia and Angola, and acted to ensure proper respect for human rights in El Salvador.

Conclusions

According to General Assembly Resolution 46/182 humanitarian assistance should be provided 'in principle on the basis of an appeal by the affected country' and that 'the affected state has the primary role in the initiation, organization, coordination and implementation of humanitarian assistance within its territory'. Wherever possible, therefore, the structures of the recipient states should, accordingly, be fully involved with the operation, and help to formulate their own demands of the international community. There are cases where this principle does not seem to have been followed. For instance, the Kenyan authorities felt that their own Drought Recovery Programme (DRP) had been dealt with in a fairly cavalier way in the Special Emergency Programme for the Horn of Africa (SEPHA) consolidated appeal in 1992. The Kenyans had drawn up an appeal in close consultation with the agencies involved, so that when the programme was launched in October 1992 they were confident that it had the full backing of the UN. But subsequently 'they felt uncertain about how far funds contributed to SEPHA would be used for the DRP' — to use the tactful words of a report written by an official. In this instance the principle of working through national structures and helping with their operations did not seem to have been respected.

A great difficulty for the humanitarian assistance process is encountered at this point. In general it is, of course, necessary to work with and to sustain national authorities. The traditional view of sovereignty would lead to a relative indifference to the character of the regime except in extreme cases. But how can a decision be reached that a government has become excessively abhorrent so that to work with it in some areas of humanitarian assistance is to defend the indefensible? And at what point, and how, is a judgement to be made that the failure of a government has been so catastrophic that some kind of rebuilding from a lower level of organization in the state is necessary? Working with acceptable regimes in what appears to be a manageable crisis could be via the UNDP system and in particular the Resident Coordinator; but if there were a collapse of such a magnitude as to constitute a complex emergency, and if the government were discredited, then a different mechanism would be indicated and brought afresh into the country as already discussed. The more serious the crisis and the greater the necessity for humanitarian assistance, the more important it is to make a judgement about a regime's acceptability: this question cannot be evaded just because of a greater capacity to intervene.

This reveals an irony in the position of the UN with regard to sovereignty and Article 2(7) of the UN Charter. A more flexible view of sovereignty is sought in order to facilitate more effective humanitarian assistance. At first sight, as the Secretary General admitted (BBC Radio 4 programme, 'The Thin Blue Line' Sunday, 25 April 1993), this might appear to be a licence for the richer states to act as a world policeman and to trample on the interests of the weaker and less developed states. But the purpose of UN activities at the end of the day is to make states stronger not weaker, to make the world safe for sovereignty. It is recognized that the Geneva Conventions, and international law regarding human rights, rest on the sovereignty of states. It is the states that sanction it and that are required to uphold it. States that are properly constituted, in respecting human rights and in promoting human welfare effectively, are more likely to be the strong and stable pillars of such a system.

Notes

1. What follows relies heavily upon research carried out by the author in Geneva, New York and Washington for his *Options for the Reform of the International System for Humanitarian Assistance*, which was written with the generous support of the Centre for the Study of Global Governance at the LSE and the Save the Childen Fund in 1992-3. This will be published in 1994 by Pinter, London.
2. See contributions from Yufan Liang and Wang Baoliu in the proceedings of the conference, *The New World Order and the Role of the United Nations*, Seoul, Republic of Korea, September 21-2 1993. See also *The White Paper on Human Rights in China* (Beijing: State Council, 1991).
3. Major UN pronouncements of 20 March 1989, and 14 April 1992 respectively.
4. See Development Studies Association, *The United Nations Humanitarian Response* (November 1992).
5. See Maggie Black, *A Cause for our Times: OXFAM the First 50 Years* (Oxford: Oxford University Press, 1992), pp. 219-21.
6. Boutros Boutros Ghali, *An Agenda for Peace* (New York: Unites Nations Publication, 1992).
7. See John Zametica, *The Yugoslav conflict*, Adelphi Paper no. 270 (London: Institute of International and Strategic Studies, 1992).
8. See *The Guardian*, 29 October 1993.

12

ECONOMIC COOPERATION AND HUMAN RIGHTS IN THE ASIA-PACIFIC REGION: THE ROLE OF REGIONAL INSTITUTIONS

LAWRENCE T. WOODS*

Introduction

The conceptual debate over human rights in the Asia-Pacific region rages at many levels.[1] State and societal attitudes towards human rights within national jurisdictions also provoke a variety of questions, regardless of how one defines the concept or the intellectual space within which the debate occurs. Some of these questions pertain to the place of global international governmental organizations (IGOs) such as the United Nations (UN), or subregional IGOs like the Association of Southeast Asian Nations (ASEAN).

This chapter looks at the institutional space between the UN and ASEAN—the regional space. The chapter will focus on the present and potential roles of regional institutions. It will review the earlier contributions of the defunct Institute of Pacific Relations (IPR). Then it will examine the three international non-governmental organizations (INGOs) with regional economic cooperation mandates: the Pacific Trade and Development Conference (PAFTAD), the Pacific Basin Economic Council (PBEC), and the Pacific Economic Cooperation Council (PECC). Finally, the impact of an intergovernmental newcomer—the Asia Pacific Economic Cooperation (APEC) forum—will be evaluated.[2]

The non-governmental regional institutions discussed in this chapter are not like dedicated, issue-specific INGOs such as Amnesty International or Asia Watch which monitor and publicize human rights violations, pressure governments to respect and defend human rights, mount letter-writing campaigns on behalf of political prisoners, seek to build global consciousness and shape societal values, and participate directly in the debate over human rights via their own activities and UN agencies.[3] None the less, together with IPR they are worthy of being assessed because of their prominence within the Pacific economic cooperation movement, a movement joined in 1989 by APEC. If this governmental entity continues to gather momentum, these regional institutions may take on new and influential positions beyond economic development, and may shape the regional human rights agenda. This said, the conclusion which emerges from the analysis that follows is that the regional option today is reminiscent of an expedient, hypocritical gap where ethics need not apply. At best, this option is indicative of a trend which sees human rights issues allegedly addressed through the back door and in an even more indirect way than during the days of the IPR.

Regional institutions and the hypocrisy gap

Regionalism tends to be fostered in the first instance by those interested in military/strategic or economic issues (what Ralph Pettman would call high or low politics), not social issues like human rights (for Pettman, the stuff of even lower politics).[4] When human rights are taken seriously at the governmental level, it tends to be within the context of a bilateral relationship between states or a global organization. Contemporary examples of the former would be US-China and Canadian–Indonesian relations, with the American government intermittently attempting to use legislation affecting trade to influence the Chinese government's attitude towards human rights and the Canadian government belatedly seeking to tie the delivery of development assistance to the Indonesian government's human rights record. The Japanese government and the European Community have also sought to tie development assistance to human rights. In each case, it must be remembered that the need to placate the outcry from one's own voting public may provide as much impetus for such policy initiatives as the observed foreign indiscretions.[5]

The global approach is exemplified by the use of the UN as a forum and instrument in the human rights debate. Its assemblies and agencies have concerned themselves with human rights issues since the organization's inception, the Universal Declaration of Human Rights and subsequent covenants (on civil and political rights and on economic, cultural and social rights), protocols, conventions and declarations being the standards against which behaviour is measured. The June 1993 World Conference on Human Rights held in Vienna is the most recent manifestation of this global approach—which has been and is being used in related issue areas where problems requiring global solutions have been identified (i.e. the environment, the rights of indigenous peoples, the status and treatment of women).

The logic of states and societal groups pursuing human rights through the UN is based upon a belief in the universality and indivisibility of human rights. The desirability and attainability of universal agreement of human rights are also assumed, the existence of the Universal Declaration supposedly making this more than an assumption. Yet we know that this belief is disputed. The creation of the other UN documents on specific human rights suggests that these rights are divisible. The universality and indivisibility of human rights are further challenged in much the same way that those who proclaimed the value of collective security at the global level were undercut by the encouragement offered to regionalism within Chapter VIII of the UN Charter itself. This opening fostered the emergence of regional collective security organizations and alliances such as the North Atlantic Treaty Organization (NATO), the Organization of American States (OAS), the Organization of African Unity (OAU), the South Asian Association for Regional Cooperation (SAARC), and the Australia–New Zealand–United States security treaty (ANZUS). Similarly, those who saw utility in a global trade agreement are now being challenged by the problematic negotiations on trade liberalization under the General Agreement on Tariffs and Trade (GATT) and the emergence of regional and subregional trading arrangements and blocs in Europe, North America, Southeast Asia, the South Pacific, and the Asia-Pacific region as a whole.

What is evident beyond these conceptual disputes and practical challenges is that state interests in geopolitics or economics often drive the movement toward a regional option before human rights concerns are considered. Europe has witnessed the creation of NATO and the construction of the European Coal and Steel Community in 1952 prior to the entering into force of the European Convention on Human Rights in 1953. Politics and economics have continued to drive the European Economic Community and European Community, with the social legislation within the Maastricht Treaty arising more recently.

In the Americas, the intervals were even greater, with the North American Aerospace Defence Command (NORAD), NATO and OAS in place well before the signing of the American Convention on Human Rights in 1978.[6] The Canada–US Free Trade Agreement and the nascent North American Free Trade Agreement were presented without regard for human rights; the issue only arose after the Canadian and American publics—fearing job losses and the further erosion of national control over economic, environmental and energy policies—began asking questions about working conditions and environmental protection legislation in Mexico. Pettman would say that this sequence reflects the priorities of states. In other words, it mirrors state interests (which some would equate with class interests) and states are bound to be interested in the preservation and enhancement of the state before they become interested in the preservation and enhancement of human rights, especially those vested in the individual rather than the collective.

It is possible then that participation in or support for regional non-governmental and governmental institutions is really a way to get around the need to address human rights or to pay it lip-service while pursuing economic priorities. If a state is not interested in defending the rights of the individual and equates state-making with wealth-making rather than person-, culture- or society-making, then the regional option may be a way to circumvent concern for human rights. In this case the observation that human rights ought to be universally accepted and therefore addressed by global institutions would serve as a justification for failing to address the issue in the regional context, the UN Charter's encouragement of regional mechanisms notwithstanding. A hypocrisy gap could thus emerge as regional bodies assert that human rights issues are better addressed through bilateral relations or global institutions, the regional bodies themselves becoming vehicles for the pursuit of economic growth and profit.

Non-governmental institutions sometimes become the vehicles of choice in these limited regional pursuits, especially in the early stages of regionalism, precisely because they enable the states and societal players involved to avoid protocol. What is going on in these fora may also be projected as of little significance when compared with official governmental interaction. These fallacious public/private and official/unofficial dichotomies are used by some to skirt the scrutiny of the otherwise closely monitored diplomatic process so that understandings can be reached and deals made behind closed doors without transparency and without explicit commitments being given by the parties involved. However, by operating via private, unofficial channels, bolder and innovative initiatives aimed at addressing perennially thorny problems such as human rights may also evolve.

Region-wide economic cooperation has been supported by Asian governments whose priorities were based on the assumptions that geopolitical and economic stability promotes or is a prerequisite for the personal well-being of the citizen. To proponents in so-called developed democracies, this means that the promotion of good government (read 'democracy') and economic development will naturally enhance human rights by addressing basic human needs (or subsistence rights)[7] and creating enlightened domestic political institutions in so-called developing (read 'non-democratic') economies. These institutions will be enlightened because they will be shaped by a citizenry seeking to uphold notions of pluralism and individual freedom.

This is apparently the view in Canada where the federal government established the International Centre for Human Rights and Democratic Development in 1988 and attempted to link the provision of foreign aid to the recipient nation's demonstrated respect for human rights.[8] However, equating democracy with human rights can lead to platitudes rather than action. Similarly, the term 'good government' (or 'good governance') is conveniently rubbery. It could just as easily be code for orderly, authoritarian government serving the interests of state agencies and business enterprises seeking a stable, malleable and inexpensive work-force alongside as little environmental regulation as possible.[9]

So if an indirect or back-door approach to human rights is taken, the regional option may prove helpful for state leaders with little interest in enhancing human rights. They could agree to participate knowing that their primary interest in geopolitical security and economic growth would be at the top of the institutional agenda. If they were to emphasize the first two ideas in the oft-heard phrase 'peace, order and good government', they could justify their actions by claiming that good government depends upon the maintenance of peace and order, concepts which may not always be consonant with democratic ideals. Thus while suiting the domestic political needs of governments in industrialized Western democracies, given constituent demands to address perceived human rights violations overseas, the back-door approach may at the same time suit unsympathetic leaders who want access to foreign investment, development assistance, technology, markets, information and diplomatic support. 'Who is coopting whom?' is perhaps the most important question.

In the Asia-Pacific region, the indirect approach to human rights has been the approach of choice within the INGOs which led the contemporary regional cooperation movement from the mid-1960s to the late 1980s — PAFTAD, PBEC and PECC — and within the governmental APEC forum established in 1989. All four bodies focus on trade issues and economic development. Only the IPR (1925–60) addressed human rights issues in anything approximating a direct way and even these efforts were for the most part confined to the Institute's earliest years. Recently geopolitical/strategic issues have been taken up in an explicit fashion via non-governmental and governmental channels. The previous practice had been to adopt the view that enhancing regional economic development would enhance geopolitical security in a region where overt discussion of the latter was until the end of the Cold War seen as an emotive non-starter because of historical and political sensitivities.

For proponents of human rights, the most hopeful aspect of this initiative is that the term being used in this dialogue is 'cooperative security', although the sincerity of those who claim that the rise of this concept signals an interest in security broadly defined (including military, economic, social and environmental concerns requiring multilateral cooperation) must be carefully questioned. It is also noted that this dialogue has for the most part and by design focused upon the North Pacific subregion.[10] Indeed, part of the motivation for this activity was dissatisfaction with the slow pace at which ASEAN states were willing to let pan-Pacific regional cooperation movement progress. Should PECC and APEC come to play roles in this dialogue, it may be possible to achieve meaningful cooperative security. If these fora look both ways, deal directly with human rights as well as strategic problems, and widen the scope of their trade liberalization and promotion agenda to include social issues even more basic than human resources development and education, all Asia-Pacific peoples will have a greater appreciation of and stake in the regional cooperation process.

To the extent that academic economists, business people and government officials involved have seen wealth-making as synonymous with state-making, their approach to regional cooperation via PAFTAD, PBEC, PECC and APEC has been prudent. It is admittedly easier to get potential participants to the table to discuss economic development than it would be to get consent to discuss potentially divisive military matters. While there has been a tacit understanding that this functional approach would serve both military security and economic security interests, there has not been a sufficient commonality of perspectives on human rights to allow this heading to be placed on the regional agenda in a direct way, even in non-governmental settings.

The Institute of Pacific Relations

Most observers and participants forget that the regional cooperation movement has a history which extends back well beyond the 1960s. Indeed, the rise of PAFTAD and PBEC in the mid-1960s and the subsequent emergence of PECC can be directly linked to the death of the IPR in 1960.[11] The Institute was founded in 1925 and rose to prominence as a respected forum for the study and debate of regional issues prior to, during and immediately following the Second World War. Regular IPR conferences were attended by as many as thirteen national delegations consisting of academics, business people, labour leaders, journalists, former government officials and (during the Second World War) active diplomats. A victim of McCarthyism in the United States during the 1950s, the Institute's national councils voted to disband the organization in December 1960.

Early in its life, the IPR engaged in human rights-related activities through surveys of race relations, immigration, the legal status of aliens, the plight of indigenous peoples, and standards of living on both sides of the Pacific. For example, human security issues such as immigration and race relations served as the primary focuses of the inaugural IPR meeting in 1925, with only seven of twenty-seven roundtables and fora diverging into the economic or military security realm.[12] These surveys and discussions were conducted on the premise that understanding the role of culture and race in international affairs would lessen conflict and increase cooperation amongst states and peoples. It must be acknowledged that some participants sought to protect corporate or national interests, while others (usually North Americans) were involved because they held what today might be termed racist views towards Asian immigration and wanted to support the maintenance of policies which would uphold these views.[13]

But to the extent that the IPR was symbolic of the Wilsonian idealism which pervaded the post-First World War period, many participants were clearly more interested in attaining social norms similar to those put forward by contemporary human rights proponents. In their eyes, the prevention of war and the preservation of peace was largely dependent upon the resolution of basic social issues. Hence, while some participation found the regional cooperation forum as a way to defend and justify the status quo, most believed that the humanitarian need to tear down the status quo would become self-evident as a result of the IPR's research and dialogue.[14] As stated in the foreword to the Institute's 1927 conference proceedings, IPR participants

wished to study the factors that underlie racial contacts and the adjustment of conflicting interests and to examine the possibility of creating a new type of international community in the Pacific area built upon reciprocity and mutual understanding.[15]

Taking this statement of intent a step further, the following year's conference observed that the IPR was a diplomatic mechanism which arose from 'a new vision of human relations based upon the concept of the rights of the weak, international interdependence, the power of facts, the intelligence of people and their participation in government'.[16]

These initial social concerns were quickly overwhelmed by international events such as the Sino-Japanese conflict, the Second World War and the Chinese communist revolution. Geostrategic issues came to dominate the IPR agenda with human rights concerns resurfacing in a less than substantial way in post-war gatherings.[17] Unfortunately the prominence of the IPR and its conferences in the 1930s and 1940s as a result of its involvement in high politics had most probably turned it into a target and scapegoat in the 1950s in the United States.[18] Had the IPR remained closer to the vision of its founders and limited itself to studying the impact of social and human rights issues upon international relations, it may still be with us today, given that in

organizational terms the creation of PECC in 1980 was tantamount to the
reinvention of the IPR wheel.

The Pacific Trade and Development Conference

Shortly after the IPR's demise, two new non-governmental institutions interested in regional affairs, PAFTAD and PBEC, began to take shape. PAFTAD
arose out of the Japanese economist Kiyoshi Kojima's proposal of a Pacific
Free Trade Area (PAFTA) involving the five industrialized countries of the
region. In 1968, economists from the Pacific Five—Australia, Canada, Japan,
New Zealand, and the United States—met to discuss the PAFTA plan under
the sponsorship of Japan's Ministry of Foreign Affairs. This gathering led to
an ongoing conference series, a research network approaching 500 alumni
from over two dozen economies and numerous international organizations, a
publishing programme, a central secretariat at Australian National University
in Canberra, and the financial support of governments, the Asian Development Bank and private foundations. Convened every eighteen months, the
conferences provide a regional perspective upon issues salient to multilateral
negotiations.[19]

The PAFTAD agenda has been dominated by neoliberal economic thinking,
believing that the greater good will be served by freer trade regulated via
international regimes which enhance policy consultation and coordination.
The need for some regulation of the market-place is consonant with the
suggestion that PAFTAD participants are economists who are aware of and
sensitive to the political realities and policy dilemmas in individual countries.
PAFTAD's leaders have never launched an explicit study of the link between
economics and human rights, coming closest in 1976 when employment issues
were addressed. Instead, they have focused upon ways to reduce and resolve
trade or economic policy conflicts regionally and globally.

PAFTAD participants focused their attention on economic issues because
they believed that national security will be served by encouraging trade and
economic development. By giving people a stake in international trading
relationships, they believed, the likelihood of military conflict would be reduced, and democratic institutions are more likely to arise and be sustained
when economic development and growth are encouraged. This does not, of
course, mean that democracy will flourish (witness the Chinese government's
response to the democracy movement of May–June 1989, intractable political
problems in the Philippines, false starts in Russia, and resistance to democratization and individual rights in Southeast Asian countries), although some
signs of this logic bearing fruit can be cited (including perhaps recent political
changes in South Korea, Taiwan and even Japan).

Finally, it should be noted that PAFTAD held its 1991 conference in
Beijing—just two years after the Tiananmen Square Massacre—and that its
1994 conference in Hong Kong will address the theme, 'Corporate Links and
Direct Foreign Investment in Asia and the Pacific'. One is tempted to ask if
these events reveal the narrow interests of the organization and/or on which
side of the human rights debate PAFTAD participants might stand.

The Pacific Basin Economic Council

PBEC first brought together business executives from the industrialized Pacific Five in an attempt to enhance corporate contacts and to maintain a favourable environment for free enterprise through the provision of policy guidance to governments. Having emerged in 1967–8 from discussions between Japanese and Australian business leaders, the limited geographic scope of the initial membership led some observers and prospective members to view PBEC as a paternalistic rich man's club.

The Council has since grown to include some 850 fee-paying member firms and its general meetings each May now boast member committees drawn from Chile, Fiji, Hong Kong, Malaysia, Mexico, Peru, the Philippines, South Korea, Taiwan (as Chinese Taipei) and the five charter nations. PBEC's central secretariat was transferred to the Honolulu office of the Center for Strategic and International Studies in 1992.[20]

This group is the regional non-governmental institution least likely to be interested in human rights because the objectives of individual corporate members are profit maintenance and enhancement. These goals are not seen as dependent upon the maintenance and enhancement of human rights, especially when it comes to working conditions or wage rates which might cut into profit margins.

The portability of capital and corporate concern for fostering a policy climate which will protect free enterprise is not consonant with the defence of personal freedom and workers' rights. To a great extent, corporate interest in regional institutions arises from a concern to ensure that profits are not adversely affected by the cooperative arrangements. As in the case of some early IPR participants, the literature on non-decision-making is pertinent here.[21]

The Pacific Economic Cooperation Council

In a direct extension of these sectoral non-governmental activities, scholars, business leaders and state officials acting in their private capacities gathered in Canberra in 1980 for a Pacific Community Seminar sponsored by the prime ministers of Japan and Australia. Organizers invited representatives from PAFTAD and PBEC to attend alongside tripartite national delegations designed to obtain balanced sectoral input. The tripartite format (having become multipartite with the inclusion in disparate cases of delegates from the labour, media and legislative sectors) has become a dominant trait of what is today known as the Pacific Economic Cooperation Council (PECC, formerly the Pacific Economic Cooperation Conference).

The building of a Pacific consensus on global economic issues has become PECC's *raison d'être*. General meetings are held every eighteen months to review a work programme involving task forces, fora and working groups on agriculture, fisheries, human resources, the Pacific Island nations, science and technology, transportation–telecommunications–tourism, tropical forests, minerals and energy, and trade policy.

The institutionalization of the PECC process has included the 1986 adoption of the Vancouver Statement on Pacific Economic Cooperation, the subsequent proclamation of a PECC Charter, the creation of a PECC Central Fund to assist the participation of developing economies, the annual publication of a regional economic forecast (*Pacific Economic Outlook*), and the creation of a central secretariat in Singapore.[22]

The Council now encompasses member committees from the Pacific Five, Brunei Darussalam, Chile, China, Hong Kong, Indonesia, Malaysia, Mexico, the Pacific Island nations (via the South Pacific Forum), Peru, the Philippines, Russia, Singapore, South Korea, Taiwan (as Chinese Taipei), and Thailand. Delegates from PAFTAD and PBEC continue to sit as non-voting members on PECC's executive committee. Some academics and government officials will see their efforts as upholding human rights, albeit in a much less direct way than the 110 non-governmental organizations that participated in the drafting of the Bangkok NGO Declaration on Human Rights in March 1993.[23] Human resources development is the PECC agenda item which embodies this indirect approach in keeping with the 'good government' and 'democracy with human rights' logic noted earlier.

Asia-Pacific economic cooperation

The heightened diplomatic profile of the ASEAN—Brunei, Indonesia, Malaysia, the Philippines, Singapore, and Thailand—presented an opportunity to go beyond the non-governmental phase in the 1980s. Initially convened in 1984, the annual ASEAN-Pacific Dialogue (APD or, in its subsequently enlarged form, the ASEAN Post-Ministerial Conference), renamed the ASEAN Regional Forum in 1993, now involves the foreign ministers of ASEAN and their counterparts from the Pacific Five (the initial guests), the European Community, South Korea, China, Russia, Vietnam, Laos, and Papua New Guinea.[24]

The APD was the first pan-Pacific IGO (excluding the less specific regional commission of the UN and Asian Development Bank). It reflected ASEAN's willingness to participate in shaping regional cooperation efforts while at the same time controlling the pace. A set of joint projects was conceived under the heading ASEAN-Pacific Cooperation, but the limited geographic scope of this arrangement, the tenuous nature of the projects, and perceived problems in the global and regional trading environment caused some to see the creation of a more effective regional governmental institution as imperative.[25]

In January 1989, Australia's Prime Minister Bob Hawke launched what became known as the Hawke Initiative. He observed that a formal regional mechanism for policy consultation and coordination would enable Western Pacific countries in particular to defend themselves through collective action should the multilateral trading system collapse and/or other countries be determined to conduct relations via regional blocs. The Australian government outlined a strategy to foster the development of an institution which would go beyond PECC's informal and non-binding activities. The immediate goals were to improve the chances for success in the GATT talks, provide an official forum for the discussion of regional trade liberalization, and enable the identification of common and complementary economic interests.

An inaugural ministerial meeting took place in Canberra in November 1989 amidst continuing turmoil within the GATT's Uruguay Round. Delegates agreed to proceed with an initial work programme under the title Asia Pacific Economic Cooperation (APEC) in accordance with a set of cautious principles which hold that cooperation should be pursued through informal consultations, open dialogue and consensus-building. In 1991, these principles were enshrined in the APEC Declaration. Annual ministerial meetings are now convened with senior officials gathering two to four times per year to set the agenda for the ministerial sessions and monitor the progress of working groups on trade and investment data, trade promotion, investment and industrial science and technology, human resources development, energy operation, marine resources conservation, fisheries, telecommunications, tourism, and transportation.[26]

With the admission of China, Chinese Taipei and Hong Kong in 1991 and Mexico and Papua New Guinea in 1993, seventeen economies have entered APEC, the Pacific Five, ASEAN Six and South Korea having been founding members. Chile is to be admitted in 1994.[27] Membership enquiries have also come from several other Latin American countries, India, Mongolia and Russia. Although observer status has been granted to ASEAN, PECC and the South Pacific Forum (SPF), concerns about the relationship between APEC and previously existing bodies have not been totally defused.

ASEANs vigorous defence of its organizational integrity manifested itself in December 1990 with the Malaysian prime minister's proposal of an exclusive East Asian Economic Grouping to be led by Japan, an idea since tempered to that of an East Asian Economic Caucus within (or in some versions without) APEC.[28] Appeals by the PECC leadership brought assurances that the Hawke Initiative was not designed to overshadow or supplant the PECC process. Rather, PECC was characterized as a leading component of a long-standing and independent research network upon which a new IGO could and should draw. Thus far, the pursuit of a symbiotic relationship between APEC and PECC has proved amenable to both sides, a development which should augur well for the future of each organization and placate those who fear the creation of an APEC bureaucracy. This said, an APEC support mechanism was established in Singapore in 1992 and there is growing suspicion that in some national contexts APEC is expected to replace PECC in the near future.

Predictably perhaps, the direct discussion of human rights issues has not found a prominent place on the APEC agenda. Instead, the broad areas of economic, educational and environmental cooperation encompassed by the working groups listed above are considered to subsume human rights by those who believe that economic development necessarily enhances individual freedoms. However, the fifth APEC ministerial meeting, hosted by the United States in November 1993, witnessed an important departure when, amidst discussions of how APEC might move towards forging a regional free trade area and addressing military/strategic issues,[29] Secretary of State Warren Christopher spoke openly and critically of China's human rights record. President Bill Clinton also raised the issue with China's President and Communist Party Secretary Jiang Zemin (who provided a fifteen-minute rebuttal based on the realist concepts of state sovereignty and non-interference) during the leaders' summit appended to the APEC sessions.[30] While it is possible to see these pointed remarks as manifestations of an ongoing bilateral dispute[31] and to criticize the selectivity apparent in targeting China, the timing was clearly calculated to ensure that the American administration's preferences were known throughout the region (the American public included), and the airing of human rights concerns has gained legitimacy within the region's most important intergovernmental economic cooperation forum.

It will be interesting to see if the APEC context is subsequently utilized to shine the ethical spotlight directly upon the environmental and economic aspects of human rights, Indonesian actions in East Timor (the next APEC summit will be held in Jakarta), and the treatment of indigenous peoples throughout the region, and North American and Asian attitudes towards immigration. If it is, the 1993 Seattle gathering, occurring as it did in the same year as the UN-sponsored World Conference on Human Rights, may come to be characterized as an example of how regional IGOs can complement global IGOs and how the hypocrisy gap can be bridged.

Conclusions

The active INGOs and IGOs surveyed in this chapter do have a role to play in the debate over and pursuit of human rights in the Asia-Pacific region, but they are not addressing such issues in a direct fashion at present and their future roles will depend upon the perspectives of the participants in the regional cooperation movement. Among the regional institutions reviewed, PBEC is not well situated to play a supporting role given that its members' interest in corporate profits will often be in conflict with the notion of enhancing human rights if this means raising living standards, increasing wage rates, improving the sociopolitical status of women, and protecting the environment.

The roles of PECC and APEC also appeared to be limited. For instance, one governmental participant from Canada contacted during the course of this research initially bristled and responded firmly in the negative when asked if PECC and APEC dealt with human rights, claiming that the international contexts and economic focuses of these organizations precluded the consideration of such unrelated (and contentious) domestic matters! However, even this official later allowed that INGOs like PAFTAD and PECC have attempted to place the issue on the regional diplomatic agenda in an indirect way to the extent that participants in these organizations see economic development as bolstering the promotion of human rights.

This said, it will be difficult to address human rights issues in a more constructive or direct way via a regional governmental arrangement such as APEC because of the political sensibilities (or insensibilities) and ulterior motives of states and their leaders. INGOs such as PAFTAD and PECC can thus serve a useful purpose by placing and keeping human rights on the diplomatic agenda, even if a back-door approach is the best one can expect. The symbiotic working relationship between PECC and APEC provides perhaps the greatest hope,[32] inasmuch as this might at least allow PECC to prod APEC into attending in a consistent manner to this divisive but vital issue area.

The inability of states to control national economic policy or to avoid policy linkages in our increasingly interdependent world enhances the probability of INGOs and IGOs playing such roles. Accordingly, if PECC survives and, with the support of PAFTAD and consent of APEC, begins behaving like the IPR did in its early years, the neo-idealist moment noted by observers of the post-Cold War world may be positively extended through economic cooperation in the Asia-Pacific region.[33] Should PECC wither away, alternative channels for societal input into the APEC process will have to be found in order to ensure that human rights concerns remain prominent on the regional diplomatic agenda.

Notes

*The author is an English-speaking Caucasian Canadian male who was born and raised in Canada (urban British Columbia, to be exact), went to school in Canada and Australia, and now works as a university professor in Canada. I offer this biographical sketch because I believe it is important for someone writing about human rights to indicate their background and possible biases. The regional focus of this volume makes this act even more necessary given the pointed cultural diversity therein.

I wish to thank Iris Almeida, Stan Beeler, Paul Bowles, Paul Irwin, Brian Job, Frank Langdon, Barbara Stark and James Tang for their assistance in the preparation of this chapter.

1. See, for instance, Bilahari Kausikan, 'Asia's different standard', and Aryeh Neier, 'Asia's unacceptable standard', *Foreign Policy*, no. 92 (Fall 1993), pp. 24–41 and 42–51 respectively. For discussions of the human rights and the cultural relativism thesis, see Christopher Tremewan, 'Human rights in Asia', *Pacific Review*, vol. 6, no. 1 (1993), pp. 17–30 ; Christopher C. Joyner and John C. Dettling, 'Bridging the cultural chasm: cultural relativism and the future of international law', *California Western International Law Journal*, vol. 20 (1990), pp. 275–314; R. J. Vincent, *Human Rights and International Relations* (Cambridge: Cambridge University Press/Royal Institute of International Affairs, 1986), pp. 37–57; Michael Vatikiotis and Robert Delfs, 'Human rights cultural divide', *Far Eastern Economic Review*, 21 November 1993, p. 20; and Elaine Sciolino, 'U.S. rejects notion that human rights vary with culture', *New York Times*, 15 June 1993, pp. Al, A18.
2. For detailed historical and organizational overviews of these four INGOs, see Lawrence T. Woods, *Asia-Pacific Diplomacy: Nongovernmental Organizations and International Relations* (Vancouver: University of British Columbia Press, 1993). On APEC, see also Andrew F. Cooper, Richard Higgott and Kim Richard Nossal, *Relocating Middle Powers: Australia and Canada in a Changing World* (Vancouver: University of British Columbia Press, 1993), pp. 83–115; and Michael Paulson,

'Heads of state sensitivities crimp Seattle party plans', *Vancouver Sun*, 16 September 1993, p. D3.

3. Peter Van Ness, 'Human rights and international relations in East Asia', *Asian Studies Review*, vol. 16, no. 1 (July 1992), pp. 49–52; Lawrence T. Woods, 'Nongovernmental organizations and the United Nations system: reflecting upon the Earth Summit experience', *International Studies Notes*, vol. 18, no. 1 (Winter 1993), pp. 9–15; Vincent, op. cit., pp. 97–9; Woods, *Asia-Pacific Diplomacy*, op. cit., pp. 11–28.

4. Ralph Pettman, *International Politics: Balance of Power, Balance of Productivity, Balance of Ideologies* (Melbourne/Boulder: Longman Cheshire/Lynne Rienner, 1991).

5. Steven A. Holmes, 'Clinton reverses policies in U.N. on rights issues', *New York Times*, 9 May 1993, pp. 1, 8; Christopher J. Dagg, 'Linking aid to human rights in Indonesia: a Canadian perspective', *Issues* (Asia Pacific Foundation of Canada), vol. 7, no. 1 (Winter 1993), pp. 3–12; 'Japan ties aid to human rights in recipient nations', *Straits Times*, 6 October 1992, p. 8; Shada Islam, 'Under Western eyes', *Far Eastern Economic Review*, 14 March 1991, pp. 20–1.

6. Vincent notes that the experience was similar in Africa. It is instructive that he provides no discussion of Asia. See Vincent, op. cit., pp. 95–6. See also Scott Davidson, *Human Rights* (Buckingham: Open University Press, 1993).

7. On basic human needs and the distinction between human rights and subsistence rights, see Vincent, op. cit., pp. 83–8, 143–50; and Panayiotis C. Afxention, 'Basic needs: a survey of the literature', *Canadian Journal of Development Studies*, vol. 11, no. 2 (1990), pp. 241–58.

8. For a view of Canadian perspectives on the links between human rights, economic development and foreign policy, see Kim Richard Nossal, 'The limits of linking aid and trade to human rights', in Mark Charlton and Elizabeth Riddell-Dixon (eds), *Crosscurrents: International Relations in the Post-Cold War Era* (Scarborough: Nelson Canada, 1993), pp. 443–50; Kathleen E. Mahoney, 'Human rights and Canada's foreign policy', *International Journal*, vol. 47, no. 3 (Summer 1992), pp. 555–94; Svend Robinson, 'Justice and human rights: inspiring Canadian foreign policy', *Canadian Foreign Policy*, vol. 1, no. 1 (Winter 1992–93), pp. 17–35; Irving Brecher (ed.), *Human Rights, Development and Foreign Policy: Canadian Perspectives* (Halifax: Institute for Research on Public Policy, 1989); Robert O. Matthews and Cranford Pratt (eds), *Human Rights in Canadian Foreign Policy* (Kingston and Montreal: McGill-Queen's University Press, 1988); Dagg, op. cit., pp. 3–12; and Cooper, Higgott and Nossal, op. cit., pp. 156–62.

9. David Gillies, 'Human rights, democracy, and "good governance": stretching the World Bank's policy frontiers', paper prepared for the President, International Centre for Human Rights and Democratic Development, Montreal, 1 June 1992.

10. On the North Pacific Cooperative Security Dialogue, see Paul M. Evans, 'The emergence of Eastern Asia and its implications for Canada', *International Journal*, vol. 47, no. 3 (Summer 1992), pp. 504–28; Stewart Henderson, 'Zone of uncertainty: Canada and the security architecture of Asia Pacific', *Canadian Foreign Policy*, vol. 1, no. 1 (Winter 1992–93), pp. 103–20; and Cooper, Higgott and Nossal, op. cit., pp. 152–6.

11. Lawrence T. Woods, 'Regional diplomacy and the Institute of Pacific Relations', *Journal of Developing Societies*, vol. 8, no. 2 (July–October 1992), pp. 212–22; Woods, op. cit., *Asia-Pacific Diplomacy*.

12. *Institute of Pacific Relations: Honolulu Session June 30–July 14, 1925* (Honolulu: IPR, 1925).

13. See, for example, John Nelson, 'Canadian view of Pacific relations', in *Institute of*

Pacific Relations: Honolulu Session, op. cit., pp. 65–8. The similarities between such expressions and the contemporary North American debate over Asian immigration is striking and disturbing to this observer. See John Berthelsen, 'Politics of exclusion: anti-immigrant lobbyists target Asians again', *Far Eastern Economic Review*, 18 November 1993, pp. 27–8.

14. For overviews of the IPR's research programme and conference agenda, see Paul F. Hooper, 'The Institute of Pacific Relations and the origins of Asian and Pacific studies', *Pacific Affairs*, vol. 61, no. 1 (Spring 1988), pp. 98–121; and William L. Holland, 'Source materials on the Institute of Pacific Relations', *Pacific Affairs*, vol. 58, no. 1 (Spring 1985), pp. 91–7.

15. J. Merle Davis, General Secretary, IPR, 'Foreword', in J.B. Condliffe (ed.), *Problems in the Pacific: Proceedings of the Second Conference of the Institute of Pacific Relations, Honolulu, Hawaii, July 15 to 29, 1927* (Chicago: University of Chicago Press, 1928), p. v.

16. J. Merle Davis, General Secretary, IPR, 'Preface', in J.B. Condliffe (ed.), *Problems of the Pacific, 1929* (Chicago: University of Chicago Press, 1930), p. v.

17. This cycle can be observed by reviewing IPR conference proceedings, research programmes and publication lists. In addition to the conference volumes cited above, see Bruno Lasker (ed.), *Problems of the Pacific, 1931* (Chicago: University of Chicago Press, 1932); Bruno Lasker and W. L. Holland (eds.), *Problems of the Pacific, 1933: Economic Conflict and Control* (Chicago: University of Chicago Press, 1934); W. L. Holland and Kate Mitchell (eds), *Problems of the Pacific, 1936: Aims and Results of Social and Economic Policies in Pacific Countries* (Chicago: University of Chicago Press, 1937); Mitchell and W. L. Holland (eds), *Problems of Pacific Countries, 1939* (New York: IPR, 1940); *War and Peace in the Pacific* (New York: IPR, 1945); *Problems of Economic Reconstruction in the Far East* (New York: IPR, 1949); and *Asian Nationalism and Western Policies* (New York: IPR, 1951).

18. Hooper, op. cit., pp. 120–1.

19. Woods, *Asia-Pacific Diplomacy*, op. cit., pp. 41–65.

20. Woods, *Asia-Pacific Diplomacy*, op. cit., pp. 66–88.

21. Peter Bachrach and Morton S. Baratz, *Power and Poverty: Theory and Practice* (New York: Oxford Unviersity Press, 1970).

22. Woods, *Asia-Pacific Diplomacy*, op. cit., pp. 89–148.

23. Bangkok NGO Declaration on Human Rights, Bangkok, 27 March 1993.

24. Michael Leifer, 'Maintain APEC on its economic trajectory', *International Herald Tribune*, 8 November 1993, p. 8.

25. James Clad, 'Rising sense of drift', *Far Eastern Economic Review*, 10 July 1986, p. 15.

26. Woods, *Asia-Pacific Diplomacy*, op. cit., pp. 119–23.

27. Clyde Graham, 'Canada looks to Pacific, GATT for Trade', *Prince George Citizen*, 22 November 1993, p. 11.

28. David E. Sanger, 'On eve of Seattle talks, wary Asians suspect Clinton of overreaching', *International Herald Tribune*, 15 November 1993, pp. 1, 12; Michael Richardson, 'ASEAN aims to hold its own at talks in Seattle', *International Herald Tribune*, 16 November 1993, pp. 1, 13; Philip Shenon, 'Malaysian is glad he stayed at home', *International Herald Tribune*, 22 November 1993, p. 5; Leifer, op. cit., p. 8.

29. Paul F. Horvitz, 'Clinton seeks to open markets: APEC prods Europe on trade', and 'A nonstarter in Seattle: "Asian-Pacific Community" ', *International Herald Tribune*, 20–1 November 1993, pp. 1, 5; Susumu Awanohara and Nayan Chanda, 'Uncommon bonds', *Far Eastern Economic Review*, 18 November 1993, pp. 16–17; 'Now let's build an Asia-Pacific economy community', *International Herald*

Tribune, 4 November 1993, p. 4; Richard W. Baker, 'Pacific summit in Seattle: testing Clinton's Asia-Pacific policy', *Asia Pacific Issues* (East–West Center), No. 9, November 1993.

30. Canadian Broadcasting Corporation (CBC) Radio News, 17 and 19 November 1993; 'Jiang won't budge on human rights', *Daily Yomiuri*, 21 November 1993, p. 1; Paul F. Horvitz, 'From Seattle, contradictions among smiles', *International Herald Tribune*, 19 November 1993, pp. 1, 7; Paul F. Horvitz, 'Clinton cites talks as positive, but divisions remain: Pacific leaders make little headway on arms and human rights issues', and R. W. Apple, 'No missteps for President, but no clear gains either', *International Herald Tribune*, 22 November 1993, pp. 1, 4; Daniel Williams, 'Chinese stick to their hard-line ways', *International Herald Tribune*, 22 November 1993, pp. 1, 5.

31. Nayan Chanda, 'Misguided complacency', *Far Eastern Economic Review*, 18 November 1993, p. 22.

32. Woods, *Asia-Pacific Diplomacy*, op. cit., pp. 118–25.

33. Charles W. Kegley, Jr., 'The neo-idealist moment in international studies? Realist myths and the new international realities', *International Studies Quarterly*, vol. 37, no. 2 (June 1993), pp. 131–46. For expressions of guarded optimism about the possibility of non-governmental organizations playing positive roles in support of human rights in Asia, see Tremewan, op. cit., pp. 17–30; and Van Ness, op. cit., pp. 43–52.

13
HUMAN RIGHTS AND REGIONAL ORDER: ASEAN AND HUMAN RIGHTS MANAGEMENT IN POST-COLD WAR SOUTHEAST ASIA

AMITAV ACHARYA

Introduction

Although human rights became an 'established subject of international relations' immediately after the Second World War, it has not figured widely in
the political agenda of regional organizations.[1] The regional process in the
promotion of human rights has largely been confined to Europe. Human
rights protection institutions and processes in the developing world have
been far more modest in scope and authority. In Asia, no regional human
rights institutions exist.[2] The most political and prominent regional grouping
in Asia—the Association of Southeast Asian Nations (ASEAN)—had until
very recently little to say or do in the area of human rights.[3]

In the post-Cold War era, the human rights issue has become more important for ASEAN states. Unlike human rights processes in other parts of the
world such as Europe, the regional human rights agenda in ASEAN is not
about regional monitoring and enforcement responsibilities and action. Human rights have been regarded by ASEAN states as a powerful instrument
directed against them in the hands of the developed countries in the emerging
'New World Order'. Thus a new challenge for them is to take collective action
to protect regional norms and autonomy against 'external' pressure. This is
akin to the role of regional organizations in responding to Great Power rivalry
and intervention during the Cold War period.

The ASEAN collective agenda in addressing human rights issues has been
shaped by a number of recent developments in the region. First, the human
rights record of individual ASEAN governments has come under intense
international scrutiny. Apart from regular and periodic reports issued by
Western human rights organizations (such as Amnesty International and Asia
Watch) and the mass media, a number of events have brought human rights
issues in ASEAN countries into the international limelight.

The most famous of these is the shooting by Indonesian security forces of
anti-state demonstrators in the East Timorese capital of Dili in November
1991. In the midst of an outcry from the international media, two Western

donor countries, the Netherlands and Canada, suspended aid to Indonesia. While Indonesia retaliated by organizing an aid consortium excluding the Netherlands, Jakarta's international image suffered a major blow. Other ASEAN countries, especially Malaysia and Singapore, have been criticized by human rights watchdogs for their internal security detention laws and lack of press freedom. Faced with loss of jobs to foreign competition (especially East Asian), trade unions and human rights groups in the United States demanded linking trade privileges with workers' rights in countries such as Malaysia. Violent military suppression minority groups in Thailand, the Philippines and Indonesia have also attracted a great deal of international attention with regard to human rights.

Second, human rights have rapidly become a threat to ASEAN's collective image and role in promoting regional and inter-regional cooperation. The European Community's (EC) refusal to negotiate a new economic treaty with ASEAN following the Dili incident underscores the link. In September 1991, a foreign ministers meeting between ASEAN and the EC in Luxembourg saw serious disagreement over whether human rights and environmental concerns should be part of any new economic cooperation agreement between the two sides.[4] In October the vice-president of the EC Commission warned in Kuala Lumpur that failure to respect human rights would have a 'severe impact' on the EC's relations with developing countries, including ASEAN.[5] ASEAN and its Western interlocutors have clashed repeatedly over the issue of sanctions against the regime in Myanmar.[6] Even Japan, which takes a much softer position than the Western countries on the ASEAN states' human rights record, has disagreed with ASEAN on the issue of aid conditionality. At the Asian regional meeting on human rights in Bangkok in April 1993, Japan took the position that human rights should not be sacrificed for economic growth and that foreign aid would be linked to human rights performance of the regime in power. Thus, human rights is a challenge to ASEAN's efforts to develop a multilateral security forum for the Asia-Pacific region.

Third, ASEAN's success as a regional grouping was based on its ability to generate intra-mural consensus on a set of norms for the conduct of international relations in Southeast Asia. Two of the core norms include: (1) non-interference by one member state in the internal affairs of another and (2) non-intervention by outside powers in the affairs of the region. The human rights thrust of the 'New World Order' challenges ASEAN on both these norms.

Last but not least, ASEAN countries face increasing demands for political liberalization and respect for human rights from domestic circles, including human rights non-governmental organizations (NGOs), especially in Thailand, Malaysia and the Philippines.[7] Despite scant resources and government suppression, these groups have been encouraged in recent years in a more favourable international climate for their cause. Thus, a combination of external and internal factors ensures that ASEAN can no longer ignore human rights issues in its collective effort to shape a new regional order in Southeast Asia and the Pacific. Human rights, along with the environment and democracy, have become one of the 'new areas of ASEAN reaction'.[8]

This chapter examines ASEAN's role in human rights management in the post-Cold War regional order. The chapter is divided into two parts. The first looks at ASEAN governments' attitudes towards the emerging significance of human rights in international relations, the universality of human rights, the scope of human rights (political versus non-political rights), and the impact of policy instruments such as aid conditionality. The second part attempts to illuminate the ASEAN approach to managing human rights difficulties through a detailed analysis of the ASEAN policy of 'constructive engagement' towards Myanmar.

At the outset, some qualifying observations are necessary. This chapter is concerned with analysing a regional position on human rights as an element of the evolving global debate on human rights. As such, it does not intend to provide an assessment of the human rights record of individual ASEAN governments. There are a number of publicly available sources which provide such assessments (including Amnesty International and Asia Watch), although such reports are often viewed by ASEAN governments as biased and inaccurate. Secondly, as with many other issues, ASEAN members do not necessarily speak in one voice over the human rights issue. The United States for example, ranked China, Pakistan, Indonesia and sometimes Singapore as among the 'worst' group of 'vocal' human rights 'violators' and 'particularizers', while Malaysia, Myanmar and India were regarded as 'unhelpful'. The position taken by the Philippines, Japan and South Korea was viewed as 'correct' and constructive, although these states were seen as being unwilling to take on their Asian colleagues.[9]

These intra-mural differences should not, however, obscure elements of a broad consensus on the need to respond collectively to Western pressures on human rights among ASEAN states. It is this exercise in consensus formation, the range of views and factors contributing to it, and its implications for ASEAN's international role, which constitute the analytical focus of this chapter.

The post-Cold War human rights agenda in ASEAN

The ASEAN states consider the rising prominence of human rights in recent years as a direct result of the end of the Cold War. The anti-communist thrust of Western policy, which tolerated blatant human rights abuses by pro-Western Asian governments in the past, is no more. Instead, the promotion of human rights constitutes the core element of the 'New World Order'. As Lee Kuan Yew, Singapore's elder statesman, put it in an Asian context:

Unfortunately, with the end of the Cold War, U.S. policies toward China, Japan and the countries of East Asia have not been guided by strategic and economic considerations as they used to be. Issues of human rights and democracy have become an obsession with the U.S. media, Congress and the administration.[10]

The relatively simplistic East–West geopolitical framework of the Cold War period has shifted to a more complex setting in which North–South conflicts over humanitarian norms have become the major faultline of the international system with direct bearing on the economic, social and political conditions in the developing countries. Some ASEAN policy-makers see the promotion of universal human rights standards by Western countries as a highly selective exercise. Singapore's Foreign Minister Wong Kan Seng argues that 'Concern for human rights [in the West] has always been balanced against other national interests'.[11]

Attesting to 'hypocrisy' in the West's application of its human rights standards, the case of Western concern for Saudi Arabia has been contrasted with Algeria, where the Western governments acquiesced with a military *coup* which overthrew an elected government with a strongly Islamic orientation.[12] The enforcement of human rights standards by the West is therefore seen not only as selective, but also intensely political. Ali Alatas, Indonesia's Foreign Minister, wondered whether or not the West's human rights campaign might have been designed to 'serve as a pretext to wage a political campaign against another country'.[13] Malaysia's Prime Minister Mahathir Mohammed has provided his own answer to this question by casting human rights as an instrument of dependency. Citing the example of Eastern Europe, Mahathir contended that the campaign of human rights and democracy is a prescription for disruption and chaos in weaker countries, a campaign which makes the target ever more dependent on the donor nations of the West.

Furthermore, the Western campaign for human rights is regarded as reflective of the power disparities in the international system. As the Malaysian Foreign Minister Ahmed Badawi put it: 'Attempts to impose the standard of one side on the other . . . tread upon the sovereignty of nations.'[14] As the current Chair of the Non-Aligned Movement, Indonesia also warned:

In a world where domination of the strong over the weak and interference between states are still a painful reality, no country or group of countries should arrogate unto itself the role of judge, jury and executioner over other countries on this critical and sensitive issue.[15]

The characterization of the West's human rights campaign as being selective and self-seeking is followed by a plea against accepting the definition of human rights in terms of Western values, norms and application procedures. 'Human rights questions,' contends Singapore, 'do not lend themselves to neat general formulas.'[16] Instead, as the Thai prime minister argued, implementation of human rights should 'vary because of differences in socioeconomic and cultural backgrounds'.[17] At the Bangkok Regional Preparatory Meeting, ASEAN worked with other like-minded Asian countries (including China) to draft a declaration which stated that human rights 'must be considered in the context of a dynamic and evolving process of international norm-setting, bearing in mind the significance of national and regional particularities and various historical, cultural and religious backgrounds'.[18]

In presenting the ASEAN case, Singapore's foreign minister referred to differences among the Western countries. He suggested that the definition of human rights has changed over time, having been influenced by centuries of history and culture. Britain, France and the United States had taken over 200 years to evolve into full democracies.

Can we therefore expect the citizens of many newly-independent countries of this century to acquire the same rights as those enjoyed by the developed nations when they lack the economic, educational and social pre-conditions to exercise such rights fully?[19]

What might be called an ASEAN human rights position combines aspects of cultural relativism, communitarianism and developmentalism.[20] The cultural relativist viewpoint, for example, was put forward forcefully by the Malaysian Prime Minister Mahathir Mohammed in the following words:

We in ASEAN never disputed that democracy for the people and opportunity for the individual to develop his or her own greatest potentials are indeed important principles. We disagree, however, that political systems qualify as democratic only when they measure up to certain particular yardsticks. Similarly, the norms and percepts for the observance of human rights vary from society to society and from one period to another within the same society. Nobody can claim to have the monopoly of wisdom to determine what is right and proper for all countries and peoples.[21]

Elaborating on the communitarian underpinnings of human rights, Ali Alatas, speaking at the Vienna United Nations World Conference on Human Rights, argued that Indonesia and the developing world have to maintain a balance between an 'individualistic approach' to human rights and the interests of the society as a whole. 'Without such a balance, the rights of the community as a whole can be denied, which can lead to instability and even anarchy.'[22] Singapore went further by invoking the Confucian principle of 'community over self',[23] while ASEAN foreign ministers collectively support Alatas' idea of 'balance' which is necessary not only to ensure 'freedom, progress and national stability' within the region, but also to create a political framework 'through which many individual rights are realized'.[24]

A communitarian approach to human rights is also essential if the state is to fulfil its developmental objectives. To ensure economic growth, Mahathir maintained, ASEAN states have been correct in placing 'a high premium on political stability by managing a balance between the rights of the individual and the needs of society as a whole'.[25] The multi-ethnic composition of states in Southeast Asia and the sensitive relationship between the dominant and minority ethnic groups adds to the need for governments to emphasize social stability and national security by exercising strict control over media and freedom of speech.

The salience of developmental objectives justifies the need for a conception of human rights based on the principle of 'non-selectivity', or the notion that political freedom and justiciable rights should not be stressed over the economic and the social. At the Vienna World Conference on Human Rights, Malaysia called for a universal conception of human rights to go beyond political rights, and to establish 'particularly its linkage with development'.[26]

The ASEAN position was summarized in a statement issued by ASEAN foreign ministers in Singapore in July 1993:

human rights are interrelated and indivisible comprising civil, political, economic, social and cultural rights. These rights are of equal importance. They should be addressed in a balanced and integrated manner and protected and promoted with due regard for specific cultural, social, economic and political circumstances . . . the promotion and protection of human rights should not be politicized.[27]

In championing 'non-selectivity', ASEAN states have sought to detract attention from the emphasis placed by the West on the restrictions on political rights within ASEAN.[28] They argued that without fulfilling the basic economic needs of their societies, developing countries cannot ensure the necessary conditions under which the political rights of citizens could be upheld.[29]

A linkage between human rights and development also provides a convenient and powerful justification for continued authoritarianism. An excessive concern with political liberalization and human rights could subvert developmental objectives of the state. As Lee Kuan Yew argued: 'The exuberance of democracy leads to undisciplined and disorderly conditions which are inimical to development.'[30] Although this view is not necessarily shared by other ASEAN leaders (such as President Ramos of the Philippines, who reminded Mr Lee that the authoritarianism of the Marcos era contributed in no small way to the country's economic ruin), there is a recognition that the Western campaign on human rights could undermine the favourable economic climate for ASEAN. Mahathir in particular sees Western attempts to link economic relations with human rights as a new set of 'conditionalities and protectionism by other means', aimed at undermining the economic prosperity and well-being of the East Asian region.[31]

In stressing the communitarian and developmental context of human rights, Singapore's leaders have put forward the notion of 'good government'. The key element of this notion is 'wise and honest' leadership. A 'good' government must be efficient and able to deliver on the economic front, but not necessarily political openness. As noted, Lee Kuan Yew believes that the two goals are negatively correlated. The notion of good government, however, incorporates a core group of human rights, such as absence of torture, slavery, arbitrary killings, disappearances or 'shooting down of innocent demonstrators'.[32] Beyond this, human rights, especially those of a political nature, would depend upon the political, economic and societal circumstances of the country.

While some common elements in the ASEAN member governments' attitude towards human rights can be identified, the very idea of a common regionalist ASEAN position remains highly problematic. The definition of what constitutes cultural norms is not uniform between or within ASEAN societies. Singapore's invoking of Confucian values is not shared by Islamic Malaysia or Catholic Philippines or Buddhist Thailand. Nor do values converge within individual ASEAN states. In multi-ethnic ASEAN states, any attempt by the ruling élite to articulate a 'national' position on human rights would, like the notion of 'national security' become an 'ambiguous symbol'. In the words of one critic, 'attempts to define the community as co-terminus with the state . . . may have less to do with culture than with political self-interest [of the ruling élite]'.[33] Thus, one cannot talk about a national or regional collective cultural/communitarian position on human rights when individual countries cannot overcome inter-ethnic competition within their own territories and when such competition feeds inter-state rivalry within the region (as in the case of Singapore–Malaysia relations).

The primacy of the political (regime security) over the cultural underpinnings of human rights is evident in the larger Asian context. Governments who emphasize that human rights must relate to culture often highlight only those elements among traditional cultural norms which justify their authoritarian political control and serve the regime's political and economic agenda. It is interesting that in Asia, governments which had once rejected traditional culture when it conflicted with their modernisation goals (e.g. China's earlier rejection of Confucianism as a factor behind its economic backwardness) are now invoking it to deflect criticism of their human rights record.

While ASEAN governments protest the politicization of human rights by the West, they themselves have indulged in a conscious political exercise to create a common ASEAN position which obscures the remarkable diversity within the grouping in terms of colonial heritage, post-colonial political/ constitutional system, and cultural, social, linguistic and ethnic milieu. This exercise in consensus-building has taken on a formal dimension.[34] It is noteworthy that while the first ASEAN summit of the post-Cold War era, held in Singapore in 1992, was silent on human rights, the 1993 annual ASEAN foreign ministers meeting, also held in Singapore, 'agreed that ASEAN should coordinate a common approach to human rights and actively participate and contribute to the application, promotion and protection of human rights'. Moreover, the foreign ministers 'agreed that ASEAN should also consider the establishment of an appropriate regional mechanism on human rights',[35] although the nature and scope of such a mechanism remains to be defined.

ASEAN states may find it easy to engage in debates with the West about the meaning and scope of human rights, but to come up with an alternative approach for real-life human rights problems is an entirely different exercise with serious implications for ASEAN's regional managerial ambitions. In this context, ASEAN's policy of 'constructive engagement' towards Myanmar assumes significance, providing both a challenge and an opportunity for the management of regional order. On the one hand, it has strained ASEAN's political relations with the West and undermined Western support for ASEAN's management of regional order when it relates to human rights issues. On the other hand, it has given ASEAN an opportunity to prove that it could provide an alternative approach to human rights management which is more sensitive to regional circumstances and therefore likely to prove more effective in the management of regional order.

ASEAN and 'constructive engagement'

In September 1988, after a wave of nationwide pro-democracy demonstrations, political power in Myanmar (then Burma) was seized by a military junta consisting of many of the key supporters of the previous regime of General Ne Win. The junta set up the State Law and Order Restoration Council (SLORC) and in May 1990 organized the first parliamentary polls in three decades. The elections were won decisively (392 out of 485 seats) by an opposition coalition, the National League for Democracy. But the results notwithstanding, the SLORC refused to convene parliament and transfer power. It also carried out large-scale arrests of opposition politicians and activists. The leader of the National League, Aung San Suu Kyi, had been placed under house arrest since July 1989.

Developments in Myanmar presented a new test for ASEAN as it entered the 1990s. It came at a time when ASEAN's own leadership in the Cambodian peace process, the major regional issue of the 1980s, was marred by intra-ASEAN bickering (over the Thai policy towards Indochina) and overshadowed by the role of the Great Powers and the UN. ASEAN was facing questions about its unity and relevance in the post-Cambodia era. And while Cambodia was on balance a cementing factor in the evolving relationship between ASEAN and the West, the situation in Myanmar, and the human rights questions it posed, seemed to be a powerful recipe for discord between ASEAN and its 'dialogue partners'.

The 1988 *coup* led to the suspension of Western and Japanese aid to Myanmar, although Japan partially resumed its aid the following year. The ASEAN countries, however, saw the Myanmar situation in very different terms. A distinction was made between issues of human rights and democracy. Lack of democracy in Myanmar, however regrettable, was not a human rights question. At the same time, Western sanctions against Myanmar were seen as ineffective, and constituting an interference in its internal affairs. ASEAN refused to go along with the Western response to the political crisis in Myanmar.

As Muthiah Alagappa pointed out, this was not the first time that ASEAN had declined to equate human rights and democratization and considered the latter to be an internal matter of the country concerned. ASEAN had chosen not to address the genocidal acts of the Pol Pot regime during 1975–8 on similar grounds. It initially chose to ignore the 1985–6 political revolt in the Philippines against the Marcos regime, a stance broken only in February 1986 with a statement calling upon Philippine leaders to resolve their differences peacefully.[36]

ASEAN responded to the Myanmar situation with a policy of 'constructive engagement'. The origins of this approach are unclear, but there is no evidence that this was a deliberate, well-calculated response. But like ASEAN's earlier policy on Cambodia, 'constructive engagement' seemed to respond to Thai interests—not just security interests, but political and economic interests as well.

In December 1988, three months after the Myanmar junta (SLORC) assumed power, the then Thai Armed Forces Supreme Commander General Chaovalit Yongchaiyut was the first foreign leader to visit Yangoon since the SLORC's coup. The visit was followed by a new economic and security relationship between the two countries. Myanmar troops were allowed to cross into the Thai border to attack Karen and Mon guerrilla positions. At the same time, Thai logging companies, facing a ban on logging within Thailand, were allowed to operate within the Myanmar border. Thai fishing companies negotiated major new contracts in Myanmar waters in the Andaman Sea.

This led some analysts to suggest a possible quid pro quo between the Thai military and the Myanmar junta, whereby the latter could carry out lucrative logging operations (through companies with strong links to the Thai military) within Myanmar in exchange for tolerating Myanmar troops' operations against its ethnic rebels inside Thai territory.[37] Indeed, some years later, the short-lived government of Suchinda Kaprayoon, after reviewing Thai policy towards Myanmar, concluded that it had to continue the old policy of opposing economic sanctions against Myanmar because the 'two countries are close and share many benefits and interests'.[38]

Like its origin, the nature and scope of the policy of constructive engagement remain obscure. But as a Singaporean newspaper, the *Straits Times*, suggested: Constructive engagement means gentle persuasion and quiet diplomacy to prod the regime [in Myanmar] into political liberalisation. This means keeping the dialogue with the SLORC leaders.' The newspaper also cited an Indonesian foreign ministry official who described the policy in the following terms: 'We are telling them [the Myanmar regime] very quietly, in a Southeast Asian way, without any fanfare, without any public statements: "Look, you are in trouble, let us help you. But you have to change, you cannot continue like this." ' Indonesia therefore refrained from taking steps against the Myanmar junta 'which embarrass and isolate them'.[39]

This policy of restraint was consistent not only with the ASEAN principle of non-interference in the internal affairs of a state, but was also a pragmatic move. This is because, as Mochtar Kusumaatmadja, a former foreign minister of Indonesia, pointed out, 'The kind of regime Myanmar has may not take kindly to advice from outside'.[40] Singapore's foreign minister similarly argued that 'there is nothing to be gained from isolating Myanmar'.[41] Thus, a key aspect of constructive engagement was to exclude economic sanctions against Myanmar. Instead, the policy allowed ASEAN countries quietly to increase economic and military links with the SLORC. Prime Minister Mahathir of Malaysia advocated such links as a means of helping economic reform in Myanmar introduced by SLORC:

Poor neighbours are no asset to anyone. The problems of the poor are likely to spill-over in the form of refugees, smuggling, black markets, etc. . . . Helping neighbours to become prosperous is therefore mutually beneficial.[42]

According to a report compiled by the US human rights group, the Institute for Asian Democracy,[43] ASEAN–Myanmar economic links since 1988 included fishing rights for Thailand in Myanmar waters (valued at US$70 a month per ton with a total of 60 vessels with total tonnage of 6806), as well as investments by Singapore in oil, automobiles, timber products, by Malaysia in hotel business, and by Thailand in brewery, hotel, road construction and a department store. The report also cited military sales by Singapore, denied by the Singapore government, consisting of mortars, rockets and ammunition, to Myanmar and training by the Malaysian Air Force of Myanmar army officers.

Despite its brave justification of constructive engagement, ASEAN was facing increasing tension with its Western dialogue partners in their annual series of consultations known as ASEAN post-ministerial conferences (ASEAN–PMC). A key argument against ASEAN's approach was whether constructive engagement meant no engagement when it came to applying diplomatic pressure on Myanmar to undertake political liberalization. At the Manila PMC in July 1992, Foreign Minister Gareth Evans of Australia contrasted constructive engagement with ASEAN's diplomacy on the Cambodian conflict, lamenting the fact that ASEAN had chosen not to apply the 'kind of energy that it demonstrated for so long in seeking to resolve the Cambodian problem' to address the situation in Myanmar. The US Under-Secretary of State Robert Zoellick challenged ASEAN to give substance to constructive engagement by 'tell[ing] the military regime it must release all political prisoners' and 'engag[ing] them in good-faith dialogue to restore constitutional government at an early date'.[44]

ASEAN responded by arguing that the policy had delivered 'some results' in extracting concessions from the regime such as the release of some political prisoners and a reunion between Aung San Suu Kyi and her family (a claim dismissed by the Western countries as being too 'limited').[45] But independent reports showed the policy had little to show for itself. Interestingly, Thai media and academic analysts were among the harshest critics of constructive engagement. A respected Thai academic, who called it 'a very bad policy', argued that, 'one cannot expect the regime to change by such a policy', adding that the continuation of the policy was due to 'persons [in Thailand] who have vested interests in Burma'.[46]

In this respect, it may be pointed out that ASEAN's policy of constructive engagement had little resemblance with the US policy towards South Africa in the 1980s bearing the same name. The US policy featured direct high-level contacts and painstaking multilateral negotiations with the apartheid regime aimed at producing movement towards political liberalization in South Africa and settlement of regional conflicts in Namibia and Angola.[47] In the case of ASEAN's Myanmar policy, the diplomatic engagement of SLORC was limited and half-hearted, at least in the public arena. Only after intense international criticism and direct pressure from its dialogue partners did ASEAN send the then Foreign Secretary of the Philippines Raul Manglapus on an 'unofficial human rights mission' to Myanmar in December 1991.[48]

But the mission was largely unsuccessful as the SLORC refused to allow Manglapus to meet with the detained opposition leader Aung San Suu Kyi. Although ASEAN officials have subsequently claimed to have applied private pressure on Myanmar, the extent and effect of this cannot be ascertained.[49] In any case, ASEAN's quarrels with the West on human rights have received far greater publicity than its contacts with Myanmar aimed at prodding the regime towards political liberalization.

Moreover, a key assumption of constructive engagement—that it would improve Myanmar's economic position and thereby induce peaceful domestic political change—remains to be proved. As *The Economist* argued: 'Constructive engagement may make sense when dealing with a regime—like China's—that will respond with long-term economic policies to improve the common man's lot. It makes no sense if it sustains regimes that practise only repression.'[50]

A passive course of constructive engagement is also at odds with ASEAN's professed desire to assume an activist role in regional security. As ASEAN leaders have sometimes acknowledged, the political situation in Myanmar is not a purely internal matter; it could threaten regional stability. Bilateral tensions created by refugee exodus from Myanmar attest to this prospect. Hostile reactions from Malaysia and Indonesia to the plight of its Rohingya Muslim population, driven by Myanmar troops into neighbouring Bangladesh, is a case in point. Continued political instability in Myanmar has also created the basis for competitive foreign intervention. For example, the dependence of the Myanmar regime on China for weapons to be used for domestic repression, which has resulted in sales worth nearly US$1.5 billion in recent years, has invited India's suspicions and could set the stage for Sino-Indian competition in Southeast Asia.

Moreover, as with other major political issues handled by the grouping, constructive engagement has been a source of intra-ASEAN frictions. Despite the apparent show of ASEAN solidarity in PMC meetings, constructive engagement, in the words of an official source in ASEAN, 'means that each [ASEAN] country can do what it wants, say what it wants as it sees fit, but not to take a collective six-country position'.[51]

Intra-ASEAN differences were starkly evident when the July 1992 ASEAN Foreign Ministers' Meeting in Manila debated whether to invite Myanmar's foreign minister to attend the meeting as a guest. The Philippines, as the host nation, and Indonesia both supported the invitation. Indonesia argued that such an invitation would give a new seriousness to constructive engagement and would be consistent with ASEAN's vision of 'One Southeast Asia', a regional community encompassing all ten states of Southeast Asia. But Malaysia resisted the move, arguing that the ASEAN Foreign Ministers' Meeting was not an appropriate venue for engaging the Myanmar junta in a dialogue. But Malaysian officials privately explained their position as retaliation against Myanmar's persecution of the Rohingya Muslims, about 150,000 of whom had fled to Bangladesh by March 1992.[52] As a Muslim nation, Malaysia wished to project solidarity with the Rohingyas whose plight had been protested by Islamic elements within Malaysia. The Malaysian posture was the first major hint of a shift in ASEAN's attitude towards Myanmar, based on a realization of the inadequacies of the constructive engagement approach practised until then.

The context of ASEAN's policy shift had been set by the decline and eventual demise of the military-dominated regime in Thailand. The civilian administrations under Anand Panyarachun and Chuan Lekpai had a domestic need to distance themselves from the close ties developed with Myanmar by the previous military-dominated regimes. But the exodus of Rohingya Muslims was the key factor behind the need to rethink constructive engagement. As the Indonesian daily, the *Jakarta Post*, argued: 'it is probably time for ASEAN to take a fresh look into the question and work out a viable formula before the seemingly never-ending problems that beset Myanmar become a threat to regional stability.'[53] In Thailand, the *Bangkok Post* was far more blunt. In an editorial, the *Post* asked: 'A pertinent question is whether ASEAN's "constructive engagement" can make a leopard change its spots.'[54] Another

Thai newspaper, the *Nation*, argued that by shifting from constructive engagement and applying pressure on the SLORC, ASEAN could exploit divisions within the junta and encourage those 'elements pushing for reform within military circles in Rangoon'.[55] Malaysia's official position on Myanmar reflected similar sentiments. It urged ASEAN to demand a timetable for political liberalization in Myanmar so as to 'stimulate' change, rather than allow change to 'evolve naturally'.[56]

Against this backdrop, ASEAN decided not to confer on Myanmar the status of observer at the 1993 ASEAN Foreign Ministers' Meeting in Singapore. This was at least partly in deference to the views of ASEAN's dialogue partners, especially the United States and the EC. After the conclusion of the Manila meeting in 1992, the US Secretary of State James Baker had signalled Washington's opposition to observer status for Myanmar. 'We congratulate ASEAN for not taking that step. As far as the US is concerned, we would be underwhelmed if they do.'[57]

While there continue to be disagreements between ASEAN and the West on the merits of constructive engagement, ASEAN states have recently claimed success in getting the latter to accept its position on Myanmar. At the Singapore PMC, the debate between ASEAN and its Western dialogue partners were reported to have become 'less confrontational' with several Western ministers making conciliatory remarks, thereby heading off a divisive debate at a time when ASEAN was announcing the launch of a new regional forum (the ASEAN Regional Forum) for security consultations in the Asia-Pacific region. Thai Foreign Minister Prasong Soonsari set the tone of moderation by acknowledging that the changes brought about by constructive engagement were 'slow', but he also added that these changes were 'going in the direction we all want'.[58] Foreign Minister Gareth Evans of Australia was especially conciliatory, stating that the West and ASEAN were 'moving in the same direction' and that there was 'no quarrel' between them, 'just a [matter of] different judgement'. Evans also acknowledged 'a willingness on the part of ASEAN governments to . . . exercise a significant degree of leverage, whether it's seen in public or not, against the Myanmar regime, based on the cards that ASEAN does hold'. The Assistant Secretary of State Winston Lord, who acknowledged 'differences in tactics', spoke of 'a common concern and the same goal' between ASEAN and its dialogue partners. The EC, however, continued to be sceptical of ASEAN's policy, with the EC Commission president announcing the grouping's determination to go on with political and economic sanctions against Myanmar.

Conclusion

This chapter has dealt with human rights management by ASEAN in the context of its overall approach to regional autonomy and order. The subject-matter of this chapter will continue to occupy a major place in ASEAN's collective political agenda in the post-Cold War era. The ASEAN governments' response to what used to be called 'internal threats' will be increasingly judged in terms of their human rights implications. ASEAN governments can no longer count on Western tolerance of harsh and violent suppression of internal dissent for the sake of regime stability and economic growth. In addition, many ASEAN states are likely to see a rise of domestic human rights groups (NGOs), drawing encouragement from the favourable international climate for their cause. Human rights management in the New World Order may no longer be conceptualized simply as a division between ASEAN and the West, but as a division between NGOs and their own governments.

Individual ASEAN governments, especially Malaysia, Singapore and Indonesia, have spoken out strongly and rhetorically against the universalization of human rights in terms of a given set of Western values, concepts and approaches, although divisions within the grouping over the extent of particularization are manifest. In general, the ASEAN governments' interest in human rights continues to be a reactive, defensive concern, and the idea of an ASEAN human rights regime for monitoring and enforcement is highly premature. But despite verbal attacks on the West, ASEAN's ability to exclude human rights from the agenda of its dialogue with the West is clearly limited. Thus, 'the initial reticence in some quarters [in ASEAN] towards the notion of human rights is now being dispelled.'[59] But in contrast to Cambodia, human rights are likely to remain a divisive issue in ASEAN's political and economic relationship with the West. Coupled with divisions within ASEAN and between ASEAN and other East Asian countries, the issue of human rights sets limits to ASEAN's ability to anchor a new regional cooperative order involving the nations of Southeast Asia and the relevant external powers.

To the extent that it embraces 'relativism' and 'particularism', ASEAN's position of human rights cannot be confined simply to refutation and rejection of values and views which are 'foreign'. It must also suggest a credible indigenous alternative to facilitate human rights management within the region. This is especially so when human rights questions are not strictly national concerns, but also affect regional stability and cooperation. ASEAN's first major effort to provide such an approach was tried out in Myanmar, in the form of the policy of 'constructive engagement'. But in pursuing constructive engagement, ASEAN has been constrained by a fear of setting a precedent which might be construed as interference in the internal politics of Myanmar. Thus, while constructive engagement is consistent with ASEAN's commitment to non-interference (by one regional state in the domestic affairs of another) and non-intervention (by external powers in regional affairs), it is no substitute for active engagement which can bring about the desired political change in Myanmar.

ASEAN's unwillingness to deal with human rights as an issue in conflict management within the region could overshadow whatever success it could claim in debating the outside world (the West in particular) about the virtue of a 'relativism'. Unless a regional organization creates a framework that would deal fairly and directly with human rights problems arising within an essentially 'domestic' milieu, its managerial role in regional order would remain incomplete.

Notes

1. On regional approaches to human rights, see Jack Donnelly, *Universal Human Rights in Theory and Practice* (Ithaca: Cornell University Press, 1989), and 'Human rights in the New World Order', *World Policy Journal*, vol. 9, no. 2 (Spring 1992), pp. 252–3.
2. Comparative assessment of regional enforcement agencies can be found in Burns H. Weston, Robin Ann Lukes and Kelly M. Hnatt, 'Regional human rights regimes: a comparison and appraisal', in Richard P. Claude and Burns Weston (eds), *Human Rights in the World Community*, 2nd edn. (Philadelphia: University of Pennsylvania Press, 1992).
3. The Declaration of the Fourth ASEAN Summit in Singapore in January 1992 did not mention human rights.
4. Michael Vatikiotis, 'Dollar democracy', *Far Eastern Economic Review*, 26 September 1991, p. 35.
5. *New Straits Times*, 31 October 1991.
6. 'Private Pressure', *Far Eastern Economic Review*, 13 February 1992, p. 9.
7. On the role of human rights NGOs in Asia, see Sidney Jones, 'The organic growth', *Far Eastern Economic Review*, 17 June 1993, p. 23.
8. 'Vienna showdown', *Far Eastern Economic Review*, 17 June 1993, p. 17.
9. ibid.
10. Michael Richardson, 'For the planners, a time to decide', *International Herald Tribune*, 18 November 1993, p. 5.
11. 'Take pragmatic line on human rights: Kan Seng', *Straits Times*, 17 June 1993, p. 1.
12. This point is made by a senior Singapore Foreign Ministry official. See Kishore Mahbubani, 'The West and the rest', *National Interest* (Summer 1992), p. 9. See also Kishore Mahbubani, 'News areas of Asean reaction: environment, human rights and democracy', *Asean-ISIS Monitor*, Issue no. 5 (October–December 1992), p. 13.
13. 'Alatas: no nation can judge others on human rights', 16 June 1993, p. 1.
14. *Straits Times*, 23 July 1991.
15. 'Alatas: no nation can judge others on human rights', op. cit.
16. 'Take pragmatic line on human rights: Kan Seng', op. cit.
17. Gordon Fairclough, 'Standing firm', *Far Eastern Economic Review*, 15 April 1993, p. 22.
18. 'Vienna showdown', op. cit.
19. 'Take pragmatic line on human rights: Kan Seng', op. cit.
20. See the discussions on these arguments in Chapters 1 to 4.
21. Cited in *New Straits Times* (Kuala Lumpur), 20 July 1991, p. 1.
22. 'Alatas: no nation can judge others on human rights', op. cit.
23. Mahbubani, op. cit., p. 15. Such an emphasis on communitarianism has not escaped criticism. According to one critic: 'The pre-industrial societies of Asia, as elsewhere, did place community and the obligation to it ahead of individuals and their rights. But this observation does not license a leap to the claim that modern East Asian societies are consequently not suited to the observance of human rights or liberal democracy because of residual Confucianism. This ignores the historical discrediting of Confucianism, the emergence of revolutionary left-wing politics and the development in South Korea, Taiwan, Hong Kong and Singapore of the most un-Confucian practices associated with rapid industrial growth such as corporate conglomerates with 12-hour working days for the executives, the breaking up of community through massive

urbanization, the necessity of parliamentarism for legitimacy, government by military élites and the militarization of politics.' Christopher Tremewan, 'Human rights in Asia', *Pacific Review*, vol. 6, no. 1 (1993), p. 27.

24. Joint Communiqué of the Twenty-Sixth ASEAN Ministerial Meeting, Singapore, 23–4 July 1993, p. 8.
25. *International Herald Tribune*, 22 July 1991.
26. 'KL will continue to speak up: foreign minister', *Straits Times*, 22 June 1993, p. 8.
27. Joint Communiqué of the Twenty-Sixth ASEAN Ministerial Meeting, op. cit., p. 7.
28. *The Environment and Human Rights in International Relations* (Jakarta: ASEAN-ISIS, undated), pp. 13–15.
29. See, for example, 'Take pragmatic line on human rights: Kan Seng', op. cit.
30. *China News* (Taipei), 21 November 1992.
31. *Straits Times*, 23 July 1991.
32. Mahbubani, op. cit., p. 15.
33. Sidney Jones, 'Human rights: basic elements of effective protection', paper prepared for the ASEAN–ISIS Asia Pacific Roundtable, 6–9 June 1993, Kuala Lumpur, Malaysia, p. 4.
34. Critics of cultural relativism have argued that such a position can mask cultural arrogance. Moreover, cultural particularities need not preclude a set of values common to all cultures which would provide the basis for universal standards of behaviour with respect to human rights. See Jack Donnelly, 'Cultural relativism and universal human rights', *Human Rights Quarterly*, vol. 6, no. 4 (1984), pp. 400–2; Christopher Tremewan, 'Human rights in Asia', op. cit. p. 23.
35. Joint Communiqué of the Twenty-Sixth ASEAN Ministerial Meeting, op. cit., p. 7. It should be noted that ASEAN governments continue to be suspicious of the idea of setting up a regional human rights watchdog.
36. Muthiah Alagappa, 'Confronting the SLORC', *Burma Review*, no. 30 (November–December 1991), p. 13.
37. John Bray, 'Burma: resisting the international community', *Pacific Review*, vol. 5, no. 3 (1992), p. 293.
38. 'Government to pursue friendly ties with Burma', *Nation*, 23 April 1992.
39. *Straits Times*, 26 August 1992, p. 27.
40. *Sunday Times* (Singapore), 11 October 1992, p. 17.
41. *Straits Times*, 27 July 1992, p. 15.
42. 'Myanmar's monsters', *Economist*, 15 March 1992, p. 17.
43. *Towards Democracy in Burma*, 2nd edn. (Washington, DC: Institute of Asian Democracy, 1993).
44. 'Asean stand on Burma draws flak', *Nation*, 25 July 1992.
45. ibid.
46. 'Full marks for foreign policy', *Nation*, 18 March 1992, p. A6.
47. For a discussion of 'constructive engagement' in Southern Africa, see Kevin Danaher, *The Political Economy of US Policy towards South Africa* (Boulder, C0: Westview Press, 1985), pp. 181–218.
48. *New Straits Times*, 3 December 1991.
49. For example, Singapore claimed that before hosting the ASEAN Foreign Ministers' Meeting in July 1993 it had invited a delegation of Myanmar cabinet ministers led by SLORC's First Secretary Lt.-Gen. Khin Nyunt as part of ASEAN's constructive engagement policy. The visit was used to tell the SLORC 'how much the world has changed' and international concerns about Myanmar's political situation. 'Singapore has expressed concern to junta leaders', *Straits*

Times, 29 July 1993, p. 20.

50. 'Myanmar's monsters', op. cit.
51. *Straits Times*, 26 August 1992, p. 27.
52. ibid.
53. 'Myanmar's problems', editorial, *Jakarta Post*, FBIS-EAS-92-062, 31 March 1992, p. 37.
54. 'Asean should rally behind KL to condemn Burma', editorial, *Nation*, FBIS-EAS-92-050, 13 March 1992, p. 50.
55. 'No reason to trust the men in Rangoon', *Nation*, 2 May 1992.
56. 'West backs ASEAN approach on Burma', *Bangkok Post*, 29 July 1993, p. 8.
57. *Straits Times*, 27 July 1992, p. 15.
58. 'West backs ASEAN approach on Burma', op. cit.; 'West moves towards Asean view on Burma', *Nation*, 29 July 1993, p. A1.
59. *The Environment and Human Rights in International Relations* (Jakarta: ASEAN–ISIS, undated).

PART IV
CONCLUSIONS

14

TOWARDS AN ALTERNATIVE APPROACH TO INTERNATIONAL HUMAN RIGHTS PROTECTION IN THE ASIA-PACIFIC REGION*

JAMES T. H. TANG

As human rights issues return to the international agenda, the record of East Asian countries has been subjected to critical scrutiny by the global community. While there may be some scope for interpreting human rights differently and perhaps even assigning different priorities to specific human rights according to the region's special circumstances, East Asian states are on the defensive.

In mounting an intellectual challenge and political offensive to the 'Western version' of international human rights protection, East Asian states may have identified some inconsistencies in Western human rights policies, and highlighted certain self-contradictory tendencies in an area which is as diverse and contentious as human rights. The acceptance of universality clearly does not necessarily mean that the reality of cultural diversity can be rejected. More-over, given the range of human rights which is being advanced in the contemporary world, it is by no means surprising that some of these rights are in conflict, and the priorities of different societies over human rights demands are not always the same.

Economic and social developments, considered by many Asian governments as crucial elements in measuring human rights conditions, are widely supported by the human rights community. A study commissioned by the United Nations Centre for Human Rights identified poverty as a key obstacle to the advancement of human rights. As the report suggests, world-wide poverty and increasing disparity between the North and the South 'is endangering the ethical foundation of our Planet'.[1] The economic dimension of human rights protection can be highly complicated involving difficult social and political questions. The report concludes that poverty is a human rights violation and 'an economic problem linked to national and international development policies, and a social and political issue that has to do with entitlements of liberties and freedoms, popular participation, and above all democracy'.[2] Asian governments are clearly not alone in claiming that economic rights are important.

As contributors to Part I of this work have demonstrated, however, East

Asian states cannot claim victory in the debates. Michael Freeman, Joseph Chen, Mely Caballero-Anthony and Yash Ghai all agree (albeit with different emphasis and varying degrees of sympathy for the Asian position) that the emphasis of Asian governments on development needs and cultural differences is not entirely groundless. But they are also unanimous in stating that East Asian states have failed to justify their policies in the suppression of human rights demands or in claiming that they are the only representatives of the community, and thereby also the only adjudicators of human rights standards. While development is a legitimate human rights concern in the developing world, as many human rights activists have observed that all too often state development policies in such countries become a source of human rights violations when people are forced to leave their homes for development projects, or deprived of their means of livelihood.[3]

The power relationship between the state and the people in many parts of the region is overwhelmingly in favour of the state. Many East Asian governments therefore cannot avoid confronting the responsibility of widespread human rights abuses in their countries. The human rights conditions in many East Asian countries have been consistently rated as poor by international human rights monitoring groups. The Humana human rights country rating, for example, has ranked most East Asian countries as below average. Several Asian countries are in fact at the bottom of the scale (see Table 14.1).

The Humana ranking is in some ways problematic, and reflects a Western bias, since economic, and social rights have not been properly incorporated. None the less, a widely used and respectable source of human rights monitoring, its assessment is an influential yardstick in measuring human rights conditions.[4] In fact most reports by independent human rights organizations have been highly critical of the situation in East Asia. Governments in the region are not only notorious for their poor human rights record, they also have a poor record in making commitments to internationally recognized norms.

In spite of growing importance of human rights issues in world politics, Asian states prefer to deal with human rights within their own domestic jurisdiction, resisting international monitoring. They are reluctant to sign major instruments of international human rights protection. Countries such as China, Indonesia, Malaysia, Singapore and Thailand are not signatories to the International Covenant on Civil and Political Rights (ICCP) and the International Covenant on Economic Social and Cultural Rights (ICESC) (see Table 14.2).

The influence of international opinion and external pressure on human rights development in Asia has proved to be rather mixed for a variety of reasons. William Barnds suggests that the capacity of the United States to change human rights conditions overseas has been exaggerated. In fact during the Cold War, US security objectives, for example, often took precedence over human rights concerns. American support for right-wing military regimes has long been a bitter issue for human rights advocates from Latin America. When the news that the Joint Planning Committee of the NGO forum in Vienna had invited former US President Jimmy Carter as a speaker for the closing session was reported, Latin American NGO delegates denounced him as 'the ex-president of a state that is principally responsible for the major violations of human rights and of the international law around the world'.[5]

Table 14.1 Humana human rights rating in the Asia-Pacific region, 1991 (%)

Country/area	Human rights rating*	
	Above average	Below average
Australia	91	
Burma (Myanmar)		17
Cambodia		33
Canada	94	
China		21
Hong Kong	79	
Indonesia		34
Japan	82	
Korea, North		20
Korea, South		59
Malaysia		61
New Zealand	98	
Papua New Guinea	70	
Philippines	72	
Singapore		60
Thailand	62	
USSR**		54
USA	90	
Vietnam		27

*World average: 62%
**Up to August 1991 at the dissolution of the 1917 Union.

Source: Charles Humana, *World Human Rights Guide*, 3rd edn. (Oxford: Oxford University Press, 1992).

In Asia, China's human rights conditions were accorded low priority in the agenda of US–China relations during the 1970s when a tacit strategic alliance against the Soviet Union was formed between the two countries. US human rights policy, seen from Asia as Francisco Nemenzo observes in his chapter on the Philippines, appeared to apply only to the communist states. American criticism of human rights situations in East Asia as both Mely Callabero-Anthony and Amitav Acharya demonstrate in their chapters, has been perceived as hypocritcal in many Asian capitals.

Since the end of the Cold War many East Asian states have continued to adopt an uncompromising attitude towards human rights difficulties with the West, denying human rights non-governmental organization (NGO) activities at home. They are often ruthless in dealing with political dissidents, considering them as a threat to regime stability. The Chinese government's unyielding position was demonstrated when the American Secretary of State Warren Christopher visited Beijing in March 1994. After the discussions on human rights problems which had been linked to the Clinton administration's re-

Table 14.2 Selected international human rights treaties (as of 31 March 1993)

	1	1a	1b	1c	2	3	4	4a
Brunei								
Cambodia	X				X	X	X	X
Canada	X	X		X	X	X(22)	X	X
China						X(22)	X	X
Indonesia						s		
Japan	X				X		X	X
Korea (DPRK)	X				X			
Korea (ROK)	X	X		X	X		X*	X*
Laos								
Malaysia								
Myanmar (Burma)								
Philippines	X	X		X	X	X	X	X
Russian Fed.	X	X		X	X	X(22)	X	X
Singapore								
Thailand								
USA	X*			X	s	s		X
Vietnam	X				X			

1 International Covenant on Civil and Political Rights (ICCPR).
1a Optional Protocol to ICCPR.
1b Second Optional Protocol to ICCPR.
1c Declaration Regarding Article 41 of ICCPR.
2 International Covenant on Economic Social and Cultural Rights (ICESCR).
3 Covention Against Torture and Other Cruel, Inhumane or Degrading Treatment of Punishment.
4 Convention relating to the State of Refugees (1951).
4a Protocol relating to the status of Refugees (1967).

* signed or become a party in 1992.
s signed but not ratified.

Source: Amnesty International Report 1993, pp. 353–43; *Human Rights: Major International Instruments* (UNESCO, 1993).

newal of the most-favoured-nation treatment for China, Foreign Minister Qian Qichen bluntly stated that 'China is under no obligation to implement the executive order of the US President'.[6]

But external pressure has clearly played a part in shaping government policies and the human rights agenda in the region. As Seichiro Takagi has shown, the Japanese government found it necessary to adopt a tougher posture towards China after the Tinanmen tragedy in 1989 as a result of Western pressure, despite its intuitive tendency for a friendly political relationship with its giant neighbour. Even hard-line states like China found it difficult to ignore human rights issues, and made a significant policy shift by encouraging scholarly research on human rights. As Zhou Wei has demonstrated, state sponsorship of scholarly human rights study in the PRC was largely a direct response to Western condemnation of the human rights conditions in China following the Tiananmen incident in 1989. The diversification of international contacts by human rights activists in the Philippines, and high-profile campaigns of human rights groups gradually made a significant impact on international public opinion about the Marcos regime which was highly dependent on foreign economic aid.

Moreover, political liberalization in several East Asian states since the 1980s such as the Philippines, South Korea, Taiwan and Thailand has forced governments in these countries to be more accountable. They have become more ready to confront their own human rights problems, thus creating a more encouraging environment for regional cooperation over human rights protection. In the Philippines 'people's power' removed the Marcos regime from power. In South Korea the election of Roh Tae-Woo marked the first proper presidential election for years. Roh's successor Kim Young Sam, a former opposition leader, is the first civilian president since the 1960s. The ruling party in Taiwan, Kuomintang, has relaxed its political grip on the Taiwanese society and has accepted open competitive elections as an integral part of the island's political process. Political developments in Russia, as Constantine Pleshakov's chapter demonstrates, proved to be even more dramatic as a result of the collapse of Soviet communism. Political liberalization has clearly led to a more positive attitude towards human rights protection in these countries.

Thus two self-contradictory tendencies on human rights problems can be observed. First, the intensification of international tensions over human rights issues is taking place as the transformation in world politics provides new opportunities for establishing a new and peaceful regional order for the Asia-Pacific region. The economic success of many East Asian states have also facilitated strong international links both across the Pacific and within East Asia, providing the basis for other forms of security arrangements and economic cooperation including multilateral frameworks involving Western and Asian countries.[7] Second, improvement in economic conditions and political liberalization in the region are taking place while at the same time political dominance of many East Asian states remains overwhelming and systemic and blatant human rights abuses continue. Even in 'newly liberalizing states' human rights violations obviously have not disappeared overnight. Traditional practices die hard and wide-spread human rights violations can still be observed. Moreover, sweeping economic changes in the region have occurred primarily in states whose economic policies are market-focused. In some cases such forces have weakened state power, but they have also created new social and economic problems with human rights implications.

The role of the international intervention in human rights problems has been a controversial one. However, as Paul Taylor indicates, the international community clearly has a role to play in assisting countries which suffer from natural disasters or war when individual rights are transgressed by warring groups or governments. In discussion the limitations of the UN humanitarian assistance programme, Taylor has argued that a more flexible view of sovereignty should be accepted, and reminds us that states which respect human

rights and promote human welfare effectively are more likely to be the strong
and stable pillars of the state system.

While East Asian states may be reluctant to tolerate international involvement in human rights protection, rejecting it as a Western attempt to impose
standards inconsistent with Asian traditions and realities, they have not produced a convincing alternative approach. In different ways, Lawrence Woods
and Amitav Acharya have demonstrated specific problems attached to the
Asian alternatives to human rights protection.

Woods explores whether human rights protection could be developed
through the existing regional economic institutions. International relations in
the Asia-Pacific region have not been as institutionalized as Europe, and
region-wide fora for discussing human rights issues are therefore limited. The
rapid pace of economic development in the region has made an institutionalized framework of economic cooperation possible both at the non-
governmental and inter-governmental levels. Woods concludes that at
present the prospect that such organizations might facilitate a human rights
dialogue does not look promising. But as Woods also suggests, some of these
organizations may provide a useful forum for keeping human rights issues
on the agenda.

Acharya reveals the limits of the Asian approach by examining in some
depth ASEAN's policy of constructive engagement towards Myanmar.
ASEAN was forced to revise its position when it became clear that the
problems in Myanmar may threaten unity among ASEAN states, and jeop-
ardize their relations with Western countries. Amitav Acharya's contribution
demonstrated the limitation of Asean's 'pragmatic alternative' regional approach. His verdict is that ASEAN's aspiration in regional management
would not be fully realized unless a framework which would deal fairly and
directly with human rights problems could be created.

In this concluding chapter an attempt will be made to explore the prospect
for developing a regional institutional approach to human rights protection
in the light of post-Cold War international and domestic changes in the Asia-
Pacific region.

Regional human rights arrangements

Contemporary human rights protection has been defined initially in universal
terms. Regionalism was not supported at the UN in the early post-Second
World War years because it was regarded by some as 'a breakaway movement, calling the universality of human rights into question'.[8] Since the 1960s,
however, regional conventions on human rights have been adopted in Europe, the Americas and Africa. The European version, which is the most
institutionalized one with strong monitoring power, can be regarded as a
successful example of regional cooperation over human rights protection by
a group of politically like-minded states which share a common cultural
tradition.[9]

If many Asian states have resisted committing themselves to international
instruments of human rights protection, they have displayed even less inter-

est in the establishment of a regional human rights system. They have rejected proposals for human rights protection mechanisms even at the subregional level, not to mention region-wide arrangements.[10] The idea of a regional approach to human rights protection in Asia has been dismissed as impractical if simply because of geography, history and culture. Asia covers a huge area, with a large population whose cultural traditions are diverse, and share little in common with each other in terms of political and economic development. It has been suggested that 'an approach which considers the whole of Asia as one region for the purpose of international human rights is unrealistic'.[11] With the exception of some South Pacific islands, Australia and New Zealand—countries on the margin of Asia—most governments in the region are not even enthusiastic about a subregional approach.

In a topology on human rights regimes, Jack Donnelly classified human rights regimes into declaratory, promotional, implementation and enforcement regimes. All regimes, by definition, have standard norms, or at least guidelines but their capacities to monitor and/or enforce the observation of norms vary. Declaratory regimes involve international norms but no international decision-making. Promotional regimes involve international exchange of information and efforts to promote the national implementation of norms. Implementation regimes involve monitoring procedures and policy coordination which are weak and are entirely under national control; enforcement regimes involve binding international decision-making and strong forms of international monitoring of national compliance with international norms.[12]

Using his own topology, Donnelly briefly reviewed the evolution of human rights regimes since the end of the Second World War. In 1945 no international regimes on human rights existed. Ten years later by 1955 a declaratory global regime had been established, another ten years later in 1965 the global regime became a strong declaratory regime, and it turned into a promotional regime by 1975, and a strong promotional regime by 1985. Among regional regimes, the European version constituted the only enforcement regime by 1985. The Inter-American regime which was only a declaratory regime in 1965, however, had become a strong promotional/enforcement regime by 1985. The declaratory African regime only came into existence in the early 1980s. The absence of a human rights regime even of the declaratory kind in Asia, one of the world's largest and economically most dynamic regions, is conspicuous (see Table 14.3).

In spite of the vast size and the complex cultural differences of Asia, region-wide human rights protection schemes have been put forward from time to time. As early as 1964 a UN seminar on human rights in developing countries held in Kabul discussed the drafting of an Asian convention on human rights. The idea was discussed again in 1965 at the Southeast Asia and Pacific Conference of Jurists in Bangkok. The Philippines proposed to the UN Commission on Human Rights in 1967 that regional commissions should be set up in regions where there were no such institutions. While proposals for regional arrangements were often discussed the idea has not enjoyed wide support in Asia.

During the 1982 Colombo seminar, for example, representatives from Asian governments did not favour the establishment of an Asian human

Table 14.3 Changes in international human rights regimes, 1945–1985

	1945	1955	1965	1975	1985
Global regime	None	Declaratory	Strong declaratory	Promotional	Strong promotional
European regime	None	Implementation	Implementation/ enforcement	Enforcement	Enforcement
Inter-American regime	None	Declaratory	Weak promotional	Promotional	Strong promotional/ enforcement
African regime	None	None	None	None	Declaratory
Asia and the Middle East	None	None	None	None	None

Source: Adapted from Jack Donnelly, *Universal Human Rights in Theory and Practice* (Ithaca, NY.: Cornell University Press, 1989) p. 224

rights commission. Proponents of a global approach feared that a regional or subregional framework might actually pose a threat to the cause of human rights because regional arrangements would run the risk of being overwhelmed by the representatives of authoritarian regimes.[13] Thus, a combination of geographical situation, physical factors, historical circumstances, cultural diversities, political opposition from different directions has prevented the establishment of a regional human rights commission in Asia.

But countries in Asia exhibited similarities, such as vast populations and highly complex social organizations that were in existence long before the reception of Western laws and legal concepts.[14] Communities in the East Asian area, a core subregion of Asia, for example, share a long history of economic, social and political interaction, even if some of the interactions have not always been cordial. In the contemporary era most of them also experienced Western colonialism in one form or another. The end of the Cold War, which removed the ideological divide among the independent states, should facilitate closer political cooperation among them. Moreover, many East Asian states embarking on a similar export-oriented economic strategy do share common interests in the face of Western economic protectionism. The increasing importance of human rights in the post-Cold War international agenda may therefore force East Asian states to rethink their approach to human rights problems.

ASEAN states, for example, have attempted to develop an alternative approach to human rights management. In July 1992 the regional think-tank ASEAN–ISIS submitted a note on human rights to the ministers' meeting in Manila with a set of guiding principles for dealing with human rights issues—incorporating the ASEAN arguments on situational uniqueness—and comprehensive human rights. The submission, however, also emphasized the importance of cooperation rather than conflict and expressed support for an impartial international monitoring body with comprehensive values. ASEAN–ISIS also proposed that ASEAN should examine the feasibility of establishing an ASEAN Commission on Human Rights. The establishment of such a commission, argued ASEAN–ISIS, would enable ASEAN to develop and formulate human rights policies in accordance with its specific historic, economic and political circumstances. The Commission would also be the 'embryo or catalyst' of a region-wide commission for the Asia-Pacific region or even Asia as a whole.[15]

Other proposals for international governmental institutions on human rights in the region include the establishment of a US–China human rights commission. According to one supporter of the proposal, the bilateral US–China human rights commission would consist of government and non-government members. The commission would provide a forum for discussing systemic human rights issues such as political crime, religious freedom, and would act as a channel for regular exchange of human rights information.[16] Such official institutions, if they are to be established, may help to ease international tensions in the region, but they are still on the drawing board and many NGOs are suspicious that they may become an instrument of human rights management rather than human rights protection.

If there is an absence of governmental support for establishing region-wide

human rights protection systems in the Asia-Pacific region, the same definitely cannot be said of the non-governmental groups. In fact most initiatives
for regional human rights protection have been made by NGOs. Since the
1970s Asian NGOs have been more and more active in promoting human
rights protection in the region. Today's Asian NGOs, as an observer re-
marked, 'are more numerous, better organized and more outspoken than
ever before'.[17] Most of them are national organizations, but some are organizations with wider-regional concerns.

One review of the regional NGO scene listed, for example, Lawasia (the
law association for Asia and the Pacific), the Asian Coalition of Human Rights
Organizations (established in Bangkok), the Asean-based Regional Council on
Human Rights in Asia, and the Asian Human Rights Commission and the
Asian Legal Resource Centre (set up in Hong Kong in 1983).[18] These are not
the only human rights NGOs with a regional focus. Other groups such as the
Asian Center for the Progress of Peoples, and the Asian Regional Exchange
for New Alternatives, for example, have been actively involved with human
rights promotion work in the region. The considerable number of regional
organizations which attended the Bangkok NGO conference in 1993 is also
indicative of the interests in human rights issues at the region-wide level.
Many of these groups, however, may have different agendas and subregional
focus. The Asia Pacific Forum on Women, Law and Development, for example, places greater emphasis on women's issues, and the Asian Students
Association is more concerned with student problems. In terms of resources
and the range of activities, they may also have significant differences, but all
of them are groups with a regional focus.[19]

The many proposals and/or initiatives for developing regional-wide human rights protection arrangements by Asian NGOs can be classified into
three major categories. The first is the ideal model characterized by a comprehensive and highly institutionalized human rights system complete with
a human rights convention, a set of monitoring and investigative machinery
as well as an enforcement mechanism. The second category is more action-
oriented, involving coordinating human rights campaigns and organizing
regional human rights promotion activities. A third category involves proposals for establishing human rights institutions for research and information-
exchange purposes with varying degrees of institutionalization.

The best example of the ideal model is represented by proposals put forward by those from the legal perspective. As early as 1968 the International
Commission of Jurists recommended the establishment of a Council of Asia
and the Pacific. Amnesty International also discussed the possibility of regional human rights protection machinery in its first Pacific regional conference in 1976 which took place in Japan. In fact Japanese NGOs have
continued their support for a regional human rights institution in the 1980s.

Among the numerous Asian NGOs, Lawasia has been particularly active
in putting forward concrete proposals on regional human rights institutions.
Lawasia has drafted ten basic principles on human rights and has also produced a model Pacific Charter of human rights. In 1988 the organization
recommended the establishment of a regional human rights research institute
which would conduct research on human rights, offer human rights study

courses, monitor human rights abuses, and serve as an information clearing-house for the region. One of the most recent proposals was put forward in a 1993 Lawasia meeting in Sri Lanka. The proposal envisages the establish-ment of the Asian convention on human rights, to be supported by an Asian Human Rights Commission and a Court of Human Rights.[20]

The action-oriented category initiatives have been brought about by neces-sity because human rights advocates increasingly found it useful to coordi-nate their efforts in the promotion of human rights and in advancing Asian concerns in major international fora. The setting up of the regional NGO facilitating group in early 1994 greatly facilitated such efforts by Asian NGOs' involvement in the Bangkok regional human rights meeting in March and April and the Vienna meeting in June 1993.

On both occasions their common position has helped to forge a greater sense of common purpose and cooperative interaction. In fact during the Vienna World Conference, Asian NGOs were regarded as the best-organized group and, with 270 representatives, represented the second-largest group in the NGO forum after Western Europe.[21] As a follow-up to the Vienna World Conference many Asian NGOs have also put forward ideas for strengthening their links and coordinating their activities. In early 1994 a new regional NGO facilitating group was created during a meeting in Bangkok which was at-tended by seventy human rights advocates from fifty-eight organizations based in fifteen different countries in the Asia-Pacific region. The group intends to facilitate human rights campaigns and activities by enhancing information exchange and access to data about human rights issues and events of common interests, and by improving the effectiveness of human rights protection actions and appeals.[22]

The category of information and research-oriented organizations is closely related to the ideal model and action-oriented categories of regional NGO initiatives. Information exchange and obtaining access to information about human rights violations in the region are clearly critical for developing a legal protection framework or an action-oriented, region-wide campaign. Several organizations have begun work in building up information networks on hu-man rights issues. Japanese NGOs, for example, have secured financial sup-port and have made concrete suggestions about establishing an Asia-Pacific human rights information centre. The centre is expected to become fully functional by the end of 1994. The centre is envisaged to 'play an important role in influencing Japanese public opinion and Japanese policy-makers to play a more active role in the promotion and protection of human rights globally and in the Asia-Pacific region'. The centre is to achieve its goal by 'contributing to greater interaction among human rights activists as well as generating and strengthening resources available to promote and protect human rights in the region'.[23]

Another initiative on human rights information networking was made in September 1993 when an Asian regional meeting on human rights informa-tion exchange and networking took place in Hong Kong. The meeting, co-hosted by the Human Rights Database project at the University of Hong Kong and HURIDOCS (Human Rights Information and Documentation Sys-tem International), was attended by representatives of nine human rights documentation centres from eight countries. The participants agreed to set up a regional focal point called HURIDOCS Asia. Participants agreed to encourage the use of standard HURIDOCS tools to document and report human rights violations. The meeting also decided that a pilot study should be conducted to explore the technicalities about information exchange via computer floppy disks and on-line information based on accumulated databases.[24] Table 14.4 provides a summary of several NGO initiatives for regional human rights protection.

Of the three broad categories the ideal type offers a possible model of development based on the global process, but does not provide an immediate solution to existing problems. The action type is a continuation of existing advocates activities, albeit better coordinated, and probably would generate more pressure on governments in the region. But it is not very institutionalized and would probably be more responsive to urgent *ad hoc* situations and specific cases rather than serving as the model for a comprehensive system. The research and information category clearly is no replacement for either a longer-term vision human rights system or a concrete human rights protection mechanism. Increasingly, however, Asian NGOs have accepted that fundamental problems such as how human violations could be documented and how such information could be analysed and shared among human rights advocates should be properly addressed.

Human rights monitoring and information networking

Measuring human rights violations is clearly no easy task. While human rights groups such as HURIDOCS and Leiden University's PIOOM (interdisciplinary programme of Research on Root Causes of human rights violation) have studied and developed useful monitoring standards, no comprehensive human rights data with reference to the particularities of human rights violations in the region are available. At present comprehensive and regular reports on human rights situations in the world are published either by government agencies such as the US State Department and international advocate NGOs such as Asia Watch, Amnesty International and Freedom House.

The most important and comprehensive governmental source on the human rights situation in different parts of the world is clearly the US State Department report. In other Western countries official human rights reports are often linked to government aid policies. Human rights groups in a number of Scandinavian countries, for example, evaluate conditions in developing countries receiving aid from their governments. All these sources, however, have their limitations. Apart from technical problems which have been discussed in a number of works,[25] existing reports have also been criticized on political grounds. Reports produced by individual governments are very often linked to specific policies objectives. Many independent observers, for example, have found the State Department reports useful, but as a governmental report its neutrality is suspect because its findings inevitably could have implications for US foreign policies.[26]

Table 14.4 NGO initiatives for regional human rights protection arrangments

Proposer	Category	Scope	Institution	Stage of development
Lawasia	Ideal	Comprehensive	Human Rights Commission; Court of Human Rights	Discussion
Bangkok Group	Action-oriented	Campaign work; information exchange; coordination	Facilitating team/electronic mail network	Networking and coordination begun
HURIDOCS and Asia-based human rights information centres	Research/ information	Documentation; data-collection; monitoring	Documentation centre based in Pakistan	Being set up
Japanese NGOs	Research/ information	Documentation; data-collection; monitoring	Information centre based in Japan	To be established mid-1994

Source: Author's compilation based on NGO reports.

International NGO reports on human rights have provided useful information on human rights and their findings have been often cited by human
advocates. Many of these reports cover the general human rights situation in
the Asian region, and on specific human rights problems in Asian countries.
Asia Watch, for example, released a report on *Human Rights in the APEC
Region* during the Asia Pacific Economic Cooperation Forum meeting in
Seattle in November 1993.[27] But such reports suffered from different limitations and none of them addressed the economic and social context of such
problems. The emphasis of some of these international NGOs may not be the
same as their Asian counterparts. Compared with some Asian NGOs, Amnesty International, for example, may be more preoccupied with prisoners of
conscience than with broader concerns about political and social structures.
The Freedom House annual report, *Freedom in the World*, is another example.
While the report is a conscious attempt to use standard data, the measures
are vague, and more emphasis is placed on political and civil liberties, with
scant reference to the social and economic dimensions of human rights. Similarly Asia Watch seldom ventures into these dimensions in its annual documentation of human rights violations.[28]

If economic and social dimensions are as important as political and civil
rights in the Asian approach to human rights implementation, then a system
of monitoring reflecting such emphasis could be incorporated into the measurement of human rights conditions in the region. As sociologist Ray Pawson
has observed, 'measurement is not just a matter of observation but also of
conceptualization'.[29]

Thus, a system of human rights protection should involve more conscientious efforts to examine the conceptual dimension of human rights protection
in Asia. In a UN-sponsored seminar in preparation for the Vienna World
Conference, the problems of measuring the economic, social and cultural
dimensions of human rights and developing indicators were discussed at
length.[30] The major problem in developing indicators for measuring human
rights is the subjective and qualitative nature of human rights. The interdependence and sometimes conflicting nature of certain economic, social,
political and civil rights have further complicated attempts to develop a set
of reliable and consistent indicators. While universal standards have been
widely accepted in contemporary human rights debates, the North–South
divide does have implications for measuring achievements and understanding the source of human rights violations.

Attempts by the United Nations Development Agency (UNDA) at producing country ranking on human rights performance based on Humana's report, for example, led to 'a storm of criticism'. Many developing states
accused the ranking as a biased scheme based on Western notions. The group
of 77 maintained that inclusion of 'freedom for homosexuality activity' was
an example of Western human rights standards being applied to Asian countries.[31] But both Asian governments and Asian NGOs have not produced
their own regular and comprehensive region-wide human rights reports.
While monitoring human rights violations and measuring them are complicated tasks, the absence of data which incorporate the social and economic
dimensions is clearly a handicap to developing human rights protection

mechanisms in the region.

Experts taking part in the 1993 UN seminar on human rights indicators have observed that a large amount of useful information and data is available within the UN system. They also stressed that the assessment of economic, social and cultural rights should be derived from a wide range of sources and not limited to information supplied by governmental agencies. The panel of experts also cautioned that while statistical data are useful, not all indicators can be expressed in quantifiable terms. The seminar did not come up with a set of indicators, but it highlighted the need to develop human rights data and information which is more relevant to the developing world.[32]

The development of an Asian approach to human rights protection requires the refinement of conceptual understanding of human rights in the Asian context and greater expertise in measuring human rights standards as well as formulating better indicators. While many people in Asia would accept that political and civil rights, and economic and social rights are indivisible, there has not been any comprehensive review of how such concepts can be applied in the regional context. The conceptualization of human rights in a regional- and cultural-specific context remains highly problematic. The establishment of region-wide human rights protection mechanisms remains difficult. But efforts to develop information centres/networks, better data collection capacities, and the promotion of region-wide information exchange may facilitate the emergence of what could be called 'principled issue-networks on human rights'.[33] Such issue-networks, characterized by their transnational nature, will help to promote greater human rights protection in the region.

Human rights in the post-Cold War Asia-Pacific Region

There is no immediate solution for resolving the human rights conflict between Western industrialized countries and Asian states in the Asia-Pacific region. This book does raise some fundamental questions about whether the development of human rights protection would be benefited by incorporating the perspectives from East Asia. But the conflicts between East Asia and the West are not based entirely on different interpretations of human rights standards and international politics; these are also conflicts arising from different state–society power relations and political arrangements in East Asia and in the West. The position of many East Asian states on human rights very often is simply an excuse for their policies. Unless dramatic political changes occur in the Asia-Pacific region, different interpretations and emphasis of human rights standards and values will remain an important source of international conflict and tension.

The Asia-Pacific region clearly has the potential to develop a human rights protection system. Economic developments have rendered many East and Southeast Asian societies affluent. The standards of living and social and economic conditions of some parts of the region have caught up with the industrialized world. International relations in the region are no longer governed by the capitalist and communist divide. Economic linkages and common political interests in the post-Cold War era may facilitate closer interaction among Asian countries. In fact regional security concern has given rise to a number of initiatives to establish multilateral regional security arrangements. Intra-regional economic activities have also led to the establishment of more institutionalized inter-governmental economic cooperation.

Important political, economic and social changes have already forced East Asian states to re-examine their positions towards human rights problems at home. The promotion of human rights protection is a long-term process. A more general improvement of human rights in East Asia requires, among other things, greater social awareness, sustained economic development and more fundamental political changes. Efforts to develop a greater sense of common purpose with regard to human rights protection, to encourage political liberalization, to establish more channels of institutionalized regional cooperation, and to promote greater awareness will certainly go some way towards the reduction of international tensions over human rights and create a better climate for human rights protection. But a regional alternative will only emerge when there is not merely an awareness of different regional conditions, but also a genuine commitment to human rights protection.

Some years ago R. J. Vincent pointed out the inescapable tension between human rights and foreign policy. As Vincent put it: 'the society of humankind stands opposed to the club of states, and one of the primary rules of the latter was to deny membership to the former.'[34] While human rights may not always enjoy the same degree of attention in the international system of states, after several decades of development, a global human rights regime has been consolidated. The ideals and concerns of human society will not be easily removed from the international agenda. Growing economic prosperity in East Asia will create greater pressure for human rights improvement in the region, leading to possible domestic political friction within Asian states with implications for regional stability. Governments in the region ignore human rights at their own peril.

Notes

*I am grateful to Ms Jo Jo Tam of the Human Rights Database Project at the Faculty of Law, University of Hong Kong for directing my attention to and supplying me with useful NGO reports on human rights information centres in Asia.

1. Paulo Sergio Pinheiro with the collaboration of Malak El-Chichini and Tulio Khan, 'Poverty, marginalization, violence and the realization of human rights', a study commissioned by the Centre for Human Rights pursuant to General Assembly Resolution 45/155 of 18 December 1990 and 46/116 of 17 December 1991. Paper submitted to the Fourth Session of the Preparatory Committee for the World Conference on Human Rights. A/CONF.157/PC60/Add.3, 1 April 1993, p. 29.
2. ibid.
3. See, for example, Clarence J. Dias, 'Relationship between human rights, development and democracy: South/North NGO solidarity in fostering popular participation', discussion paper for a workshop on the relationship between development democracy and human rights, NGO forum held in conjunction

with the World Conference on Human Rights, Vienna, 10–12 June 1993.

4. For a discussion of the report's methodology and a defence of its limitations, see the introduction in Charles Humana, *World Human Rights Guide*, 3rd edn. (Oxford: Oxford University Press, 1992), pp. 3–10.

5. *Terra Viva*, 12 June 1993, p. 11. Carter's speech was drowned by the booing from Latin American and Caribbean delegates. See also *Terra Viva*, 14 June 1993, pp. 1, 6.

6. *South Morning China Post*, 17 March 1994.

7. A useful source on international security issues in the Asia-Pacific region and possible post-Cold War international structures there can be found in working papers produced by the research programme of the North Pacific Cooperative Security Dialogue organized by the Centre for International and Strategic Studies and the Joint Centre for Asia-Pacific Studies, York University.

8. Karel Vasak, 'Introduction' to 'Sub-part II: Regional institutions for the protection of human rights', in Karel Vasak, (ed.), *The International Dimension of Human Rights*, revised and edited for the English version by Philip Alston, Vol. 2 (Westport, Connecticut: Greenwood, 1982) p. 451.

9. A solid discussion of the European arrangements can be found in Karel Vasak, 'The Council of Europe', in Vasak (ed.), *The International Dimension of Human Rights*, op. cit., chapter 16. A more up-to-date and straightforward account of the Council's work can be found in *The Council of Europe and Human Rights*, report prepared by the Council of Europe for the World Conference on Human Rights (Strasbourg: Council of Europe, 1993).

10. The term international regime is used with reference to the existing literature on regimes theory. See Stephen Krasner (ed.), *International Regimes* (Ithaca, NY: Cornell University Press, 1983). See also Stephen Haggard and Beth A. Simmons, 'Theories of international regimes', *International Organization*, no. 41 (1987), pp. 491–517. A discussion of international human rights protection and regimes theory is in Jack Donnelly, 'International human rights: a Regime analysis', *International Organization*, no. 40 (1986), pp. 599–642.

11. Virginia A. Leary, 'Asia and the international human rights movement', in Claude E. Welch, Jr. and Virginia A. Leary (eds.), *Asian Perspectives on Human Rights* (Boulder: Westview, 1990), p. 16. See also James W. Morley (ed.), *Driven by Growth, Political Change in the Asia-Pacific Region* (New York: M. E. Sharpe, 1993) for discussions on East Asia's diverse political and economic experiences since the end of the Second World War.

12. Jack Donnelly, *Universal Human Rights in Theory and Practice* (Ithaca, NY: Cornell University Press, 1989), p. 206.

13. Seminar on national, local and regional arrangements for the promotion of human rights in the Asian region, Colombo, 21 June–2 July 1982. Government representatives attended were from: Afghanistan, Australia, Bangladesh, China, Democratic Kampuchea, France, India, Maldives, Mongolia, Nepal, New Zealand, Pakistan, Republic of Korea, Sri Lanka, Thailand, the Soviet Union, Britain, the US, and Vietnam. See Virginia A. Leary, 'Asia and the international human rights movement', op. cit., pp. 16–18.

14. Hiroko Yamane, 'Asia and human rights', in Vassak (ed.), op. cit., p. 653.

15. See a detailed discussion of the ASEAN–ISIS proposal in Jusuf Wanandi, 'Human rights and democracy in the ASEAN nations: the next 25 years', *Indonesian Quarterly*, vol. 21, no. 1, First Quarter (1993), pp. 14–24.

16. For a discussion of the commission, see John Kamm's opening address to the International Colloquium on Human Rights and Foreign Policy, 11 March 1993, University of Hong Kong. John Kamm, a former president of the American

Chamber of Commerce in Hong Kong, has been a key supporter of the US–China Commission on Human Rights.

17. Sidney Jones, 'The organic growth: Asian NGOs have come into their own', *Far Eastern Economic Review*, 17 June 1993, p. 23.

18. Virginia Leary, 'Asia and the international human rights movement', op. cit.

19. A full list of NGOs which attended the Bangkok NGO Conference on Human Rights in March 1993 can be found in *Our Voice: Report of the Asia Pacific NGO Conference on Human Rights and NGOs' Statements to the Asia Regional Meeting* (Bangkok: Asian Cultural Forum on Development, 1993), pp. 263–86.

20. See various issues of Lawasia's *Human Rights Bulletin*. For discussions on the regional charter and human rights commission, see Nihal Jayawickrama, 'An Asian convention on human rights', paper presented at Lawasia 1993, Sri Lanka, 13 and 16 September, 1993; and Tony Deklin, 'Current initiatives in the Pacific for the development of a regional human rights organization', paper presented at a seminar on human rights organizations in the Asia and the Pacific, Taipei, October 1990; and also Yougindra Khushalani, 'Human rights in Asia and Africa', *Human Rights Law Journal*, vol. 4, part 4 (1983), pp. 403–42.

21. The breakdown of organizations by region as provided by the Ludwig Boltzmann Institute of Human Rights (BIM), which was the coordinating organization for the forum, is as follows: Africa—202; North America—178; Latin America—236; Asia—270; Australia/Oceania—38; Western Europe—426; Eastern and Central Europe—179. *NGO-Newsletter*, no. 4, July 1993.

22. See, for example, 'Asia Pacific regional NGO network established' in *Human Rights Defender*, vol. 3 no. 1 (1994), (Human Rights Centre, University of New South Wales).

23. *Introduction to the Proposed Asia-Pacific Human Rights Information Centre*, report by the preparatory committee for the Asia-Pacific Human Rights Information Centre.

24. *Report on the Asia Regional Meeting on Human Rights Information Exchange and Networking*, 1993. Full details about HURIDOCS standard formats can be found in Judith Dueck *et al.*, *HURIDOCS Standards Formats: A Tool for Documenting Human Rights Violations* (Oslo: HURIDOCS, 1993); and Judith Dueck and Aida Maria Noval *et al.*, *HURIDOCS Standard Formats: Supporting Documents* (Oslo: HURIDOCS, 1993).

25. See, for example, Michael Stohl, David Carleton, George Lopez and Stephen Samuels, 'State violations of human rights: issues and problems of measurement', *Human Rights Quarterly*, vol. 8, no. 4 (November 1986); and also Harry M. Scoble and Laurie S. Wiseberg, 'Problems of comparative research in human rights', and John F. McCamant, 'A critique of present measures of "human rights development" and an alternative', in Ved. P. Nanda, James R. Scarritt and George W. Shepherd, Jr. (eds), *Global Human Rights: Public Policies, Comparative Measures and NGO Strategies* (Boulder: Westview, 1981).

26. Analysis of the State Department reports can be found in McCamant, op. cit., Wiseberg, op. cit.

27. Asia Watch, *Human Rights in the APEC Region* (New York: Asia Watch, November 1993).

28. See for example, Asia Watch's contribution to *Human Rights Watch World Report, 1993* (New York: Human Rights Watch, 1992) pp. 147–193.

29. Ray Pawson, *A Measure for Measure: A Manifesto for Empirical Sociology* (London: Routledge, 1989), p. 49, also quoted in Russell Lawrence Barsh, 'Measuring human rights: problems of methodology and purpose', *Human Rights Quarterly*, vol. 15 no. 1 (February 1993).

30. Report of the seminar on appropriate indicators to measure achievements in the progressive realization of economic, social, and cultural rights, Geneva, 25–29 January 1993. A/CONF.157/PC/73 20 April 1993.
31. See discussions in Barsh, op. cit. See also the foreword by William H. Draper III in *Human Development Report 1992* (New York: Oxford University Press for the United Nations Development Programme, 1992).
32. Seminar report in A/CONF.157/73 (20 April 1993), op. cit. Some useful works on data collection and statistical application of human rights measurement have been published in recent years. See for example, Thomas B. Jabine and Richard P. Claude (eds), *Human Rights and Statistics: Getting the Record Straight* (Philadelphia: University of Pennsylvania Press, 1992).
33. Kathryn Sikkink, 'Human rights, principled issue-network, and sovereignty in Latin America', *International Organization*, vol. 47 no 3 (Summer 1993), pp. 411–41.
34. R. J. Vincent, *Human Rights and International Relations* (Cambridge: Cambridge University Press, 1986), p. 129.

APPENDIX I
BANGKOK DECLARATION

The Declaration adopted by the Ministers and Representatives of Asian States, who met Bangkok from 29 March to 2 April 1993, pursuant to General Assembly Resolution 46/116 of 17 December 1991 in the context of preparations for the World Conference on Human Rights:

Emphasizing the significance of the World Conference on Human Rights, which provides an invaluable opportunity to review all aspects of human rights and ensure a just and balanced approach thereto,

Recognizing the contribution that can be made to the World Conference by Asian countries with their diverse and rich cultures and traditions,

Welcoming the increased attention being paid to human rights in the international community,

Reaffirming their commitment to principles contained in the Charter of the United Nations and the Universal Declaration on Human Rights,

Recalling that in the Charter of the United Nations the question of universal observance and promotion of human rights and fundamental freedoms has been rightly placed within the context of international cooperation,

Noting the progress made in the codification of human rights instruments, and in the establishment of international human rights mechanisms, while expressing concern that these mechanisms relate mainly to one category of rights,

Emphasizing that ratification of international human rights instruments, particularly the International Covenant on Civil and Political Rights and the International Covenant an Economic, Social and Cultural Rights, by all States should be further encouraged,

Reaffirming the principles of respect for national sovereignty, territorial integrity and non-interference in the internal affairs of States,

Stressing the universality, objectivity and non-selectivity of all human rights and the need to avoid the application of double standards in the implementation of human rights and its politicization,

Recognizing that the promotion of human rights should be encouraged by cooperation and consensus, and not through confrontation and the imposition of incompatible values,

Reiterating the interdependence and indivisibility of economic, social, cultural, civil and political rights, and the inherent interrelationship between development, democracy, universal enjoyment of all human rights, and social justice which must be addressed in an integrated and balanced manner,

Recalling that the Declaration on the Right to Development has recognized the right to development as a universal and inalienable right and an integral part of fundamental human rights,

Emphasizing that endeavours to move towards the creation of uniform international human rights norms must go hand in hand with endeavours to work towards a just and fair world economic order,

Convinced that economic and social progress facilitates the growing trend towards democracy and the promotion and protection of human rights,

Stressing the importance of education and training in human rights at the national, regional and international levels and the need for international cooperation aimed at overcoming the lack of public awareness of human rights,

1. Reaffirm their commitment to the principles contained in the Charter of the United Nations and the Universal Declaration on Human Rights as well as the full realization of all human rights throughout the world;
2. Underline the essential need to create favourable conditions for effective enjoyment of human rights at both the national and international levels;
3. Stress the urgent need to democratize the United Nations system, eliminate selectivity and improve procedures and mechanisms in order to strengthen international cooperation, based on principles of equality and mutual respect, and ensure a positive, balanced and non-confrontational approach in addressing and realizing all aspects of human rights;
4. Discourage any attempt to use human rights as a conditionality for extending development assistance;
5. Emphasize the principles of respect for national sovereignty and territorial integrity as well as non-interference in the internal affairs of States, and the non-use of human rights as an instrument of political pressure;
6. Reiterate that all countries, large and small, have the right to determine their political systems, control and freely utilize their resources, and freely pursue their economic, social and cultural development;
7. Stress the universality, objectivity and non-selectivity of all human rights and the need to avoid the application of double standards in the implementation of human rights and its politicization, and that no violation of human rights can be justified;
8. Recognize that while human rights are universal in nature, they must be considered in the context of a dynamic and evolving process of international norm-setting, bearing in mind the significance of national and regional particularities and various historical, cultural and religious backgrounds;
9. Recognize further that States have the primary responsibility for the promotion and protection of human rights through appropriate infrastructure and mechanisms, and also recognize that remedies must be sought and provided primarily through such mechanisms and procedures;
10. Reaffirm the interdependence and indivisibility of economic, social, cultural, civil and political rights, and the need to give equal emphasis to all categories of human rights;

11. Emphasize the importance of guaranteeing the human rights and fundamental freedoms of vulnerable groups such as ethnic, national, racial, religious and linguistic minorities, migrant workers, disabled persons, indigenous peoples, refugees and displaced persons;

12. Reiterate that self-determination is a principle of international law and a universal right recognized by the United Nations for peoples under alien or colonial domination or foreign occupation, by virtue of which they can freely determine their political status and freely pursue their economic, social and cultural development, and that its denial constitutes a grave violation of human rights;

13. Stress that the right to self-determination is applicable to peoples under alien or colonial domination or foreign occupation, and should not be used to undermine the territorial integrity, national sovereignty and political independence of States;

14. Express concern over all forms of violation of human rights, including manifestations of racial discrimination, racism, apartheid, colonialism, foreign aggression and occupation, and the establishment of illegal settlements in occupied territories, as well as the recent resurgence of neo-nazism, xenophobia and ethnic cleansing;

15. Underline the need for taking effective international measures in order to guarantee and monitor the implementation of human rights standards and effective and legal protection of people under foreign occupation;

16. Strongly affirm their support for the legitimate struggle of the Palestinian people to restore their national and inalienable rights to self-determination and independence, and demand an immediate end to the grave violations of human rights in the Palestinian, Syrian Golan and other occupied Arab territories including Jerusalem;

17. Reaffirm the right to development, as established in the Declaration on the Right to Development, as a universal and inalienable right and an integral part of fundamental human rights, which must be realized through international cooperation, respect for fundamental human rights, the establishment of a monitoring mechanism and the creation of essential international conditions for the realization of such right;

18. Recognize that the main obstacle to the realization of the right to development lies at the international macroeconomic level, as reflected in the widening gap between the North and the South, the rich and the poor;

19. Affirm that poverty is one of the major obstacles hindering the full enjoyment of human rights;

20. Affirm also the need to develop the right of humankind regarding a clean, safe and healthy environment;

21. Note that terrorism, in all its forms and manifestations, as distinguished from the legitimate struggle of peoples under colonial or alien domination or foreign occupation, has emerged as one of the most dangerous threats to the enjoyment of human rights and democracy, threatening the territorial integrity and security of States and destabilizing legitimately constituted governments, and that it must be unequivocally condemned by the international community;

22. Reaffirm their strong commitment to the promotion and protection of the rights of women through the guarantee of equal participation in the political, social, economic and cultural concerns of society, and the eradication of all forms of discrimination and of gender-based violence against women;

23. Recognize the rights of the child to enjoy special protection and to be afforded the opportunities and facilities to develop physically, mentally, morally, spiritually and socially in a healthy and normal manner and in conditions of freedom and dignity;

24. Welcome the important role played by national institutions in the genuine and constructive promotion of human rights, and believe that the conceptualization and eventual establishment of such institutions are best left for the States to decide;

25. Acknowledge the importance of cooperation and dialogue between governments and non-governmental organizations on the basis of shared values as well as mutual respect and understanding in the promotion of human rights, and encourage the non-governmental organizations in consultative status with the Economic and Social Council to contribute positively to this process in accordance with Council Resolution 1296 (XLIV);

26. Reiterate the need to explore the possibilities of establishing regional arrangements for the promotion and protection of human rights in Asia;

27. Reiterate further the need to explore ways to generate international cooperation and financial support for education and training in the field of human rights at the national level and for the establishment of national infrastructures to promote and protect human rights if requested by States;

28. Emphasize the necessity to rationalize the United Nations human rights mechanism in order to enhance its effectiveness and efficiency and the need to ensure avoidance of the duplication of work that exists between the treaty bodies, the Sub-Commission on Prevention of Discrimination and Protection of Minorities and the Commission on Human Rights, as well as the need to avoid the multiplicity of parallel mechanisms;

29. Stress the importance of strengthening the United Nations Centre for Human Rights with the necessary resources to enable it to provide a wide range of advisory services and technical assistance programmes in the promotion of human rights to requesting States in a timely and effective manner, as well as to enable it to finance adequately other activities in the field of human rights authorized by competent bodies;

30. Call for increased representation of the developing countries in the Centre for Human Rights.

APPENDIX II
THE ASIA-PACIFIC NON-GOVERNMENTAL ORGANIZATIONS' BANGKOK STATEMENT AND RESPONSE TO THE BANGKOK DECLARATION

(A) Summary of Bangkok NGO Declaration

Joint statement of several human rights and development NGOs presented at the Regional Meeting for the Asia-Pacific in preparation for the United Nations World Conference on Human Rights.

Bangkok, Thailand, Monday, 29 March 1993

Introduction

On the eve of the Preparatory Meeting of Asian Governments, some 240 representatives of more than 110 non-governmental organizations (NGOs) from about 26 countries across the Asia-Pacific region have put forward a detailed human rights agenda for immediate implementation.

The Bangkok NGO Declaration sets out the human rights challenges facing our region and the recommendations designed to meet them.

The representatives in this landmark document leave no doubt as to what is expected of governments and to the determination of human rights and development NGOs to have such expectations met.

II. Key Challenges

The Bangkok NGO Declaration has put stress on the following:

There is emerging a new understanding of universalism encompassing the richness and wisdom of Asia-Pacific cultures. As human rights are of universal concern and are universal in value, the advocacy of human rights cannot be considered to be an encroachment upon national sovereignty.

We affirm our commitment to the principle of the indivisibility and interdependence of human rights, be they economic, social and cultural rights, or civil and political rights. There must be a holistic and integrated approach to human rights. One set of rights cannot be used to bargain for another.

The issue of women's rights has not been sufficiently visible. Women's rights are human rights. Crimes against women are crimes against humanity. The failure of governments to prosecute those responsible for such crimes implies complicity.

We are entitled to join hands in solidarity to protect human rights world-wide. International solidarity transcends the national border, to refute claims of State sovereignty and of non-interference in the internal affairs of State.

We emphasize the need for balanced and sustainable development, bearing in mind maximization of people's development; integrated approaches on civil, political, economic, social and cultural rights; equity and social justice; income distribution and fair resource allocation. There is an urgent call to democratize the development processes at both the national and international levels so as to ensure a harmonious relationship between humanity and the natural environment, and to create processes to enhance gender equality and the empowerment of women. The thrust is to promote human and humane development.

Democracy is a way of life. It pervades all aspects of human life: in the home, workplace, in the local community and beyond. Democracy must be fostered and guaranteed in all countries.

We express our deep concern over the increasing militarization through the region and the diversion of resources. The quest for peace and human rights is intertwined with the need to demilitarize.

We affirm that all peoples have the right to self-determination. By virtue of that right, they may freely determine their political status, and freely pursue their economic, social and cultural development. The right of peoples to self-determination must, therefore, be observed by all governments.

The practice of torture, and other inhuman, degrading or cruel treatment and punishment in the Asia-Pacific region gives rise to increasing concern. These practices must be abolished.

The pretext for constraining the channels of freedom of expression is often internal, for national security and law and order. This is a façade for authoritarianism and for the suppression of democratic aspirations and institutions.

If we wish to promote democracy and respect for human rights, we must develop comprehensive human rights education and training in both governmental and non-governmental programmes, in and out of school.

The Asia-Pacific region is home to many indigenous peoples. A basic issue among the indigenous peoples is the fact that many are neither recognized as indigenous nor as peoples by governments and as such are denied the right to self-determination.

Implementation of the rights of children to survival, protection, development and participation as embodied in the UN Convention on the Rights of the Child must be a paramount concern of every State, regardless of considerations of national capacity and security.

Too often, peasants and workers endure the worst cases of human rights abuses in the region.

The human rights of internally displaced persons and refugees as a direct result of militarization and armed conflict are violated in the name of restrictive national policies.

We emphasize that states are bound to respect all human rights in their 'countries' under all circumstances.

As human right activists and development workers voice the interests of the people and work for their advancement, it is imperative that they be permitted to work freely; their rights to participate in community life and to enjoy the totality of human rights must be respected.

We affirm the need for the independence of the judiciary and call for judicial responsibility to render justice more accessible to the people.

III. Key Recommendations

A. International Human Rights Laws

Agreed on the urgent need to address women's rights as human rights as one of the principal issues, with a determination to see effective protection for the rights of indigenous peoples, children, peasants, workers, Dalits (the Untouchables), disabled persons and all other marginalized groups, the meeting is putting to Governments of the Asia-Pacific region a number of specific recommendations.

1. Governments of the region must accede, without further delay, to the principal United Nations Covenants, Conventions, Protocols, Rules, Codes of Conduct and other human rights instruments.
2. Governments of the region must, without further delay, withdraw reservations on those human rights instruments to which they are High Contracting Parties, including the Convention on the Elimination of All Forms of Discrimination Against Women (CEDAW).
3. These international instruments must be given force not only in domestic law but more importantly in practice.

B. U.N. Mechanisms

In addition, the representatives of NGOs are putting forward specific recommendations aimed at strengthening the capacity of the United Nations to promote and protect human rights, including:

1. The establishment within the U.N. of a Special Commissioner for Human Rights as a new high-level authority to bring a more effective and rapid response, coherence and coordination of the United Nations in the protection of human rights;
2. Improvement in the operation of existing treaty monitoring bodies and mechanisms; and,
3. Support for the establishment of effective regional human rights instruments and mechanisms subject to explicit guarantees of its independence and effectiveness and public access, including by NGOs.

(B) The Asia-Pacific Governments' final draft Declaration: an NGO response

Representatives of the Asia-Pacific NGOs met this morning to consider a response to the Final Draft Declaration prepared by governments. This NGO response reflects the challenges and issues presented during this week in the form of the Bangkok NGO Declaration prepared by some 240 representatives of 110 NGOs in this region.

2 April 1993

The NGO representatives stress the following points:

i) There are several points to be commended in the Final Draft Declaration prepared by government. In this regard:
—we welcome the specific sections on the rights of women and the rights of children;
—we are relieved to find a reaffirmation of the principles in the UN Charter and the Universal Declaration on Human Rights;
—we support the reaffirmation of the universality, indivisibility and interdependence of human rights;
—we share a concern for effective implementation of the right to development and the need arising from the situation in our region to recognise the impact of macroeconomic issues and the disastrous results of poverty, evident in the widening gap between the North and the South, the rich and the poor.
ii) We are encouraged by the recognition of NGOs in the Final Draft Declaration and the fact that governments responded to the concerted representations by so many Asia-Pacific NGOs from day one of this Asia Regional meeting.
   Yet the Final Draft Declaration in several significant respects reflects the continued attempt by many Governments of the Asia-Pacific region to avoid their human rights obligations, to put the state before the people and to avoid acknowledging their obligations to account for their failures in the promotion and protection of human rights.
iii) Most disturbing is the apparent intention to restrict the right of self-determination to peoples under alien or colonial domination or foreign occupation. Again these governments have proved themselves incapable of giving proper recognition to the most fundamental rights of indigenous peoples. This issue will clearly continue to be a matter of priority for NGO action.
iv) The fear of governments in our region to account for the continued violation of human rights is evident in their attempt to give primacy to national human rights mechanisms—mechanisms which we know too well that they will direct and control themselves. This is NOT accountability and offers little hope of appropriate remedies.
v) This fear is similarly evident in the apparent attempt to limit the operations of the UN Centre for Human Rights.
vi) Given the encouragement for States to ratify international human rights instruments in the preambular paragraphs, we cannot understand the failure to give more direct effect to this call by its inclusion in the so-called operative paragraphs.
vii) In this regard we reiterate that governments must commit themselves to ratification without reservations of the major international human rights instruments, including the Convention on the Elimination of all forms of Discrimination Against Women (CEDAW) and that on the Rights of the Child (these steps would be consistent with the relevant sections on these issues in the Final Draft Declaration).
viii) We could not help but note that specific references to torture, freedom of expression and the lack of the rule of law have been deleted in the final draft. We are

left to ask WHY!

ix) Further evidence of the attempt to avoid accountability for their failures to protect human rights is apparent in the specific discouragement of conditionality in
relation to development assistance. Governments have again got it wrong by failing
to put the emphasis where it should lie, that is on the necessity that aid must always
promote and protect human rights.

In other sections the draft Final Declaration is vaguely worded and ambiguous showing what we all know to have been a high degree of conflict and disunity between
governments on key issues.

By contrast it must be said and said again that the NGOs of the Asia-Pacific region
are united as never before. The threshold has been crossed and we will NOT allow
further erosion of human rights; we will not rest till existing rights are not just words
but become a reality for all the peoples of Asia and the Pacific.

STATEMENTS BY REPRESENTATIVES OF ASIAN GOVERNMENTS AT THE VIENNA WORLD CONFERENCE ON HUMAN RIGHTS

Statements are divided into two groups A and B: those made by Asian governments (including Russia) which are not ASEAN members and those made by ASEAN representatives. Non-ASEAN statements appear first in alphabetical order according to country, followed by ASEAN statements also in alphabetical order. All formal addresses to the chair of the meetings have been deleted.

(A) Statement by Liu Huaqiu, Head of the Chinese Delegation, Vienna, 17 June 1993

The World Conference on Human Rights is convened on the occasion of the 45th anniversary of the Universal Declaration of Human Rights. This is a noteworthy event in the international community today. We hope that this Conference will contribute positively to strengthening international cooperation in the field of human rights and to promoting full enjoyment of human rights and fundamental freedoms of people of all countries. Please allow me to take this opportunity to offer, on behalf of the Chinese Government and people, our warm congratulations to the Conference, and wish the Conference a success.

In the wake of World War II and victory over the brutal fascist forces, the United Nations worked out the Charter of the United Nations and the Universal Declaration of Human Rights which give expression to the longing desire of people across the world for the respect and protection of human rights and fundamental freedoms. It has, through relentless efforts, scored many achievements in safeguarding and promoting human rights, broke down the shackles of colonialism and won independence successively, which culminated in the total collapse of the centuries-old evil colonial system. All this has created prerequisites and opened up broad vistas for the realization of basic human rights for people of all countries in the world. The United Nations and the international community have done a great deal of work in terms of eliminating colonialism, racism, apartheid, massive and gross violations of human rights as a result of foreign invasion and occupation, safeguarding the right of small and weak countries to self-determination and the right of developing countries to development, and helping people of all countries to obtain the basic human rights. All these represent a major development of the Universal Declaration of Human Rights. Moreover, the series of programmatic documents such as the Proclamation of Teheran and the Declaration on the Right to Development adopted successively by the United Nations have further enriched the contents of and defined the objectives and guiding principles for international activities in the field of human rights. In preparation for this Conference, Africa, Latin America and Asia convened regional preparatory meetings which passed respectively the Tunis Declaration, the San José Declaration and the Bangkok Declaration. These important instruments on human rights have identified some pressing issues of concern to the developing countries which make up the overwhelming majority of the world population and put forward their practical and feasible principled propositions, thus further enriching and expanding the contents of human rights protection and promotion.

The issue of human rights has attracted universal attention in the international community as it bears on the basic rights and vital interests of the world's people. In recent years, the international situation has undergone drastic changes. The world has entered a historical juncture whereby the old pattern is giving way to a new one. The international community has before it difficulties and challenges on the one hand, and hopes and opportunities on the other. In the international human rights field, the pressing task facing the people of all countries is to sum up experience and set the correct direction and principles for the future course in light of the changing situation, with a view to effectively protecting and promoting basic human rights. This World Conference on Human Rights is an important conference linking the past and future. Its success will undoubtedly be of great significance to the realization of this objective.

We should also be soberly aware that the serious consequences of colonialism, racism, apartheid, foreign invasion and occupation are yet to be fully removed. People in countries still under foreign occupation or apartheid have not yet enjoyed basic human rights and freedom. Though the Cold War characterized by confrontation between the two military blocs has come to an end, the world today is far from tranquil as is evidenced by increasing factors of destabilization and emergence of new hot spots. People in some regions are still struggling for survival. Many developing countries find themselves in greater economic difficulties and impoverishment. Over one billion people in the world are still living below the poverty line, suffering from starvation, diseases and shortages. These, no doubt, are the stumbling blocks in the way to the realization of universal human rights. Therefore, to remove these obstacles and carry out international cooperation in this connection should be given top priority by the international community in its efforts to promote the cause of human rights.

The concept of human rights is a product of historical development. It is closely associated with specific social, political and economic conditions and the specific history, culture and values of a particular country. Different historical development stages have different human rights requirements. Countries at different development stages or with different historical traditions and cultural backgrounds also have different understanding and practice of human rights. Thus, one should not and cannot think of the human rights standard and model of certain countries as the only proper ones and demand all other countries to comply with them. It is neither realistic nor workable to make international economic assistance or even international economic cooperation conditional on them.

The concept of human rights is an integral one, including both individual and collective rights. Individual rights cover not only civil and political rights but also economic, social and cultural rights. The various aspects of human rights are interdependent, equally important, indivisible and indispensable. For the vast number of developing countries to respect and protect human rights is first and foremost to ensure the full realization of the rights to subsistence and development. The argument that human rights is the precondition for development is unfounded. When poverty and lack of adequate food and clothing are commonplace and people's basic needs are not guaranteed, priority should be given to economic development. Otherwise, human rights are completely out of the question. We believe that the major criteria for judging the human rights situation in a developing country should be whether its policies and measures help promote economic and social progress, help people meet their basic needs for food and clothing and improve the quality of their life. The international community should take actions to help developing countries alleviate economic difficulties, promote their development and free them from poverty and want.

The rights and obligations of a citizen are indivisible. While enjoying his legitimate rights and freedom, a citizen must fulfil his social responsibilities and obligations. There are no absolute individual rights and freedom, except those prescribed by and within the framework of law. Nobody shall place his own rights and interests above those of the state and society, nor should he be allowed to impair those of others and the general public. This is a universal principle of all civilized societies. Moreover, to maintain social stability and ensure the basic human rights to citizens do not contradict each other. The practice of the international community has proved once and again only when there is justice, order and stability in a country or society, can its development and the well-being as well as basic human rights of all its citizens be guaranteed.

According to the U.N. Charter and the norms of international law, all countries, large or small, strong or weak, rich or poor, have the right to choose their own political system, road to development and values. Other countries have no right to interfere. To wantonly accuse another country of abuse of human rights and impose the human rights criteria of one's own country or region on other countries or regions are tantamount to an infringement upon the sovereignty of other countries and interference in the latter's internal affairs, which could result in political instability and social unrest in other countries. As a people that used to suffer tremendously from aggression by big powers but now enjoys independence, the Chinese have come to realize fully that state sovereignty is the basis for the realization of citizens' human rights. If the sovereignty of a state is not safeguarded, the human rights of its citizens are out of the question, like a castle in the air. The views that the human rights question goes beyond boundary and that the principle of non-interference in other's internal affairs is not applicable to it and actions on these premises are, in essence, a form of power politics. They run counter to the purposes and principles of the U.N. Charter and to the lofty cause of the protection of human rights.

China believes that the protection of human rights, like the promotion of development, requires international cooperation and a peaceful and stable international environment. For the purpose of strengthening international cooperation in the field of human rights and promoting activities in the protection of human rights in the whole international community, the Chinese delegation hereby puts forth the following principled proposals and wishes to discuss them with you.

1. The international community should give its primary attention to the massive gross violations of human rights resulting from foreign aggression and occupation and continue to support those people still under foreign invasion, colonial rule or apartheid system in their just struggle for national self-determination. It should also commit itself to the elimination of the massive gross violations of human rights ensued from regional conflicts.

2. World peace and stability should be enhanced and a favourable international environment created for the attainment of the goals in human rights protection. To this end, countries should establish a new type of international relationship of mutual

respect, equality, amicable coexistence and mutually beneficial cooperation in accordance with the U.N. Charter and the norms of international law. All international
disputes should be solved peacefully in a fair and reasonable manner and in the spirit
of mutual accommodation and mutual understanding, and consultation on equal
footing, instead of resorting to force or threat of force. No country should pursue
hegemonism and power politics or engage in aggression, expansion and interference.
This is the way to ensure regional and global peace and stability and to prevent
armed conflicts which may incur massive violations of human rights.
3. The right of developing countries to development should be respected and guaranteed. To create a good international economic environment for the initial economic
development of developing countries, the international community should commit
itself to the establishment of a fair and rational new international economic order.
Developed countries, in particular, have the responsibility to help developing countries through practical measures in such areas as debt, capital, trade, assistance and
technology transfer, to overcome their economic difficulties and develop their
economy. This is the way to gradually narrow the gap between the North and the
South which may otherwise be widened and finally to bring about common development and prosperity.
4. The right of each country to formulate its own policies on human rights protection
in light of its own conditions should also be respected and guaranteed. Nobody
should be allowed to use the human rights issue to exert political and economic
pressures on other countries. The human rights issue can be discussed among countries. However, the discussions should be conducted in the spirit of mutual respect
and on an equal footing.

It is the sole objective of the Chinese Government to serve the Chinese people and
work for their interests. Therefore, China has always attached importance and been
committed to the guarantee and promotion of the basic human rights of its people.
It is known to all that the old China was an extremely poor and backward semi-
feudal and semi-colonial society where the Chinese people did not have any human
rights to speak of as they were enslaved and oppressed by the imperialists and
Chinese reactionary forces. This bitter past was not put an end to until the founding
of the People's Republic. Since then, the Chinese people have, for the first time in
history, taken their own destiny into their own hands, become masters of their own
country and enjoyed basic human rights. According to China's Constitution, all
power in the People's Republic of China belongs to the people. The law guarantees
that each and every Chinese citizen, regardless of gender, family background, ethnic
status, occupation, property status and religious belief, enjoys genuine democracy
and freedom, civil and political rights as well as extensive economic, social and
cultural rights. China is a unitary multi-national state. To strengthen national unity
and safeguard the unification of the motherland accord with the common interests
and aspiration of the Chinese people of all nationalities. To handle properly the
ethnic question and the relations among different nationalities has all along been of
vital importance to the stability, development and equality among all nationalities of
the country. The Chinese Government, therefore, attaches great importance to the
work in this regard. Equality and unity among all nationalities and regional national
autonomy are China's basic principles and policies for handling matters concerning
nationalities. As a result, people of all nationalities living in the same big family are
now marching towards common prosperity. Since China began to implement the
policy of reform and opening to the outside world, its economy has been developing
vigorously and its democratic and legal system improving steadily. The nearly 1.2
billion Chinese populace of all nationalities, who are united as one, have seen their

material and cultural well-being improved considerably. As their basic needs have been more or less met, they are briskly heading toward a fairly comfortable and affluent life. China has made steady progress in promoting and protecting human rights, which has been acknowledged and commended by all fair-minded people in the international community.

China respects and abides by the basic principles of the U.N. Charter and the Universal Declaration of Human Rights. It attaches importance to and has actively participated in the international exchanges and cooperation in the field of human rights as well as U.N. activities in this field. China has acceded, one after another, to eight international conventions on human rights and is earnestly honouring the obligation it has thereby undertaken. It is ready to further strengthen exchanges and cooperation with other countries on human rights in the international arena and to contribute its part to the effective promotion and protection of human rights in the international community and to the achievement of the lofty ideal that people throughout the world will be able to fully enjoy the basic human rights.

Statement by Nobuo Matsunaga, Envoy of the Government of Japan and Representative of Japan, Vienna, 18 June 1993

In 1945, the peoples of the United Nations, in the newly adapted Charter, proclaimed their historic determination to save succeeding generations from the scourge of war and to reaffirm their faith in fundamental human rights. Now, with the end of the Cold War, the spirit of the United Nations Charter, though nearly half a century old, should be full of fresh meaning for us. When we recall the important part that faith in human rights has played in the ongoing world-wide tide of democratization, notably in Eastern Europe and the former Soviet Union; when, with dismay, we see emerging ethnic conflicts marked by total disregard for human dignity; and as we set out to build a new international order which will guarantee all peoples and individuals lasting freedom, peace and prosperity, we must strive to give the Charter renewed vigour, and reaffirm, and act upon, our solemn commitment in the Charter to fundamental human rights and world peace.

In the decades since its establishment, the United Nations has made remarkable achievements in the promotion and protection of human rights. The Universal Declaration of Human Rights was the first landmark. A series of human rights conventions and international mechanisms to ensure their observance are part of the precious heritage of mankind. The time has now come to build on those accomplishments, overcome remaining obstacles, and meet today's new challenges. I would like to express my profound gratitude to the Government of Austria for hosting this important conference, to address our historic task.

Human rights are universal values common to all mankind. This truth, reflected in the United Nations Charter, is now generally accepted by the international community. The Universal Declaration of Human Rights is regarded as a common standard of conduct. The two basic human rights instruments, namely, the International Covenant on Economic, Social and Cultural Rights and the International Covenant on Civil and Political Rights, each of which came into effect with 35 ratifications in 1976 had, as of September 1992, been adhered to by, respectively, 116 and 113 States. And their numbers are increasing. Japan firmly believes that the international community must remain committed to the principles set forth in the Declaration and the Covenants. It is the duty of all States, whatever their cultural tradition, no matter what their political or economic system, to protect and promote those values.

Some countries argue that human rights are a matter falling essentially within the domestic jurisdiction of a State. It is true that a State has the primary responsibility to guarantee the human rights of those under its jurisdiction. However, human rights are also a matter of legitimate concern of the international community, as their enshrinement in the United Nations Charter testifies. One of the purposes of the Organization is to achieve international cooperation in promoting and encouraging respect for human rights. The Economic and Social Council is authorized to make recommendations for the purpose of promoting respect for, and observance of, human rights and fundamental freedoms for all. To express concern over any grave violation of human rights, be it arbitrary detention, enforced disappearance or torture, in whatever country such abuses may occur, and to encourage the country concerned to remedy the situation, should not be regarded as interference in internal affairs.

This Conference gives us an opportunity to address the question of the relationship between development, democracy and human rights.

While social and economic development may facilitate enhanced respect for human rights, I believe that fundamental freedoms and rights should be respected by each and every country, whatever its culture, political or economic system, or stage of development.

Human rights should never be sacrificed to development. Rather, development should serve to promote and protect rights — economic, social, cultural, civil and political. Respect for human rights will facilitate development by bringing about a society in which individuals can freely develop their own abilities.

Convinced of this, Japan believes that development assistance should also contribute to promotion of the rights of individuals.

The Official Development Assistance Charter, which the Government of Japan adopted in June last year, clearly states that when development assistance is provided, full attention should be paid to the situation regarding basic human rights and freedoms in a recipient country, and to the efforts being made by that country to promote democratization.

My country believes it important that we continue to endeavour to promote the enjoyment of human rights for those who are particularly vulnerable: children, the aged, the disabled and others.

The 1990 World Summit for Children agreed to take joint actions to protect the rights of children and to improve their situation. The Government of Japan for its part, formulated its Plan of Action in 1991, as a follow-up to the Summit. One of the main objectives of our Plan of Action, covering both domestic measures and international assistance, is to assist children in developing countries, in particular in the area of Basic Human Needs, such as food, health and medical care, sanitation and education. Japan's international assistance in the field of Basic Human Needs accounted for as much as approximately 33% of all of its bilateral aid in 1992, and the Government intends to expand such assistance in the future.

This year is the International Year for the World's Indigenous People. The Government of Japan considers this an important opportunity to strengthen international cooperation aimed at finding solutions to the problems faced by indigenous communities. Trusting that the voluntary fund established for this International Year will be used as a catalyst to stimulate activities initiated by indigenous people, Japan is contributing $50,000 to this Fund.

The advancement of women continues to be an important item on the agenda. Although progress has been made, especially through the efforts of the Commission on the Status of Women and the Committee on the Elimination of All Forms of Discrimination Against Women, there still remains a considerable gap between the *de jure* and *de facto* status of women. Continued efforts need to be made to eradicate gender discrimination, taking into consideration the importance of working towards the elimination of violence against women. I hope to see further improvement in the *de facto* status of women as we prepare for the Fourth World Conference on Women, to be held in Beijing in 1995.

Japan desires to see universal ratification of the Convention on the Elimination of All Forms of Discrimination Against Women. I also urge States to review and withdraw reservations which are inconsistent with the object and purpose of the Convention.

Technical cooperation in the field of human rights has an effective role to play in the promotion and protection of human rights. Japan evaluates highly the role played by the United Nations Centre for Human Rights in providing advisory services and technical assistance. Japan has regularly contributed to the United Nations voluntary funds in the field of human rights, including the voluntary fund for advisory services and technical assistance. I believe that the United Nations technical cooperation activities in the area of human rights should be further strengthened, and wish to appeal for additional contributions to the voluntary fund.

Given the growing responsibilities of the United Nations in the field of human rights, it is important to allocate adequate resources to the United Nations Centre for Human Rights. Japan looks constructively at the need for additional resources for the Centre to be reallocated within the United Nations regular budget. At the same time, we urge all concerned to make further efforts to enhance the Centre's efficiency.

My country also supports the proposal that a United Nations High Commissioner for Human Rights be established. It believes that the High Commissioner should play an important role in coordinating United Nations human rights activities, and in assuring that the means necessary for thematic and country rapporteurs to do their tasks adequately are available.

I believe that the countries of the Asian region should set to work to address the question of regional arrangements in the area of human rights. Given the ethnic, religious, cultural, social and legal diversity existing among the countries of Asia, we should proceed step by step, beginning with exchanges of experience and information at regional and subregional levels. I wish to call upon all fellow Asian States to work closely together for the promotion and protection of human rights, stressing enhanced dialogue among us.

In concluding I wish to pay tribute to the work of the United Nations Centre for Human Rights and to commend many non-governmental organizations for their dedicated efforts for the promotion and protection of human rights. While the effort to promote and respect human rights may sometimes seem undramatic, it is a sound and steady way to ensure both the well-being of all human beings and lasting peace for the world. I appeal to all here to work together for enhanced respect for human rights.

Statement by Han Sung-joo, Minister of Foreign Affairs of the Republic of Korea, Vienna, 15 June 1993

Forty-five years ago, the United Nations adopted the Universal Declaration of Human Rights. That same year, the United Nations helped establish the government of the Republic of Korea. Since then, for almost half a century, the Declaration has served as a guiding light for Korean people in their struggle for freedom and democracy.

In striving for the ideal, we have experienced numerous trials and tribulations. There were times when we despaired because the possibility of success seemed so remote. There were times when we rejoiced prematurely because of false hopes. As a divided nation, we had overriding security concerns. As a country ridden by century-old poverty, we had pressing economic concerns.

But against all odds, we continued our march toward full respect for human rights, building on the courage and sacrifice of those who stood up for fundamental rights and freedom.

As we gather here at the World Conference on Human Rights, I am happy to report to you that human rights have finally come of age in Korea. I stand before you representing a nation and a people who can proudly say that truth, freedom and democracy have at last triumphed in their country.

The world capitalized on the opportunities created by the end of World War II by establishing the United Nations and subsequently adopting the Universal Declaration of Human Rights. It was our first significant action for the protection and promotion of human rights. Now as we gather in this forum, we realize that a new opportunity is unfolding before us in the wake of the Cold War. Ideologically speaking, World War II was fought against fascism and the Cold War against communism.

The demise of the Cold War means that liberal democracy has survived and triumphed. In retrospect, oppressive ideologies perversely justified the systematic and wholesale violation of human rights in the 20th century. Now we can put to rest frightening Orwellian phrases such as 'freedom is slavery' or 'two and two make five'. States that ignored such basic rights as the freedom to choose where to live, not to mention the freedom to travel, are ceasing to exist.

Now, in the post-Cold War era, the trends of reconciliation and cooperation have become an integral part of the emerging new world order. These trends offer a new opportunity for the promotion of human rights, a rare opportunity comparable to the one we had forty-five years ago after World War II.

Together with this new opportunity of achieving universal human rights, we also face difficult challenges of the post-Cold War era: eruption of regional conflicts with massive violation of human rights and the persistence of poverty and underdevelopment. The essence of these challenges is reflected in the agenda items of this forum, such as the universality of human rights, and the relationship between development, democracy and human rights.

During our struggle, we found out that the fight for human rights is inherent to human nature. Human rights are something mankind is eventually bound to cherish and aspire to regardless of political or economic circumstances. Human rights are universal, indivisible and interdependent. They cannot be altered according to circumstances. It is neither justifiable nor appropriate to deny some human rights in order to guarantee others.

At the same time, we have to bear in mind that the journey toward human rights cannot be completed overnight. It will be a long and arduous one to be achieved concurrently with other tasks. Without security and economic development, human rights cannot be genuine. Democracy and human rights cannot flourish without a certain degree of economic prosperity. There is no denying that development and human rights are closely related.

It is also true that regional and national circumstances need to be taken into account in the promotion and protection of human rights. Yet, history shows us that special circumstances do not justify abuses of human rights. Lack of development, for example, can never be used as an excuse or justification for any abuse of human rights.

Clearly, we have a dilemma here. In dealing with this problem, we should bear in mind that a simplistic and self-righteous approach to the issue of human rights could be counter-productive by provoking another powerful human sentiment, namely, nationalism. Compassion and pragmatism, rather than subjective moralism, should be our guiding principle.

As we discuss ways to promote human rights, we have to pay particular attention to the importance of two interrelated elements: free flow of information and integration of the state in the international order. The days when governments controlled the flow of information among their people are over. Free information always works for the promotion and protection of human rights. In the same vein, the more a state becomes integrated in the regional and world order, the less likely it is that gross violation of human rights will occur.

Twentieth-century history bears witness to the fact that only democracy and human rights ensure the full blossoming of individual potential, which in turn forms the basis for political, social and economic development.

In this process, we have learned that individual courage and sacrifice are fundamental driving forces behind the promotion and protection of human rights. In this respect, the important role of individuals and non-governmental organizations cannot be overemphasized.

More often than not, the NGOs, as well as the individuals, can be more responsive to the implementation of human rights than governments. For that reason, the increasing number of NGOs indicates a promising trend for the universal realization of human rights.

Individuals and NGOs function within the realm of a state. It is the state that has the primary responsibility to protect and promote human rights. Thus, it is imperative that all nations become party to the international human rights instruments, including the two International Covenants on Human Rights. The states which have not yet done so should be urged to ratify or accede to these instruments as soon as possible.

As we turn our attention from the individual and the state to the world scene, we see the vital contributions made by the United Nations Human Rights Commission. The Universal Declaration, the International Covenants and other major human rights instruments were prepared and drafted by the Commission. In the actual promotion of human rights also, the role of various special rapporteurs and working groups established by the Commission has been crucial.

Now that we have a rare opportunity to promote human rights at a global level and that the United Nations is established as the most effective organization to do this, it is high time to strengthen the U.N. mechanism on human rights.

The United Nations should be provided with a more effective organizational mechanism for dealing with human rights activities. In this respect, Korea supports the proposal to establish the office of High Commissioner for Human Rights.

A High Commissioner will facilitate the coordination of activities conducted by various human rights organs of the United Nations. This institution will also be able to respond more effectively to emergency situations involving massive human rights violations.

We fully support the strengthening of U.N. activities to ensure the rights of women so that human rights violations against women can be dealt with in a more effective and comprehensive manner.

Likewise, concrete programmes of action should be adopted to facilitate the promotion and protection of the rights of vulnerable groups, such as children, minorities, indigenous people and the disabled. Such programmes of action should be prepared with the recognition that the people in these groups should not only be the objects of protection but become full participants in the development process of the society to which they belong.

The Republic of Korea is a party to most of the major human rights instruments, including the Optional Protocol to the International Covenant on Civil and Political Rights. We are now preparing to accede to the Convention Against Torture within this year, and will faithfully carry out all the obligations under these conventions.

Korea is irrevocably committed to the cause of human rights. The President of the Republic of Korea announced new foreign policy guidelines last month, which have particular bearing on human rights. Korea's new diplomacy, he said, is the one which places emphasis on such universal values as democracy, liberty, welfare and human rights.

His announcement reflects the belief in democracy shared by all people in my country. The Republic of Korea, with the firm faith that democracy is an ultimate guarantor of human rights, individual liberties, peace and development, will continue to do its part in the international endeavour to expand democratic ideals.

In 1998, we will commemorate the 50th anniversary of the epoch-making Universal Declaration of Human Rights. These intervening five years will be critical for the cause of human rights as the new world order takes clearer shape.

With our common efforts to achieve the goals set in the Declaration, we must be able to say to future generations that this conference here and now opened a new and bright chapter of human rights for the 21st century.

Statement by U Ohn Gyaw, Minister for Foreign Affairs and Chairman of the Delegation of the Union of Myanmar, Vienna, 15 June 1993

I should like, at the outset, to congratulate you, Sir, on behalf of the Myanmar Delegation and on my own behalf, on your assumption of the high office of the presidency of the conference. I am confident that given your wide experience and well-known diplomatic skills and personal attributes you will be able to guide this conference to a fruitful conclusion.

Allow me also to take this opportunity to express a personal note of friendship and appreciation to Mme Warzazi who has devoted so much of her time to the cause of human rights. My Delegation fully appreciates her endeavours and notes with satisfaction the exemplary manner in which she guided the work of the Preparatory Committee.

We are meeting, Mr President, at a time when vast transformations are taking place and when events are unfolding at a dramatic pace. Who would have foreseen, a quarter of a century ago, when nations gathered in Teheran for the first World Conference on Human Rights, that the Cold War and its attendant power struggles would forever be relegated to history or that the political map of a good part of the European continent would be so dramatically altered? Yet it will be some time before the faint outlines of a new order become clearer. While we welcome the positive transformation taking place around us, we view with concern the strife and turmoil that prevail in many regions of the world. It is essential that we have an appreciation of where the momentum of present day events is leading us to. We should take care not to be intimidated by the problems we face or be swept overboard by the euphoria over the changes. We must seek to build a truly better world for all the peoples of the world.

It is therefore appropriate that we meet at this juncture to take stock of the developments in the field of human rights, assess the effectiveness of the International Bill of Human Rights, consisting of the Universal Declaration and the two International Covenants, complemented be a corpus of other instruments, and to reflect on how best we can ensure a higher degree of international cooperation in the promotion of human rights world-wide without attempting to create novel doctrines that would upset established understandings. Indeed if there is to be a better tomorrow we must, while consolidating the positive accomplishments gained so far, seek to enhance international cooperation to encourage genuine respect for human rights.

There is in our world today no cause which is being accorded more attention than human rights. But I would like to emphasize here that concern for human rights is neither new nor unique to any one culture. Even before the advent of the UN Charter which in its Preamble reaffirms the faith of the Peoples of the United Nations, 'in fundamental human rights, in the dignity and worth of the human person, in the equal rights of men and women . . ', many a society upheld the dignity of the human person through cultural and religious teachings about correct behaviour, the just society and wise leader. Religious teachings of all faiths emphasize tolerance for fellow human beings. In our own Myanmar culture, there are precepts about the duties and obligations of the wise ruler to his subjects, parents to their offspring, husband to wife, and vice versa. I believe therefore that even as we seek universality of human rights, our diversity in historical, cultural and religious backgrounds must never be minimized or forgotten. There is no unique model of human rights implementation that can be superimposed on a given country. What we should strive for then is not the imposition of one's view on another but universal acceptance of agreed norms through dialogue and persuasion. Any international endeavour to promote and protect human rights must be made in accordance with the Charter of the United Nations.

In order to narrow the gap between aspiration and reality in the field of human rights, we firmly believe that certain facts must be recognized.

First and foremost, the clear signals sent by the Bangkok, San José and Tunis meetings which were convened under UNGA Resolution 45/155 of December 1990 must be given the attention they deserve. The three regional meetings provided an opportunity for representatives of sovereign nations as well as non-governmental organizations to discuss and coordinate views. The concluding documents of these regional meetings represent the considered views of the overwhelming majority of the international community. Much has been included in these mutually reinforcing declarations providing the seeds of a universal culture of human rights. The Bangkok Declaration reaffirms the principle of national sovereignty, territorial integrity and non-interference in the internal affairs of States, while the San José Declaration complements that by stressing the principles of peaceful coexistence and respect for pluralism. The Tunis Declaration too sends an important message in reaffirming the importance that Africa attaches to collective rights of peoples.

My delegation was pleased to have taken an active part in the deliberations in Bangkok and to be associated with the final declaration. We were happy to join our neighbours and friends from the Asian region in reaffirming our commitment to principles contained in the Charter of the United Nations and the Universal Declaration of Human Rights. It is clear that any attempt to use human rights to encroach on the essential domestic jurisdiction of States and to erode their sovereignty can only result in confrontation and spell chaos for the world. The last thing the world needs now is another round of rivalry and confrontation. We therefore are encouraged by the reaffirmation of the principles of respect for national sovereignty, territorial integrity and non-interference in the internal affairs of states. That is not to say that human rights can be systematically violated with impunity behind the protective barrier of the principle of non-interference. Far be it. We wish to see a consensus on accepted norms of human rights and to encourage the promotion of those rights through international cooperation and consensus-building, and not through confrontation and the imposition of incompatible values. What we should strive for is not the right of intervention but genuine international cooperation to bring relief and redress to human rights situations wherever they may occur—whether in the inner cities of Developed Countries or in some poverty-stricken area of the Developing World.

It must also be clearly understood that the principle of protection of human rights, like any other principle, cannot be invoked in a particular situation and disregarded in another. The call for the promotion and protection of human rights will become a vacuous claim if the principle of human rights is applied selectively. This is a clear need to avoid double standards and the temptation to use human rights as a means to achieve political ends.

This leads me, Mr President, to my third point. It is simply that when we speak of human rights we must not fail to address the whole spectrum of economic, social, cultural, civil and political rights. In recent years while civil and political rights have been highlighted the right to development has not been given the attention it deserves. One has only to look at the millions in developing countries who live below the poverty line to see the urgent need for the promotion of their right to development as an integral part of basic human rights. It is worth recalling that the right to development as a fundamental human right has already been recognized by the UN General Assembly which in 1986 adopted the Declaration on the Right to Development. In my own country priority is being given to the elimination of poverty and we are striving to promote all round development of our citizens — city dwellers as well as our brethren who live in the remote border areas. We consider it important that they have equal opportunity in their access to food, housing, transportation, employment, education and health services. The national races living in remote border areas had traditionally been economically and socially backward as they struggled to survive under the yoke of terrorism. They lived in abject poverty and had no rights to speak of. Today with the return to the legal fold of many terrorist groups and the restoration of law and order the situation has changed. The Government is taking comprehensive measures for the development of the border areas and national races as a national priority. This has not only raised the living standards of those peoples but has made it possible for them to enjoy fully their political and civil rights for the very first time. Representatives of the remote border areas are today taking part in the National Convention that would pave the way to a genuine democratic state.

Developing countries, particularly the least developed among them, continue to be faced with the problem of negative net financial transfers, large foreign debts, deterioration in terms of trade, shortage of foreign exchange and falling commodity prices. In view of this situation the developed countries should cooperate with the developing countries to eliminate all obstacles to development. This can be achieved only through constructive dialogue based on the shared belief that the right to development is as important a human right as any other. Any attempt to link developmental assistance with human rights is to debase those very rights. It bears to be repeated that poverty is a major obstacle preventing the full enjoyment of human rights.

In view of the growing attention being given to the theme of human rights and the role of the UN in protecting and promoting those rights I cannot but agree with those who see the need to rationalize the work of the UN bodies dealing with human rights and the need to avoid the multiplicity of parallel mechanisms. Instead of encouraging the proliferation of new mechanisms, what is required is the improvement of existing procedures to make them more efficient.

There is no doubt in my mind that this conference in Vienna will mark an important milestone in our quest to promote human rights. Much can be achieved if we can proceed with an appreciation of the rich and varied cultural, racial, linguistic, economic and religious backgrounds that make up our world. If genuine efforts are made here in Vienna, obstacles in the way may no longer prove insuperable. The atmosphere of confrontation that has characterized human rights debates needs to be replaced by cooperation and understanding. That, I believe, is an impelling call if our quest to promote human rights is to succeed.

Statement by A. V. Kozyrev, Minister for Foreign Affairs of the Russian Federation (unofficial translation), Vienna, 15 June 1993

A state, which violates the rights of its own citizens poses danger for the outside world.

A public statement of this truth in our country was quite recently considered to be an act of civil courage for which its best people, such as Andrei D. Sakharov, paid with years of exile, ostracism or even imprisonment.

Today, A. Sakharov's idea of the relationship between human rights and international security finds an ever growing response in world politics. The collapse of communist totalitarianism has expanded the world democratic space.

Our people, who have upheld their rights and freedoms at the barricades of August 1991, have again voiced their support of the democratic policy at the referendum in April 1993. Adoption of a new Constitution will be a next step, which will complete the process of establishment of a genuine democratic republic in Russia.

This is not an intention to adopt to somebody else's values but a firm belief in that democratic statehood is not counter-indicated to the Russian traditions or national identity of its peoples. Rather, they cannot be preserved without it.

A potentially very rich country with a great cultural capacity, Russia has paid for the isolated 'Soviet democracy' and 'socialist' human rights with social backwardness. This is why we have a definite moral right to warn against 'special' concepts of human rights for Asia of the 'South', as well as against a selective approach to some categories of rights as compare to others.

Certainly, genuine democracy can be easier established in a rich, rather than in a poor, country. But our own experience proves that in countries where freedom is traded for bread both are deprived eventually.

We understand how difficult it is for many countries to secure material guarantees of human rights. In this regard, we too have quite a few outstanding problems. In order to solve them, the Russian government is open for cooperation with national and international organizations. We consider it a way to support our reforms rather than interference into internal affairs.

Therefore, we cannot accept references to the non-interference principle with regard to other countries either, when violation of individual rights and freedoms is involved. Moreover, international solidarity is often the only means for victims of repression to prevent the authorities from the use of physical reprisals. That was the case in the former USSR. That is what is happening now in the countries where dissent is still considered a crime.

I believe that a unanimous recognition of the fact that human rights are indivisible would be a great achievement of our Conference. The international obligations to protect them should be honoured by all countries.

The necessity to make the rules of humanitarian law universal is all the more urgent now that mass violations of human rights do not only continue to take place but acquire a new nature and threatening dimensions.

While in the past, there was mainly a need for protection of people from encroachments of totalitarian regimes, now it is the victims of aggressive nationalism who need primarily to be protected. Civilian populations are mercilessly dragged into armed inter-ethnic conflicts. The most sophisticated weapons, including heavy artillery and aviation are used against them. Tortures, mass executions, marauding, deportations, rape, the taking of hostages have become widespread.

All this is not simply a result of the criminal actions of individuals. Rather it is a consequence of an international realization of doctrines aimed at the creation of 'monoethnic states' at whatever sacrifice.

'Ethnic cleansing' is also performed in, shall we say, 'white gloves'. A democracy cannot be recognized as genuine if it is only established for the 'indigenous' population, while members of national minorities are either forced out of the country or made outcasts.

We are already paying a dear price for underestimating that danger in the territory of former Yugoslavia. Today, the lack of attention to the rights of national minorities carries the risk of damaging the Baltic region and turning Europe into a zone of special standards, though lower and double rather than higher.

We cannot accept this because, at the very least, we do not wish to give such a present to the communist and fascist, red and brown opposition in Russia.

You may argue that I am exaggerating. But one cannot help being alarmed when on the very next day after joining the Council of Europe one of its new members enacted a discriminatory law on local self-government. And the authorities of this state's capital took a decision to forcibly evict thousands of people from their apartments, using the police.

The main task is to ensure that in the territory of the former USSR the highest standards of human rights become firmly established. We are actively working in this direction within the Commonwealth of Independent States.

In his message to the participants at this conference President Yeltsin expressed hope that it would contribute towards the elaboration of a general strategy for international humanitarian cooperation on the verge of the 21st century.

In our view, the priorities in this strategy could be outlined as follows.

First, joint efforts in the struggle against aggressive nationalism as a global threat to international stability and human rights. The joint Russian–French initiative within the CSCE was just a starting point of this process. We hope that states from other regions will join it too. Ultimately, an atmosphere of rejection by world public opinion of any manifestations of national and religious intolerance should be created.

Second, comprehensive measures to protect the rights of national minorities. Adoption of the relevant U.N. Declaration was an important step in this direction. Now it is necessary to translate its principles into a language of legal and administrative safeguards.

Third, setting up a U.N. emergency mechanism for addressing critical situations caused by flagrant and massive violations of human rights, as well as for establishing a post of U.N. High Commissioner for human rights.

Fourth, protection of victims of armed conflicts. We believe the time has come to start creating global and regional monitoring systems in order to safeguard their rights, including procedures for examining individual complaints of victims. Moreover, it is important that the punishment of those who are guilty be inevitable.

During the period of confrontation, human rights were the focus of the struggle between forces of democracy and those of totalitarianism. Hopefully, in a new multipolar world they will become a uniting factor for all of us. Thus, we would come close to the goal proclaimed by the U.N. founders: 'to reaffirm faith in fundamental human rights, in the dignity and worth of the human person.'

(B) Statement by Prince Mohamed Bolkiah, Minister of Foreign Affairs, Brunei Darussalam, Vienna, 21 June 1993

I would like to congratulate you on your election, Mr President, and present my best wishes to the members of your bureau. At the same time, I would like to thank his excellency Ibrahima Fall, and his secretariat for their work in preparing this conference.

May I also express my appreciation, through you, to the Government and people of Austria for their warm hospitality.

In the twenty-five years since the first world conference, much has been done in the promotion and protection of human rights. Governments and non-government organizations, private groups, ordinary citizens and many distinguished individuals have helped to do this. As a result, human rights are on the annual agenda of the United Nations and have become important matters for discussion at many international and regional meetings. To this extent, I think we all understand much more about this sensitive subject.

I believe our conference offers us a chance to see how we can add to that progress by promoting international consensus. I hope we can listen to each other with respect, seek mutual understanding and try to reach common ground. In this way, we may be able to build upon what the United Nations has already achieved.

This is called for in the United Nations Charter. Of course, it is not a simple task. There are clearly differences of opinion and approach. These do not necessarily mean that we have opposing principles; they do, however, reflect differing national priorities.

Some governments must recognize the special needs of individuals who have been able to reach a high level of social and economic development. By contrast, others must satisfy the pressing needs of people who lack the basics for a life with dignity. Whereas some try to apply universal principles, others feel that human rights development has to follow the pace of political and economic development.

None of these positions can be simply described as right or wrong. Any set of truly universal principles must recognize that they are all legitimate. The questions we are asking at this conference are therefore complex.

Attempting to change conditions by economic and political pressure will raise crucial questions about national sovereignty. These could lead to serious misunderstandings between nations and stand in the way of any improvements that may be needed.

Rightly, the international community must express concern where it believes human rights have been violated. However, if the measures it takes to encourage change are to be successful, broad-based agreement is needed.

Hence, I would like to see this conference helping to develop a process which will lead to international cooperation and dialogue. After we end here, I hope we will carry on listening to each other and learning from each other.

I think it is essential for us to do this if we are to ensure that the provisions of the United Nations Charter are applied consistently. This would also be most timely when violations of human rights in some places threaten what we in Brunei Darussalam hold to be the most important right of all the rights of the individual—to live in harmony with the other members of his or her community and nation.

Statement by Ali Alatas, Minister for Foreign Affairs and Head of the Delegation of the Republic of Indonesia, Vienna, 14 June 1993

Indonesia deems it a singular privilege to participate in this Second World Conference on Human Rights for it constitutes another landmark event in our long journey to arrive at a world order that is worthy of the spiritual kinship of all humankind.

It has been twenty-five years since the First World Conference on Human Rights was held Teheran and forty-five years since the United Nations General Assembly proclaimed the Universal Declaration of Human Rights which laid down the inalienable rights vested in all persons and all peoples by the simple virtue of their being human. This is indeed an opportune time for the United Nations again to convene a World Conference to evaluate the progress we have made since then, to identify the obstacles and challenges to further progress, and to devise the ways to overcome them.

Allow me, therefore, to express Indonesia's deep appreciation to the Government and people of Austria for hosting this Conference, for the gracious hospitality extended to my Delegation, and for the excellent arrangements made to ensure the efficiency of our proceedings. May I add that this Conference could not have had a more appropriate setting than this historic city of Vienna, cradle of some of the world's greatest philosophers and composers, and, in more recent times, the cultural and intellectual bridge between the East and the West.

Indonesia comes to this Conference with a profound awareness of the vital stakes involved in the outcome of our deliberations, for we are a developing nation which recently regained its national independence and therefore knows only too well how it is to hunger and to struggle for the most fundamental of human rights: the freedom to be free, the freedom from want, ignorance, social injustice and economic backwardness. We are also here as a country from Asia, that vast continent which, over the millennia, has given to the world its major religions, the wisdom of its philosophical thoughts and the rich diversity of its age-old cultures and civilizations. Hence, we do realize the constructive contribution that we can and should make to this World Conference. As the State currently holding the Chair of the Non-Aligned Movement, we are also entrusted to reflect the consensus position on human rights taken by 108 member states of the Movement which met in a Summit Conference in Indonesia last year, a position that is embodied in the Jakarta Message and the Final Documents which emanated from that Conference. And lastly, but by no means least important, we are here as a responsible member of the United Nations and as such fully conscious of the commitment of all members to adhere to the Charter of the United Nations and to the Universal Declaration of Human Rights.

We are therefore constrained to voice our concern at the recent spate of international media reports that tend to give the impression that the success of this Conference is being threatened by a clash of values between the developed countries of the North and the developing countries of the South, by a confrontation between the perceived universal, mostly Western, concept of human rights that stresses political and civil rights, and the purported 'dissident' view, particularly of Asian countries, which emphasizes the indivisibility of all categories of rights and the need to take into account the diversity of socio-economic, cultural and political realities prevailing in each country.

This depiction is not only erroneous but also unwarranted and therefore counterproductive. Speaking for Indonesia and, I believe, also for the other Asian countries, signatories to the recently adopted Bangkok Declaration, and the Non-Aligned Countries which all subscribe to the provisions on human rights as contained in the Final Documents of the Jakarta Summit, I can say in all truthfulness that we have not come to Vienna to engage in confrontation, nor to advocate an alternative concept of human rights, based on some nebulous notion of 'cultural relativism', as spuriously alleged by some quarters.

On the contrary, as clearly stated in the Bangkok Declaration on Human Rights, we recognize that the observance and promotion of human rights *should be encouraged by cooperation and consensus and not through confrontation and the imposition of incompatible values'*.

Indeed, there can and should be no room for confrontation or acrimony, considering that we all proceed from the same basic premises: our shared view on the universal validity of basic human rights and fundamental freedoms; our common adherence to the Universal Declaration of Human Rights and our commitment to the Charter of the U.N. which requires us to cooperate in promoting respect for human rights for all without distinction as to race, sex, language or religion.

If this is the case, then I cannot see how and why anyone can have any quarrel with the central proposition we have always advanced, namely that in considering human rights issues and in promoting and protecting these rights, we should all base our approaches and actions on what the U.N. Charter enjoins us to do rather than on the particular perceptions and preferences of any one country or group of countries. While the question of human rights has of late become the focus of heightened international concern, it is, of course, not a new issue. Since 1945, human rights have been enshrined in the Charter of the U.N. and since then our Organization has developed a growing corpus of covenants, conventions, declarations and other instruments which constitute a veritable International Bill of Human Rights. In the process, commonly agreed conceptual perceptions, principles, procedures and mechanisms have been established within the United Nations System. I therefore believe, and it is, as I earlier stated, our central proposition, that the promotion and protection of human rights will be far better served if all of us were to adhere more conscientiously to those common understandings and procedures as already agreed upon over the years rather than be diverted into a futile debate over misperceived alternatives or dichotomies.

Neither can it be said that the present concept of human rights, the theoretical basis of which was first conceived and developed in the West, is unknown or unappreciated in the countries of Asia or Africa. We in Indonesia do know how this concept sprang from the libertarian writings of such European political and legal thinkers as Thomas Hobbes, John Locke, Montesquieu, Jean Jacques Rousseau, Cesare Beccaria, and John Stuart Mill—and from their various postulations and juridical constructions of a 'social contract' and of the inherent, 'natural' rights of individuals in facing the powers of the State and of governmental authority. These were the ideas that eventually gave birth to the modern state and the attendant civil and political rights of the citizen. But these were also among the same ideas that inspired the struggle of many new nations of Asia and Africa to cast off the yoke of colonialism, just as they helped ignite, during an earlier time, the French and American Revolutions.

Thus, if today there appears to be still a debate on the concept of human rights, it is not so much from any contention between East and West or between North and South but, it seems to me, the lingering echo of an earlier clash between two Western traditions, between the principle of individual liberty which, for example, Thomas Jefferson passionately espoused and the principle of a strong, lawful authority which Alexander Hamilton just as passionately advocated.

On the rights of the individual as measured against those of the State, the view of the latter tradition is that:

When it comes to a decision by a Head of State upon a matter involving its life (the State's), the ordinary rights of individuals must yield to what he deems the necessities of the moment.

These are not the self-justifying words of some leader of the developing world. They constitute the considered view, in the Hamiltonian tradition, of one of America's most perceptive judicial minds, Justice Oliver Wendell Holmes.

I believe, however, that in essence the conflict between these two traditions or principles has some time ago already been resolved and for our age the writer Walter Lippmann summed its resolution in the following terms:

> The conflict of the two principles can be resolved only by uniting them. Neither can live alone. Alone, that is, without the other, each is excessive and soon intolerable. Freedom, the faith in man's perfectibility, has always and will always lead through anarchy to despotism. Authority, the conviction that men have to be governed and not merely let loose, will in itself always lead through arbitrariness and corruption to rebellion and chaos. Only in their union are they fruitful. Only freedom which is under strong law, only strong law to which men consent because it preserves freedom, can endure.

It is certainly not my intention, Mr President, to dwell on the past or to indulge in theorizing, for that is decidedly not the purpose for which we are gathered here today. But the point I do wish to make is that while we in the developing world do understand and appreciate the genesis of the thinking and motivation underlying present-day Western policies and view on human rights, we should at least expect similar understanding and appreciation of the historical formation and experiences of non-Western societies and the attendant development of our cultural and social values and traditions. For many developing countries, some endowed with ancient and highly developed cultures, have not gone through the same history and experience as the Western nations in developing their ideas on human rights and democracy. In fact, they often developed different perceptions based on different experiences regarding the relations between man and society, man and his fellow man and regarding the rights of the community as against the rights of the individual. In saying so, it is not my intention therefore to propose a separate or alternative concept on human rights. But this *is* a call for greater recognition of the immense complexity of the issue of human rights due to the wide diversity in history, culture, value systems, geography and phases of development among the nations of the world. And therefore this is also a call addressed to all of us to develop a greater sensitivity toward this complexity—and greater humility and less self-righteousness in addressing human rights issues.

What then are the commonly agreed understandings and perceptions to which I referred earlier and which should appropriately guide us in addressing the issue of human rights? Allow me to highlight a few and comment on them from the point of view of a Non-Aligned, developing country like Indonesia.

The universal validity of basic human rights and fundamental freedoms is indeed beyond question. But the United Nations Charter has rightly placed the question of their universal observance and promotion within the context of international cooperation. And I am sure we all agree that international cooperation presupposes as a basic condition respect for the sovereign equality of states and the national identity of peoples. In this spirit of cooperation and mutual respect, there should be no place for the practice of exchanging unfounded accusations or preaching self-righteous sermons to one another. In a world where domination of the strong over the weak and interference between states are still a painful reality, no country or group of countries should arrogate unto itself the role of judge, jury and executioner over other countries on this critical and sensitive issue of common concern to the entire international community.

Human rights questions are essentially ethical and moral in nature. Hence, any approach to human rights questions which is not motivated by a sincere desire to protect these rights but by disguised political purposes or, worse, to serve as a pretext to wage a political campaign against another country, cannot be justified.

Human rights are vital and important by and for themselves. So are efforts at accelerated national development, especially of the developing countries. Both should be vigorously pursued and promoted. Indonesia, therefore, cannot accept linking questions of human rights to economic and development cooperation, by attaching human rights implementation as political conditionalities to such cooperation. Such a linkage will only detract from the value of both.

On such conditionalities, the Leaders of the Non-Aligned Movement, during their Tenth Summit in Jakarta last year, emphasized that:

> any attempt to use human rights as a condition or socio-economic assistance, thus sidelining the relevance of economic, social and cultural human rights, must be rejected. No country should use its power to dictate its concept on human rights or to impose conditionalities on others.

It is now generally accepted that all categories of human rights — civil, political, economic, social and cultural, the rights of the individual and the rights of the community, the society and the nation — are interrelated and indivisible. This implies that the promotion and protection of all these rights should be undertaken in an integral and balanced manner and that inordinate emphasis on one category of human rights over another cannot be justified. Likewise, in assessing the human rights conditions of countries, and of developing countries in particular, the international community should take into account the situation in relation to all categories of human rights.

This, I believe, is what Secretary-General Boutros Boutros-Ghali meant when on the occasion of Human Rights Day 1992, he stated:

> Full human dignity means not only freedom from torture but also freedom from starvation. It means freedom to vote as it means the right to education. It means freedom of belief as it means the right to health. It means the right to enjoy all rights without discrimination.

This is also consistent with the basic principles contained in the Universal Declaration of Human Rights. Article 29 of that Declaration addresses two aspects that balance each other. On the one hand, there are principles that respect the fundamental rights and freedoms of the individual; on the other, there are stipulations regarding the obligations of the individual toward the society and the state.

It is clear, therefore, that implementation of human rights implies the existence of a balanced relationship between individual human rights and the obligations of individuals toward their community. Without such a balance, the rights of the community as a whole can be denied, which can lead to instability and even anarchy, especially in developing countries. In Indonesia, as in many other developing countries, the rights of the individual are balanced by the rights of the community, in other words, balanced by the obligation equally to respect the rights of others, the rights of the society and the rights of the nation. Indonesian culture as well as its ancient well-developed customary laws have traditionally put high priority on the rights and interests of the society or nation, without however in any way minimizing or ignoring the rights and interests of individuals and groups. Indeed, the interests of the latter are always fully taken into account based on the principles of 'musyawarah-mufakat' (deliberations in order to obtain consensus), which is firmly embedded in the nation's socio-political system and form of democracy.

Indeed, Mr President, we in Indonesia, and perhaps throughout the developing world as well, do not and cannot maintain a purely individualistic approach toward human rights for we cannot disregard the interests of our societies and nations. We hold that, flowing from the innate quality of the human being as an individual person and at the same time as a member of the community, his or her existence, rights and duties, can only become meaningful within the social context of the community and where, in the words of Article 29 of the Declaration of Human Rights, the free and full development of his or her personality becomes possible.

In promoting human rights in developing countries, including our own, it should also be borne in mind that there are other fundamental rights and concerns besides certain civil and political freedoms to which equally urgent attention should be devoted, such as the right of the vast majority of the people to be free from want and from fear, from ignorance, disease and backwardness. At the same time, most developing countries are presently at a stage of development which necessitates increasing focus on the human being as both the principal agent and ultimate beneficiary of all development, thus requiring primary efforts to be devoted to human resources development. This is why developing countries attach such great importance to the right to development and to the right to pursue development in an environment of peace and national stability.

The right to development has been recognized in the UNGA Declaration of 1986 and in UNGA Resolution 41/128. Article 1 of that Declaration clearly states that the right to development is an inalienable human right by virtue of which every human person and all peoples are entitled to participate in, contribute to and enjoy economic, social, cultural and economic development in which all human rights and fundamental freedoms can be fully realized.

While human rights are indeed universal in character, it is now generally acknowledged that their expression and implementation in the national context should remain the competence and responsibility of each government. This means that the complex variety of problems, of different economic, social and cultural realities, and the unique value systems prevailing in each country should be taken into consideration. This national competence not only derives from the principle of sovereignty of states, but also is a logical consequence of the principle of self-determination.

In this context, I fully concur with the view expressed by former Secretary-General Javier Perez de Cuellar in his 1991 annual Report that

the principle of non-interference with the essential jurisdiction of States cannot be regarded as a protective barrier behind which human rights can be massively or systematically violated with impunity.

But, as he also observed in the same Report,

maximum caution needs to be exercised lest the defense of human rights becomes a platform for encroaching on the essentially domestic jurisdiction of States and eroding their sovereignty. Nothing would be a surer prescription for anarchy than an abuse of this principle.

Indonesia is also of the firm view that in evaluating the implementation of human rights in individual countries, the characteristic problems of developing countries in general, as well as the specific problems of individual societies, should be taken fully into account. In other words, to be objective and credible, the complete picture rather than the partial view should be presented. It is important to note that the United Nations General Assembly has acknowledged these requirements as evidenced by its adoption in 1977 of Resolution 32/130 which *inter alia* reads as follows:

(Preambular Paragraph 3) Convinced that such cooperation should be based on a profound understanding of the variety of problems existing in different societies and on the full respect for their economic, social and cultural realities.

(Operative Paragraph 1, sub-para.d) Consequently, human rights questions should be examined globally, taking into account both overall context of the various societies in which they present themselves as well as the need for the promotion of the full dignity of the human person and the development and well-being of the society.

For its part, Indonesia has consistently endeavoured to adhere to the humanitarian precepts and fundamental human rights and freedoms as embodied in its State Philosophy, the *Pancasila*, its 1945 Constitution and its relevant national laws and regulations. As a member of the U.N. and of the Commission on Human Rights, Indonesia will continue to work vigorously to ensure that human rights are promoted and protected on the basis of universality, objectivity, indivisibility and non-selectivity.

The international scene has changed profoundly since the first World Conference on Human Rights in Teheran twenty-five years ago. Scientific and technical progress has triggered the processes of globalization, cross-cultural interlinks and the internationalization of value systems. The Cold War and the bipolar East–West conflict have ended. The tumult of their attendant global corollaries — ideological rivalry, bloc politics, nuclear brinkmanship and the scramble for spheres of influence — is fading away. The issue of human rights has ceased to be a bloc controversy and once again it has acquired a life of its own in the consciousness of the international community.

The desire of the international community to promote human rights is manifested by the fact that even during the period of greatest tension between East and West significant and meaningful progress was nevertheless made. The instruments adopted during this period have broadened the scope and dimensions of human rights, further extending protection to all peoples. In recent times the concept of human rights has come to incorporate the rights of women, of children, of migrant workers and their families, as well as the right to development. This year, we observe the International Year of the World's Indigenous People as a further example of the scope to which human rights have been extended.

But there is, unfortunately, still a wide gap between international aspirations on human rights and the reality of their implementation. For in various parts of the world the human rights of millions of people are still in grave jeopardy. Human rights cannot thrive in a world burdened with widespread poverty, environmental crisis and rapid population growth, by unresolved disparities and inequities in the world economic system and a steadily widening gap between the rich and the poor. And in the terrifying surge of national, ethnic and religious conflicts, human rights are among the first victims. Indonesia, therefore, joins the signatory-countries to the Bangkok Declaration and the Tunis Declaration in condemning the persistence of institutionalized racism in the form of Apartheid in South Africa, and the continued massive and systematic violations of the fundamental national and human rights of the Palestinian people. I should also like to cite the painful irony and incongruence of this Conference discussing the fundamental rights and freedoms of human beings and nations while a few hundred kilometres from here an entire nation is being subjected to brutal aggression, mass murder, systematic rape and the inhuman practice of ethnic cleansing.

It has not helped the cause of promoting and protecting human rights that the way in which concerns on human rights are expressed at the international level has so far failed to reflect the immense political, economic, social and culture diversity of the world we live in. When this diversity is disregarded, as it often is, then we are confronted by imbalances in such forms as politicization, selectivity, double standards and discrimination. As a result, some countries have too often become the target of unfair censure and trial by prejudicial publicity. On the other hand, there are countries that deserve opprobrium but are spared from censure for reasons that have nothing to do with human rights.

To improve the universal promotion and the protection of human rights, we have to address these imbalances through the adoption of an integrated and balanced approach that takes into account the diversity of the societies in which human rights are to be observed and implemented; the indivisibility and non-selectivity of all human rights; and the inherent relationship between development, democracy, social justice and the universal enjoyment of human rights.

Endeavours toward the establishment of uniform international human rights norms should go hand in hand with sincere efforts to work toward a just and equitable world economic order. Above all, the misuse of human rights as an instrument of political pressure or of a politically motivated campaign should be eschewed. And this applies and, in this context, I am pleased to announce the recent establishment of an independent National Commission on Human Rights in Indonesia.

We have noted the proposal to establish the office of a High Commissioner for Human Rights. We believe that this proposal needs further careful study in the context of our overall effort to enhance the efficiency and effectiveness of the United Nations human rights mechanisms so as to avoid duplication of efforts as well as wastage of resources.

Indonesia has always been of the view that the primary objective of international action in the field of human rights is not to indulge in acrimony nor to sit in self-righteous judgement over one another but, together, to enhance the common consciousness of the international community in promoting the observance of these fundamental rights. Indeed, what is needed at this present stage of international developments is not heightened confrontation but rather increased cooperation, compassion and mutual tolerance. We should not try to remake the world in our own image, but we can and should try to make the world a more humane, tolerant, peaceful and equitably prosperous place for all.

In the field of human rights, the concepts, the instruments and the international understandings are already there for us to build upon. This we must continue to nurture so that in time they will be also to bridge the vast diversity of cultures, traditions, and social, economic and political systems in the world today without disregarding any one of them or allowing one of them to dominate the others. Then we shall be able to weave together the three major strands as reflected in the U.N. Charter — the resolution of conflicts, the promotion of development and observance of human rights — which together compose the precious tissue of lasting peace.

Statement by Datuk Abdullah Haji Ahmad Badawi, Minister of Foreign Affairs, Malaysia, Vienna, 18 June 1993

We are meeting at a time when the world is undergoing a process of unprecedented change. Since the Teheran Conference twenty-five years ago, human rights have moved to the forefront of the international agenda because of the alarming increase in human rights violations, many of which were tolerated under the cover of East–West ideological rivalry. With the end of the Cold War, the situation has not improved and the need for effective global action on this vital issue has assumed an even greater urgency. Our presence here today testifies to our abiding commitment to constructive dialogue and international cooperation in the pursuit of human rights, human dignity and the essential worth of the human person.

In Malaysia, we have been closely studying developments in the field of international cooperation on human rights. A great deal of progress has been made in strengthening the instruments for the promotion and protection of human rights. The procedures at the Commission on Human Rights that provide for the appointment of representatives of the Secretary-General or Special Rapporteurs, Working Groups and monitoring mechanisms, along with the Confidential 1503 procedure have been developed over the years. Unfortunately, all of them reflect the preoccupation with civil and political rights. We are also witnessing signs of the increasing politicization of human rights issues by the developed countries and at the United Nations.

Forty-five years after the Universal Declaration of Human Rights, the world, regrettably, is no closer to a consensus on the universality of all human rights. While there is no question that we want human rights to be protected and promoted, there is a conceptual divide, arising from differing perceptions and positions on this complex issue. It is important that this is recognized and redressed. The objective, after all, is to harmonize and reconcile diverse viewpoints so that we may arrive at a meaningful global consensus. On the question of human rights there is no place for confrontation but there is a need for global partnership.

Malaysia takes a holistic view of human rights. We believe that civil, political, economic, social and cultural rights are indivisible and interdependent. We wish to stress that the right to development is a fundamental and inalienable human right. The 1968 Teheran Conference proclaimed that the full realization of civil and political rights would be impossible without the enjoyment of economic, social and cultural rights. The international community must address the totality of this issue in an integrated manner and with the same equality and urgency.

The Teheran Conference also established that the realization of human rights was impeded by the widening gap between the developed and developing countries. It further acknowledged that meaningful progress in implementing human rights depended upon sound and effective national and international policies of economic and social development. Yet, today, the goals of the Teheran Declaration remain unfulfilled and the gap between developed and developing countries has further widened. Increasingly, the policies of the North are constraining the developmental objectives of the South and seriously undermining their economic growth. Without development, without an integrated approach to human rights, in which developmental needs are incorporated, international cooperation on human rights cannot be sustained. A senior World Bank official at a seminar organized here last Wednesday said: 'It is unfair to talk about political rights only. There is no doubt that freedom from poverty comes first for the poor, although everybody aspires to all freedoms and rights.' The time has come to give due weight and attention to implementing the Declaration on the Right to Development.

The relationship between development and democracy is an essential condition for the full and effective enjoyment of human rights. Unfortunately, however, there has been a retreat from the commitment reached in Teheran on the linkage between human rights and development. Bilateral and multilateral attempts to link development assistance to the observance of human rights only undermine our collective commitment to and pursuit of human rights. It is right and proper that we do not condone violations of human rights, wherever and whenever they occur, but selective approaches, be they monitoring or pressure tactics, will not be conducive to the fostering of international cooperation for the promotion and protection of human rights.

It is our hope that this Conference will go beyond the simple recognition of the relationship between human rights and development and move into concrete programmes of action. In this respect, we are deeply concerned at attempts by donor countries to incorporate conditionalities in their development assistance programmes. Malaysia shares the view of the UNDP and the World Bank against the introduction of conditionalities which encourage political prejudices and selectivity and victimize the poor twice over.

Human rights and democracy are meaningless in an environment of political instability, poverty and deprivation. Let us admit and recognize this. The West had an enormous advantage of history, and the plundering of economic resources of their colonies as well as the luxury to hew and hone its democratic instincts, political values, military power and civilian rule. For many developing countries, meeting basic needs for food, shelter, education and health remains a daily struggle. In such situations, civil and political rights have little meaning without their social and economic underpinning. Neither has a priority on the other and the two must develop in tandem.

Let me be clear that Malaysia is not advocating that the promotion of human rights be conditional upon development. Nor are we saying that we should use discipline to curb individual freedom. What we are seeking is a balanced and democratic approach that incorporates the views and concerns of all of us and not just those of a privileged and powerful few. Another conceptual lacuna in the current debate on human rights is the manifest emphasis on individual rights at the expense of the rights of the community. The rights of the individual are certainly not in splendid isolation from those of the community. Excessive individual freedom leads to a decay in moral values and weakens the whole social fabric of nations. In the name of individual rights and freedom, racial prejudices and animosities are resurfacing to the extent that we are witnessing the rise of new forms of racism and xenophobia, increasingly manifested in violence.

The international community must take stock of the practical linkages between development and democracy for human rights to be fully enjoyed. Every opportunity should be given to the developing countries to shape their own political, social and economic institutions which reflect their own traditions and values. After all, as colonies, many of them had been subjected to human rights abuses by the very same self-righteous proponents and defenders of human rights today.

The United Nations Secretary-General has observed that both the principles and the practices of human rights are under stress. He recently wrote and I quote:

This is a time for serious discussions, for quiet diplomacy and step-by-step problem-solving. Solutions cannot be imposed from the top down. Proposals for new bureaucracies, high-level positions, more procedures and permanent forums, as admirable and well-intentioned as they are, may only arouse discontent and resistance at a time when liberality and leeway are called for. This is a year for dialogue.

Our concern now is not about the need for human rights but rather about how we achieve reasonable standards of human rights, as to who sets those standards and as to how aberrations created by double standards can be effectively addressed.

Against this dismal backdrop, we hear a rising clamour for new institutions including the proposed post of High Commissioner for Human Rights. In Malaysia's view, what is perhaps needed is a thorough study to revamp the existing United Nations human rights machinery, in particular the Commission on Human Rights and the Centre for Human Rights. As regards the proposals for the establishment of an International Court of Human Rights and an International Penal Court, our view is that we should await the outcome of studies being undertaken by the Commission on Human Rights and the International Law Commission before taking a final decision.

Nowhere is the double-standard approach to human rights more glaring than in the West's evasion of its responsibilities through its inaction in the face of the massive and gravest violations of human rights in Bosnia-Herzegovina. Surely, their apathetic and meek response to genocide, ethnic cleansing and rape, in the heart of Europe, makes a total mockery of their preaching and posturing on the promotion and protection of human rights in far corners of the world. We ask ourselves what credentials do they still have to preach about human rights when the most blatant abuse of those rights before their very eyes goes unpunished. The murderous acts and cruelty perpetrated by the Serbs on Bosnian men, women and children, the horror of which confronts all of us on our television screens every day, are stark expressions of a deliberate and cynical humiliation of the human spirit and dignity, not to mention the destruction of life itself. Must a whole community be annihilated for another community to achieve its nationalistic aspirations? What mare is needed to move the West to take forceful action provided for in the Charter of the United Nations to end killings, aggression and the mutilation of a sovereign and independent nation, a member of the United Nations, when all peaceful diplomatic efforts have failed? Their failure is an impeachment of their credibility.

The Security Council too has failed to fulfil its obligations under Article 24 of the Charter to take prompt and effective action to restore peace and uphold the sovereignty, independence and territorial integrity of the Republic of Bosnia-Herzegovina. At the same time, the Council is denying the Government of this Republic its inherent right to self-defence under Article 51. This is immoral, unjust and totally unacceptable.

Today, as we are gathered to take stock of international progress in the field of human rights, we must be courageous, honest and responsible enough to address the acute and tragic human rights situation in Bosnia-Herzegovina. Failure to do so is to condone and to connive at aggression and massive violations of human rights, and to be an accessory to the crimes being committed by the Serbs. Like many others, my delegation was deeply moved by the heart-rending appeal made by the Bosnian Foreign Minister on Tuesday and we were extremely gratified that this Conference spontaneously endorsed his plea for our meeting to request the U.N. Security Council to take all necessary measures immediately to end the genocide in Bosnia-Herzegovina especially in Gorazde.

Our worst fear of the consequence of a policy of apathy and appeasement is now surfacing with the abandonment of the Vance–Owen Plan in favour of the Tudjman–Milosevic proposal for the partition of Bosnia-Herzegovina into three states based on ethnic lines. Although full details of the proposal are not yet available to us, the fact remains that its acceptance means legitimizing Serbian acquisition of territory through the use of force and the abhorrent practice of ethnic cleansing. We are troubled by the notion that European nations and the United States of America, at the dawn of the 21st century, find it practical and proper for a country to be divided along ethnic and religious lines, when Bosnia-Herzegovina has long been multi-ethnic and multi-religious. It contravenes international law and is in violation of all Security Council Resolutions and General Assembly Resolutions 46/242 (1991) and 47/121 (1992).

In the light of this latest development, it is important that this crucial initiative be further reinforced and complemented by a comprehensive plan of action. In this connection, members of the Organization of Islamic Countries (OIC) have proposed that this World Conference issues a declaration to pledge its solidarity with the people and the Government of the Republic of Bosnia-Herzegovina and urge the Security Council to fulfil its responsibilities under the U.N. Charter, particularly, under Article 24, by taking prompt and effective measures in order to restore peace, to affirm the independence, sovereignty and territorial integrity of the Republic of

Bosnia-Herzegovina and to uphold the human rights of its people. In the context of this Conference having to address the issue of human rights, the tragedy of Bosnia-Herzegovina is an acid test. Where is the protection of the most basic of human rights — the right to life itself? The need to support the OIC proposed Special Declaration is in my view imperative.

I certainly agree with the view that there is no single model or panacea that would help tackle the threat of the revival of ethno-nationalist and religious conflicts. In Malaysia, we are blessed with a multi-racial society, the majority of which are indigenous people. It is no coincidence that through the secret ballot box, people in my country enjoy full participation in the democratic process . . . In the villages and in the forests there are also minority indigenous groups. Often, there are conflicting and forceful demands on the Government to respect and sustain the traditional way of life of some of these groups, and at the same time, to encourage them to contribute to, and participate fully in the mainstream of national life.

This morning at the Conference we observed a special commemoration of the International Year of the World's Indigenous People. As a nation with more than thirty indigenous groups, we in Malaysia rejoice in celebrating this historic day. In Malaysia, we certainly do not wish to see any of our indigenous people become marginalized in our society or become mere tourist attractions. There is ample opportunity, room and land for all our citizens and ethnic groups. Our vision of the future is a nation, whose people are highly motivated, resilient, tolerant and compassionate. For us, the underlying foundation of a democratic and successful nation remains the need for strong and good governance for a disciplined and productive society, for continuing emphasis on political stability and quality economic growth with human beings at the centre of development efforts, while we continuously strive for the upholding of human dignity and the essential worth of the human person.

In conclusion, I would like to underline that progress in the field of human rights and democracy must be pursued within the context of democratization in international relations. It is important that the principles of democracy are practised within the United Nations. All States, big and small, rich and poor, must be given the opportunity to participate in the work of the Organization to enhance cooperation in human rights as well as in other areas of international cooperation. This is the only way to avoid replacing the ideological rivalry of the Cold War period with that of North–South antagonism. After all, in the words of the Charter, the United Nations both symbolizes and reflects the harmonization of the collective action by nations in the pursuit of common ends. Let this inspire us to work towards our common goals in the spirit of constructive dialogue, consensus and genuine cooperation.

Statement by Roberto R. Romulo, Secretary of Foreign Affairs and Head of the Philippine Delegation, Vienna, 16 June 1993

My delegation and I join all of those who have already spoken at this podium and the others who will follow me here in extending to you warm felicitations on your assumption of the presidency of the World Conference on Human Rights.

Our conference in this magnificent city recalls for us another international gathering more than one and three-quarter centuries ago — the congress of Vienna of 1815.

We are confident, Mr President, that, with your experience and skill, you will guide our deliberations to a successful conclusion, much as Prince Metternich was a moving force in that *other* congress of Vienna.

There is, however, a fundamental difference between that gathering and this. The congress of Vienna of 1815 sought to guide the behaviour of states in their relations with one another. The subject of this conference is no less than the very nature of human beings and of the communities that they compose, and the rights and freedoms inherent in their nature.

We are gathered here to renew the commitment of our Governments and peoples and that of the international community to the protection and promotion of the human rights and freedoms of all persons who inhabit our planet.

This is not the first time that the international community specifically addresses the question of the rights of man. The founding fathers of the United Nations, including my late father, declared, at the very beginning of the Charter of the United Nations, the determination of the World's Peoples 'To reaffirm faith in fundamental human rights, in the dignity and worth of the human person, in the equal rights of men and women and of nations large and small', and, at the same time, 'To promote social progress and better standards of life in larger freedom'.

Three years later, that same international community through the United Nations General Assembly, reaffirmed its commitment to those fundamental human rights in even more specific and explicit terms. In the ringing eloquence of the Universal Declaration of Human Rights, the World's Peoples proclaimed: 'All human beings are born free and equal in dignity and rights . . . Everyone has the right to life, liberty and security of person.' In a later article, the Universal Declaration affirms: 'Everyone has the right to a standard of living adequate for the health and well-being of himself and of his family.'

We are gathered amid the splendour of this city, Mr President, to give to the words of the Charter and of the Declaration further meaning and substance for the Peoples of the World. No task could be nobler.

If it is possible for us to hold this conference, Mr President, it is because there is some common ground on which we can all agree with respect to certain concepts of the rights of human beings and of peoples. To deny the existence of that common ground is to deny the value of this conference. It is to deny the fundamental validity of the Charter of the United Nations and of the Universal Declaration of Human Rights. Indeed, it is to deny our common humanity.

Surely, we can all agree on the existence of certain individual rights. We can all agree that all of us and our other fellow-human beings have 'the right to life, liberty and security of person', as the Universal Declaration proclaims. We all have the right not to be tortured, the right not to be discriminated against on the basis of race, sex, religion, language or culture. We can all agree that all women have the right to their dignity and to the integrity of their womanhood. We can all agree that the world's children have the right to be sheltered from abuse. We can all agree that the very poor and other vulnerable groups, including migrant workers, the disabled, and indigenous peoples, have the right to be protected from any exploitation of their weakness.

Surely, we can all agree on the inherent nature of these rights regardless of our differences in history, tradition, culture, and empirical circumstances.

Certainly, we in the Philippines believe in it, indeed insist on it. The constitution of the Philippines declares: 'The state values the dignity of every human person and guarantees full respect for human rights.'

The Bill of Rights in that same constitution begins: 'No person shall be deprived of life, liberty, or property without due process of law, nor shall any person be denied the equal protection of the laws.' It goes on to promulgate provisions that give flesh to this undertaking.

Our constitution establishes an independent commission on human rights, which is functioning fully today, with broad powers to ensure the observance and protection of the rights of all persons in the Philippines.

Because we believe that not only Filipinos but all human beings possess fundamental human rights by virtue of their being human, we reserve the right, and respect the right of others, to express concern about particularly flagrant violations of human rights wherever they may occur.

In the political realm, we believe, and again insist, that the leadership of the state must have the mandate of the people, that the government must govern with the consent of the governed and that the people must have a voice in the formulation and implementation of public policy. This to us is the substance of democracy.

Countries may differ, and do differ, in how the mandate is given, the consent is expressed, and the participation is carried out. Here, states have no right to impose their system on others. What democracy demands, in our view, is that the mandate be legitimate, the consent genuine, and the participation effective. At the same time, as the Secretary-General stressed in *An Agenda for Peace*, 'democracy within nations requires respect for human rights and fundamental freedoms, as set forth in the Charter.'

We believe, of course, that our system of democracy is best for our People, with its checks and balances, its pluralism, its openness, its atmosphere of freedom. It is a functioning democracy. If that imperfect system of Government has its weaknesses, it has also its strengths, and the guarantee of individual rights is one of them.

Essential no less to the dignity of the human person is the right to development. For an integral part of human dignity is a person's ability to raise himself and his family to a level of living fit for a human being. Only with development can the right of human beings to food, clothing, shelter, medical care, employment, and education be adequately fulfilled.

There is a broader dimension to the right to development. There cannot be peace without development. There cannot be development without peace. And there cannot be universal enjoyment of human rights if there is no peace and no development.

It was in this light that the General Assembly adopted, in December 1986, the Declaration of the right to development, which proclaims: 'The right to development is an inalienable human right by virtue of which every human person and all peoples are entitled to participate in, contribute to, and enjoy economic, social, cultural and political development, in which all human rights and fundamental freedoms can be fully realized.'

Some of those who deny the existence of this right seem to have so easily forgotten that they themselves, at an earlier stage in their history, placed such a high value on *their* right to development that, in the pursuit of that right, they saw nothing deplorable in setting aside the human rights of their workers, including child laborers, those of persons of a different race, or those of peoples of different climes.

The truth is that individual rights, democracy and the right to development are indivisible and interdependent. All of them together make up the sum and substance of the rights of each one of us as human beings. They, together, are an inseparable part of our nature. They, together, are an inalienable portion of our selves.

The Philippine experience has shown that there is in reality no lasting and real bargain between the rights of man and progress, between democracy and dictatorship, between bread and freedom.

It is thus a tragedy for human rights that, upon the end of the Second World War, for their own political and strategic purposes, governments selectively used human rights as ideological weapons or as justification for state policy rather than for the sake of the human persons and peoples who possessed them. They treated human rights in their distinct and discrete components instead of the integrated whole that they are and must be — and as they are enshrined in the Universal Declaration of Human Rights.

The West laid almost exclusive emphasis on the rights of the individual and on civil and political rights as an affront to its totalitarian adversaries, while ignoring violations of those rights in states that were politically aligned with it. Others championed economic, social and cultural rights either as a defensive measure or as their justification for their repression of individual and political rights, even as many of them failed to ensure for their own peoples those same economic, social and cultural rights that they so fervently espoused.

A consequent part of this tragedy is that the international community was completed to conclude, in December 1966, two separate covenants—one on civil and political rights and another on economic, social and cultural rights—when all these rights, belonging as they do to the same human person, should be treated as an integrated whole.

It is time, at this conference, to begin to regard these two covenants, together with the Universal Declaration of Human Rights, as one inseparable set of rights. The ideological divide between East and West is no more. The march of democracy around the world is far advanced. The dissension between North and South is emerging from its confrontational stage. There should no longer be any excuse, even if there were one before, for the separate advocacy of the various sets of human rights.

In any case, we in the Philippines strongly hold that, because these rights are indivisible and interrelated, they should be promoted simultaneously and *not* sequentially. We cannot give the non-fulfilment of one set of rights as an excuse for our failure to protect another.

This, I submit, Mr President, is a measure of our commitment to human rights in their totality.

We have come to Vienna to renew that commitment and to reaffirm, at this particular stage in history, our abiding faith in human rights.

Many will be tempted to call that faith misplaced. They will point to the massive violations of human rights in Bosnia-Herzegovina; to societies where the weight of tradition continues to crush the right of women to equality and dignity; to countries that exploit and abuse their children; to places where peoples have their cultures and very existence threatened with extinction; to states that use torture as a matter of policy and incarcerate, without trial or charges, persons who disagree with them; to areas where grinding poverty so demeans people that human rights have lost all meaning for them.

But it is precisely in the midst of such violations that we must keep alive our faith in human rights and strengthen our determination to advance and protect them. Indeed, to a significant extent, recent developments have confirmed us in our faith and encouraged us in our resolve.

The codification of the International Bill of Human Rights, its translation into National Legislation, and the Establishment of National and International Institutions to monitor compliance are landmark achievements which have defined and fixed forever the international community's recognition of the transcendental nature of human rights.

The radical political changes that the world has undergone in recent years now provide new opportunities and wider scope for international cooperation in the promotion and protection of human rights.

Above all, there has been a rapid awakening among the World's Peoples to the fact that human-rights violations are neither a necessary nor an inevitable evil. This awakening has taken many shapes and forms, the resurgence of popular aspirations for economic growth, social justice, democracy, and fundamental freedoms being only one, but certainly the most compelling, of its manifestations.

Certainly, the holding of this conference is another of those manifestations. But it is more than an expression of our faith in human rights and of our commitment to them, important as that is.

This conference is also an occasion for us, as nations and as an international community, to call for and agree upon measures to strengthen our collective and individual ability to protect and promote human rights throughout the world.

We might begin by calling upon states to accede to and ratify the international human-rights conventions. For our part, the Philippines has so far signed and ratified nineteen of those conventions. We might, in this regard, also call upon governments to refrain from making reservations that vitiate the spirit and purposes of those conventions.

Let us establish national institutions for the promotion and protection of human rights. We in the Philippines are ready to offer to others the experience and expertise of the Philippine commission on human rights.

We support the proposal to institute in Asia regional arrangements for human rights, provided such arrangements genuinely promote human rights and not mask their violation or neglect.

As an international community, we need to intensify international cooperation on human rights and to strengthen the institutional mechanisms, especially those in the United Nations, through which to carry out such cooperation. One way of strengthening those mechanisms would be to reduce, if not eliminate, the many duplications in their functions, another would be to provide them with adequate financing, particularly for the technical and advisory services.

Not least, we need to enlist in our cause the profound wisdom and tremendous energy of the non-governmental organizations which have, on their own, made that cause their mission and their crusade. We in the Philippine Government regard them as partners, sharing the same cause and carrying out the same mission. We welcome their participation in this conference.

As the world enters the new era of international relations and international cooperation, the promotion and protection of human rights present mankind with the greatest and most rewarding challenge of our times.

In meeting here in Vienna, we take up that challenge, convinced of the rightness of our task.

We have come to Vienna in search of a better future for mankind. We know that the road to peace and security, prosperity and justice is often littered with the mangled bodies and broken spirits of those whose rights we have trampled upon.

That awful truth must now give us the courage and the wisdom to try and make sure that it never happens again.

Statement by Wong Kan Seng, Minister for Foreign Affairs of the Republic of Singapore, Vienna, 16 June 1993

The Real World of Human Rights

How a state treats its citizens is no longer a matter for its exclusive determination. Other countries now claim a concern. No country has rejected the Universal Declaration of Human Rights. A body of international law on human rights is evolving. These developments will eventually make for a more civilized world. We should work towards it.

But the international consensus on human rights is still fragile. Although everyone professes support for the ideal of human rights, conflicts still abound. The prepara-

tory process for the World Conference on Human Rights has been mired in fundamental disagreements. Even now, we cannot assume that a consensus will be
reached. This is not simply due to bad faith or hypocrisy.

Human rights do not exist in an abstract and morally pristine universe. The ideal
of human rights is compelling because this is an imperfect world and we must strive
to make it better. There is no need for human rights in heaven. But precisely because
this is an imperfect world, making progress on human rights will be marked by
ambiguity, compromise and contradiction.

Differences of opinion over human rights are inevitable in the real world of competing states and contending interests. The promotion of human rights by all countries has always been selective. Concern for human rights has always been balanced
against other national interests. Those who deny this protest too much.

Universal recognition of the ideal of human rights can be harmful if universalism
is used to deny or mask the reality of diversity. The gap between different points of
view will not be bridged if this ignored. We deceive only ourselves if we pretend this
is not so.

Forty-five years after the Universal Declaration was adopted as a 'common standard of achievement', debates over the meaning of many of its thirty articles continue.
The debate is not just between the West and the Third World. Not every country in
the West will agree on the specific meaning of every one of the Universal Declaration's thirty articles. Not everyone in the West will even agree that all of them are
really rights.

Let us take the United States of America as an example. Not every state of the
U.S.A. interprets such matters as, for example, capital punishment or the right to
education in the same way. Despite U.S. Supreme Court rulings, abortion is still a
hotly contested issue. But this multiplicity of state and local laws is not decried as a
retreat from universalism. On the contrary, the clash and clamour of contending
interests is held up as a shining model of democratic freedom in the U.S.A.

For that matter, the right to trial by jury, so precious in Britain and the United
States, has never prevailed in France. Are we therefore to conclude that human rights
are repressed by the French? This would be absurd. Sweden, to give another example, has more comprehensive and communal social arrangements than some other
Western countries may find comfortable. Is Sweden therefore a tyranny? Naturally
not. Order and justice are obtained in diverse ways in different countries at different
times.

Therefore, are the common interests of humanity really advanced by seeking to
impose an artificial and stifling unanimity? The extent and exercise of rights, in
particular civil rights, varies greatly from one culture or political community to
another. This is because they are the products of the historical experiences of particular peoples.

When the Universal Declaration was being formulated in 1947, no less an authority
than the American Anthropological Association cautioned that 'what is held to be a
human right in one society may be regarded as anti-social by another people' and
that 'respect for differences between cultures is validated by the scientific fact that no
technique of qualitatively evaluating cultures has been discovered'.[1]

Time has not refuted, but unfortunately has dimmed the memory of this sensible
advice. The point is now subject to fierce disputes with a pronounced theological
flavour. Moralizing in the abstract is seldom productive. I believe that a more pragmatic approach is in order, if we want to be effective rather than just feel virtuous.

The momentum of international cooperation on human rights will not be sustained
by mere zealotry. Only if we all recognize the rich diversity of the human community
and accept the free interaction of all ideas can the international consensus be deep-

ened and expanded. No one has a monopoly of truth. Claiming an unwarranted authenticity for any single point of view may prove futile and unproductive. We must all humbly acknowledge this fact before we can help each other grope towards a practical application of the ideals we all share.

Of course, there is a risk that tolerance for diversity will be used as a shield for dictators. This is unacceptable. But pragmatism and realism do not mean abdication. We need not, indeed we should not, cease to speak out against wanton cruelty or injustice. We can strike a realistic balance between the ideal of universality and the reality of diversity if we adopt a clinical approach.

Our aim should be to promote humane standards of behaviour without at the same time claiming special truths or seeking to impose any particular political pattern or societal arrangement.

Diversity cannot justify gross violations of human rights. Murder is murder whether perpetrated in America, Asia or Africa. No one claims torture as part of their cultural heritage. Everyone has a right to be recognized as a person before the law sentence on children. There are other such rights that must be enjoyed by all human beings everywhere in a civilized world. All cultures aspire to promote human dignity in their own ways. But the hard core of rights that the truly universal is perhaps smaller than we sometimes like to pretend.

Most rights are still essentially contested concepts. There may be a general consensus. But this is coupled with continuing and, at least for the present, no less important conflicts of interpretation. Singaporeans, and people in many other parts of the world do not agree, for instance, that pornography is an acceptable manifestation of free expression or that homosexual relationships are just a matter of lifestyle choice. Most of us will also maintain that the right to marry is confined to those of the opposite gender.

Naturally, we do not expect everyone to agree with us. We should be surprised if everything were really settled once and for all. This is impossible. The very idea of human rights is historically specific. We cannot ignore the differences in history, culture and background of different societies. They have developed separately for thousands of years, in different ways and with different experiences. Their ideals and norms differ. Even for the same society, such norms and ideals also differ over time. For example, how rights were defined in Europe or America a hundred years ago is certainly not how they are defined today. And they will be defined differently a hundred years hence.

Take Britain for illustration. Its Parliament was established in 1215 with the signing of the Magna Carta. But women only had the right to vote in 1928. Up till 1948, Oxbridge university graduates and businessmen had extra votes.

The United States of America gained independence in 1776. Only those who paid poll tax or property tax had the right to vote from 1788. There were barriers of age, colour, sex and income. In 1860, income and property qualifications were abolished but other barriers like literacy tests and poll tax still discriminated against African-American and other disadvantaged groups. Women only had the vote in 1920. It was not until 1965 that the African-Americans can vote freely after the Voting Rights Act suspended literacy tests and other voter qualification devices which kept them out.

So full democracy was only established in Britain in 1948, 733 years after Magna Carta, and in the United States in 1965, 189 years after Independence. In France, liberté, fraternité and egalité in 1788 did not succeed as a democracy until this century.

The U.S.A., Britain and France took 200 years or more to evolve into full democracies. Can we therefore expect the citizens of the many newly independent countries of this century to acquire the same rights as those enjoyed by the developed nations when they lack the economic, educational and social pre-conditions to exercise such rights fully? If all the countries in the world are merged into one, and everyone has the same right, will this be acceptable to all?

We should therefore approach this conference with humility. We are not the prophets of a secular god whose verities are valid for all time. We should act more pragmatically, and I hope modestly, as diplomats dealing with a difficult international issue. Our work, while important, will in due course be displaced by the shifting tides of history.

How, for example, we interpret and apply Article 14 of the Universal Declaration on the right to asylum today is different from when it was first drafted at the beginning of the Cold War. With the dismantling of communist regimes and with modern communications, massive population shifts are now under way. Desperate peoples, or just those newly free to travel, are on the move, searching for better security or a better life. This has forced contiguous countries to adopt more restrictive standards for admission. No country has been consistent in its application of the rights of refugees. The very manner in which we conceive of refugees has changed.

All international norms reflect a specific historical configuration of interests and power. History moves on continually. Every international norm must therefore evolve. If this dynamic is not to be driven by the clash of steel and blood, then it must entail a process of debate, interpretation and re-interpretation, in which most agreements are contingent. This is how an international consensus is built and sustained.

A pragmatic approach to human rights is one that tries to consolidate what common ground we can agree on, while agreeing to disagree if we must. More effort should be devoted to clinically identifying the specific rights that we can all agree on now, and which others must await further discussion before we reach consensus. This will be a more productive approach than one grounded in self-righteousness.

But identifying the core rights which are truly universal will not always be easy. Many will argue that the 'non-derogable' rights in the International Covenant on Civil and Political Rights must be among them. I agree. But some fervent advocates of these civil and political liberties will dispute that development is also, as I and many others hold, an inalienable right. This has a direct impact on the important and contentious question of human rights conditionality for development assistance.

Clearly, the purpose of aid is to enable the peoples to which it is given to live with dignity. It should not be misused. No one has a 'right' to squander aid. The question is how to ensure that aid will be used effectively. Here the human rights debate merges into broader questions of political theory and public administration. 'Human rights', 'democracy' and 'good government' are sometimes used as if they were synonyms. There is certainly a degree of overlap. But they are not the same thing.

Repression is wrong. It is unhealthy and will stifle development. Growth both promotes and is promoted by the ability of the individual to live with dignity.

But poverty makes a mockery of all civil liberties. Poverty is an obscene violation of the most basic of individual rights. Only those who have forgotten the pangs of hunger will think of consoling the hungry by telling them that they should be free before they can eat. Our experience is that economic growth is the necessary foundation of any system that claims to advance human dignity, and that order and stability are essential for development.

Good government is necessary for the realization of all rights. No one can enjoy any rights in anarchy. And the first duty of all governments is to ensure that it has the power to govern effectively. And they must govern fairly.

If political institutions fail to deliver a better life to their peoples, they will not endure over the long term. Human rights will not be accepted if they are perceived as an obstacle to progress. This is a fact that some zealots would do well to ponder.

There is already evidence that at some stage an excessive emphasis on individual rights becomes counterproductive.

Life in any society necessarily entails constraints. The exercise of rights must be balanced with the shouldering of responsibility. To claim absolute freedom for the individual is to become less a human being with rights than an animal, subject only to the law of the jungle.

Development and good government require a balance between the rights of the individual and those of the community to which every individual must belong, and through which individuals must realize their rights. Where this balance will be struck will vary for different countries at different points of their history. Every country must find its own way. Human rights questions do not lend themselves to neat general formulas.

In the early phase of a country's development, too much stress on individual rights over the rights of the community will retard progress. But as it develops, new interests emerge and a way to accommodate them must be found. The result may well be a looser, more complex and more differentiated political system. But the assumption that it will necessarily lead to a 'democracy', as some define the term, is not warranted by the facts.

Singapore's political and social arrangements have irked some foreign critics because they are not in accordance with their theories of how societies should properly organize themselves. We have intervened to change individual social behaviour in ways other countries consider intrusive. We maintain and have deployed laws that others may find harsh. For example, the police, narcotics or immigration officers are empowered by the Misuse of Drugs Act to test the urine for drugs of any person who behaves in a suspicious manner. If the result is positive, rehabilitation treatment is compulsory. Such a law will be considered unconstitutional in some countries and such urine tests will lead to suits for damages for battery and assault and an invasion of privacy. As a result, the community's interests are sacrificed because of the human rights of drug consumers and traffickers. So drug-related crimes flourish.

The Singapore Government is accountable to its people through periodic secret and free elections. But we do not feel guilty because the opposition parties have consistently failed to win more than a handful of seats. We have made alternative arrangements to ensure a wide spectrum of view is represented in our Parliament through non-elected Members of Parliament and put in place other channels for good communication between the government and the people.

We make no apology for doing what we believe is correct rather than what our critics advise. Singaporeans are responsible for Singapore's future. We justify ourselves to our people, not by abstract theories or the approbation of foreigners, but by the more rigorous test of practical success.

Our citizens live with freedom and dignity in an environment that is safe, healthy, clean and incorrupt. They have easy access to cultural, recreational and social amenities, good standards of education for our children and prospects for a better life for future generations. I can say without false modesty that many of our well meaning critics cannot claim as much. We do not think that our arrangements will suit everybody. But they suit ourselves. This is the ultimate test of any political system.

We need to remind ourselves that the purpose of this conference is not to score debating points or just to produce a Declaration. We ought to try and expand consensus on very difficult issues. Without a genuine political commitment any Declaration is just another piece of paper. We can force states to pay lip service to a Declaration. But we cannot force states to genuinely respect human rights. In the real world of sovereign states, respect and political commitment can only be forged through the accommodation of different interests.

Unless we all remember this, I fear that we will only fracture the international consensus on human rights. If this happens, the responsibility must lie with those who are so blinded by their own arrogance and certainties as to lose the capacity for imagination and empathy. I venture to suggest that a more modest approach not only behooves our common humanity, but is more likely to lead to a successful outcome for this conference. There is too much at stake over us to fail.

Note

1. 'Statement on human rights', *American Anthropologist*, vol. 49 (1947): 539–43.

Statement of Prasong Soonsiri, Minister of Foreign Affairs of Thailand, Head of Thai Delegation, Vienna, 16 June 1993

I wish to join the previous speakers in congratulating the distinguished Federal Minister for Foreign Affairs of the Republic of Australia in his election, by acclamation, President of the World Conference on Human Rights. I wish to assure you of the Thai delegation's full support and cooperation in all efforts to reach a successful conclusion of this historic Conference.

I wish also to congratulate the election of the other members of the General Committee. In thanking the Conference for electing Thailand to serve as one of the Vice-Presidents, I wish to pledge that Thailand will faithfully serve the Conference to the best of our ability in whatever task is assigned to us in the interest of the body as a whole and especially of the developing countries of the world.

At the outset, I wish to thank most wholeheartedly the Government of the Republic of Austria for taking the brave and daring decision to host this meeting. The road to Vienna has been long and arduous. To be greeted with the traditionally warm hospitality of the Austrian people and the excellent facilities extended by the host country to all delegations has made the hardship of the arrival worthwhile. I hope that the rich historic and cultural setting of Vienna will inspire all of us to represent all of mankind with responsibility during our participation at this Conference.

The statements delivered by Their Excellencies the President, the Federal Chancellor, and the Federal Minister of Foreign Affairs of the Republic of Austria at the opening session of the Conference strongly underlined the importance of this Conference in setting the course of the promotion of human rights back on the track that was envisaged by the United Nations Charter and the Universal Declaration of Human Rights. The brilliant statement to the opening session of the Conference of the Secretary-General of the United Nations brought clear and balanced messages which should provoke all participants to creative thoughts and reactions capable of inspiring this Conference and the international community to strive for joint and separate actions to promote human rights on the basis of the highest common factors achievable by the international community through a process of consensus-making at this Conference where, as the Secretary-General of the Conference said, the principle of the equality of nations is real.

Two months ago, Thailand had the privilege to serve as the venue of the regional meeting for Asia, which was the first of its kind in bringing together states from the Asian region to discuss human rights issues of concern to the region in preparation for this Conference. Thanks to the spirit of compromise and mutual respect that prevailed during the meeting, Asian states were able to adopt the 'Bangkok Declaration' containing the aspirations and commitments of states in the Asian region to human rights, as Asia's contribution to the World Conference. If the discourse on human rights is to be genuinely international with a view to making human rights truly universal, the 'Bangkok Declaration' and the final outcome of the other regional meetings, which taken together represent the views of two-thirds of the world's population, should be made the determinant and integral part of the Final Outcome of this Conference.

The discussions which have taken place within the context of preparations for the World Conference on Human Rights have shown that there is world-wide interest in the promotion of human rights. This is indeed a healthy development towards strengthening the universality of human rights.

Universalization of human rights must start from the premise that the Universal Declaration of Human Rights embodies the basic rights and fundamental freedoms that are universally recognized, and should, therefore, be kept at the forefront of international efforts to achieve a common standard on human rights. At the same time, it is recognized that the United Nations has made great strides in codifying standards for promoting the respect for and observance of human rights, The progressive accession to international human rights instruments and the implementation of human rights by individual states at a suitable and manageable pace taking into account local conditions should be encouraged.

As states have the primary responsibility to promote the respect for and observance of human rights, efforts to achieve the full realization of human rights must begin at home. In this connection, every individual and organ of society, including national institutions, the media and non-governmental organizations, have major roles to play in promoting public awareness and appreciation of human rights, and should be encouraged to do so. This, however, does not mean that the international community has no role to play in such efforts, since the United Nations Charter has placed universal observance and promotion of human rights and fundamental freedoms within the context of international cooperation. In encouraging the observance and promotion of human rights, international assistance should be made readily available to States at their request.

Today, no society can ignore the atrocities committed against fellow human beings arising from intolerance, racial discrimination, xenophobia and sexual violation, harassment and exploitation, especially when the victims are women, children and vulnerable groups. Nor can we refrain from sharing the suffering of peoples caused by hunger, extreme poverty and economic hardship or the absence of the rule of law. More often than not, these obstacles to and violation of human rights lead to, or threaten to lead to, displacement of populations across borders which become burdensome to countries of first refuge, receiving third countries, and the international community as a whole.

Violations of, and obstacles to the realization of, human rights and fundamental freedoms are therefore matters of concern to the international community as a whole. It must be made clear from the very beginning, however, that this concern should in no way be translated into interference in domestic affairs or serve as a pretext for encroachment on the national sovereignty of a state. In addressing such situations, the international community must work on the basis of cooperation, not confrontation, in order to ensure that the letter and spirit enshrined in the United Nations Charter are not compromised. A balanced and non-selective and objective approach should become the basis for international efforts to address human rights, so that human rights do not become instruments of political and/or economic pressure.

The Thai delegation is convinced that the promotion of human rights at the international level cannot be achieved in isolation from other equally important considerations. Recognition of the inherent relationship between development, democracy and human rights is a step in the right direction. They should be understood to be complementary and mutually reinforcing. The pursuit of these crucial concepts has as its common objective the overall development of society whereby the inherent dignity and worth of the human person can be fully enhanced.

The pillars of the relationship between democracy, development and human rights are mutually supportive as a result of the interdependence and indivisibility of civil and political rights and economic, social and cultural rights. Thailand believes that both sets of rights have to be achieved progressively in a balanced and simultaneous manner in order for democracy, development and the full realization of human rights to be sustainable. It should also be recognized that just as development should not be used to justify violation of human rights or the suppression of democracy, neither should development assistance be subject to conditionalities on the grounds of the rate of progress in the other two areas.

Over the years, improvements in the promotion of human rights have been achieved at the international level thanks partly to the United Nations human rights institutions, machineries and procedures. While this is welcome, there is a clear need to rationalize them in order to ensure their effectiveness and efficiency and to avoid duplication of work. The Centre for Human Rights, as the focal point for United Nations human rights activities, should be given the necessary resources to carry out its work effectively, in particular those relating to the provision of advisory services and technical assistance to the states in the Asian region.

I would like to take this opportunity to inform this august meeting of some significant measures Thailand is carrying out to further promote human rights at national level. At the moment, the Thai Government is undertaking the necessary steps for Thailand to accede to the International Covenant on Civil and Political Rights.

The Parliamentary Committee on Justice and Human Rights and the Sub-Committee on Human Rights, which have been established recently, would afford elected representatives the opportunity to consult actively with governmental agencies on human rights issues. The distinguished chairman of the Sub-Committee on Human Rights is also participating at this Conference as a member of the Thai delegation. In accordance with the decision of the Government, the Thai authorities concerned are closely and actively examining the possibility of establishing a national institution to promote the respect for and observance of human rights in Thailand. These, and other steps that are being taken by the Thai Government, are part and parcel of its overall development strategy to advance further democracy, economic development and social justice in Thailand.

In closing, the Thai delegation believes that this Conference is capable of great achievement, if all participants present in Vienna appreciate the diversity of the human family, and with an open mind, approach human rights from the basis of mutual respect and understanding, for only then will human rights become truly universal.

(A) Documents

Official Statements in the World Conference on Human Rights, Vienna, June 1993, by government representatives from the following countries: Brunei, China, Indonesia, Japan, Republic of Korea, Malaysia, Myanmar, the Philippines, Singapore, Thailand, the United States.

Statement by Prince Mohamed Bolkiah, Minister of Foreign Affairs, Brunei Darussalam at the World Conference on Human Rights, Vienna, 21 June 1993.

Statement by Liu Huagiu, Head of the Chinese Delegation at the World Conference on Human Rights, Vienna, 17 June 1993.

Statement by Ali Alatas, Minister for Foreign Affairs and Head of the Delegation of the Republic of Indonesia at the World Conference on Human Rights, Vienna, 14 June 1993.

Statement by Nobuo Matsunaga, Envoy of the Government of Japan and Representative of Japan at the World Conference on Human Rights, Vienna, 18 June 1993.

Statement by Han Sung-joo, Minister of Foreign Affairs of the Republic of Korea at the World Conference on Human Rights, Vienna, 15 June 1993. .

Statement by Datuk Abdullah Haji Ahmad Badawi, Minister of Foreign Affairs, Malaysia at the World Conference on Human Rights, Vienna, 18 June 1993.

Statement by U Ohn Gyaw, Minister for Foreign Affairs and Chairman of the Delegation of the Union of Myanmar at the World Conference on Human Rights, Vienna, 15 June 1993.

Statement by Roberto R. Romulo, Secretary of Foreign Affairs and Head of the Philippine Delegation at the World Conference on Human Rights, Vienna, 16 June 1993.

Statement by A. V. Kozyrev, Minister for Foreign Affairs of the Russian Federation at the World Conference on Human Rights, Vienna, 15 June 1993.

Statement by Wong Kan Seng, Minister for Foreign Affairs of the Republic of Singapore at the World Conference on Human Rights, 'The real world of human rights', Vienna, 16 June 1993.

Statement by Prasong Soonsiri, Minister of Foreign Affairs of Thailand, Head of Thai Delegation at the World Conference on Human Rights, Vienna, 16 June 1993.

Statement by Warren Christopher, Secretary of State of the United States of America, Vienna, 14 June 1993.

Other governmental documents

Asean

Joint Communiqué of the Twenty Sixth ASEAN Ministerial Meeting, Singapore, 23–4 July 1993.

China

Constitution of the People's Republic of China, esp. Articles 42, 46, 52, 53 and 54.

The White Paper on Human Rights in China (Beijing: Information Office of the State Council of China, 1991).

India

Constitution of the Republic of India, esp. Articles 14, 15, 17, 23 and 51, and Directive Principles of State Policy.

Japan

Gaimusho (Ministry of Foreign Affairs), *Waga Gaiko no kinkyo* (Recent Development in Japanese Diplomacy) (1957, 1962, 1967, 1973).

Gaimusho (n.d.), 'Chugoku no Jinkenmondai nitaisuru Wagakuni no Taioh' (Japan's response to human rights problems in China), mimeo.

Gaimusho, *Gaikou Seisho: Waga Gaiko no Kinkyo* [Diplomatic Bluebook: Recent Developments in Japanese Diplomacy] (1988, 1990, 1991).

Gaimusho Keizai Kyoryoku kyoku (Department of Economic Cooperation, Ministry of Foreign Affairs), *Wagakuni no Seifu Kaihatsu Enjo* (Japan's Official Development Assistance) (1991, 1992).

Otsuka, S., 'Statement by Seiichiro Otsuka, Minister, Embassy of Japan in Thailand and Representative of Japan to the Regional Meeting for Asia of the World Conference on Human Rights', *Jiyu to Seigi* (Liberty and Freedom), vol. 44, no. 11 (1993), pp. 105–6.

Philippines

Constitution of the Republic of Philippines, (1935), esp. Articles 7, Section 10 (2).

Presidential Proclamation No. 1081, 'A state of martial law in the Philippines', 21 September 1972.

The Philippines Supreme Court Reports: Annotated, Vol. 46, 17 August 1972 (Republic of the Philippines versus William H. Quasha), 21 August 1972 (Anti-Dummy Board versus Luzon Stevedoring Company), Vol. 50, 31 March 1973 (Javellana versus the Executive Secretary), Vol. 59, 17 September 1974 (Benigno Aquino versus Juan Ponce Enrile).

Singapore

Shared Values, Cmd. 1 (Singapore: Singapore National Printers, 1991).

The United States

US Senate Committee on Foreign Relations and US House of Representative Committee on Foreign Affairs, *Legislations on Foreign Relations through 1992* (Washington, DC: Government Printing Office, 1993), Vols. I, II, III.

Country Reports on Human Rights Practices, State Department.

United Nations and other Inter-governmental Organizations

Compilation of International Human Rights Instruments (Geneva: The Human Rights Centre, 1991).

Manual on Human Rights Reporting (New York: United Nations, 1991).

Poverty, Marginalization, Violence and the Realization of Human Rights, by Paulo Sergio Pinheiro *et al.*, a study commissioned by the UN Center of Human Rights in preparation for the UN World Conference on Human Rights. (A/CONF.157/PC/60/Add.3).

Report on Appropriate Indicators to Measure Achievements in the Progressive Realization of Economic, Social, and Cultural Rights, Geneva, 25–9 January 1993. (A/CONF.157/PC/73) (20 April 1993).

United Nations Pronouncements (A/43/131) of 20 March 1989 and (A/46/182) of 14 April 1992.

The Final Outcome of the World Conference on Human Rights. (A/CONF.157/DC/1/Add.1) (24 June 1993).

UNDP, *Human Development Report 1992* (New York: Oxford University Press for the United Nations Development Programme, 1992).

UNESCO, *Human Rights: Major International Instruments* (Paris: UNESCO, 1993).

Council of Europe, *The Council of Europe and Human Rights* (Strasbourg: Council of Europe, 1993).

Council of Europe, *Human Rights at the Dawn of the 21st Century*, proceedings of the inter-regional meeting organized by the Council of Europe in advance of the World Conference on Human Rights, Strasbourg, 28–30 January 1993 (Strasbourg, Council of Europe Press, 1993).

World Bank, *The East Asian Miracle: Economic Growth and Public Policy* (New York: Oxford University Press for the World Bank, 1993).

Non-governmental documents and reports

(In alphabetical order according to organizations)

Amnesty International, *Human Rights Violations in the Philippines: An Account of Torture, Disappearances, Extrajudicial Executions and Illegal Detentions* (New York: Amnesty International U.S.A. Publication, 1982).

Amnesty International, *Arrest, Detention and Political Killing of Priests and Church Workers in the Philippines* (London: Amnesty International Publications, 1988).

Amnesty International, *Unlawful Killings by Military and Para-military Forces* (London: Amnesty International Publications, 1988).

Amnesty International, *The Killing and Intimidation of Human Rights Lawyers* (London: Amnesty International Publications, 1988).

Amnesty International, *Philippines: The Killing Goes On* (London: Amnesty International Publications, 1992).

Amnesty International, *Facing Up to the Failures: Proposals for Improving the Protection of Human Rights by the United Nations* (Amnesty International: December 1992).

Amnesty International, *Amnesty International Report 1993* (London: Amnesty International Publications, 1993).

Asia Cultural Forum on Development, *Our Voice: Bangkok NGO Declaration on Human Rights, Reports of the Asia-Pacific NGO Conference on Human Rights and NGOs' Statements to the Asia Regional Meeting* (Bangkok: Asia Cultural Forum on Development, 1993).

Asia-Pacific Forum on Women, Law and Development, *Women's Rights Human Rights: Asia-Pacific Reflections* (Kuala Lumpur: Asia-Pacific Forum on Women, Law and Development, 1992).

Asia-Pacific Information Centre, *Introduction to the Proposed Asia-Pacific Human Rights Information Centre*, Preparatory Committee for the Asia-Pacific Human Rights Information Centre, Osaka, Japan (3 March 1993).

Asia Watch, *Human Rights in the APEC Region* (New York: Asia Watch, November 1993).

(BIM) Ludwig Boltzman Institute of Human Rights, *NGO-Newsletter*.

Chinese Association for Human Rights, *Seminar on Human Rights Organizations in Asia and the Pacific*, summary proceedings (1990).

Freedom House, *Freedom in the World: Political Rights and Civil Liberties* (New York, Freedom House).

Hong Kong Human Rights Database Project, *Report of the Asian Regional Meeting on Human Rights Information Exchange and Networking*, the Hong Kong Human Rights Database Project, Faculty of Law, University of Hong Kong, and HURIDOCS (24–8 September 1993).

Human Rights Centre, University of New South Wales, *Human Rights Defender*.

Human Rights Watch, *Indivisible Human Rights: The Relationship of Political and Civil Rights to Survival, Subsistence and Poverty* (1 September 1992).

Human Rights Watch, *Human Rights Watch World Report, 1993* (New York: Human Rights Watch, 1992).

HURIDOCS, *HURIDOCS Standards Formats: A Tool for Documenting Human Rights Violations* (Oslo: HURIDOCS, 1993).

HURIDOCS, *HURIDOCS Standard Formats: Supporting Documents* (Oslo: HURIDOCS, 1993).

Institute of Pacific Relations, *Institute of Pacific Relations: Honolulu Session, June 30-July 14 1925, History, Organization, Proceedings, Discussions and Addresses 1925* (Honolulu: IPR, 1925).

Institute of Pacific Relations, *Problems in the Pacific: Proceedings of the Second Conference of the Institute of Pacific Relations, Honolulu, Hawaii, July 15 to 29, 1927*, edited by J. B. Condliffe (Chicago: University of Chicago Press, 1928).

Institute of Pacific Relations, *Problems of the Pacific, 1929: Proceedings of the Third Conference of the Institute of Pacific Relations: Nara and Kyoto, Japan, October 23 to November 9, 1929* edited by J. B. Condliffe (Chicago: University of Chicago Press, 1930).

Institute of Pacific Relations, *Problems of the Pacific, 1931: Fourth Conference of the Institute of Pacific Relations, Hangchow and Shanghai, China, October 21 to November 2*, edited by Bruno Lasker (Chicago: University of Chicago Press, 1932).

Institute of Pacific Relations, *Problems of the Pacific, 1936: Aims and Results of Social and Economic Policies in Pacific Countries - Proceedings of the Sixth Conference of the Institute of Pacific Relations, Yosemite National Park, California, 15–29 August 1936*, edited by W. L. Holland and Kate Mitchell (Chicago: University of Chicago Press, 1937).

Institute of Pacific Relations, *Problems of Pacific Countries, 1939: Proceedings of the Study Meeting of the Institute of Pacific Relations, Virginia Beach, Virginia, November 18–December 2 1939*, edited by Kate Mitchell and W. L. Holland (New York: IPR, 1940).

Institute of Pacific Relations, *War and peace in the Pacific: A Preliminary Report of the Eighth Conference of the Institute of Pacific Relations on Wartime and Post-war Cooperation of the United Nations in the Pacific and the Far East, Mont Tremblant, Quebec, December 4–14, 1942* (New York: IPR 1943).

Institute of Pacific Relations, *Security in the Pacific: A Preliminary Report of the Ninth Conference of the Institute of Pacific Relations, Hot Springs, Virginia, January 6–17, 1945* (New York: IPR, 1945).

Institute of Pacific Relations, *Problems of Economic Reconstruction in the Far East: Report of the Tenth Conference of the Institute of Pacific Relations, Stratford-on-Avon, England, September 5–20, 1949* (New York: IPR, 1949).

Institute of Pacific Relations, *Asian Nationalism and Western Policies: Preliminary Report of the Eleventh Conference of the Institute of Pacific Relations, Lucknow, India, October 1–15, 1950* (New York: IPR, 1951).

International Service for Human Rights, *Human Rights Monitor*.

Lawasia, *Human Rights Bulletin*.

PIOOM, A Manual for the Assessment of Country Performances, in computer diskette, by A. J. Jongman, A. Schmid, D. Gupta, T. Gurr, B. Harff, F. Bluiminck, R. Rakers et. al. (Leiden: Center for the Study of Social Conflicts, 1993).

PIOOM, *PIOOM Report*, newsletter and progress report of Programma Interdisciplinair Onderzoeknnaar Oorzaken van mensenrechten-schendingen (Interdisciplinary Programme of Research on Root Causes of Human Rights Violations), Leiden University, The Netherlands (Vol. 5, no. 1, summer 1993).

(B) Newspapers and news magazines

Asahi Shimbun (Tokyo)
Bangkok Post (Bangkok)
China News (Taipei)
Daily Yomiuri (Tokyo)
Earth Times (New York, special edition covering the World Conference on Human Rights)
Far Eastern Economic Review (Hong Kong)
Guardian (London)
International Herald Tribune (Neuilly-sur-Seine)
Jakarta Post (Jakarta)
Nation (Bangkok)
New Straits Times (Kuala Lumpur)
New York Times (New York)
Nihon Keizai Shimbun (Japan)
South China Morning Post (Hong Kong)
Star (Kuala Lumpur)
Straits Times (Singapore)
Sunday Times (Singapore)
Terra Viva (Vienna, World Conference on Human Rights)
Wall Street Journal (New York)
Vancouver Sun (Vancouver)

(C) Books

Ahmad, Zakaria Hj. (ed.), *Government and Politics of Malaysia* (Singapore: Oxford University Press, 1987).

Alston, Philip (ed.), *The United Nations: A Critical Appraisal* (Oxford: Clarendon Press, 1992).

Bachrach, Peter and Baratz, Morton S., *Power and Poverty: Theory and Practice* (New York: Oxford University Press, 1970).

Bailey, George, *The Making of Andrei Sakharov* (London: The Penguin Press, 1989).

Bedau, H. A., 'International human rights', in Regan and van De Veer (eds), *And Justice for All: New Introductory Essays in Ethics and Public Policy* (New Jersey: Rowman and Littlefield, 1973).

Benn, David W., *From Glasnost to Freedom of Speech* (London: The Royal Institute of International Affairs, 1992).

Binyon, Michael, *Life in Russia* (New York: Pantheon Books, 1983).

Black, Maggie, *A Cause for our Times: OXFAM, the First Fifty Years* (Oxford: Oxford University Press, 1992).

Bonner, Elena, *Alone Together* (New York: Alfred A. Knopf, 1986).

Brecher, Irwing (ed.), *Human Rights, Development and Foreign Policy: Canadian Perspectives* (Halifax: Institute for Research on Public Policy, 1989).

Cane, David, *Soviet Society Under Perestroika* (Boston: Unwin Hyman, 1990).

Chan, J. and Ghai, Yash (eds), *The Hong Kong Bill of Rights: A Comparative Approach* (Hong Kong: Butterworths Asia, 1993).

Chan, Hang Chee, *The Dynamics of One-Party Dominance: The PAP at the Grass-roots* (Singapore: Singapore University Press, 1976).

Clark, Cal and Chan, Steve (eds), *The Evolving Pacific Basin in the Global Political Economy: Domestic and International Linkages* (Boulder: Lynne Rienner Publishers, 1992).

Cooper, Andrew F., with Higgot, Richard and Nossal, Kim Richard, *Relocating Middle Powers: Australia and Canada in a Changing World* (Vancouver: University of British Colombia Press, 1993).

Cranston, M., *What are Human Rights?* (New York: Basic Books, 1973).

Crouch, Harold, *The Army and Politics in Indonesia* (New York: Cornell University Press, 1978).

Dahl, Robert A., 'Democracy and human rights under different conditions of development', in Asbjorn Eide and Bernt Hagtvet (eds), *Human Rights in Perspective: A Global Assessment* (Oxford: Basil Blackwell Ltd., 1992).

Danaher, Kevin, *The Political Economy of U.S. Policy towards South Africa* (Boulder: West View Press, 1985).

Davidson, Scott, *Human Rights* (Buckingham: Open University Press, 1993).

Day, Erin, *Economic Sanctions Imposed by the United States Against Specific Countries; 1979 through 1992* (Washington, DC: Congressional Research Service, 1993).

Deyo, Frederick (ed.), *The Political Economy of the New Asian Industrialism* (Ithaca: Cornell University Press, 1987).

Donnelly, Jack, *Universal Human Rights in Theory and Practice* (Ithaca: Cornell University Press, 1989).

Dworkin, Ronald, *Taking Rights Seriously* (London: Duckworth, 1978).

Evans, Peter B., Rusechemeyer, Dietrich and Skocpol, Theda, *Bringing the State Back in* (Cambridge: Cambridge University Press, 1985).

Feinberg, J., *Social Philosophy* (New Jersey: Prentice-Hall, 1973).

Gewirth, Alan, *Human Rights: Essays on Justification and Application* (Chicago: University of Chicago Press, 1982).

Ghali, Boutros Boutros, *An Agenda for Peace* (New York: United Nations Publication, 1992).

Goodno, James B., *The Philippines: Land of Broken Promises* (London: Zed Books, 1991).

Halle, Louis J., *Dream and Reality* (New York: Harper and Brothers, 1958).

Halperin, Morton H. and Scheffer, David with Small, Patricia, *Self Determination in the New World Order* (Washington DC: Carnegie Endowment for International Peace, 1992).

Henkin, L. (ed.), *The International Bill of Rights: The Covenant on Civil and Political Rights* (New York: Columbia University Press, 1981).

Hsiung, James C., *Human Rights in East Asia, A Cultural Perspective* (New York: Paragon Books, 1985).

Jabine, Thomas B., and Claude, Richard P. (eds), *Human Rights and Statistics: Getting the Record Straight* (Philadelphia: University of Pennsylvania Press, 1992).

Javate-De Dios, Aurora and Daroy, Petronilo Bn., Kalaw-Tirol, Lorna (eds), *Dictatorship and Revolution: Roots of People's Power* (Manila: Conspectus, 1988).

Keane, John (ed.), *Civil Society and the State: New European Perspectives* (London: Verso, 1988).

Kent, Anne, *Between Freedom and Subsistence* (Hong Kong: Oxford University Press, 1993).

Krasner, Stephen (ed.), *International Regimes* (Ithaca, NY: Cornell University Press, 1983).

Kymlicka, Weil, *Liberalism, Community and Culture* (Oxford: Clarendon Press, 1989).

Lacquear, Walter, *The Long Road to Freedom* (London: Unwin Hyman, 1990).

Lo, Chung-sho, 'Human rights in the Chinese tradition', in UNESCO (ed.), *Human Rights: Comments and Interpretations* (Westport: Greenwood Press, 1993).

Locke, John, *The Second Treatise of Government* (Cambridge: Cambridge University Press, 1970).

Mathews, Robert O. and Pratt, Cranford (eds), *Human Rights in Canadian Foreign Policy* (Kingston and Montreal: McGill-Queens University Press, 1988).

Merrills, J. G., *The Development of International Law by the European Court of Human Rights* (Manchester: Manchester University Press, 1988).

Milne, A. J. M., *Human Rights and Human Diversity: An Essay in the Philosophy of Human Rights* (London: Macmillan, 1986).

Morley, James W. (ed.), *Driven by Growth, Political Change in the Asia-Pacific Region* (New York: M. E. Sharpe, 1993).

Muyot, Alberto T., *Human Rights in the Philippines, 1986–91* (Quezon City: University of the Philippines Law Centre, 1992).

Nanda, Ved. P., Scarritt, James R. and Shepherd, George W. Jr. (eds), *Global Human Rights: Public Policies, Comparative Measures and NGO Strategies* (Boulder: Westview, 1981).

Nardin, Terry and Mapel, David R., *Traditions of International Ethics* (Cambridge: Cambridge University Press, 1992).

Nickel, James W., *Making Sense of Human Rights* (Berkeley: University of California Press, 1987).

Parker, Tony, *Russian Voices* (London: Jonathan Cape, 1991).

Pawson, Ray, *A Measure for Measure: A Manifesto for Empirical Sociology* (London: Routledge, 1989).

Pettman, Ralph, *International Politics: Balance of Power, Balance of Productivity, Balance of Ideologies* (Melbourne/Boulder: Longman Cheshire/Lynne Rienner, 1991).

Quah, Jon S. T. (ed.), *Government and Politics of Singapore* (Singapore: Oxford University Press, 1987).

Raz, Joseph, *The Morality of Freedom* (Oxford: Clarendon Press, 1986).

Regan, T. and VanDeVeer, D. (eds), *And Justice for All: New Introductory Essays in Ethics and Public Policy* (New Jersey: Rowman and Littlefield, 1973).

Regional Outlook: Southeast Asia 1993–1994 (Singapore: Institute of Southeast Asian Studies, 1993).

Rielly, John E. (ed.), *American Public Opinion and U.S. Foreign Policy 1991* (Chicago: The Chicago Council on Foreign Relations (IL), 1991).

Rorty, Richard, *Contingency, Irony, and Solidarity* (Cambridge: Cambridge University Press, 1989).

Shalom, Stephen R., *The U.S. and the Philippines: A Study of Neo-Colonialism* (Philadelphia: Institute for the Study of Human Rights, 1981/Quezon City: New Day Publishers, 1986).

Shue, H., *Basic Rights: Subsistence, Affluence, and U.S. Foreign Policy* (New Jersey: Princeton University Press, 1980).

Sieghart, P., *The International Law of Human Rights* (Oxford: Clarendon Press, 1983).

Suryadinata, Leo, *Military Ascendancy and Political Culture: A Study of Indonesia's Golkar* (Ohio: Ohio University Press, 1989).

The Environment and Human Rights in International Relations, (Jakarta: ASEAN–ISIS, undated).

Towards Democracy in Burma, second edn. (Washington, DC: Institute of Asian Democracy, 1993).

Taylor, A. J. P., *The Struggle for Mastery in Europe, 1848–1878* (Oxford: Clarendon Press, 1954).

Vasak Karel (ed.), *The International Dimension of Human Rights*, revised and edited for the English version by Philip Alston (Westport: Greenwood, 1982).

Vincent, R. John, *Human Rights and International Relations* (Cambridge: Cambridge University Press/Royal Institute of International Affairs, 1986).

Waldron, Jeremy (ed.), *Nonsense upon Stilts: Bentham, Burke and Marx on the Rights of Man* (London: Methuen, 1987).

Welch, Claude E. Jr. and Leary, Virginia A. (eds), *Asian Perspectives on Human Rights* (Boulder: Westview, 1990).

Woods, Lawrence T., *Asia Pacific Diplomacy: NGO and International Relations* (Vancouver: University of British Colombia Press, 1993).

Yanov, Alexander, *The Russian Challenge and the Year 2001* (New York: Basil Blackwell, 1987).

Zametica, John, *The Yugoslav conflict*, Adelphi Paper no. 270 (London: Institute of International and Strategic Studies, 1992).

(D) Articles and chapters

(Articles in newspapers or news magazines used by contributors are only listed below when the authors of the articles are referred to in the text or the notes. Other unsigned articles and news reports otherwise cited can be found in the notes at the end of each chapter.)

Afexention, Panayiotis C., 'Basic needs: a survey of the literature', *Canadian Journal of Development Studies*, vol. 11, no. 2 (1990).

Alagappa, Muthiah, 'Confronting the SLORC', *Burma Review*, no. 30 (November–December 1991).

Alatas, Ali, 'No nation can judge others on human rights', *Straits Times*, 16 June 1993.

Almendral, Gemma N., 'The fall of the regime', in Aurora Javate-De Dios *et al.* (eds), *Dictatorship and Revolution: Roots of People's Power* (Metro-Manila: Conspectus, 1988).

Apple, R. W., 'No missteps for president, but no clear gains either', *International Herald Tribune*, 22 November 1993.

Awanohara, Susumu, 'Do unto others ...', *Far Eastern Economic Review*, 1 July 1993.

Awanohara, Susumu, Vatikiotis, Michael and Islam, Shada, 'Vienna showdown', *Far Eastern Economic Review*, 17 June 1993.

Awanohara, Susumu and Chanda Nayan, 'Uncommon bonds', *Far Eastern Economic Review*, 18 November 1993.

Baker, Richard W., 'Pacific summit in Seattle: testing Clinton's Asia Pacific policy', *Asia Pacific Issues* (East-West Center) no. 9, November 1993.

Barsh, Russell Lawrence, 'Measuring human rights: problems of methodology and purpose', *Human Rights Quarterly*, vol. 15, no. 1 (February 1993).

Berthelson, John, 'Politics of exclusion: anti-immigrant lobbyists target Asians again', *Far Eastern Economic Review*, 18 November 1993.

Boo, Tion Kwa, 'Righteous talk', *Far Eastern Economic Review*, 17 June 1993.

Bray, John, 'Burma: resisting the international community', *Pacific Review*, vol. 5, no. 3 (1992).

Chan, Steven and Clark, Cal, 'Changing perspectives on the evolving Pacific Basin: international structures and domestic processes', in Cal Clark and Steve Chan (eds), *The Evolving Pacific Basin in the Global Political Economy: Domestic and International Linkages* (Boulder: Lynne Rienner, 1992).

Chanda, Nayan, 'Misguided complacency', *Far Eastern Economic Review*, 18 November 1993.

Ching, Frank, 'Asia: West reach compromise on human rights in Vienna', *Far Eastern Economic Review*, 15 July 1993.

Clad, James, 'Rising sense of drift', *Far Eastern Economic Review*, 10 July 1986.

Crouch, Harold, 'The military and politics in Southeast Asia', in Zakaria Hj. Ahmed and Harold Crouch (eds), *Military Civilian Relations in Southeast Asia* (Singapore: Oxford University Press, 1985).

Dagg, Christopher J., 'Japan ties aid to human rights in recipient nations', *Straits Times*, 6 October 1992.

Dagg, Christopher J., 'Linking aid to human rights in Indonesia: a Canadian perspective', *Issues* (Asia Pacific Foundation of Canada), vol. 7, no. 1 (Winter 1993).

Development Studies Association, 'The United Nations humanitarian response' (November 1992).

Donnelly, Jack, 'Cultural relativism and universal human rights', *Human Rights Quarterly*, vol. 6, no. 4 (1984).

Donnelly, Jack, 'Human rights: a regime analysis', *International Organization*, no. 40 (1986).

Donnelly, Jack, 'Human rights in the New World Order', *World Policy Journal*, vol. 9, no. 2 (Spring 1992).

Donnelly, Jack, 'Twentieth-century realism', in Terry Nardin and David Mapel (eds), *Traditions of International Ethics* (Cambridge: Cambridge University Press, 1992).

Evans, Paul M., 'The emergence of Eastern Asia and its implications for Canada', *International Journal*, vol. 47, no. 3 (Summer 1992).

Fairclough, Gordon, 'Standing firm: Asia sticks to its view of human rights', *Far Eastern Economic Review*, 15 April 1993.

Ghai, Yash, *Whose Rights to Development?* (London: Commonwealth Secretariat, 1989).

Ghai, Yash, 'Capitalism and the rule of law: reflections on the Basic Law' in Raymond Wacks (ed.), *Legal Theory: China, Hong Kong and 1997* (Hong Kong: Hong Kong University Press, 1989).

Ghai, Yash, 'Derogations and limitations in the Hong Kong Bill of Rights', in Johanes Chan and Yash Ghai (eds), *The Hong Kong Bill of Rights: A Comparative Approach* (Hong Kong: Butterworth Asia, 1993).

Graham, Clyde, 'Canada looks to Pacific, GATT for trade', *Prince George Citizen*, 22 November 1992.

Green, Jeannie, 'The Philippines: human rights issues in United States foreign policy', *Harvard Human Rights Year Book*, Vol. II (Spring, 1989).

Gurevitch, Peter A., 'The Pacific Rim: current debate', *The Annals*, vol. 505 (September 1989).

Halperin, Morton H., 'Guaranteeing democracy', *Foreign Policy*, (Summer 1993).

Hatano, R., 'Jinken Shohiinkai no Kino: Sono "dokuritusei" to "seijisei" ' (The function of the Human Rights Sub-Commission: its 'independence' and 'political nature'), *Kokusai Jinken* (Human Rights International), vol. 1 (1990).

Henderson, Jeffrey and Appelbaum, Richard, 'Situating the State in East Asian development', in Richard Appelbaum and Jeffrey Henderson (eds), *State and Development in the Asian Pacific Rim* (Newbury Park: Sage, 1992).

Henderson, Stuart, 'Zone of uncertainty: Canada and the security architecture of Asia Pacific', *Canadian Foreign Policy*, vol. 1, no. 1 (Winter 1992–93).

Hoffman, Stanley, 'The hell of good intentions', *Foreign Policy*, no. 29 (1977–78).

Holland, William L., 'Source materials on the Institute of Pacific Relations', *Pacific Affairs*, vol. 58, no. 1 (Spring 1985).

Holmes, Steven A., 'Clinton reverses policies in U.N. on rights issues', *New York Times*, 9 May 1993.

Hooper, Paul F., 'The Institute of Pacific Relations and the origins of Asian and Pacific Studies', *Pacific Affairs*, vol. 61, no. 1 (Spring 1988).

Horvitz, Paul F., 'From Seattle, contradictions among smiles', *International Herald Tribune*, 19 November 1993.

Horvitz, Paul F., 'Clinton seeks to open markets: APEC prods Europe on trade', and 'A nonstarter in Seattle: Asian Pacific community', *International Herald Tribune*, 20, 21 November 1993.

Horvitz, Paul F., 'Clinton cites talks as positive, but divisions remain: Pacific leaders make little headway on arms and human rights issues', *International Herald Tribune*, 22 November 1993.

Huntington, Samuel, 'The clash of civilizations?' *Foreign Affairs*, vol. 72, no. 3 (September 1993).

Islam, Shada, 'Under Western eyes', *Far Eastern Economic Review*, 14 March 1991.

Jones, Sidney, 'The organic growth: Asian NGOs have come into their own', *Far Eastern Economic Review*, 17 June 1993.

Joyner, Christopher C. and Dettling, John C., 'Bridging the cultural chasm: cultural relativism and the future of international law', *California Western Law Journal*, vol. 20 (1990).

Kausikan, Bilahari, 'Asia's different standard', *Foreign Policy*, no. 92 (Fall 1993).

Kegley, Charles W. Jr., 'The neo-idealist moment in international studies? Realist myths and the new international realities', *International Studies Quarterly*, vol. 37, no. 2 (June 1993).

Kiss, A.C., 'Permissible limitations on rights', in L. Henkin (ed.), *The International Bill of Rights: The Covenant on Civil and Political Rights* (New York: Columbia University Press, 1981).

Koh, Tommy, 'The 10 values that undergird East Asian strength and success', *International Herald Tribune*, 11–12 December 1993.

Kurth, James, 'The Pacific Basin versus the Atlantic Alliance: two paradigms of international relations', *The Annals*, vol. 505 (September 1989).

Leary, V., 'The Asian region and the International Human Rights Movement', in Claude E. Welch Jr. and Virginia A. Leary (eds), *Asian Perspectives on Human Rights* (Boulder: Westview, 1990).

Leifer, Michael, 'Maintain APEC on its economic trajectory', *International Herald Tribune*, 8 November 1993.

Mahbubani, Kishore, 'The West and the rest', *The National Interest* (Summer 1992).

Mahbubani, Kishore, 'New areas of ASEAN reaction: environment, human rights and democracy', *ASEAN–ISIS Monitor*, no. 5 (October–December 1992).

Mahbubani, Kishore, 'Live and let live: allow Asians to choose their own course', *Far Eastern Economic Review*, 17 June 1993.

Mahoney, Kathleen E., 'Human rights and Canada's foreign policy', *International Journal*, vol. 47, no. 3 (Summer 1992).

McMamant, John F., 'A critique of present measures of "human rights development" and an alternative', in Ved. P. Nanda, James R. Scarritt and George W. Shepherd, Jr. (eds), *Global Human Rights: Public Policies, Comparative Measures and NGO Strategies* (Boulder: Westview, 1981).

Muzzaffar, Chadra, 'Ethnicity and ethnic conflict in Malaysia', in Claudia E. Welch, Jr. and Virginia A. Leary (eds), *Asian Perspectives on Human Rights* (Boulder: Westview, 1990).

Neier, Aryeh, 'Asia's unacceptable standard', *Foreign Policy*, no. 92 (Fall 1993).

Nelson, John, 'Canadian view of Pacific relations', *Institute of Pacific Relations: Honolulu Session* (Honolulu: IPR, 1925).

Nossal, Kim Richard, 'The limits of linking aid to human rights', in Mark Charlton and Elizabeth Riddel Dixon (eds), *Cross-currents: International Relations in the Post-Cold War Era* (Scarborough: Nelson Canada, 1993).

Paulson, Michael, 'Heads of states sensitivities crimp Seattle party plans', *Vancouver Sun*, 16 September 1993.

'Private pressure', *Far Eastern Economic Review*, 17 June 1993.

Redding, Andrew, 'Clinton is right on international human rights', *Wall Street Journal*, 15 July 1993.

Richardson, Michael, 'ASEAN aims to hold its own at talks in Seattle', *International Herald Tribune*, 16 November 1993.

Robinson, Svend, 'Justice and human rights: inspiring Canadian foreign policy', *Canadian Foreign Policy*, vol. 1, no. 1 (Winter 1992-93).

Samudavanija, Chai-anan, 'Thailand: a stable democracy', in Larry Diamond, Juan Linz and Seymour Martin-Lipset (eds), *Democracy in Developing Countries: Asia*, vol. 3 (Colorado: Lynne Rienner Publishers, 1989).

Sanger, David E., 'On eve of Seattle talks, wary Asians suspect Clinton of overreaching', *International Herald Tribune*, 15 November 1993.

Sciolino, Elaine, 'U.S. rejects notion that human rights vary with culture', *New York Times*, 15 June 1993.

Scoble, Harry and Wiseberg, Laurie S., 'Problems of comparative research in human rights', in Ved. P. Nanda, James R. Scarritt and George W. Shepherd, Jr. (eds), *Global Human Rights: Public Policies, Comparative Measures and NGO Strategies* (Boulder: Westview, 1981).

Shenon, Philip, 'Malaysian is glad he stayed at home', *International Herald Tribune*, 22 November 1993.

Sikkink, Kathryn, 'Human rights, principled issue-network, and sovereignty in Latin America', *International Organizations*, vol. 47, no. 3 (Summer 1993).

Stohl, Michael, Carleton, David, Lopez, George and Samuels, Stephen, 'State violations of human rights: issues and problems of measurement', *Human Rights Quarterly*, vol. 8, no. 4 (November 1986).

Sundhausen, Ulf, 'The durability of military regimes in Southeast Asia', in Zakaria Hj. Ahmad and Harold Crouch (eds), *Military Civilian Relations in Southeast Asia* (Singapore: Oxford University Press, 1985).

Tao, Julia, 'The Chinese moral ethos and the concept of individual rights', *Journal of Applied Philosophy*, vol. 7 (1990).

Train, John, 'When can sanctions succeed?' *Wall Street Journal*, 14 June 1989.

Tremewan, Christopher, 'Human rights in Asia', *Pacific Review*, vol. 6, no. 1 (1993).

Van Ness, Peter 'Human rights and international relations in East Asia', *Asian Studies Review*, vol. 16, no. 1 (July 1992).

Vasak, Karel, Introduction to Sub-Part II: 'Regional institutions for the protection of human rights', in Karel Vasak (ed.), *The International Dimension of Human Rights*, revised and edited for the English version by Philip Alston (Westport: Greenwood, 1982).

Vasak, Karel, 'The Council of Europe', in Karel Vasak (ed.), *The International Dimension of Human Rights*, revised and edited for the English version by Philip Alston, (Westport: Greenwood, 1992).

Vatikiotis, Michael, 'Dollar democracy', *Far Eastern Economic Review*, 26 September 1992.

Vatikiotis, Michael and Delfs, Robert, 'Human rights cultural divide', *Far Eastern Economic Review*, 21 November 1993.

Wanandi, Jusuf, 'Human rights and democracy in ASEAN nations: the next 25 years', *Indonesian Quarterly*, vol. 21, no. 1, (1993).

Weston, Burns, H., Lukes, Robin Ann and Hnatt, Kelly M., 'Regional human rights regimes: a comparison and appraisal', in Richard P. Claude and Burns Weston (eds), *Human Rights in the World Community*, second edn. (Philadelphia: University of Pennsylvania Press, 1992).

Williams, Daniel, 'Chinese stick to their hard-line ways', *International Herald Tribune*, 22 November 1993.

Wong, Kan Seng, 'Take pragmatic line on human rights', *Straits Times*, 17 June 1993.

Woods, Lawrence T., 'Regional diplomacy and the Institute of Pacific Relations', *Journal of Developing Societies*, vol. 8, no. 2 (July–October 1992).

Woods, Lawrence T., 'Nongovernmental Organizations and the United Nations system:

reflecting upon the Earth Summit experience', *International Studies Notes*, vol. 18, no. 1 (Winter 1993).

Yamane, Hiroko, 'Asia and human rights', in Karel Vasak (ed.), *The International Dimension of Human Rights*, revised and edited for the English version by Philip Alston (Westport: Greenwood, 1982).

(E) Unpublished papers and other sources

Alston, Philip, 'Human rights in 1993: how far has the United Nations come and where should it go from here?' workshop discussion paper, NGO forum, Vienna, June 1993.

Angeles, Leonora, Gonzales, Brenda; Guan, Mary Jean and Magno, Anna Lisa, 'The quest for justice: obstacles to the redress of human rights violations in the Philippines' (unpublished research paper submitted to the University of Philippines Centre for Integrative and Development Studies, July 1989).

Canadian Broadcasting Corporation (CBC) Radio News.

Dias, Clarence J., 'Relationship between human rights, development and democracy: South/ North NGO solidarity in fostering population participation', workshop discussion paper, NGO forum, Vienna, June 1993.

Gillies, David, 'Human rights, democracy and good governance: stretching the World Bank's policy frontiers', paper prepared for the President, International Center for Human Rights and Democratic Development, Montreal, 1 June 1992.

Jones, Sidney, 'Human rights: basic elements of effective protection', paper prepared for the ASEAN-ISIS Asia Pacific Round Table, Kuala Lumpur, Malaysia, 6-9 June 1993.

Neary, Ian, 'The Hyongpyongsa, the Suiheisha and the struggle of human rights in East Asia' (unpublished, 1993).

Taylor, Paul, *Options for the Reform of the International System for Humanitarian Assistance* (London: Pinter, to be published in 1994).

(F) Chinese-language materials

(Below is a list of Chinese-language works published in the People's Republic of China referred to in Chapter 7. All publications are in Chinese and the authors' names are given in their original order, i.e. surnames preceding given names.)

Bai Guimei, 'State sovereignty and international law', *Peking University Law Journal*, vol. 5 (1990), pp. 31-5.

Bai Guimei, 'Labour law and protection of human rights', *Studies in Law*, vol. 5 (1991), pp. 7-12.

Bao Xin, 'China respects and protects human rights', *Outlook Weekly* (*Overseas Edition*), 15 April 1991, p. 15.

Chen Chunlong, 'Marxist concept of human rights and law', *Peking University Law Journal*, vol. 4 (1992), pp. 39-42.

Chen Shiuyi *et al.*, 'The meeting of conversation by writing concerning issues about human rights', *Peking University Law Journal*, vol. 3 (1991), pp. 34-45.

Cheng Jirong, 'Adhere to Marxist human rights approach: a critical analysis of France's Declaration of the Rights of Man and the Citizen', *Politics and Law*, vol. 2 (1990), pp. 1-5.

Ding Xueliang, 'Marxism is coherent with humanism', *Wenhui Daily*, 12 April 1982.

Dong Ling, 'The origin and class nature of human rights', *Practice*, vol. 7 (1979), pp. 22-4.

Dong Yunhu and Liu Wuping, *World Documents of Human Rights* (Shichuan: People's Press, 1990).

Du Gangjian, 'Absolute and relative theory of human rights in the U.S.A.', *Studies in Law*, vol. 2 (1992), pp. 81-7.

Duan Qizeng, 'On human rights viewpoints of classical Marxist authors', *Quarterly Journal of the Shanghai Academy of Social Science*, vol.4 (1990), pp. 66-73.

Fu Xuezhe, 'On problems about human rights', *Universities' Social Science*, vol. 1 (1990), pp. 10-17.

Gu Chunde, 'Two opposing approaches to human rights', *Legal System Daily*, 11 November 1989.
Gu Chunde, 'Protection and guarantee of human rights in China', *Liberation Army's Daily*, 8 May 1991.
Guo Daohui, 'On the class nature and universality of human rights', *Peking University Law Journal*, vol. 5 (1991), pp. 20-4.
Guo Qingxun, 'On human rights and rights of the citizen', *Journal of Hainan Normal College*, vol. 2 (1990), pp. 19-22.
He Hairen, 'Ideology: equality and human rights', *Journal of Jianghai Academia*, vol. 4 (1990), pp. 45-50.
Hu Dong, 'On the administrative law guarantee of human rights in China', *Jurisprudence and Practice*, vol. 2 (1992), pp. 2-4.
Hu Dachu, 'Human rights are a bourgeois slogan', *Changjiang Daily*, 19 April 1979.
Hu Qiaomu, *On Some Problems about Humanism and Alienation* (Beijing: People's Press, 1984).
Hu Yicheng, 'An analysis of human rights', *Shanxi Daily*, 19 April 1979.
Huang Nansheng, 'Some theoretical problems about humanism', *People's Daily*, 4 June 1981.
Huang Nansheng, 'Marxist philosophy and human rights', *Peking University Law Journal*, vol. 3 (1991), pp. 38-9.
Jiao Fengui, 'A talk on human rights', *Hebei Daily*, 12 April 1979.
Jie Hua, 'Do not talk abstract human rights', *Study and Research*, vol. 10 (1989), pp. 36-8.
Jie Tongwen, 'On some theoretical problems of Marxist human rights theory', *Journal of China University of Political Science and Law*, vol. 1 (1992), pp. 1-9; vol 2: pp. 1-10.
Jin Keshi, 'The Chinese Society of International Law and the Chinese Association of United Nations Symposium on the 40th Anniversary of Universal Declaration of Human Rights', *Chinese Yearbook of International Law* (1989), p. 518.
Lai Weifang, 'Right and wrong of the problems of human rights', *Study and Research*, vol. 10 (1989), pp. 39-40.
Lan Ying, 'Are human rights a bourgeois slogan? Discussion with Comrade Xiao Weiyun', *Social Science*, vol. 3 (1979), pp. 34-7.
Li Buyun, 'On the three forms of human rights', *Studies in Law*, vol. 4 (1992), pp. 11-17.
Li Buyun, 'On the basic theory of protection of human rights in socialist countries', *Studies in Law*, vol. 4 (1992), pp. 1-8.
Li Guoliang, 'Brief introduction to the origin and evolution of the theory of human rights', *Peking University Law Journal*, vol. 5 (1991), pp. 25-31.
Li Huaping, 'Reflections on legal philosophy concerning certain problems of human rights', *Journal of China University of Political Science and Law*, vol. 3 (1990), pp. 64-70.
Li Lin, 'A summary of symposium: under the guidance of Marxism, deepening the study of the human rights theory', *Studies in Law*, vol. 5 (1991), pp. 13-22.
Li Lin, 'International human rights and state sovereignty', *Chinese Legal Science*, vol. 1 (1993), pp. 37-44.
Li Linmei, 'Principle of sovereignty and international protection of human rights', *Journal of Foreign Affairs College*, vol. 1 (1992), pp. 48-53.
Li Ming, 'Human rights in the Charter of the United Nations and problems of non-intervention in internal affairs', *Chinese Legal Science*, vol. 3 (1993), pp. 34-43.
Li Renzhen, 'On the subjective status of Human Beings in international law based on international protection of human rights', *Law Forum*, vol. 1 (1984), pp. 33-8.
Li Shiju, 'Engels' thought on human rights and socialist viewpoint on human rights', *Journal of Hebei Normal College (Social Science Edition)*, vol. 4 (1990), pp. 6-11.
Li Zherui, 'A theoretical inquiry into international human rights law', *Chinese Yearbook of International Law* (1983), pp. 3-116.
Lin Rendong, 'On human rights and citizens' rights', *Nanjing Social Science*, vol. 1 (1992), pp. 43-8.
Lin Rongnian and Zhang Jinfan, 'On the rights of man', *Study and Exploration*, vol. 1 (1980), pp. 30-7.
Lin Xiangquan and Li Qunxing, 'On labour law protection of human rights in China', *Wuhan University Law Journal*, vol. 2 (1992), pp. 7-12.
Ling Jingyao, 'My views of humanity and humanism', *Wenhui Daily*, 8 February 1983.
Liu Huaqing, 'Speech at the UN World Human Rights Conference in Vienna' (Hong Kong), *Mingpao*, 21 June 1993, p. 32.
Liu Shoufen, 'On the protection mechanics of Chinese criminal law and human rights', *Peking*

University Law Journal, vol. 4 (1992), pp. 43–9.

Liu Wenzong, 'On human rights and "human rights diplomacy" of USA: an international law perspective', *People's Daily*, 10 May 1992.

Lu Deshan, 'Also talking about the subject of human rights', *Chinese Legal Science*, vol. 2 (1992), pp. 22–4.

Luo Mingde and He Hangzhou, 'On the individual character of human rights', *Journal of China University of Political Science and Law*, vol. 1 (1993), pp. 56–61.

Ma Zheming, 'A critical analysis of the philosophy of man', *Study and Research*, vol. 1 (1982), pp. 12–15.

Meng Chunjin, 'Insisting on the Marxist human rights view, rejecting the bourgeois human rights view: a brief summary of the Universities' Theoretical Conference on Human Rights', *People's Daily*, 17 September 1990.

Ni Zengmao, 'On the rule of law and humanism', *Journal of Northwest Politics and Law College*, vol. 1 (1987), pp. 1–4.

Nu Xin, 'Is humanism the same as revisionism?' *People's Daily*, 15 August 1980.

Pan Baocun, 'Theoretical exploration concerning human rights', *Journal of Jianghai Academia*, vol. 1 (1987), pp. 68–70.

Qiao Congqi, 'Chinese bourgeois theory of human rights and the rule of law', *Peking University Law Journal*, vol. 3 (1992), pp. 50–7.

Qiao Wei, 'Commenting on the rights of man', *Journal of Literature, History and Philosophy*, vol. 6 (1989), pp. 3–11.

Qiu Ping, 'On the people's democratic dictatorship and protection of human rights in our country', *Politics and Law Journal*, vol. 2 (1990), pp. 1–4.

Shao Jin, 'Holding high the banner of human rights: in memory of the 20th anniversary of two covenants of human rights', *World Knowledge*, vol. 23 (1986), pp. 18–20.

Shen Baoxiang, 'On human rights in the international forum', *Theory Development*, vol. 339 (1982), pp. 11–12.

Shen Zongling, 'What kind of rights are human rights?' *Chinese Legal Science*, vol. 5 (1991), pp. 22–5.

Shen Zongling *et al.*, 'Views on human rights and legality', *Peking University Law Journal*, vol. 4 (1991), pp. 46–56.

Sheng Zuhong, 'Human rights and the rule of law', *Democracy and Legality*, vol. 2 (1979), pp. 11–17.

Shi Daxin, 'On human rights and international protection of human rights', *Journal of Anhui University*, vol. 3 (1982), pp. 52–7.

Shi Tanjing, 'On emerging human rights', *Studies in Law*, vol. 5 (1991), pp. 1–6.

Si Pingping, 'Judicial independence and protection of human rights', *Science of Law*, vol. 5 (1989), pp. 13–16.

The State Council, *The White Paper of Human Rights in China*, Beijing, Information Office of the State Council of China, 1991.

Sun Xiaochun, 'Confucian theory of human nature and the traditional humanistic thought of China', *Northern Forum*, 1 January 1991, pp. 5–11.

Sun Xiaoxia, 'Human rights in the process of law', *Chinese Legal Science*, vol. 3 (1992), pp. 39–45.

Wan Erxiang, 'On international standards of human rights', *Chinese Legal Science*, vol. 1 (1993), pp. 45–51.

Wang Dexiang, 'The constitutional guarantee of human rights in China', *Studies in Law*, vol. 4 (1992), pp. 18–23.

Wang Fusan, 'Humanism is no principle of Marxism', *Journal of Eastern China Normal College*, vol. 4 (1981), p. 14–18.

Wang Hongyan, 'On legal protection of human rights in civil action', *Tribune of Political and Law*, vol. 3 (1993), pp. 73–9.

Wang Jianyuan, 'Legal protection of human rights in China', *Journal of Zhengzhou University*, vol. 5 (1992), pp. 69–74.

Wang Mingfu, 'Value explanation and legal realization of human rights', *Nanjing Social Science*, vol. 2 (1992), pp. 74–9.

Wang Ruosui, 'A defence for humanism', *Wenhui Daily*, 12 April 1982.

Wang Tiancheng, 'Those who govern are governed by law: administrative laws and human rights', *Peking University Law Journal*, vol. 5 (1992), pp. 29–36.

Wang Yilian and Zheng Zhongchao, 'On Marxism and humanism', *Journal of Central China Normal College*, vol. 2 (1983), pp. 34-7.

Wei Min, 'International protection of human rights and non-interference in internal affairs', *Peking University Law Journal*, vol. 3 (1991), pp. 44-9.

Wu Baoding, 'International human rights practice and human rights guarantee in China', *Journal of Anhui University (Social Science)*, vol. 3 (1992), pp. 3-8.

Wu Daying, 'Analysing human rights historically and concretely', *Jurisprudence Study*, vol. 4 (1979), pp. 10-12.

Xia Yong, 'The reasoning and implementing of human rights: on A. J. M. Milne's point of view on human rights', *Peking University Law Journal*, vol. 1 (1992), pp. 26-31.

Xiao Weiyun, 'How does Marxism treat human rights?' *Honggi Journal*, vol. 5 (1979), pp. 22-6.

Xing Fensi, *Humanism in European Philosophical History* (Beijing: People's Press, 1978).

Xu Bing, 'On human rights and rights of citizens', *Guangming Daily*, 19 June 1979.

Xu Bing, 'The rise and historical development of human rights theory', *Studies in Law*, vol. 3 (1989), pp. 1-10.

Xu Congde, 'Fighting for human rights is not a slogan for the proletariat', *Guangzhou Daily*, 7 May 1979.

Xu Congwen, 'Human rights and sovereignty', *Journal of Postgraduate School of Chinese Social Science Academy*, vol. 6 (1992), pp. 40-52.

Xu Guodong, 'Freedom of movement and the gap between urban and rural areas', *Peking University Law Journal*, vol. 5 (1979), pp. 37-42.

Xu Goujin, 'The limit of fulfilling duties of international human rights by the state', *Chinese Legal Science*, vol. 2 (1992), pp. 13-21.

Xu Jianyi (ed.), *Answers to Questions from the White Paper on Human Rights in China* (Beijing: Chinese Youth Press, 1991).

Xu Weidong, Shen Zhengwu and Zheng Chengliang, 'On the ideological and legal standards of human rights', *Chinese Legal Science*, vol. 1 (1992), pp. 21-5.

Xu Xianming, 'Several theoretical problems from the subject of human rights', *Chinese Legal Science*, vol. 5 (1992), pp. 35-9.

Xu Yiujun, 'Chinese criminal procedure law and human rights', *Peking University Law Journal*, vol. 2 (1992), pp. 38-43.

Yang Bing, 'How young Marx and Engels treated humanity and humanism', *Jianghuai Forum*, vol. 6 (1980), pp. 8-11.

Yang Dunxian and Chen Xingliang, 'Existence and repudiation of capital punishment and protection of human rights', *Peking University Law Journal*, vol. 6 (1991), pp. 57-63.

Yang Jianrong, 'An approach to human rights', *Academic Research*, vol. 5 (1979), pp. 23-7.

Yang Naichu, 'On human rights and human liberation', *Xin-jiang Social Science*, vol. 6 (1990), pp. 51-6.

Yang Xinghua, 'A critical analysis of the human rights foreign policy of the USA', *Zhengming*, vol. 1 (1992), pp. 6-10.

Ye Lixuan and Li Shizhen, *Human Rights Theory* (Fuzhou: Fujian People's Press, 1991).

Yi Jia, 'A critical analysis of bourgeois human rights', *Modern Jurisprudence*, vol. 1 (1990), pp. 1-5.

Yu Liang, 'Human rights are a bourgeois slogan', *Wenhui Daily*, 8 April 1979.

Zhang Chunjin, *On Human Rights* (Tianjin: People's Press, 1989).

Zhang Guangbo, 'Adhere to Marxist views on human rights', *Chinese Legal Science*, vol. 4 (1990), pp. 10-17.

Zhang Guangxin and Shi Peixin, 'On human rights', *Journal of Nanjing Political Science College*, vol. 2 (1990), pp. 37-40.

Zhang Jinfan (ed.), *Legal History of China: Law Textbook for Universities* (Beijing: Masses Press, 1987).

Zhang Kuiliang, Bi Zhiguo and Wang, Yialin, 'On the value of man in the socialist system', *Study and Exploration*, vol. 1 (1981), pp. 12-16.

Zhang Mengmei, 'On the bourgeois rights of man', *Journal of Hubei Finance and Economics College*, vol. 2 (1972), pp. 7-12.

Zhang Shenghua, 'Development, jurisdiction and other questions about human rights: summary of the 4th National Conference of the Youth Scholars of International Law', *Legal System Daily*, 2 July 1990, p. 3.

Zhang Wenxian, 'On the subject of human rights and the subject's human rights', *Chinese Legal Science*, vol. 5 (1991), pp. 26–34.

Zhang Wenxian, 'Human rights, rights, collective human rights: answers to Comrade Lu Deshan', *Chinese Legal Science*, vol. 3 (1992), pp. 116–18.

Zhang Wei, 'Changes and the nature of human rights protection in Western constitutional law', *Peking University Law Journal*, vol. 5 (1992), pp. 43–5.

Zhang Xibo, 'Also talking about human rights legislations in the revolutionary base areas', *Study and Research in Law*, vol. 3 (1992), pp. 35–41.

Zhang Xiuping, 'Marxism including humanism', *Qilu Academic Journal*, vol. 3 (1983), pp. 11–14.

Zheng Fulin, 'An analysis of human rights', *Changchun Daily*, 9 May 1979, p. 3.

Zheng Yong, 'The origins and development of the human rights issue in the international arena', *Chinese Legal Science*, vol. 4 (1990), pp. 18–23.

Zhi Qun, 'Which class do human rights belong to?' *Xinhua Daily*, 19 April 1979, p. 3.

Zhou Yang, 'Inquiring into some theoretical questions of Marxism', *People's Daily*, 16 March 1983.

Zuo Yu and Shu Sheng, 'The basic content of human rights: human rights and citizens' rights', *Chinese Legal Science*, vol. 6 (1991), pp. 14–22.

INDEX